SEX ROLES: A RESEARCH BIBLIOGRAPHY

by

Helen S. Astin, Ph.D.
Editor and Director of Research

Allison Parelman
Anne Fisher

Center for Human Services
Washington, D.C.
1975

NATIONAL INSTITUTE OF MENTAL HEALTH
5600 Fishers Lane
Rockville, Maryland 20852

This bibliography was compiled pursuant to Contract
#HSM 42-72-140 with the National Institute of Mental
Health, U.S. Public Health Service, Department of
Health, Education, and Welfare

DHEW Publication No. (ADM) 75-166
Printed 1975

For sale by the Superintendent of Documents, U.S. Government Printing Office
Washington, D.C. 20402 - Price $3.30
Stock Number 017-024-00422-7
Catalog Number HE20.8112:SE9

FOREWORD

The National Institute of Mental Health has a deep interest in the contemporary roles of women and men and recognizes the need for careful research investigations into the influence of sex roles on individual behavior and on societal institutions. A selective bibliography of research conducted over the past decade seemed an essential tool for further efforts, and the Institute is proud to offer such a reference work in this publication.

Over the past 2½ years, the Institute has held a series of research workshops to identify and encourage needed studies on sex roles, their biological and social bases and their consequences for behavior and society. This research bibliography and a growing number of innovative and excellent studies are the result.

The bibliography covers literature originating in investigations published both here and abroad and is directed toward social and behavioral scientists. It is hoped that it will also be an important research tool that will stimulate graduate students as well as experienced scientists to pursue the increasingly important problems of sex roles and their determinants.

Bertram S. Brown, M.D.
Director

ACKNOWLEDGMENTS

The development of this bibliography required the efforts and commitment of many people.

We first thank our sponsors, the Division of Extramural Research Programs, NIMH, who made this work possible.

We also thank the friends and colleagues who shared their time and ideas about selection and classification of the research literature on sex roles: Jessie Bernard, Alice Rossi, Eleanor Maccoby, Beatrix Hamburg, Janet Giele, and Elise Boulding, who very generously provided her listings of the international literature on sex roles.

Thanks are also due to Ronnie Parelman, for her expert assistance in abstracting, and to those who translated and developed abstracts from the foreign research literature: Birgitta Engvall, for the Scandinavian literature; and Michele Herman and Ann Finkelstein, for the French literature. Mary Gospodarek, who monitored the keywording and indexing, and Semeion B. Pyles, Jr., who coded and taped the draft, also contributed to this document.

This project would not have been possible without the assistance of Jeanne Barrett, who edited the abstracts and supervised the preparation of the final manuscript.

Nevertheless, the authors assume responsibility for any errors in the interpretation and representation of the research findings reported in this bibliography.

Helen S. Astin
Allison Parelman
Anne Fisher
November 1973

PREFACE

Although the present-day sex-role debate is popularly viewed as a "movement" reflecting the changing needs of women in defining their lives, no one can ignore the fact that the roles of both men and women today are changing. This "movement" is also not an isolated event perpetrated by a few, but a reflection of a host of economic, social, and psychological pressures emerging from the demands of the rapidly changing environments of the world. In the Western world, this public debate has primarily focused on the role of women and has already resulted in new legislation and changes in education, employment, and the structure of family roles. However, change affects both sexes, if not equally, and role changes for one sex to meet new demands will necessarily affect the roles of the other. It is hoped that an examination of the research literature on sex roles will lead to a better understanding of the roles of men and women: Their origins, their development, and how they are manifested.

The study of sex roles has been of concern to psychologists, anthropologists, sociologists, economists, biologists, physiologists, and others for a long time: Developmental psychologists have examined sex differences in cognitive and personality development and have explored the impact of socialization and childrearing practices on sex roles; anthropologists have investigated the cross-cultural variations in sex-typed behavior; biologists and physiologists have been concerned with how anatomical, hormonal, and other biological characteristics differentiate the sexes; sociologists have studied the socialization of sex roles, sex-role expectations, and sex-role perceptions, as well as sex stereotyping; and economists have examined the numbers and status of women in the professional and nonprofessional job markets and have inquired into the economic impact of an influx of women workers. Thus, a literature search in the subject of sex is necessarily multidisciplinary.

Selection of the Contents

One of the early steps in this project was to identify the major areas of research as well as the primary scholars in the field. This required an examination of bibliographic material, presentations, and symposia at national meetings of professional associations. Letters requesting reprints and publications from scholars in the field provided some of the source materials used. Numerous publishers were also asked to provide copies of their most recent publications on the subject of sex roles. A computer search of the NIMH National Clearinghouse for Mental Health Information and MEDLARS at the National Library of Medicine identified some of the relevant literature. The research team also made use of such library facilities as the National Library of Medicine, the Library of Congress, and the libraries of nearby academic institutions: The Johns Hopkins University, George Washington University, the University of Maryland, and the American University.

The selected items cover the publishing years 1960 to 1972, but the timespan actually represented is much greater given the inclusion of historical studies and longitudinal research studies. The literature search concentrated on a broad representation of the various disciplines, with selections that exemplify research approaches and theoretical frames of reference as well as the knowledge amassed concerning sex differences and sex roles. The final selection for the bibliography, however, generally permitted inclusion of only one or two entries from each author. This allowed us to highlight the kinds and directions of research being performed, but precluded a comprehensive approach that would also indicate the actual quantity of research.

Most of the entries included in the bibliography are published and available from libraries. However, some unpublished papers were chosen for inclusion either for their theoretical contribution or because they suggest a new direction in research; these papers are available from the respective authors. Since the emphasis of the bibliography is on literature with an empirical basis, only a few feminist commentaries and essays are included.

Also covered are some theoretical papers deemed especially useful in defining specific research concerns. Our purpose was to present a selective overview and not to critically review the research literature. The selections therefore not only broadly represent different theories and approaches, but varying degrees of rigor in methodologies as well. Consequently, this bibliography reflects the "state of the art" of the research on sex roles.

Each abstract provides the user of this bibliography with the most important elements of the research piece: its purpose, original hypotheses, theoretical orientation, study sample(s), methodology (including measures used), findings, and conclusions. Each abstract also includes the number of references cited in the original document and additional sources, if it was published more than once.

Our team of translators searched and abstracted 38 documents from the French and Scandinavian literature. These articles were selected primarily on the basis of accessibility of original document, visibility of author, and variation in research topics. Other countries are well-represented in the English language literature, including both translations from the original language and studies by English-speaking researchers.

Classification of Research

Our initial examination of the research and theoretical literature on sex roles allowed us to develop a conceptual framework to define the categories of research. This classification was then used to select the articles and books to be included.

The first category of research topics consists of descriptive studies of measured or observed sex differences in personality characteristics, cognitive functioning, game behavior, etc. Studies of this type do not attempt to account for the differences found; they simply describe them. Correlational studies that do not examine causal relationships are also included in this category. Some of these studies examine gender identity and other personality characteristics as possible mediators of sex-role behavior. Moreover, some of the studies compare sex differences by inference or by reference to earlier studies with male data, rather than by collecting data on both sexes and analyzing them simultaneously. Laboratory or experimental studies that examine behavioral differences are also included.

The second category consists of studies on the origin of sex differences and development of sex roles. The research included identifies primarily the determinants of sex differences in behavior and, ultimately, of sex roles. These research efforts attempt to examine the biological and/or sociocultural origins of sex differences and the pertinent factors in the socialization process. Research on the effect of hormones on behavior, brain lateralization and its effect on differential cognitive functioning, and genetic determinants and their differential effects on the sexes exemplifies such studies. Research designed to examine socialization processes, such as childrearing practices and the influence of peers and others, is included in this second category. Also included are studies that describe and attempt to explain the process by which awareness of and attitudes toward sex roles emerge at different stages of life. Studies which illustrate how and when sex-role behavior is understood and incorporated were also placed in this category.

The third major category in the classification includes studies concerning the manifestation of sex roles: how sex roles are expressed within the social structure, and what the various roles of men and women are in such settings as the world of work, the family, and educational institutions.

The fourth major category includes overviews and historical accounts of the relative status of the sexes in the United States and in other cultures and nations. However, foreign or cross-cultural studies of sex differences, determinants of sex differences, and manifestations of sex roles are classified under the appropriate topic headings in the other sections.

The fifth category includes general reviews and theoretical position papers on the process of socialization and development of sex roles as well as methodological issues and concerns for research on sex roles.

Animal studies were classified as developmental studies if they examined biological or sociocultural factors as determinants of sex differences. Some of these animal studies highlight aspects of social organization and socialization that result in differential behavior of the sexes.

Of course, as with any attempt to categorize complex subject matter, we encountered difficulties in classifying studies that cut across a number of substantive concerns. Especially difficult was the classification of studies of sex-role behavior in the family which discuss determinants as well as manifestations. Similarly, many studies concerning women and the world of work also deal with determinants of career choices for women. In some instances, the categorical disposition of some references was necessarily arbitrary. Thus, although these categories offer a convenient taxonomy of the concerns and topics of research on sex roles, the bibliography user will probably find the keywords preceding each abstract and in the subject index to be the most useful tools in actually locating research findings of interest.

For the 346 journal articles abstracted in this bibliography, the table below categorizes the source journals by subject. The bibliography also contains 54 summaries of books relevant to sex role research and 49 summaries of relevant chapters within books of a broader nature. Also summarized are the proceedings of two conferences and five unpublished papers and speeches.

Number of Abstracts by Source

Source	Number of Abstracts
Journals	
Sociology	109
Psychology	110
Child development	52
Anthropology	7
Political science	6
Economics and labor	9
Medicine and related fields	20
Education	15
Miscellaneous	18

CONTENTS

SEX DIFFERENCES
Measurement and Description

1

Barron, Nancy. Sex-typed language: The production of grammatical cases. *Acta Sociologica,* 14(1-2):24-42, 1971.

Cognitive styles. Language.

As part of a larger research program on the dynamics of speech in social interaction, this study tested a rationale regarding sex-typed language. Various studies of nonlinguistic sex-typed behaviors have suggested that men have an analytic cognitive style and a self-assertive interaction style, and that women have a synthetic cognitive style and an other-oriented interaction style. It was hypothesized in this study that linguistic features would correspond to these nonlinguistic features.

The specific language variable studied was case, which gives the relational meaning and use of nouns in a sentence. Hypotheses were developed from corresponding features of sex-role behaviors and case categories. The eight subjects were one 6th-grade and three 11th-grade teachers from black, working-class inner-city schools, and a corresponding group from white, upper middle-class suburban schools. Four of the teachers were male, four were female; four teachers were over age 40, four were under age 30. Portions of the natural language of classroom interaction were videotaped and transcribed. Reconstruction, a method of making covert language overt, was used to process the language data. Variables investigated were sex of teacher, case features of teachers' noun phrases, and the explicitness or implicitness of the case-marked nominals.

Most of the hypotheses were confirmed: Case use was sex typed. Women used significantly more explicit participative and purposive cases than men, apparently demonstrating their greater concern with internal psychological states. Men used significantly more instrumental, source, and objective cases, thus emphasizing implementation of action by means of and upon objects. Contrary to expectations, the agentive and locative cases did not discriminate between men and women, and men did not specify more spatial-temporal orientations.

Sex differences held constant for both socioeconomic and racial groups. It is concluded that men and women are predisposed by experience to be concerned with different classes of cognitive meaning, and that they therefore speak in different patterns and with different emphases and content. (37 references)

2
Beller, E. Kuno, and Neubauer, Peter B. Sex differences and symptom patterns in early childhood. *Journal of Child Psychiatry,* 2:417-433, 1963.

Preschool children. Psychological adjustment.

An empirical study was designed to classify psychosocial disturbances of the preschool child; to analyze the frequency and distribution of these disturbances in a clinical population of children; and to study the pattern of these problems, particularly in relation to sex differences. Subjects were 55 boys and 55 girls, children of urban middle-class and lower middle-class parents. Most of the parents were Jewish second-generation immigrants from Europe. The children were selected from among clients at a New York City clinic devoted to the study and treatment of psychological disturbances in early childhood. Mean age for the sample was approximately 3 years. The age difference between boys and girls was small but statistically significant, suggesting that parents tend to seek professional help somewhat earlier for girls than boys. Information on behavior problems and symptoms was extracted from clinical records of diagnostic interviews with the parents and diagnostic summaries, and the problems were classified in 25 categories.

Disturbances in feeding and sleeping constituted the largest share of early difficulties. There was also a relatively high incidence of fear and aggression problems. There was a low incidence of bladder and bowel control problems and of such autoerotic manifestations as thumbsucking and masturbation. With regard to sex differences, parents reported significantly more aggression, hyperactivity, lack of bowel control, and speech disturbances in boys. For girls, parents reported significantly more problems of overdependence, emotional overcontrol, bowel retention, and sibling rivalry. When symptom patterning was examined, the majority of significant relationships among different symptoms were found in one or the other sex, but not equally in both. Aggression, hyperactivity, and temper tantrums constituted an interrelated cluster which appeared more often in boys than in girls. This cluster was associated with defiance of parental demands and with an absence of separation anxiety. Although there was less patterning of symptoms in girls than in boys, impulse control emerged as a central difficulty. However, the interrelated problems of girls pointed toward overcontrol and indirect expression of impulses. Data suggested that boys in our culture tend to express defiance by lack of impulse control, whereas defiance by overcontrol is more common in girls. (18 references)

3

Berger, Charles R. Sex differences related to self-esteem factor structure. *Journal of Consulting and Clinical Psychology,* 32(4):442-446, 1968.

Self-esteem. College students.

This two-phase study explores the factorial nature of the self-esteem construct. In phase one, data from a prior study of self-esteem in 298 college men and women were factor analyzed to identify the factors involved in self-esteem. In phase two, a second overall analysis and separate analyses of 194 male and 78 female undergraduates were performed to explore sex differences in self-esteem.

Results of the first phase yielded five relatively independent factors of self-esteem: Communicative propensity, other-anxiety, negative self-evaluation, positive self-evaluation, and other-certainty. The second overall analysis produced a similar factor structure. However, the separate analysis of the female data revealed that the negative self-evaluation and other-certainty factors formed a single dimension. This connection, which does not appear for males, suggests that the self-evaluation of females is partially contingent on their degree of certainty that other people like them. Explanation of this apparent sex difference would require further inquiry into the developmental aspects of self-esteem. (6 references)

4

Carlson, Rae. Sex differences in ego functioning: Exploratory studies of agency and communion. *Journal of Consulting and Clinical Psychology,* 37(2):267-277, 1971.

Self-concept. Cognitive styles.

A series of two empirical studies and one literature review tested two related theoretical formulations on sex differences in personality: D. Gutmann's formulation of ego functioning in the two sexes and D. Bakan's constructs of agency and communion.

Study I used a sample of 213 college students and adults in the community to test four hypotheses, derived from Gutmann's formulation, which specify the ways in which males and females differ in experiencing and representing the self, others, the physical environment, and the future. Measures used were the Carlson Adjective

Checklist, a modified version of the Role Construct Repertory Test, subjects' brief written personality sketches of a well-known other, descriptions of their childhood physical environment, and responses to a question on what sort of person each expects to be 15 years later. Tests of all the hypotheses yielded significant results in the expected direction: Males represented the self in individualistic terms and others in objective terms; females represented the self in terms of interpersonal relations and the physical environment in self-centered terms. Males represented the future in instrumental, external terms; females, in expressive, internal terms.

Study II tested the utility of the agency-communion formulation in conceptualizing sex differences in ego functioning. Agency is a male-related principle exemplified in psychological functioning by differentiation of self from the field; intellectual functions involving separating and ordering; and interpersonal styles involving objectivity, competition, exclusion, and distance. Communion is a female principle represented by merging of self with the field; intellectual functions involving communication; and interpersonal styles involving subjectivity, cooperation, acceptance, and closeness. The hypothesis tested was that males would express more agentic themes in reporting significant affective arousal; whereas females, because of their greater bisexuality, would express more communal and mixed themes. College students (18 males and 23 females) were asked to report on life experiences that produced feelings of shame, fear, anger, disgust, joy, excitement, or surprise. The predicted sex differences were supported by the results.

Study III evaluated the ability of the agency-communion formulation to assimilate existing knowledge about sex differences. Two samples of 100 each were drawn from abstracts of the published literature relating to the development of sex differences. Each abstract was categorized as relevant or irrelevant to a series of seven hypotheses derived from the agency-communion formulation. If relevant, each study was evaluated as confirming, nonconfirming, or disconfirming. In the two samples of abstracts, 81 and 84 percent were judged relevant. Of the relevant studies in both samples which reported significant sex differences, 97 percent of each sample were judged to confirm one or more of the predictions. (30 references)

5
Cattell, Raymond B., and Lawson, Edwin D. Sex differences in small group performance. *Journal of Social Psychology*, 58:141-145, 1962.

Group performance. College students.

This study deals with sex differences in small-group performance. Specifically, it was hypothesized that groups of men would perform differently than groups of women on standardized tasks, and that these differences would not be explainable in terms of individual male and female performance. University of Illinois undergraduates comprised 10 groups of men and 7 groups of women (10 members per group). Subjects were randomly selected from psychology classes and told that a $100 prize for task performance would be awarded to the best men's group and to the best women's group. Each group elected a leader and met for three daily sessions of 3 hours each. Standardized tasks consisted of cryptogram deciphering; construction of models, giving an aspiration-level score for estimation of completion time; timed group self-evaluation discussion; jury judgment, giving a level of persuadability score; card sorting; a guessing game; group answers to factual questions; attitudes (group decisions on controversial political and social statements); and interests (group votes on how to spend an evening).

Differences were found between the male and female groups on the construction task, with the man having a faster time for completion of models and a higher level of aspiration. Male groups had a significantly higher level of persuadability in jury judgments than female groups. There were no clear-cut differences in attitudes expressed in group discussion, although trends indicated that women were slightly more conservative. In the interests situation, men preferred seeing a movie and playing handball significantly more than women, and women preferred studying more than men. Despite the differences in levels of aspiration and persuadability, it was concluded that the group performances of men and women are substantially similar. (5 references)

6
Clark, John P., and Haurek, Edward W. Age and sex roles of adolescents and their involvement in misconduct: A reappraisal. *Sociology and Social Research,* 50(4):495-508, 1966.

Adolescents. Delinquency. Sex-role perceptions.

This study investigated the relationships between age and sex and adolescent misconduct. Subjects were 495 male and 621 female public school students, ages 11 to 19, from an urban, lower-class community, an upper middle-class suburb, an industrial city, and a prosperous farm community. Data on possible participation in 38 offenses during the preceding year were gathered by anonymous questionnaires.

Although the ratios of males to females who admitted committing each offense varied widely by offense, all ratios obtained were substantially lower than those derived from official statistics. However, sex ratios in admitted delinquency still indicated a greater amount of male than female misconduct, especially among those who admitted committing the offenses four or more times. Sex ratios derived from official statistics appeared to more accurately reflect this chronic delinquent group than adolescents in general. The remaining discrepancy between this study's sex ratios for chronic delinquents and official statistics suggests some male-female differentiation in the arrest and conviction of juvenile offenders. The higher ratio of male to female offenders found in rural areas perhaps results from a more traditional differentation of sex roles there. Offenses associated with the cultural role of the child (throwing cans at cars) appear to decrease through adolescence; offenses less deviant for adults than for children (hanging around pool halls) increase. Offenses involving risk and aggression (theft, assault, defying a teacher) increase to midadolescence for males, presumably because these acts are seen as a testimonial to masculinity, and then decrease as anxiety concerning masculine identity decreases in later adolescence. (18 references)

7
Clifton, Marguerite A., and Smith, Hope M. Comparison of expressed self-concepts of highly skilled males and females concerning motor performance. *Perceptual and Motor Skills,* 16:199-201, 1963.

Self-concept. Athletic ability. College students.

It was hypothesized that males and females who are highly skilled in athletic ability would give comparable self-ratings to their motor performances. Subjects were 36 male and 49 female University of California at Los Angeles students who were varsity or nationally ranked athletes and high scorers on motor ability batteries. Each subject first performed a sequence of running, catching, throwing, and standing broad jump and then completed a checklist of self-ratings for each motor skill performance.

Although both sexes responded positively to their overall performance of the motor skills sequence, the females rated themselves much less favorably than the males in their performance of the standing broad jump. Their actual performance on this skill did not warrant the low self-ratings. Thus, this study supported previous findings that males and females differ in expressed self-concepts of their motor performances, although fewer differences were found between these highly skilled males and females than in the general population. (2 references)

8
Dowse, Robert E., and Hughes, John A. Girls, boys and politics. *British Journal of Sociology,* 22(1):53-67, 1971.

Political behavior. Adolescents. Great Britain.

This study explores sex differences in political behavior of British school children by age and economic class. The hypotheses tested were that political sex differences apparent in childhood will increase with age as sex roles become more clearly defined, and that middle-class girls will resemble middle-class boys in political behavior more than working-class girls will resemble working-class boys. A sample of Exeter, England, school children between the ages of 11 and 17 was randomly selected from a girls' and a boys' grammar school (N=148 girls and 146 boys), two girls' secondary modern schools (N=193), and a boys' secondary modern school (N=140). Data on the political knowledge, attitudes, and behavior of these subjects were gathered by questionnaires.

At the cognitive level, tested by the political knowledge scale, girls (especially working-class girls) scored below boys; in the cognition of likely voting patterns, girls were less aware than boys. In most of the affective or attitudinal items, girls were very much more likely to be undecided than boys. However, when girls did have an opinion, it was not significantly different from that of boys. Neither the age nor the social class hypothesis was confirmed. Findings suggested that these marginal sex differences in childhood combine with the structural restraints of married women's lives (i.e., familial responsibilities, isolation from the outside world) to produce adult sex differences in levels of political awareness and activity. (31 references)

9
Droege, Robert C. Sex differences in aptitude maturation during high school. *Journal of Counseling Psychology,* 14(5):407-411, 1967.

High school students. Academic ability. Aptitude maturation.

This longitudinal study conducted by the U.S. Employment Service examined sex differences in aptitude maturation. A sample of 20,541 lower high school (9th-, 10th-, and 11th-grade) students and 6,167 12th-grade students from 168 schools was initially administered the General Aptitude Test battery. The experimental group of lower high school students was retested as 12th graders. Aptitudes measured were intelligence; verbal, numerical, and spatial aptitudes; form perception; clerical perception; and motor coordination, finger dexterity, and manual dexterity.

Boys averaged consistently higher than girls on spatial aptitude, and girls averaged consistently higher on form perception, clerical perception, motor coordination, and finger dexterity. There were significant differences between boys and girls in average increase in mean aptitude scores, but the differences were small throughout. Boy-girl differences in mean-score increases for most of the aptitudes were largest for the 9th-grade sample and smallest for the 11th-grade. Girls showed a slight but significant and consistent tendency toward greater score stability on motor coordination, and boys had greater score stability on numerical aptitude, spatial aptitude, and clerical perception. It is concluded that separate aptitude test forms for lower high school and 12th-grade students are necessary to take into account maturation effects. However, since both stability of aptitude and effects of maturation and practice on aptitude-score levels are similar for boys and girls in high school, separate sex norms are not required. (3 references)

10
Farnsworth, Paul R. The effects of role-taking on artistic achievement. *Journal of Aesthetics and Art Criticism,* 18(3):345-349, 1960.

Sex-role perceptions. Artistic activities. Stereotypes.

This study investigated men's and women's perceptions of sex roles in the arts. The sample of 103 male and 86 female university undergraduates encompassed a wide range of musical and other artistic interests. A questionnaire asked subjects to choose the five most feminine and five most masculine items from among 34 artistic endeavors or activities. Subjects also ranked eight musical activities (other than composing) in order of femininity and ranked their own musical preferences using the same activity list.

Males and females strongly agreed on both the most feminine and the most masculine artistic items. Dancing in ballet, viewing ballet, singing in an opera, viewing an opera, and reading silently or listening to poetry were regarded as the most feminine activities. Composing or performing jazz, authoring a stage production, and composing classical music were viewed as masculine pursuits. Similarly, in femininity rankings, both sexes tended to rate the least active behaviors as feminine and the activities associated with jazz as masculine. There was some similarity between the preferred musical activities of the two sexes (listening to or collecting classical or jazz records). Performing jazz was the third-ranked preference for males, and the eighth (least-liked) activity for females. There was no relationship between preferred and feminine-rated activities for males, However, there was a moderate positive relationship between females' preferences and feminine-rated activities. Both men and women apparently regard creativity in the arts as a masculine characteristic. (8 references)

11
Goldberg, Susan, and Lewis, Michael. Play behavior in the year-old infant: Early sex differences. *Child Development,* 40(1):21-31, 1969.

Sex-role development. Infants. Play behavior. Mother-child relations.

A standardized free play situation was utilized to observe sex differences in the behavior of 13-month-old children toward mothers, toys, and a frustration situation. Data from a longitudinal study of the same sample were used to assess possible relations between behavior patterns at 6 and at 13 months. Maternal behavior in relation to differences in boys' and girls' behavior was also considered.

Observations were made of 32 girls and 32 boys and their mothers. Of the 64 infants, 9 girls and 10 boys were first borns, and the remaining infants had from one to six siblings. The procedures for the 6- and 13-month observations were similar, except for the use of a free play procedure at 13 months. A wood and mesh barrier between mother and child provided the source of child's frustration.

Striking sex differences in the infants' behavior toward their mothers and in their play were observed. Girls were more dependent, less exploratory, and quieter in play style than boys. Boys were less dependent, more exploratory and vigorous, played with toys requiring gross motor activity, and tended to run and bang in their play more than girls. In the frustration situation, girls cried more and boys tried more actively to get around the barrier. Comparisons of the mothers' behavior toward the infants at 6 months and at 13 months indicate that some of the sex differences were related to mothers' behavior toward infants. When the children were 6 months old, mothers touched, talked to, and handled their daughters more than their sons; and when they were 13 months old, girls touched and talked to their mothers more than boys did. It appears that parents behave differently toward girls and boys, even as infants, and thus reinforce sex-appropriate behavior. (13 references)

12
Greenstein, Fred I. Sex-related political differences in childhood. *Journal of Politics,* 23(2):353-371, 1961.

Political awareness. Elementary school students.

This discussion examines the childhood antecedents of sex differences in adult political behaviors and attitudes. Data are provided by literature on child development and by a survey of 659 fourth-through eighth-grade New Haven children, ages 9 to 14, of various socioeconomic levels. A selective review of the literature on sex differences in adult political behavior is included.

Media studies and political information studies from the 1920's through the 1950's indicate that boys exceed girls in interest in and information about matters related to politics. Studies conducted during World War II of children's familiarity with war suggested that differences in interest precede differences in information. The New Haven survey also confirmed the continuance of political sex differences among more contemporary school children. In all questionnaire responses, boys were found to be more political. Boys scored higher on political information (naming mayor, president) even in the fourth grade and were more likely than girls to be able to think of a news story, to prefer Washington to New Haven news, and to name a public figure as a famous person they did not emulate. All subjects were more likely to choose the father than the mother as an appropriate source of voting advice. The various data suggest that awareness of politics develops as an area of male specialization during childhood. (43 references)

13
Hall, Calvin, and Domhoff, Bill. A ubiquitous sex difference in dreams. *Journal of Abnormal and Social Psychology*, 66(3):278-280, 1963.

Dream content. Story content. Cultural differences.

Data from 11 separate investigations were pooled to determine the relative proportions of men and women represented in the dreams of each sex. Brief summaries of two anthropological dream studies and of three studies which did not concern dreams are provided as supplemental data. Subjects of the 11 dream studies comprised 1,399 men and 1,418 women. Age range was 2 to 80 years, although most subjects were college students. Men of all ages dreamed more about other men than they did about women, whereas women dreamed about men and women in almost equal proportions. Dream collections obtained from two widely separated ethnic groups, the Hopi of the American Southwest and the Yir Yoront of Australia, showed some minor differences but substantiated these findings.

Also reviewed are studies of impromptu listings of people liked and disliked, sex of characters in short stories written by men and by women, and the drawing power of male and female movie stars upon moviegoers. In each case, results showed a sex difference analogous to that found for dreams.

All of these findings are interpreted to suggest that the unresolved problems of males center on their relationships with men rather than with women, whereas those of females center on their relationships with both sexes about equally. Theoretical support for this hypothesis is derived from Freud's theory of the male and female oedipus complex. (3 references)

14

Hilton, Thomas L., and Berglund, Gosta W. Sex differences in mathematics achievement—A longitudinal study. *Journal of Educational Research,* in press, 1973.

Mathematical achievement. Intellectual maturation.

Sex-typed interests are investigated as possible causes of differences in mathematics achievement between the sexes. Longitudinal data from a growth study begun in 1961 by the Educational Testing Service were used. It was proposed that preadolescent differences in mathematics achievement would be negligible and that, beginning with adolescence, differences in achievement would appear and would widen thereafter in concert with widening differences in interests between the sexes.

Data were collected from a nationwide sample of fifth graders in 1961, and then again when they were in the 7th, 9th, and 11th grades, using the Sequential Test of Education Progress (STEP) and the School and College Ability Test (SCAT). Data from a 177-item background and experience questionnaire (BEQ) given each time except in 1961 were also utilized. Subjects were divided by academic and nonacademic curriculum. There were 632 boys and 688 girls in the academic group and 249 boys and 290 girls in the nonacademic group.

The findings supported the propositions. At grade five, there were no differences in achievement. Thereafter, boys pulled ahead of the girls, with parallel differences emerging with respect to perceiving mathematics as interesting and likely to be helpful in earning a living. (19 references)

15

Johnson, Olof, and Knapp, Robert H. Sex differences in aesthetic preferences. *Journal of Social Psychology,* 61:279-301, 1963.

Artistic preferences.

This analysis of data on sex differences in esthetic preferences draws primarily on research projects conducted by the authors. Preferences of men and women of similar backgrounds were compared for a range of art objects within an art field, as well as for styles within a medium. The preferences of several groups were analyzed to determine the magnitude of sex differences relative to differences due to other variables, such as age, social class, special art training, and vocation. Sample groups for the various studies ranged in size from 60 to 223 and consisted of high school students, college students, art students, student nurses, and teachers.

Results of these studies combined with evidence from other research suggest the following conclusions: Men and women do differ significantly in their preferences for all types of art. Differences in preference tend to be small in absolute terms when the total range of an art field is considered, but are greater in terms of specific styles within a medium of art. Sex differences are also considerably less than the differences in preference caused by such variation among groups as age, social class, special training, and vocation. A study of specific art objects preferred by men and women reflects sex differences in individual and social roles. (19 references)

16
Lester, Eva P.; Dudek, Stephanie; and Muir, Roy C. Sex differences in the performance of school children. *Canadian Psychiatric Association Journal,* 17(4):273-278, 1972.

Academic achievement. Elementary school students. Canada. Personality differences.

This longitudinal study is concerned with sex differences in the academic performance of elementary school children. The 107 children from a middle-class, suburban, English-speaking population in Montreal were tested in kindergarten through grade five. The California Achievement Test measured school achievement. To obtain correlates with achievement, psychiatric interviews with parents and children, intellectual and cognitive tests, motor and perceptual scales, and anxiety and personality scales were used.

Academic performance was markedly and consistently higher for girls in all grades. However, tests of intelligence, perceptual maturity, and conceptual ability showed no sex-linked differences; only tests of motor ability favored girls. No sex differences in academic performance were found in the interviews. To explain the higher female academic achievement, personality attributes were considered. On the Cattell Personality Questionnaire, statistically significant differences were found in three clusters: Girls were obedient and dependent, sober-minded and quiet, and practical and realistic; boys were assertive and independent, excitable and happy-go-lucky, and sensitive and free-thinking. The findings suggest that sex differences in personality may account for the higher academic achievement of girls. (8 references)

17
Lunneborg, Patricia W. Sex differences in aptitude maturation during college. *Journal of Counseling Psychology,* 16(5):463-464, 1969.

Academic ability. Aptitude maturation. College students.

This study investigated the hypothesis of equal aptitude maturation rates for the sexes in college. Subjects were 59 female and 67 male college seniors who scored above average on a multiaptitude pre-college battery given to them as high school seniors. They were retested in their senior year at college with the same battery for this study. Significant intellectual growth occurred on all tests; and although both sexes increased all scores substantially, the amounts of change between the two did not differ. A pattern of sex differences was sustained: Verbal differences were virtually absent, and males continued to score higher on quantitative tests and on spatial and mechanical reasoning. (2 references)

18

Lunneborg, Patricia W., and Lunneborg, Clifford E. Sex differences in aptitude maturation in a noncollege sample. *Journal of Counseling Psychology,* 19(6):529-536, 1972.

Academic ability. Aptitude maturation. Young adults.

To test the hypothesis of equal intellectual growth rates for the sexes, 50 women and 43 men who had taken the Washington State Pre-College Test battery but spent little or no time in college were retested 4 years after high school graduation. Mailed questionnaires provided additional personal and occupational data.

In contrast to previous findings for a college-attending sample, female subjects in this sample had lost their earlier slight verbal superiority over males and declined in quantitative abilities, whereas the males had improved somewhat with respect to aptitude scores. Questionnaire data revealed that the females had dropped out of college to work, whereas the males had temporarily interrupted their education for military service. More males than females were currently enrolled in college.

Among the employed subjects, most women held low-level office jobs, and the males held low-level technical jobs. However, the men had markedly higher educational and vocational aspirations than the women. An analysis of the subsample of subjects currently in college indicated that these aspirations were more significant in explaining the men's higher scores than their military training or current enrollment in college. Other studies are cited to support the theory that, where current educational experience is held constant, no sex differences in aptitude growth are evident. (10 references)

19

Maccoby, Eleanor E. Sex differences in intellectual functioning. In: Maccoby, Eleanor, ed. *The Development of Sex Differences.* Stanford, Calif.: Stanford University Press, 1966. pp. 25-55.

Academic ability. Academic achievement. Intellectual maturation.

This review of studies of sex differences in intellectual functioning concentrates on verbal, numerical, spatial, and analytic ability; general intelligence; creativity; and achievement. Correlations are presented for intellectual performance and personality and socialization variables, and explanations of performance differences between boys and girls are evaluated.

From various studies it appears that, in some aspects of intellectual development, impulsiveness is a negative factor for boys but not necessarily for girls. Correlations between and anxiety and aptitude or achievement are substantially negative for females, but vary for males. Aggressiveness appears to be less beneficial for intellectual development among boys than among girls. Male-female differences in the relationship between ability and achievement are more complex; although boys are less willing than girls to meet female teachers' demands, they are able to assess their abilities more realistically than girls and are less fearful of and disorganized by failure. Creativity and originality appear to be associated with cross-sex typing in both sexes, but particularly in females. In both sexes, the more passive-dependent children tend to perform poorly on intellectual tasks, and independent children tend to excel. Few studies relate parental attitudes or behavior to children's intellectual characteristics. It appears, however, that intellectual growth of boys is more dependent on a nurturant early environment than for girls.

Theories on the varied maturational timetables of the sexes, the direct effects of sex-typed interests, and differential learning opportunities are seen as insufficient explanations for sex differences in intellectual functioning. It is contended that sex-typed personality traits mediate intellectual functioning. Theories are offered to explain how the same psychological variable might have opposite effects on male and female intellectual development. Studies of possible genetic and environmental factors producing sex differences in personality traits and in intellectual performance indicate the complexity of how each sex uses its innate strengths and weaknesses to react to outside influences. (66 references)

20
Maccoby, Eleanor E., and Jacklin, Carol Nagy. Sex differences in intellectual functioning. In: *Assessment in a Pluralistic Society: Proceedings of the Educational Testing Service Invitational Conference on Testing Problems.* Princeton, N.J.: Educational Testing Service, 1973. pp. 37-51.

Academic ability. Academic achievement. Intellectual maturation. Methodological issues.

This selective review of the literature published since 1966 on sex differences in intellectual functioning emphasizes areas needing reconsideration and further research. To dispel misconceptions about intellectual sex differences, recent studies are compared and their methodological problems and weaknesses noted. In most studies using large, unselected samples of children, very few sex differences in verbal skills appear between ages 3 to 11, but girls gain an advantage at adolescence. The majority of studies of math ability show no sex differences up to adolescence, but when differences are found in the age range 9 to 13, they tend to favor boys. After age 13, boys tend to gain the advantage in math ability. In spatial ability, sex differences remain minimal and inconsistent until approximately age 10 or 11, when boys score consistently higher on a wide range of tests. The greater male vulnerability to prenatal and childhood injury and disease produces more very low scores by males on mental ability tests. However, no difference emerges in the number of boys and girls having high overall intellectual ability. Various studies of the physiological origins of intellectual sex differences suggest that spatial ability may be inherited through the opposite-sex parent, that differential brain lateralization may be related to the sexes' different ability patterns, and that either male or female hormones may promote aspects of prenatal growth affecting intellectual strength in both sexes. Little conclusive evidence exists regarding the mechanics of such processes, however. Examination of social-emotional factors has not yielded explanations adequately tying either girls' verbal superiority or boys' spatial and mathematical superiority to differing elements in their socialization or childhood activities. (No references)

21
May, Robert. Sex differences in fantasy patterns. *Journal of Projective Techniques,* 30(6):252-259, 1966. Also in: Bardwick, Judith M., ed. *Readings on the Psychology of Women.* New York: Harper & Row, 1972. pp. 301-307.

Fantasy. Sex-role perceptions.

This psychoanalytically oriented study of sex differences in personality empirically tested sex-linked fantasy patterns. Feminine masochism was expected to reveal itself in a typical sequence of negative followed by positive action and feeling in women's fantasy patterns. The typical male fantasy pattern, in contrast, was expected to be positive experience or feeling followed by negative. The predicted difference was assumed to reflect sex differences in social role, including expectations concerning one's life cycle and in the experience of one's own body.

Subjects were 60 female and 44 male college students drawn from undergraduate psychology courses at an urban coed university, a private women's college, and an engineering college. A group form Thematic Apperception Test was used, with four pictures presented in a fixed order. Instructions emphasized the rapid production of a dramatic, creative, and psychologically insightful story. The 416 stories obtained were scored to yield positive scores for the predicted female pattern (deprivation followed by enhancement) and negative scores for the predicted male pattern (enhancement followed by deprivation). Individual story scores were averaged to obtain a "person score."

The difference between the mean scores for males and females was in the predicted direction and was significant at the .0005 level. Approximately two-thirds of the subjects scored in the direction predicted for their sex (significant beyond the .001 level). Thus, the hypothesis was strongly supported, although the effect was not a categorical one. When results for the pictures were analyzed separately, the hypothesis was supported for three of the four. While the relative scores of males and females remained similar across pictures, the baseline was different for each picture. This finding emphasized the fact that the hypothesis in this study concerns relative rather than absolute shifts in emotional tone. Qualitative aspects of the stories written indicated that "giving up" or suffering has overtones of finality for men, whereas for women it could be a means to an end, or an opportunity. (32 references)

22

Morgan, Sherry Ward, and Mausner, Bernard. Behavioral and fantasied indicators of avoidance of success in men and women. 1971, 25 pp. (Mimeo.) Available from the author.

Success avoidance. Fantasy. Field dependency. High school students.

This study investigates the possibility that avoidance of success by males and females might be evidenced in their behavior without the motive expressed in fantasy. Subjects were students recruited from nonhonor chemistry classes in the high school of a predominantly white, middle-class suburb of Philadelphia. In session one, the first half of the ETS Hidden Figures Test (field dependency) was administered to 203 students. Students were also asked to respond to previously used verbal cues designed to elicit fantasy achievement responses. Students with scores in the first and last quartiles were identified as potential subjects for the second part of the study. Of the 103 students identified, only 56 were included in the next phase, which matched male-female pairs of unequal ability on the second half of the field dependency test. There were 14 pairs each of high males with low females, and high females with low males. The pairs took the test together, and an observer recorded interactions of subjects.

As expected, in fantasy boys showed as much or more evidence of
the motive to avoid success as girls; but in girls, learned sex-role
behavior outweighed ideology and produced behavioral avoidance of
success only in observed interactions. In these interactions, high males
lowered their levels of performance only slightly, while girls depressed
their performance significantly. (13 references)

23
Olesker, Wendy, and Balter, Lawrence. Sex and empathy. *Journal of
Counseling Psychology,* 19(6):559-562, 1972.

Empathy.

Sex differences in empathic ability were examined to test the
hypothesis that individuals have more empathy for persons of the
same sex than for those of the opposite sex. College students of
average tested intelligence comprised the sample of 48 males and 48
females. Empathic judgments were measured using a shortened
version of the Affective Sensitivity Scale, comprised of video-taped
excerpts from eight counseling sessions and a 42-item questionnaire
on the video-taped client's feelings about himself or herself. Subjects
were similar to the video-taped clients with regard to race
(Caucasian), age (16-26 years old), and education (college). Groups of
of 10 to 15 subjects were shown the video tapes, with the sex of the
judges (subjects) and of the person being judged (clients) systematically varied.

Results showed that males and females did not differ significantly in
empathic ability. However, significant differences were found between
same-sex and other-sex groups, supporting the hypothesis that
individuals show more empathy toward persons of the same sex. It is
suggested that contradictory findings from earlier studies of sex and
empathy may have resulted from the failure to consider the sex of
the person being judged as well as that of the judge. (28 references)

24
Reuband, Karl-Heinz. Status consciousness of women in Germany.
International Journal of Sociology of the Family, 2(1):1-5, 1972.

German Federal Republic. Self-concept. Social class aspirations.
Socioeconomic differences.

Subjective social class ratings of married men and women were
compared to test the hypothesis that women are more status-
conscious than men and therefore consider themselves in a higher
social class than do their husbands. Two random samples representa-

tive of the German Federal Republic (peasant population excluded) were combined to yield 1,101 male and 1,299 female married subjects. Data were the respondents' self-ratings on social class and the occupation of the main family earner.

The comparison of married men and women regarding subjective social-class rating showed negligible male-female differences for the aggregate. Ratings analyzed by the objective criterion of occupation (manual versus nonmanual labor) showed women as slightly more inclined than men to consider themselves in a higher class than warranted by the occupation of the main family earner. Organization of the data according to 15 occupational groups indicated that only among groups of highly skilled workers did women tend to list themselves in a higher class than men. Wives of professionals appeared more likely than their husbands to give themselves a low rating. These contradictory findings led to a rejection of the status consciousness hypothesis with respect to subjective social class. (14 references)

25
Richey, Marjorie H., and Fichter, James J. Sex differences in moralism and punitiveness. *Psychonomic Science,* 16(4):185-186, 1969.

Moralism. Punitiveness. Delinquency.

This study explored sex differences in judgments made about personal misconduct and dishonesty. Three hypotheses were tested: Females would make more moralistic judgments than males, females would be condemned more than males for personal improprieties but not for dishonesty; and both sexes would be more lenient toward their own sex in judgments of dishonest behavior. A sample of 120 male and female St. Louis University students read simulated newspaper stories in which a student was charged with one of two offenses: Cheating on an examination (dishonest behavior) or possession of marijuana (personal impropriety). There were two versions of each story, one with a male and one with a female offender. After reading whichever story they had been given, subjects rated the fictional student on character (morals), probable truthfulness of defense, and appropriate punishment.

There were no differences between male and female subjects in character or credibility ratings of offenders of either sex in either situation. In judging appropriate punishment, females were significantly more severe than males in prescribing action against female offenders for both offenses. There were, however, no differences in male and female subjects' recommendations for punishment of male offenders or in females' recommendations for male and female punishment. The findings for female offenders were therefore interpreted as indicating selective male lenience rather than female punitiveness. (5 references)

26

Singer, Judith E.; Westphal, Milton; and Niswander, Kenneth R. Sex differences in the incidence of neonatal abnormalities and abnormal performance in early childhood. *Child Development,* 39:103-122, 1968. Also in: Bardwick, Judith M., ed., *Readings on the Psychology of Women.* New York: Harper & Row, 1972. pp. 13-17.

Physiological maturation. Psychological adjustment. Preschool children. Infants.

Data from a larger study of cerebral palsy children conducted at 13 institutions across the United States were analyzed to determine sex differences among patients in physical, neurological, and psychological development from birth to 4 years. Previous research led to the expectation that sex differences would be found and that most of these would be to the disadvantage of the male. The main sample was 15,000 patients, 0-1 years old, from the study population, which was 55 percent Negro and had over 95 percent ward patients. Additional data were obtained for 100 three-year-olds from a Buffalo, N.Y., center and for 4-year-olds from Buffalo (N=71), Philadelphia (N=260), and Boston (N=100). Four sets of evaluative measures were taken for the first-year subjects and one set each for the 3- and 4-year-olds. On each of these measures, various aspects of development were categorized as normal, suspect, or abnormal.

Data were obtained at different developmental ages. On an 8-month examination, significant sex differences were found on all scales—mental, fine-motor, gross-motor, social-emotional, and overall summary. Males had significantly poorer scores on all these scales except the social-emotional. On a 12-month neurological examination, males had significantly more abnormal ratings than did females. They also had a significantly higher incidence of abnormalities on a summary of the first year of life and in the neonatal period. Of 88 three-year-olds for whom global speech and hearing scores were obtained, males had significantly more abnormal global ratings than females. Psychological examinations of the Buffalo 4-year-olds showed significant sex differences on all subscales, with males performing less well than females. Analysis of data from the Philadelphia and Boston 4-year-old groups resulted in sex differences which were in the same direction, although not as large as those in the Buffalo sample. Several possible origins and mechanisms of the sex differences found in this study are discussed. These differences are said to have implications for test standardization, for the use of controls in longitudinal studies of development, and for the understanding of mechanisms of reproductive casualty. (29 references)

27

Thagaard Sem, Tove. Sex differences in academic behavior. *Acta Sociologica*, 14(1-2):59-67, 1971.

Academic achievement. College students. Norway. Married students.

Formal aspects of academic behavior, derived from academic records of Norwegian male and female college students, were compared to examine the possible influences of marriage and children on educational outcomes. Subjects were 1,189 female and 4,502 male graduates of gymnasiums (secondary schools) from the years 1946, 1951, and 1958, who had registered at a university or college. University records provided data for each student on graduate versus dropout status, examination grades, field of study, and length of attendance. The Norwegian Government loan fund supplied information on marriage and children for the 1,373 male and 241 female students who graduated in 1958, making possible an investigation of reasons for temporary educational interruptions.

Results showed that 67 percent of the male but only 39 percent of the female students graduated from universities. A noticeable sex difference existed in field of study chosen. Sex differences in graduation varied with field of study; however, female graduation rates were not necessarily high in fields with large numbers of women. There were only slight differences in academic behavior between married and single students, with or without children. Although the data do not exclude the possibility that greater family obligations caused more women to drop out, marriage and children exerted only a small influence on the other variables. Sex differences in dropout rates were discussed in the contexts of the general selection-out process and of the existing egalitarian atmosphere within Norwegian universities. (21 references)

28

Turner, Ralph H. Some aspects of women's ambition. *American Journal of Sociology*, 70(3):271-285, 1964.

Career aspirations. Educational aspirations. Material aspirations. High school students.

This study attempts to differentiate male and female ambitions. In the past, "ambition" has been a male-oriented term, with female ambitions defined by analogy to male ambitions. Data collected from male and female high school seniors in Los Angeles were used. The questionnaire responses of 1,441 women were examined to discern patterns in the intercorrelations of women's ambitions compared with men's (based on an earlier study) and to determine career and noncareer patterns of ambition in women.

Distributions of ambition were studied by levels of material aspiration, educational aspiration, and occupational and eminence ambitions. Women were additionally questioned regarding acceptable minimum levels of future husband's occupation, education, and material standard of living. Seven ambition measures were intercorrelated, and patterns for women and men were compared. Two latent types of ambition for both men and women emerged from the correlational analysis: Material ambition, and women's career and men's eminence ambition. Although the same discrete measures of ambition appeared for men and women, they were more highly differentiated for women. Educational and occupational ambitions related substantially to material ambitions for men, but not for women, for whom educational ambition more often served intrinsic needs.

Virtually all the women expected to be homemakers, with 48 percent also expecting a lifetime career. Whereas women desiring careers stressed educational over material ambitions, women wishing only to be homemakers stressed the reverse. Since career and noncareer choosers, with minimum acceptable husband's occupation controlled, did not differ in material ambition, it seems that women expect to leave the extrinsic rewards to the husband while seeking intrinsic satisfactions from career and education. It is suggested that women who value intrinsic rewards more highly are more likely to seek careers. Comparisons between career choosers and noncareer choosers regarding value endorsements and sociometric characteristics supported this conclusion. (16 references)

29
Very, Philip S. Differential factor structures in mathematical ability. *Genetic Psychology Monographs,* 75:169-207, 1967.

Mathematical ability. College students. Cognitive styles.

Quantitative, verbal, and reasoning factors were investigated in an effort to measure and describe sex-differentiated mathematical ability. A battery of 30 tests was administered to 193 male and 162 female students enrolled in the summer term at Pennsylvania State

University. Sex differences in mathematical ability were measured by factor analyzing correlations among test scores for the total group and for each sex separately, and by comparing the mean scores.

The factorial structure identified for the total group was very similar to that found for college students in the existing literature. However, clear differences were found between the configurations of factors for the two sexes analyzed separately. There were more specific, clearly defined factors found for males than for females, particularly in the areas of reasoning and spatial ability. Additionally, the comparison of mean scores between sexes revealed significant differences in ability on 17 of the 30 tests. Males scored higher in 11 of the tests, generally those most closely related to specific mathematical processes. In six of the 17 tests, primarily those involving verbal ability and perceptual speed and accuracy, females scored higher. It is suggested that cultural pressures for greater exposure to and superior performance in mathematics may have increased male abilities. (16 references)

30
Vroegh, Karen. Masculinity and femininity in the elementary and junior high school years. *Developmental Psychology,* 4(2):254-261, 1971.

Masculinity. Femininity. Sex-typed behavior. Elementary school students. Junior high school students.

Personality correlates of "masculinity" and "femininity" were examined separately for grades 1-3, 4-6, and 7-8. The subjects were 209 boys and 201 girls in a school system in an upper middle-class Chicago suburb. Each subject completed one of three personality inventories used in the study. Masculinity and femininity were determined from peer and teacher rankings of gender identity. Although there was general agreement between teacher and peer rankings, the data from peer rankings allowed more specific conclusions.

Masculinity and femininity rankings were most strongly correlated with particular personal characteristics for students in grades 4-6. In this grade range, boys rated most masculine by their peers were socially, intellectually, and psychologically competent. Girls considered most feminine scored highest on traits of traditional femininity (e.g., patience) and social and intellectual competence. Masculine-rated boys and feminine-rated girls did not share similar personality characteristics in grades 7-8. Boys and girls during these years appear to make special efforts to distinguish themselves from one another by emphasizing their male or female qualities. In grades 7-8, masculinity was associated with venturesomeness, assertiveness, and group dependence; femininity was moderately linked to patience. Perhaps indicative of greater pressure on boys to achieve appropriate gender identity, boys more often than girls showed a definite pattern of development and greater specificity in the characteristics associated with their sex. (13 references)

31
Ward, William D. Variance of sex-role preference among boys and girls. *Psychological Reports,* 23:467-470, 1968.

Sex-role preference. Preschool children. Elementary school students.

This study tested the prediction that young girls would show greater group variance than young boys on a measure of sex-role preference. Forty-eight children from prekindergarten through the second grade were given a sex-oriented, toy preference test. The test was devised from a collection of 65 pictures of toys. The pictures were paired so that each set portrayed one masculine and one feminine toy. The measure of sex-role preference was the number of times the subject chose his or her own-sex toy.

The main hypothesis was supported by test results. With a direct measure of sex-role preference, girls showed significantly greater group variance than boys. A finding of secondary interest was that overall male-toy preferences of boys were significantly higher than the female-toy preferences of girls. The results tend to confirm the assumptions that children's toy preferences develop according to adult expectations and reinforcement of sex role, and that girls have more sex-role latitude than boys. (10 references)

32
Warshay, Diana W. Sex differences in language style. In: Safilios-Rothschild, Constantina, ed. *Toward a Sociology of Women.* Lexington, Mass.: Xerox College Publishing, 1972. pp. 3-9.

Language. Cognitive styles.

Content and style analyses were conducted to test whether men tend to use an instrumental language style and whether women tend to use an affective language style. It was hypothesized that, since males and females represent different sex statuses for which varied value systems and behavioral orientations exist, language as a behavior would reflect these differences.

A total of 263 middle-class, white, native-born students in a large Midwestern State university comprised the sample. The Important Events Test (IET) was the instrument; it requires subjects to write down all past events important to them. This instrument, devised specifically for the study, was designed to elicit responses that transcend role situation and highlight language relevant to social status. Data from the IET were grouped by sex and age. Language samples from the IET consisted of 3,311 separate events that were analyzed using categories developed from selected theoretical descriptions of social structure.

Males tend to write with less fluency, to refer to events with verb phrases, to be time-oriented, to involve themselves in references to events rather than people, and to locate events in their personal sphere of activity rather than refer to events that happened to others. Females tend to be more fluent, to refer to events with noun phrases, to be less personally involved in the events, to locate events outside their personal sphere of activity, and to refer more to events that happened to others. The interpretation is offered that the adult female, blocked or excluded from public achievement, seeks satisfaction in primary relations and in the local community. (13 references)

Mediators and Correlates

33
Becker, Gilbert. Ego defence pattern, extraversion-introversion, and sex-role adjustment. *British Journal of Social and Clinical Psychology,* 8:275-285, 1969.

Sex-role identification. Coping behavior.

An empirical study sought to replicate exploratory data on differences in the coping methods used by extraverts and introverts; to test whether there are particular extraversion-factor patterns associated with coping behavior; and to test whether a biological sex difference found in the exploratory study could be extended to psychological sex as well. It was hypothesized that scores on three extraversion-introversion scales (where a high score represents extraversion) would be negatively correlated with scores on a measure of tendency to use isolation rather than repression as a coping mechanism.

Subjects were 221 male and 210 female undergraduates in an introductory psychology course at Louisiana State University. Coping behaviors were measured by selected items from the revised Byrne R-S scale. Sex-role adjustment was assessed by comparing biological sex with scores on 38 items from the femininity scale of the

California Psychological Inventory. Extraversion-introversion was measured by 90 items from the Guilford-Zimmerman Temperament Survey, scored to assess three factors: restraint versus rhathymia (R), sociability (S), and thoughtfulness or thinking introversion (T).

Factor analysis indicated that extraversion scores on the S and T scales predicted repression tendencies, but predicted isolation tendencies on the R scale. An interaction among R, S, and T scores was interpreted to suggest that restraint in extraversion on S and T facilitates the tendency toward repression, whereas rhathymia inhibits it; and that rhathymia in introversion on S and T facilitates the tendency to use isolation, whereas restraint inhibits it.

No moderating effects were found for either sex or for femininity on the correlations between coping mechanism and R, S, or T scores. But factor analysis showed that males and females with masculine scores on the femininity scale tended to score toward the repression end of the R-S scale; conversely, females and males with feminine scores scored toward the isolation end. Well-adjusted (masculine) males tended to use more repression than isolation, whereas well-adjusted (feminine) females tended to use more isolation than repression. Those with poor sex-role adjustment behaved differently: masculine-identified females tended to score like well-adjusted males (more repression), whereas feminine-identified males tended toward an intermediate position. (10 references)

34

Bezdek, William, and Strodtbeck, Fred L. Sex-role identity and pragmatic action. *American Sociological Review,* 35(3):491-502, 1970.

Sex-role identification. Pragmatism. Idealism.

The initial purpose of this study was to evaluate experimentally the proposition that being means-oriented is structurally parallel with male sex-role requirements, whereas being goal-oriented is parallel with female role requirements. The entire junior class of a middle-class suburban high school outside Chicago provided 78 male and 96 female subjects. Sex-role identity was classified in three different ways: Biological sex, obtained from self-report; conscious sex-role preference, measured by the Gough Masculinity-Femininity Scale; and unconscious sex-role identification, measured by a projective technique, the Franck Drawing Completion Test. For the experimental treatment, one of two taped radio panel discussions was presented to the subjects in class. In each, an authority discussed water pollution either as a serious but unsolvable problem or as a not so serious problem which can be solved by citizen action. The dependent measure, taken as both a pretest and posttest, was subjects' willingness to take part in a program to reduce water pollution. This was measured by the sum of responses on a seven-point scale to eight different action proposals.

The predicted significant difference in outcomes—that feminine subjects would be readier to act in the serious/nonsolvable situation and masculine subjects would be readier to act in the not serious/solvable situation—was found only when subjects were classified on the basis of the Franck projective measure. No significant differences were found when the criterion was biological sex or score on the Gough scale. Nor were differences found when a supplementary, "nonobvious" attitude scale was used. The experimental treatment did not increase willingness to act, and the two treatments were roughly equal in their impact on willingness to act. The difference between the two experimental conditions is interpreted as the difference between a means-choice strategy without particular attention to goal, and a goal-choice strategy without particular attention to the means for its attainment. Interpretation of the projective drawing test as an index of unconscious sex-role identity is questioned, in view of the negative results for more directly sex-linked measures. It is suggested that the projective measure reflects role differences in the nuclear family and a pragmatic-versus-idealistic value distinction, which is not necessarily sex related. (19 references)

35

Connell, David M., and Johnson, James E. Relationship between sex-role identification and self-esteem in early adolescents. *Developmental Psychology,* 3(2):268, 1970.

Self-esteem. Adolescents. Sex-role identification.

This empirical study tested the hypothesis that early adolescent subjects with high appropriate sex-role identification have more positive feelings of self-esteem than those with low sex-role identification. Eighth-grade students in a Catholic parochial school, 70 boys and 73 girls, completed the Gough Femininity Scale and the Coopersmith Self-Esteem Inventory. The latter yielded a score for total feelings of self-esteem and subscores for general self-esteem and for self-esteem in relation to social interactions with peers, home life and interactions with parents, and performance in the academic area. Correlations between sex-role identification and total self-esteem were obtained. In addition, the 24 highest and 24 lowest scorers on the Gough Scale for each sex were selected to form four groups: High sex-role identification (high ID) for males and for females, and low sex-role identification (low ID) for males and for females. The data for these four groups were factor analyzed for differences in self-esteem scores.

High ID was significantly correlated with high total self-esteem for boys. For girls, there was no significant correlation between ID and total self-esteem. Factor analysis supported these general conclusions. For total, general, and social self-esteem with peers scores, there was no significant difference between high- and low-ID females, but there was a significant difference between high- and low-ID males. For the same three analyses, the interaction of ID with actual sex was also significant. That is, ID and self-esteem scores on these scales were differently related for males and females. For the total and general self-esteem scores, high-ID subjects differed significantly from low-ID subjects, and the order of findings was consistent: High-ID males scored highest, all females (high and low ID) next highest, and low-ID males lowest. The analyses for the home-parents subscale and the academic-school subscale showed no significant differences. Neither males nor females showed variations in feelings of self-esteem in these areas as a function of ID.

Results indicated that, as the adolescent male's sexual identification becomes more appropriate, his feelings of self-esteem increase, whereas there is no difference in feelings of self-esteem between early adolescent girls who identify with the masculine role and those who identify with the feminine role. It was concluded that the male role may have reward value in itself whether the role is adopted by a male or a female. (11 references)

36

Cottle, Thomas J.; Edwards, Carl N.; and Pleck, Joseph. The relationship of sex-role identity and social and political attitudes. *Journal of Personality,* 38:435-452, 1970.

Sex-role identification. Political attitudes. Social attitudes.

This study investigated the effects of conscious role preference and unconscious sexual identification on attitudes toward five categories of social and political issues. The sample of 85 men and 80 women, ranging in age from 18 to 78, from Boston working-class, middle-class, and upper-class communities, were classified into four sex-role configurations on the basis of combinations of conscious and unconscious masculinity and femininity scores. Instruments used were the Gough Masculinity-Femininity Scale, for social role preference; the Franck Drawing Completion Test, for unconscious sexual identification; and a 35-item inventory on attitudes toward political liberalism, birth control, sex-role morality, racial discrimination, and the achievement ethic.

Controlling for the effects of age, sex, marital status, occupation, education, and political affiliation, results indicated statistically significant associations between conscious and unconscious masculinity and femininity and attitudes toward all categories of social and political issues. Unconsciously masculine-consciously feminine (MF) and unconsciously feminine-consciously masculine (FM) males and females scored highest on political liberalism. FM males had the highest scores for items clustered and labeled "discrimination." MF women had the highest scores on the factor labeled "puritan achievement ethic." It is suggested that latent sexual aspects of these issues produce some of the ideological inconsistencies found. Individual aspects of unconscious and conscious identity rather than unconscious-conscious interaction were associated with the factors of birth control and sex-role morality. Both unconscious and conscious femininity were linked with support of birth control. Sex-role morality was supported by unconsciously masculine males and consciously feminine females. Sex-role identity as a value and sex-role differentiation in the integration of personality and of society are briefly discussed. (30 references)

37
Eagly, Alice H. Sex differences in the relationship between self-esteem and susceptibility to social influence. *Journal of Personality,* 37(4):581-591, 1969.

Self-esteem. Social attitudes. Sex-role identification.

This study investigated sex differences in the validity of self-esteem and sex-role identification as predictors of opinion change in response to reported opinions of peers. Subjects were 96 male and 121 female ninth-grade students from an urban Massachusetts high school. Self-esteem was measured by the Feelings of Inadequacy Scale; and sex-role identification, by the Gough Femininity Scale. Subjects completed an opinion questionnaire on social, economic, educational, and personal values before and after receiving information concerning the group's mean responses to the questions.

Males and females did not differ in amount of opinion change toward the reported averages, nor did the variability of opinion (toward or away from the mean) differ between the sexes. Among females, sex-role identification was significantly related to amount of opinion change: The more feminine girls yielded more to the reported means than did the less feminine girls. Self-esteem did not relate to opinion change for females. Among boys, however, subjects with the highest and lowest self-esteem scores tended to change their opinions less than those with self-esteem scores in the middle range. Sex-role identification did not relate to the amount of opinion change for males. No interaction between self-esteem and sex-role identification occurred for either sex. (25 references)

38
Epstein, Ralph, and Liverant, Shephard. Verbal conditioning and sex-role identification in children. *Child Development,* 34:99-106, 1963.

Conditioning. Sex-role identification. Elementary school students. Experimenter effect.

This study tested the hypothesis that, in a verbal conditioning situation, the differential reinforcement value of male and female adults would vary with the level of sex-role identification of young children. An initial sample consisted of 135 boys (ages 5 to 7) from the kindergartens and first grades of two lower middle-class public schools in Columbus, Ohio. The subjects were administered the It Scale for Children, a projective test of sex-role identification. The 40 highest and 40 lowest scorers were selected for the conditioning situation. The conditioning procedure involved the presentation of 75 questions, each of which could be answered by the response "father," "mother," "sister," or "brother." Depending on the appropriate condition, father or mother responses were rewarded by verbal approval. Differences in frequency of the rewarded response between the first (nonrewarded) and last (rewarded) trials constituted the measure of conditioning.

The major hypotheses concerning the relationship between a strong masculine-role identification and the reinforcement value of a male experimenter were confirmed. Subjects with a strong masculine identification were conditioned more effectively by a male experimenter than by a female experimenter. Both high-masculine and low-masculine identifiers conditioned more to "father" than to "mother." The generally poorer conditionability of the low-masculine identifiers was explained by the greater ambivalence and conflict experienced by boys with inappropriate identification. (14 references)

39
French, Elizabeth G., and Lesser, Gerald S. Some characteristics of the achievement motive in women. *Journal of Abnormal and Social Psychology,* 68(2):119-128, 1964.

Academic achievement. Social skills, Achievement motivation. College women.

The main hypothesis of this study was that females would respond to arousal cues with heightened achievement motivation scores and high motivation-performance relationships only when the cues were relevant to their achievement value orientations. Subjects were 432 female undergraduates from three coeducational and three women's colleges. On the basis of homogeneity of Student Attitude Scale scores, a women's and a coeducational institution were chosen to represent each of three value orientations: High intellectual-low woman's role, high intellectual-high woman's role, and low intellectual-high woman's role. Subjects were administered the Test of Insight, a measure of motivation level, under both neutral and arousal conditions. Half the sample (M group) took the motivation form with male figures, and half (F group) took the form with female figures. For each college, one M group and one F group took a vocabulary performance test under intellectual arousal conditions (being told their intelligence was being tested), and one M group and one F group took a social skills performance test under woman's role arousal conditions (being told social skills were necessary for successful marriage).

Motivation scores of subjects with intellectual orientation were found to be heightened by intellectual arousal. Scores of subjects with woman's role orientation were heightened by woman's role arousal. The sample as a whole, regardless of value orientation, had higher motivation scores when responding to male figures under intellectual arousal and to female figures under woman's role arousal. Motivation scores from the female figure test form predicted performance best in all cases except that of women under intellectual arousal who value both goals. In both motivation and performance, subjects oriented toward woman's role who took the male form motivation test responded to intellectual arousal, suggesting that they see intellectual attainment as desirable for males although not for themselves. (9 references)

40
Hammer, Emanuel F. Creativity and feminine ingredients in young male artists. *Perceptual and Motor Skills,* 19:414, 1964.

Creativity. Artistic activities. Femininity. Adolescent males.

The relationship between creativity and feminine characteristics in young male artists was examined. An initial sample of 57 high school students who won art scholarships at New York University was grouped by art professors on the basis of a two-semester workshop as artistically facile but noncreative, indefinite, or genuinely creative. A final sample of 23 males from the facile and creative groups was rated for sex-typed personality characteristics. Ratings were based on sex of the projected human images and unmasculine components on the Rorschach Test and sex misrecognition of the figures on the Thematic Apperception Test.

Creative subjects were significantly more feminine on these measures than the facile subjects. However, creative males were also differentiated from facile males by their higher measures of strength, confidence, determination, ambition, and power. It is concluded that an integration of feminine sensitivity and intuition and masculine purposive action and determination produced the capacity for creative artistry in these males. (No references)

41

Helson, Ravenna. Personality of women with imaginative and artistic interests: The role of masculinity, originality, and other characteristics in their creativity. *Journal of Personality*, 34:1-25, 1966.

Creativity. Artistic activities. College women. Parental influence.

This study tested the hypothesis that creative women with imaginative and artistic interests are more masculine, original, and intelligent and have a stronger need for accomplishment than less creative women with these interests. Subjects were 135 women from two Mills College senior classes, including 36 students nominated by the faculty as outstandingly creative, and 139 women from the University of California, 11 of whom had received "A" grades for creative term papers. The Childhood Activities Checklist provided data on imaginative and artistic interest and "tomboy" pursuits. All subjects completed at least one personality inventory. Masculinity was measured by several identity scales; need for accomplishment, by college averages; and originality, by the Unusual Uses Test, Thematic Apperception Test stories, and the Barron Originality Scale. Intelligence was measured by SAT verbal scores. Parents of creative nominees from Mills completed measures of personality and values and questionnaires on their daughter's childhood; and students from UC completed a descriptive checklist of their parents.

The imaginative-artistic syndrome (IA) was found to correlate with mistrust of personal relationships, impulsiveness, rebelliousness, introspection, independent judgment, and originality. Mothers of IA women tended to have similar characteristics, and many IA's had had difficult early relations with their mothers. Of the 43 IA's in the total sample, 18 were creative nominees. The number of UC creative IA's (six) was too small for analysis. The Mills creative IA's had significantly higher scores on intelligence and need for accomplishment than other Mills IA's. However, they were not significantly more masculine in ratings of assertion, analytical thinking, or general personality. A "tomboy" history did not consistently contribute to developing assertiveness or creative traits. Compared with other IA's, the creative women had even stronger symbolic interests and need for autonomy, avoided outside influence and acting on impulse, and were motivated to assume the role of the creative person. Fathers of creative IA's differed from the fathers of the other IA's more than the comparable groups of mothers differed. Fathers of creative IA's were intellectually oriented and placed a high value on moral integrity. (36 references)

42
Helson, Ravenna. Women mathematicians and the creative personality. *Journal of Consulting and Clinical Psychology*, 36(2):210-220, 1971. Also in: Bardwick, Judith M., ed. *Readings on the Psychology of Women*. New York: Harper & Row, 1972. pp. 93-100.

Mathematicians. Professional women. Creativity.

An empirical study of the personality, research style, and background characteristics of women mathematicians was designed to contribute to the understanding of creativity and to appraise women's creativity and potential for scientific accomplishment. It also tested the notion that creative women mathematicians must be "abnormal." Subjects were from 41 to 47 women who had obtained a Ph. D. in mathematics between 1950 and 1960 and were referred by their graduate institution or fellow mathematicians. Age range was 24-64; two-thirds of the sample were married; and most came from Jewish or Protestant backgrounds. The creativity of each subject was rated by mathematicians in her field of specialization, and subjects were categorized into creative comparison groups based on these ratings. The creative group was believed to constitute virtually all creative women mathematicians in the United States at the time. Assessment procedures included a variety of tests and measures in several areas: Intelligence, personality characteristics, interests, cognitive and esthetic abilities, mathematical style, and personal and professional history.

Findings showed that the women classified as creative were performing at a higher level of professional achievement than the comparison subjects. Results offered no support for the idea that creative women mathematicians differed greatly from other women Ph. D.'s in mathematics in cognitive abilities or for the idea that they might be more masculine on the type of measures used. However, many large differences were found between the creative and comparison subjects in background and personality. The traits most characteristic of the creative women were rebellious independence, narcissism, introversion, and a rejection of outside influence; strong symbolic interests and a marked ability to find self-expression and self-gratification in directed research activity; and flexibility, or lack of constriction, in general attitudes and in mathematical work. These traits also appeared stronger in the creative women mathematicians than in creative men mathematicians tested in another study. The creative women sought and, despite obstacles, attained more integration and simplification of life than comparison women. The present study did not investigate why so few women in this country pursue the study of higher mathematics, but the extent of foreign birth and parentage in the sample and the degree to which the creative women were found to reject outside influences suggest that countervailing social pressures are a major factor. (33 references)

43

Hollender, John. Sex differences in sources of social self-esteem. *Journal of Consulting and Clinical Psychology,* 38(3):343-347, 1972.

Self-esteem. College students.

The interaction of sex of subject with various sources of social self-esteem was examined in relation to level of social self-esteem. Source variables selected were need for approval, course grades, family sibling structure, and perceived parental identification. It was hypothesized that the level of social self-esteem would not differ between sexes, but that its correlates would differ for the two sexes. Subjects were 40 female and 38 male students in an introductory psychology course at Emory University. Social self-esteem was measured by having each subject rank order himself or herself within a set of five social roles; six such sets were ranked by each subject. The Marlowe-Crowne Social Desirability Scale measured need for approval. A nine-item semantic differential rating indicated perceived parental identification. The family structure variables were ordinal position and sex of sibling. Course grades were reported by the instructor.

Results showed a negative correlation of social desirability scores with self-esteem for females, but not for males. For males, a low course grade was associated with lower self-esteem; for females, a high grade was associated with lower self-esteem. Sex differences were also found in the relationship between family structure and self-esteem: For males analyzed separately, first borns with female second siblings had higher self-esteem than first borns with male second siblings; for females analyzed separately, family structure variables yielded no significant differences. For all first borns, self-esteem was lower in females than in males, regardless of sex of the second sibling. For both sexes analyzed together, first borns with second-born siblings of the opposite sex had higher self-esteem than those with same-sex second siblings. No significant differences were found in the parental identification analysis. (16 references)

44
Israel, Joachim, and Eliasson, Rosmari. Consumption society, sex roles and sexual behavior. *Acta Sociologica,* 14(1-2):68-82, 1971.

Sex-role perceptions. Sexual behavior. Sweden. Moralism.

Untested hypotheses and some empirical data concerning Scandinavian and American sex-role expectations are explored in relation to actual sexual behavior. The relationship between capital accumulation and puritan morality is discussed in terms of need gratification. It is postulated that rapid industrialization necessitates deferment of need gratification, including a restrictive sexual morality. In the present highly industrialized, consumption-oriented society, however, the emphasis is on gratification of needs, which extends to sexuality. Changes in the basic process of production are also seen as effecting changes in sex roles, particularly for women.

A random sample of 663 men and 634 women, ages 16 to 25, was interviewed in Stockholm, Sweden, regarding sexual behavior, norms, and attitudes. Findings suggest that the more sexually permissive the society, the less pervasive the sexual double standard. Factor analysis of various attitude scales yielded such factors as pragmatic puritanism (a restrictive sexual attitude pragmatically grounded in the risks involved); romantic love moral (an attitude stressing the necessity of being in love with one's sexual partner); and acceptance of traditional sex-role expectations (involving attitudes toward authority, division of labor in the home, and the emotional characteristics of men and women). The romantic love moral was highly correlated with being a woman, rather than with social background factors. The majority of males interviewed apparently had rejected the romantic love moral. For females, acceptance of traditional sex-role expectations was positively correlated with pragmatic puritanism. In general, a restrictive sexual attitude was correlated with acceptance of traditional sex-role expectations.

Findings are also presented comparing attitudes with actual (reported) sexual activity. Men reported more sexual activity than did women; however, most within-sex differences exceeded the between-sex differences. Men and women who had accepted a romantic love moral were more similar in extent of sexual activity than men and women who had rejected it. An interviewer bias effect was found in this study: Male subjects gave more traditional answers to male interviewers, and female subjects did the same with female interviewers. It is suggested that traditional female sex roles in a permissive society may be more controlled by the expectations of women than of men. (9 references)

45

Lansky, Leonard M.; Crandall, Vaughn J.; Kagan, Jerome; and Baker, Charles T. Sex differences in aggression and its correlates in middle-class adolescents. *Child development,* 32:45-58, 1961.

Aggression. Adolescents. Sex-role identification.

This study investigated sex differences in the relationships between aggressive behaviors and other behavioral areas, such as achievement, dependence, affiliation, sex anxiety, sex-role identification, moral standards, and defenses against guilt. Subjects were 32 male and 22 female middle-class adolescents, 13 to 18 years old, enrolled in a longitudinal study at the Fels Research Institute. Individual interview sessions explored the following behaviors: Achievement, dependence, affiliation, self-esteem, aggression toward parents and authorities, attitudinal differences with parents, anxiety over heterosexual relationships, and identification with parental models. A modified version of the Rorschach test investigated aggression and sex anxiety. At a group session, the Gough Femininity Scale and the Franck Drawing Completion Test were used to measure sex-role identification; the French Insight Test, to examine achievement, dependency/autonomy, and affiliation; a story completion test, to investigate severity of standards and defenses against guilt; and a self-rating inventory, to test aggression, acceptance, and parental identification.

On individual variables, boys scored higher than girls on reported aggression toward father (in the interview), aggression (on the self-rating inventory), independence-autonomy, and severity of moral standards. Girls scored higher than boys with respect to preoccupation with affiliation (on the French test), anxiety about sexual activity (expressed in the self-rating inventory), femininity of attitudes and interests (on the Gough test), and in taking responsibility for aggressive action toward a frustrating authority (as assessed from the story completion test).

There was a greater number of significant interrelations among aggression variables for the boys than for the girls. However, there was a greater number of significant relations for girls' aggression scores and measures of other behaviors. For the boys, both aggression toward father and Rorschach aggression were positively related to self-rated need for acceptance and dependency scores. For the girls, expressed criticism of mother was related to preoccupation with recognition for achievement, anxiety about sexuality, low concern with affiliation, low desire to be similar to mother, and minimal guilt about aggressive acts directed against a male authority. Expressed criticism of father by the girls was negatively related to desire to be similar to mother and to conform with authorities. Girls' aggressive Rorschach imagery was negatively related to high affiliation scores. Results are discussed in reference to the different sex-role demands and conflicts of middle-class adolescent boys and girls. (11 references)

46
Lipsitt, Paul D., and Strodtbeck, Fred L. Defensiveness in decision making as a function of sex-role identification. *Journal of Personality and Social Psychology*, 6(1):10-15, 1967.

Sex-role identification. Jury decisions. Sex-role conflict. Homosexuality.

Styles of defenses invoked by individuals representing varying sex-role identities were distinguished in a decisionmaking task. Subjects were 380 male naval enlisted personnel, ages 18 to 29, who were assigned to a hospital corpsman training school. Franck Drawing Completion Test scores (unconscious sex-role identity) and Gough Femininity Scale scores (conscious sex-typed attitudes and interests) were used to classify the subjects into four unconscious-conscious sex-role identity groups: MM, MF, FM, and FF. The decisionmaking task required a verdict on whether a fictional soldier was guilty of treason. Subjects heard one of four taped simulated trials: In one version, no arousal material was introduced; in another, the judge intervened to rule that evidence of the defendant's character was admissible; in a third version, homosexuality was ascribed to the defendant; and in a fourth version, both the judge's intervention and the allegation of homosexuality were included.

In the version without arousal material and the version containing only the judge's intervention, the frequencies of guilty and not guilty verdicts were not significantly different among subjects in the four sex-role categories. However, subjects who were unconsciously feminine and consciously masculine were more likely than other subjects to find a defendant guilty when homosexuality was alleged. Both unconsciously and consciously feminine subjects were significantly more likely to find the defendant not guilty when the judge's intervention was combined with the homosexual reference. Subjects with unconscious and conscious masculine identities varied least in decisions in the several versions of the trial. These findings are discussed in reference to the relationship between sex-role identity and selection of defenses against inner conflict. (7 references)

47
Lirtzman, Sidney I., and Wahba, Mahmoud A. Determinants of coalitional behavior of men and women: Sex roles or situational requirements? *Journal of Applied Psychology*, 56(5):406-411, 1972.

Group performance. Competitiveness.

A challenge is presented to the hypothesis that women in coalition formation and bargaining situations adopt an "accommodative" or anticompetitive strategy related to sex role. The alternative hypothesis is offered that, in competitive situations where the outcome is uncertain, women will follow the same strategies as men—those predicted by an expectancy model of coalition formation (CEU, or Coalition Expected Utility, theory). Outcomes predicted by each hypothesis are compared with actual behavior in an experimental situation.

Subjects were 48 female undergraduates recruited by campus advertisements and grouped into 16 triads. For each of 60 trials, each subject was randomly assigned to one of three arbitrary positions within her triad, and different predetermined "resource levels" were assigned to each position. On the basis of these resource levels, subjects then chose partners within the triad with whom to form a coalition of two. Mutual choice determined the final coalition; and if no coalition was formed, the trial was terminated. After coalition formation, subjects played a card game in which both the preassigned resources and the chance draw of cards determined the outcome. The outcome, in turn, determined small but real monetary winnings or losses. For each trial, the actual outcome of coalition formation was then compared with the predictions of CEU theory, with the noncompetitive "feminine strategy" theory, and with results previously obtained from men.

CEU predictions were verified in 73 percent or more of the cases, a higher proportion than the alternative prediction. For some trials, predictions from the two theories were the same. The difference between obtained results and a theoretical chance distribution of equal frequencies was highly significant. Results closely paralleled those for men; in fact, they matched CEU predictions somewhat more closely than the men's results had. The conclusion is drawn that, at least in situations where a norm of competition is set up and where there is uncertainty, women employ the same competitive strategies in coalition formation as do men. Thus, the common rationale for excluding women from high positions in complex organizations—that they will behave noncompetitively on the basis of their sex roles—is asserted to be a fallacy. The determining force of situational factors rather than sex roles is supported. (18 references)

48
LoPiccolo, Joseph, and Blatt, Sidney J. Cognitive style and sexual identity. *Journal of Clinical Psychology,* 28:148-151, 1972.

Cognitive styles. Sex-role conflict. Homosexuality.

This is a report of two studies that explored the relationships between style and sex-role conflict in men and women. It was hypothesized that a reversal in male (logical and fact-oriented) and female (intuitive and passive) cognitive styles would be related to problems of sexual identity.

In study I, 150 male and 50 female college freshmen were administered the information and comprehension subtests of the Wechsler Adult Intelligence Scale. As expected, males generally scored higher on the fact-oriented information test, and females scored higher on the comprehension test, which measured passive acceptance of social conventions. From this group, seven males and nine females with higher information than comprehension scores (I>C) and eight males and nine females with higher comprehension than information scores (C>I) were selected. These subjects were administered an eye-fixation test to measure homosexual tendencies and a Thematic Apperception Test (TAT) to provide data on homosexual tendencies and defensiveness about heterosexual motivation.

There were no significant differences between the I>C and C>I females on any of the sex-role conflict measures. C>I males showed significantly higher scores on the TAT homosexuality scale and greater defensiveness on the defensiveness scale. However, on all three sections of the eye-fixation test where there were significant differences between I>C and C>I males, the I>C group had the higher homosexual tendency scores.

In study II, 119 female and 55 male freshmen were administered the information and comprehension subtests plus the MMPI masculinity-femininity scale. The correlation between I-C balance and masculinity-femininity scores was not significant for females. For males, the correlation approached significance. Males obtained higher I-C balance scores than females, supporting the hypothesis that cognitive style is somewhat sex stereotyped. Although both studies showed cognitive style and sex-role conflict to be related in males, because of the lack of verified measures of sexual-identity conflict in women, it was not possible to interpret female results. (8 references)

49
Marcia, James E., and Friedman, Meredith L. Ego identity status in college women. *Journal of Personality,* 38(2):249-263, 1970.

College women. Self-concept.

Ego identity status constructs that were initially validated for men were augmented and explored to develop a consistent theory of ego identity status for college women. These constructs were examined in relation to five dependent variables: Difficulty of college major, cognitive efficiency and flexibility, self-esteem, authoritarianism, and anxiety.

Subjects were 49 senior women volunteers at the State University of New York at Buffalo. A 30-minute semistructured tape interview evaluated presence or absence of decisionmaking (crisis) and extent of personal investment (commitment) in the areas of occupation, ideology, and sexual standards (the added criterion—attitudes toward premarital intercourse). Subjects were classified into four identity status categories: Identity achievement (past crisis, current commitments); moratorium (in crisis, vague commitments); foreclosure (no crisis, firm commitments); and identity diffusion (no crisis, no commitments). Five different tests were administered to measure each subject on the five dependent variables.

Although limits were found in the range of the constructs when applied to cognitive activities, the significant findings supported the general applicability of ego-identity status constructs to women. Identity-achievement women were majoring in more difficult college subjects, than identity-diffusion women. Identity-achievement and moratorium subjects did not, however, show more cognitive flexibility than foreclosure and identity-diffusion subjects. Contrary to expectations, identity-diffusion subjects, rather than moratorium subjects, obtained the highest anxiety scores. Moratorium subjects were lowest on authoritarianism, and foreclosure subjects were highest. As expected, significantly higher self-esteem scores and lower anxiety scores were found for foreclosure subjects than for others. This particular finding is interpreted as possibly reflecting either approval-seeking test behavior or the special adaptive value of foreclosure status for women. (22 references)

50
Poffenberger, Thomas, and Norton, Donald. Sex differences in achievement motive in mathematics as related to cultural change. *Journal of Genetic Psychology*, 103:341-350, 1963.

Mathematical achievement. Sociocultural determinants. High school students. Propaganda.

This study tested the hypothesis that cultural propaganda affects the interest and achievement motivation of high school males more than females. The "propaganda" was defined as the emphasis American society placed on the importance of mathematical education following the early Russian space successes. In 1955 all freshmen (208 males and 188 females) at California State University at Davis completed questionnaires on their high school overall grade averages and grades in mathematics, their attitudes toward mathematics, and sources of their achievement motivation. Questionnaires were also administered in 1960 to all incoming freshmen at the university (309 males and 460 females). It was expected that the intervening 5 years would reflect the changes in cultural emphasis on technology.

Girls in both samples reported higher overall high school grades than boys, although boys' grades increased more over time. Both sexes in 1960 showed significantly higher grades in first-year algebra than in 1955, with the boys showing a greater increase than the girls. While girls in the 1960 sample did not vary from 1955 girls in their attitudes toward mathematics, significantly more male freshmen in 1960 than in 1955 reported preferring mathematics to other high school subjects. Both boys and girls in 1960 viewed parents as expecting higher math grades than did the 1955 sample; however, in 1960 significantly more boys than girls reported that their parents expected high grades. There was no significant difference between boys and girls in 1955 on the ratings of parental expectations about math grades. It was concluded that, while girls responded generally to the "propaganda" for excellence in scholarship, boys were stimulated more by the specific post-Sputnik cultural cues for improvement in mathematics. (4 references)

51
Sherman, Julia A. Problem of sex differences in space perception and aspects of intellectual functioning. *Psychological Review,* 74(4):290-299, 1967.

Spatial perception. Intellectual maturation. Cognitive styles.

This theoretical essay argues that sex differences in spatial perception offer an important aid in explaining sex differences in various aspects of intellectual functioning. Existing research is cited to support a critique of the analytical cognitive approach and to offer a causal explanation of sex differences on the basis of differential learning. Rod and Frame, Embedded Figures, and geometric and mathematical reasoning tests were examined as sex-biased indicators of analytical ability. Further, the criticism of the analytical cognitive approach centers on its exclusion of verbal tasks, many of which are as analytical as the nonverbal tasks currently used.

The differential learning of spatial skills argument offers evidence that these skills can be learned and that differences in learning opportunity stem from sex-role socialization—girls are early inclined toward verbal and socially mediated problem solving; and boys, toward a spatial approach. The sex-role link between personality variables and performance on perceptual tasks is briefly considered. The conclusion is that relationships between sex typing and analytical skill can be reduced by controlling for spatial perception and that, since spatial skill can be learned, it could become a significant factor in improving remedial education. (36 references)

52
Vroegh, Karen. Lack of sex-role differentiation in preschoolers' figure drawings. *Journal of Projective Techniques and Personality Assessment,* 34(1):38-40, 1970.

Preschool children. Sex-role identification. Figure drawings.

Preschoolers' figure drawings were studied to determine their validity as measures of sex-role identity. Subjects were 151 white, upper middle-class preschoolers. They were selected by pair comparisons made by 40 preschool teachers who designated most masculine boys (MM), least masculine boys (LM), most feminine girls (MF), and least feminine girls (LF) in their classrooms. Of the subjects, 38 were MM, 33 LM, 44 MF, and 40 LF; the subjects in each group were classified as younger (39 to 53 months) or older (54 to 66 months).

Analysis indicated that neither age nor teacher-rated sex-role identity is related to reported sex of figures. Biological sex membership was related to the drawing of like-sex figures. However, only 15 percent of the drawings were rated as being differentiated on the basis of sex. These findings cast doubt on the usefulness of figure drawings of preschool children as measures of sex-role or sexual identity. (4 references)

53
Vroegh, Karen; Jenkin, Noel; Black, Michael; and Handrich, Millicent. Discriminant analysis of preschool masculinity and femininity. *Multivariate Behavioral Research,* 2:299-313, 1967.

Preschool children. Masculinity. Femininity. Methodological issues.

The nature and dimensions of the constructs of masculinity and femininity as applied to preschool age children were investigated experimentally. The traditional constructs of masculinity and femininity, based on normative data from unselected male and female criterion groups, were hypothesized to be different from the constructs of masculinity and femininity actually used by people in everyday life. A second hypothesis was that masculinity and femininity are not opposite ends of a single bipolar continuum.

Forty female preschool teachers of private nursery schools ranked all boys in their classes on degree of masculinity and all the girls on femininity by the method of pair comparisons. Four criterion groups of children were then selected from the most masculine boys (MM), the least masculine boys (LM), the most feminine girls (MF), and the least feminine girls (LF) from each teacher's rankings. These 160 children (40 in each criterion group) were then rated by the teacher on eight-point unipolar scales for 60 personality variables. The personality variables were factor analyzed and four factors were identified: Extraversion-introversion, social adjustment, competence, and an unnamed factor which appeared to involve a combination of exuberant activity and problem behavior.

Discriminant analyses using the four criterion groups indicated that MM boys were more extraverted, somewhat more competent, and slightly better adjusted than LM boys. MF girls were socially better adjusted, somewhat more competent, and slightly more introverted than LF girls. The constructs of masculinity and femininity revealed in this study are related to, but not identical with, the traditional constructs. Moreover, the low coefficient of congruence found between the discriminant patterns for masculinity and femininity indicates that these constructs are not opposite ends of one continuum. (32 references)

THE DEVELOPMENT OF SEX DIFFERENCES AND SEX ROLES

Biological Determinants

54

Archer, John. Sex differences in emotional behaviour: A reply to Gray and Buffery. *Acta Psychologica*, 35:415-429, 1971.

Sex hormones. Emotionality. Rodents.

Detailed logical and empirical evidence is invoked in criticism of a particular theory of the relationship of emotionality to sex. Gray and Buffery are said to have argued that female rodents are less emotional or fearful than males, that the reverse is true for human beings, and that these sex differences in emotionality may have a specific endocrine basis and be adaptively significant in relation to social structure.

A number of specific criticisms are made of this theory in its application to rodents. First, measures from the tests cited are said not to be related in a way which is adequately described by a unitary concept. Second, it is asserted that sex differences in fear measured by these tests are not controlled by the same set of hormonal factors in each case. Third, sex differences in open field measures are said to be more variable than was suggested. An alternative view of sex differences in avoidance conditioning is presented which is said to account more adequately for recent work involving sex hormones. Alternative explanations are presented for sex differences in corticosterone levels and response to crowding. More general criticisms are then made of the theory's inferences regarding the adaptive significance of sex differences in emotionality.

Several crucial assumptions of the theory are questioned: That hormonal effects on behavior are most usefully considered in terms of major motivational variables; that all hormonally produced sex differences are the result of the direct effect of the hormones on the central nervous system; that such sex differences are relatively fixed genetic characteristics; and that an adequate foundation for a general theory of sex differences is provided by an understanding of animal societies in terms of the traditional concepts of dominance and territoriality. (71 references)

55
Broverman, Donald M.; Klaiber, Edward L.; Kobayashi, Yutaka; and Vogel, William. Roles of activation and inhibition in sex differences in cognitive abilities. *Psychological Review,* 74(1):23-50, 1968.

Cognitive ability. Sex hormones.

To construct a biological framework with which to conceptualize normal human individual differences in certain mental abilities, the hypothesis is offered that observed sex differences in cognitive abilities reflect sex-related differences in physiology. Studies concerning the effects of sex hormones on adrenergic and cholinergic processes in learning phenomena were examined with respect to cognitive sex differences: Males excel on complex tasks requiring inhibition of immediate responses to obvious stimulus attributes in favor of responses to less obvious stimulus attributes; females surpass males on simple, overlearned perceptual-motor tasks. It is hypothesized that the variation between the sexes reflects differences in relationships between adrenergic activating and cholinergic inhibitory neural processes, which are sensitive to the gonadal steroid sex hormones, androgens and estrogens.

The authors conclude that assessments of cognitive processes should examine differences between abilities that vary as a function of differences in internal organismic states. (176 references)

56
Dalton, Katharina. Ante-natal progesterone and intelligence. *British Journal of Psychiatry,* 144:1377-1382, 1968.

Prenatal influences. Sex hormones. Intellectual maturation. Physiological maturation.

This longitudinal study compared the overall growth and educational development of children whose mothers had received progesterone (a female hormone) during their pregnancy with that of children whose mothers had not. Progesterone had been administered for the treatment of toxemia. The 29 progesterone children were matched with children whose mothers had had a normal pregnancy and with children whose mothers had developed toxemia but had not been treated with progesterone. The test and control groups were compared at their first birthdays by means of mothers' and doctors' questionnaires on their development, and at age 9-10 by means of teachers' assessments of their abilities in verbal reasoning, English, arithmetic, craftwork, and physical education.

Significantly more progesterone children were breast-fed at 6 months and were standing and walking at 1 year. The groups were similar in age of first tooth, total number of teeth, and talking ability. At age 9-10, progesterone children received significantly higher grades than controls on all areas of ability except physical education. These developmental and intellectual advantages were also related to the dose of progesterone received by the mother—when mothers received over 8 grams of progesterone during pregnancy, their children stood and walked earlier and achieved higher grades in school. The intellectual advantage was greatest in children whose mothers received progesterone before the 16th week of pregnancy. Although progesterone children tended to be heavier at birth and to be breast-fed longer, probably due to increased mammary development by progesterone, this study suggests that progesterone overall produces an educational rather than a physical advantage. (8 references)

57
Davidson. Julian M., and Levine, Seymour. Endocrine regulation of behavior. *Annual Review of Physiology,* 34:375-408, 1972.

Sex hormones. Sexual behavior. Mammals. Brain differentiation.

This review of literature on the effects of hormones on reproductive and nonreproductive mammalian behavior deals primarily with work published in 1970 and the first half of 1971. Studies on reproductive behavior in laboratory animals concern the influence of gonadal hormones on sexual receptivity and maternal behavior and the production of opposite-sex behavior. The mechanisms of gonadal hormone activity encompass various physiochemical reactions in different parts of the brain and corresponding behavioral responses.

Prenatal and neonatal studies of the differentiation of sexual behavior have concentrated on the critical period when masculinization occurs in the brain. Hormone-behavior interactions in which behavior influences endocrine function include situations which may involve pheromones and situations where sexual stimuli affect hormonal mechanisms. Studies on endocrine action and human sexual behavior consider hormones in relation to pheromones, impotence, male libido, homosexuality, copulation-induced ovulation, and the effects of contraceptive steroids on female sexual behavior. In experiments on nonreproductive behavior, gonadal hormones have been found to influence sexually dimorphic behaviors, such as aggression, in rats, mice, and gerbils. The pituitary-adrenal system appears to be involved in aggressive behavior and in learning and extinction of responses, as well as in sensation and perception among laboratory animals. (227 references)

58

Gadpaille, Warren J. Research into the physiology of maleness and femaleness: Its contributions to the etiology and psychodynamics of homosexuality. *Archives of General Psychiatry,* 26:193-206, 1972.

Sex hormones. Homosexuality. Physiological determinants. Genetic determinants.

An overview of biological research on sexual differentiation in humans and other animals provides insights into the etiology and psychodynamics of homosexual development. Recent experimental studies have produced more data than can be explained by the two classic theories of homosexual development.

Neuroendocrine and neuroanatomical studies have established the role of anterior portions of the hypothalamus in governing sexual behavior. Hormonal studies show that the presence of androgens in utero at the critical period suppresses the otherwise female morphology in favor of male differentiation, regardless of genotypic sex. Differentiation of mating and other sex-related behavior appears to parallel physiological dimorphism. Parts of the brain are also distinctly male or female.

Animal behavior studies reveal sexually dimorphic differences in social behavior. They also suggest that maleness is more complex, difficult to achieve, and vulnerable to disruption than femaleness. Studies of human anomalies—chromosomal, developmental, and iatrogenic—further explain sexual differentiation in humans. Several conditions and their consequences are described, including adreno-genital syndrome, progestin-induced hermaphroditism, and the XYY syndrome. A major principle of psychosexual differentiation emerges from these studies: With few exceptions, the gender of assignment and rearing takes precedence over all physiological and genetic determinants.

Epidemiological studies indicate that men of all ages are more vulnerable than females to physical disorder, to sexual deviations and perversions, and to death at a younger age. Genetic studies of possible hereditary aspects of homosexuality are inconclusive and unreplicated. (97 references)

59

Garron, David C. Sex-linked, recessive inheritance of spatial and numerical abilities, and Turner's syndrome. *Psychological Review,* 77(2):147-152, 1970.

Sex-linked inheritance. Genetic determinants. Chromosome disorders. Spatial perception. Mathematical ability.

This paper explores the hypothesis that sex-linked, recessive transmission of superior spatial and numerical abilities can be inferred from male superiority in these abilities and from greater unlike-sex than like-sex parent-child similarity. Impairment of these abilities in women with Turner's syndrome is also viewed as implicating the sex chromosome complement. It may be shown, however, that women with Turner's syndrome should be superior in these abilities if transmission is sex linked and recessive. Although the specific hypothesis is not supported, there is evidence suggesting that the sex chromosome complement and related sex differences in biochemical processes may underlie sex differences in these abilities. (50 references)

60

Gray, Jeffrey A., and Buffery, Anthony W. H. Sex differences in emotional and cognitive behavior in mammals including man: Adaptive and neural bases. *Acta Psychologica,* 35(2):89-111, 1971.

Social structure. Sex-typed behavior. Physiological determinants.

This review of recent biological studies of mammalian social organization endeavors to show that behavioral sex differences originate from the specialized reproductive roles of males and females. It is also hypothesized that, in all mammals, certain sex differentiated, nonsexual emotional and cognitive behaviors result from natural selection rather than from recent cultural influences (in the case of humans). Moreover, a dichotomy drawn between biological and social forces is false and misleading.

Regarding behaviors attributed to adaptive and some neural bases, it is proposed that: The greater male aggressiveness observed in mammals reflects the male role in establishing dominance hierarchies; the greater female fearfulness observed in primates (in contrast to the greater nonprimate male fearfulness) reflects the nature of female participation in the dominance hierarchies; the greater male spatial abilities observed in mammals reflect the male's role in dominance interactions and (in primates) his role in protecting the group from attack; and the greater linguistic ability observed in female humans reflects the role of the mother in providing the infant's linguistic environment.

The neural overlap in the frontal neocortex connects the structures involved in submissive and fearful behavior. This connection suggests that a direct relationship exists between linguistic ability and fearfulness in humans. Thus, behavioral sex differences in humans, even though unlike those of other mammals, may reflect new evolutionary pressures that have emerged at this complex biological level. (68 references)

61
Hamburg, David A. Recent research on hormonal factors relevant to human aggressiveness. *International Social Science Journal,* 23(1):36-47, 1971.

Sex hormones. Aggression. Sexual behavior.

This review of research literature primarily from the last decade illustrates some new directions as well as the complexities involved in understanding aggressive behavior. Hormonal studies are of particular interest because research has demonstrated the effects of sex hormones on brain organization, aggression, and sexual behavior in many mammalian species. Moreover, biochemical techniques have greatly improved the precision and reliability of hormonal measurement. In humans, some hormone-behavior correlations are found. For example, such relationships have been observed in investigations of the behavior of girls who were exposed to androgens *in utero* and in female aggressiveness that is associated with progesterone and estrogen fluctuations. Moreover, the pubertal increase in testosterone levels and subsequent behavior also suggests the existence of a relationship between hormones and behavior. Some additional studies have examined the effects of factors such as population density on endocrine functions. Experimental and field studies of primates suggest that the male's early aggressive inclination, based on factors mediated by hormonal effects on brain differentiation and muscle growth, is developed through social learning and ultimately put to adaptively significant use. Given the human learning capacity, it seems unlikely that lifetime aggressive patterns are fixed by early exposure to the male sex hormone, although they may be more readily learned because of general hormonal orientation. It is concluded that the widening range of biological studies—endocrine, biochemical, genetic, evolutionary, and neurophysiological—must combine with the social sciences for a more complete understanding of human aggressiveness. (34 references)

62

Hamburg, David A., and Lunde, Donald T. Sex hormones in the development of sex differences in human behavior. In: Maccoby, E. E., ed. *The Development of Sex Differences.* Stanford, Calif.: Stanford University Press, 1966. pp. 1-24.

Sex hormones. Genetic determinants.

A review of investigations undertaken over the last decade in a variety of disciplines suggests that sex differences in human behavior are the result of complex interactions among genetic, hormonal, and environmental factors. Biochemical methods for directly determining hormones in blood and urine, plus advances made in the measurement of hormones, aid in the measurement of the effect of endocrine variation on behavior of children. Research literature on puberty suggests that the environmental impact on the onset of puberty affects boys and girls differently. Research literature on the effects of sex hormones on infrahuman species and on humans suggests developmental correlations in brain differentiation. The effects of hormones on the development of gender role are seen as significant. Also, sex differences in the behavior of infants are observed, but it remains unclear whether they are mediated by hormonal effects on the brain during fetal development. Literature on sex differences in disease susceptibility also suggests behavior consequences for males and females.

These findings point up new avenues for research on the role of sex hormones in the development of sex differences. Clarification of the complex interactions among genetic, endocrinological, and environmental variables would facilitate the successful integration of concepts and techniques from the behavioral and biological sciences. (60 references)

63

Hartlage, Lawrence C. Sex-linked inheritance of spatial ability. *Perceptual and Motor Skills,* 31:610, 1970.

Genetic determinants. Sex-linked inheritance. Spatial perception.

This study attempted to replicate an earlier finding that indicated possible involvement of a sex-linked recessive gene in the transmission of spatial abilities. The sample of 100 subjects ranged in age from 16 to 56 and represented 25 families with all combinations of father-son, father-daughter, mother-son, and mother-daughter pairs. Subjects were administered the space section of the Differential Aptitude Test (DAT), and correlations were computed between DAT scores for the four possible parent-child pairs.

Mean DAT space scores were highest for fathers, followed by sons, daughters, and mothers. Significant correlations occurred between mothers and sons and between fathers and daughters. Since the son's X chromosome comes from his mother and the father's X chromosome is transmitted only to his daughter, the correlations support the hypothesis that an X chromosome is involved in the transmission of spatial ability. The low correlation between father-son scores indicates that the Y chromosome is not significantly involved. Although this study varied from the earlier one in its use of a different population and spatial ability test, the findings from the two studies are similar. (4 references)

64
Hutt, Corinne. Males and Females. Harmondsworth, England: *Penguin Books,* 1972. 158 pp.

Physiological determinants. Sex hormones. Sex-role development.

This book draws on mammalian experiments, clinical case histories, genetic and developmental research, and sociological and psychological studies to explore the biological and cultural bases of psychological and intellectual sex differences. Chapters on the genetic determination of sex, male and female hormones, and the process of sex differentiation describe the biological roots of sex differences. Sexual dimorphism and the mechanics of hormonal control are considered in relation to sex differences in sexual and nonsexual behavior. A discussion of sexual anomalies argues that psychosexual differentiation is already present at birth and is not primarily a product of rearing. Sex differences in growth and maturation, in abilities, in attitudes, and in interests are outlined and their educational implications noted. A final chapter discusses the influence of social and cultural factors on male and female differences and how these factors result in social and economic inequities. (157 references)

65
Levine, Seymour. Sex differences in the brain. *Scientific American,* 214(4):84-90, 1966.

Brain differentiation. Sex hormones. Mammals.

A review of experimental research conducted since the 1930's suggests that the brain, as well as hormones, is involved in the sexual differentiation of mammals. Distinct differences between male and female brains determine sexual and certain nonsexual forms of behavior in mammals.

Animal experiments in which male and female sex organs were exchanged demonstrated in the 1930's that sexual differentiation occurs very early in development and is controlled by the absence or presence of testosterone. A recent extensive program of experiments has tested whether the brain itself is subject to differentiation through hormonal action. A program of hormone injection treatment of rats in the critical first few days after birth has shown that testosterone produces profound and permanent changes in the sensitivity of the brain to sex hormones. In the absence of testosterone, males and females are sensitive to female hormones and are capable of displaying female sexual behavior. In the presence of testosterone, males and females are desensitized and fail to display female sexual behavior even when given female hormones. Hormonal treatment of guinea pigs, monkeys, and other mammals in their respective critical periods resulted in the same behavioral pattern.

The precise mechanism by which testosterone produces sexual differentiation in the brain remains unknown. Broader questions requiring further research include the sex-differentiating role of nonsexual hormones and the implications of animal research for human behavior. (3 references)

66
Levine, Seymour. On becoming male. In: Ramsay, I. T., and Porter, Ruth, eds. *Personality and Science.* London: Churchill Livingstone, 1971. pp. 5-12.

Masculinity. Prenatal influences. Brain differentiation. Genetic determinants. Sex hormones.

This paper presents a summary of research on the prenatal processes involved in the development of maleness. Available evidence leads to the conclusion that the basic primordial sexual differentiation of most mammalian species is female, and that a number of additive steps in the developmental process are essential to produce the changes that characterize the male physiologically and behaviorally. These requirements include the presence in the genes of an X and a Y chromosome, since it is the presence or absence of the Y which determines maleness or femaleness in both normal and abnormal instances; and the formation of fully functioning male gonads, the testes, from the original undifferentiated embryonic gonad.

The role of the testes in physiological and reproductive development is discussed, and data are presented in support of the hypothesis of sexual differentiation of the brain and central nervous system. The central nervous system (CNS) and the hormones are said to interact. It is assumed that the function of gonadal hormones in infancy is to organize the CNS with regard to neuroendocrine control of behavior. Possible effects of CNS differentiation on sex differences in such nonsexual behavior as activity patterns and aggressive behavior are postulated. Most of the research reported deals with laboratory animals, but some studies of humans are presented. In each instance where male patterns of development are presented, the corresponding patterns in females are compared. (8 references)

67
Levine, Seymour. Sexual differentiation: The development of maleness and femaleness. *California Medicine,* 114(1):12-17, 1971.

Sex hormones. Brain differentiation. Mammals.

This discussion outlines sexual differentiation in mammals, focusing on the influence of hormones on the nervous system. Evidence from experiments on laboratory animals shows that alterations in hormonal status in newborn mammals affect subsequent biological functioning. Castration studies on newborn rats indicate that maleness depends on having a male nervous system. To produce a male nervous system, the fetal and neonatal testes must secrete androgen, which presumably acts upon the brain to differentiate it into that of a male.

The primordial sex differentiation of most mammals is female, and without male hormones the organism remains female. There is evidence that differentiation into maleness involves not only the addition of the male hormones, androgen and testosterone, but suppression of the capacity to respond to estrogen and progesterone, the female hormones. Studies involving the administration of testosterone to female rats and the castration of males show that sex hormones can act directly on the brain. Females treated neonatally with testosterone and later with androgen show some increase in male sex behavior. Conversely, males act as females when treated with progesterone and estrogen, but only when castrated soon after birth. Timing is vital in sex differentiation. In the male rat, the period of high androgen activity just before and after birth is essential for sexual differentiation of the brain.

Observations of activity patterns of male and female rats indicate that there are differences in nonsexual as well as sexual behavior. Sex differences have been shown in activity levels, emotional responses to novel situations, and aggressive behavior. The closest human analogies to these laboratory-induced situations are pathologic conditions resulting in functional sexual ambiguities. However, it is emphasized that there is an additional process in human sexual development involving the effects of upbringing on the formation of gender role. (14 references)

68

Persky, Harold; Smith, Keith D.; and Basu, Gopal K. Relation of psychologic measures of aggression and hostility to testosterone production in man. *Psychosomatic Medicine,* 33(3):265-277, 1971.

Aggression. Sex hormones. Psychological adjustment.

This study investigated the effects of aggression and hostility on testosterone production in the male. Subjects were 18 healthy young men (average age 22), 15 healthy older men (average age 45), and 6 male hospitalized psychiatric patients (average age 39). All subjects completed the Multiple Affect Adjective Check List, the IPAT Anxiety Scale, the Manifest Anxiety Scale, the MMPI Depression Scale, and the Buss-Durkee Hostility Inventory, while undergoing tests to determine their plasma testosterone levels and testosterone production rates.

In the younger men, testosterone production was found to be highly correlated with a measure of reported aggressive feelings derived from the Buss-Durkee Hostility Inventory. A multivariate regression equation was obtained for testosterone production using four psychologic measures of aggression and hostility. The equation accounted for 82 percent of the variance in the production rate of testosterone for the younger group. However, the equation was not valid for the older men. Age was the principal correlate of production rate in the older group, the rate decreasing with advancing age. Height, weight, and body surface did not relate significantly to testosterone production. Estimates of the testosterone production rates of the three psychiatric patients who were within the age range of the younger group were made, using the multivariate regression equation and their hostility-aggression scores. The two patients who scored significantly higher than the control group also had discrepancies between observed and equation-estimated production rates which were greater than those of the control group. It was concluded that, in normal males, testosterone production rises with the aggressions engendered in puberty. As these aggressions are mastered or subside in later life, age takes its progressive effects on the gonads and their testosterone output. (26 references)

69

Stoller, R. J. A contribution to the study of gender identity. *International Journal of Psycho-Analysis,* 45(Parts 2-3):220-226, 1964.

Hermaphroditism. Sex-role development. Physiological determinants.

This paper discusses gender identity and presents two case studies of anatomically intersexed patients who assumed a gender identity not produced by the anatomy and physiology of external genital organs or attitudinal influences of parents, siblings, and peers. The two case studies—a female-reared child who became a male and a male-reared child who became a female—defied these influences from infancy in assuming their dominant biological gender. They are asserted to illustrate the influence of a third determinant, a "biological force," which, though unconscious, provides some of the drive for gender identity.

The patients described are exceptional in that they did not develop the gender identity ascribed to them at birth, as do most intersexed people, and they also evaded the role assignment and attitudes of their parents in their gender identity. Both patients indicate that a congenital, perhaps inherited, biological force may provide a strong core gender identity that overrides the influence of environment and external genitalia. (8 references)

70
Walker, P. A. and Money, J. Prenatal androgenization of females: A review. *Hormones,* 3:119-128, 1972.

Prenatal influences. Sex hormones. Intelligence. Masculinity. Femininity.

This review covers the etiology and treatment of prenatally androgenized females, the effects of progestin and progesterone on intelligence, progestin psychosexual differentiation, and parallels in the andrenogenital syndrome and in animal research. The use of synthetic progestins to avert miscarriage became standard clinical procedure in the late 1940's. However, cases of masculinization of some newborn females were reported; in some cases, the condition was diagnosed as hermaphroditism. Findings of this review indicate that the degree of masculinization depends on timing of administration of progestins during pregnancy and on the strength of dosage. Progestin-induced hermaphroditism is similar to andrenogenital syndrome hermaphroditism.

The clinical data on human females indicate elevated IQ and some behavioral masculinization, without gender-identity disorders, following prenatal exposure to androgenic substances. However, suppression of feminine behavior was minor in the human subjects. This is contrary to the reports of animal studies, in which suppressed femininity is claimed. In humans, a consistently feminine sex of assignment and rearing maximizes femininity and minimizes masculinization resulting from the prenatal androgenic hormone environment. (20 references)

71

Willerman. Lee, and Stafford, Richard E. Maternal effects on intellectual functioning. *Behavior Genetics,* 2(4):321-325, 1972.

Adolescents. Intellectual maturation. Parental influence.

This study attempted to demonstrate a maternal effect on intellectual performance of teenage children by showing that these children more closely resemble the intellectual performance level of their mothers than their fathers. Subjects were 130 children, ages 13 through 17, and parents from 104 New Jersey and Pennsylvania families. Paper and pencil tests taken by all the subjects measured ability in English vocabulary, spelling, letter concepts, mental arithmetic, and perspective perception. Test scores were corrected for age and transformed to a mean and standard deviation. The scores of parents of children who scored one SD above or below the mean were compared. Mothers generally tended to score lower than fathers. It was therefore necessary to compare parents of both high- and low-scoring children to see if the proportion of mothers scoring lower or higher than the fathers differed in relationship to the child's level of performance.

Data provided partial support for the maternal-effect hypothesis. Forty-four percent of the high-scoring children, but only 23 percent of the low scorers, had higher scoring mothers than fathers. However, English vocabulary was the only test that showed statistical significance of maternal effect. (10 references)

72

Zuger, Bernard. Gender role determination: A critical review of the evidence from hermaphroditism. *Psychosomatic Medicine,* 32(5):449-467, 1970.

Hermaphroditism. Sex-role development. Methodological issues.

This paper examines clinical evidence to dispute the theory that individuals with ambiguous sex at birth will accept the sex role of rearing over that indicated by biological variables (chromosomes, gonads, hormones, internal and external genitalia). The critique focuses on methodology and conclusions from the Money, Hampson, and Hampson study of the sex assignment and subsequent gender role adjustment of hermaphrodites. (Prior to publication, Money responded to this critique; his detailed comments and this author's rebuttal are included in the paper.)

Criticism of the Money and Hampson study methodology involves the parallel rather than serial ordering of the biological variables that possibly determine gender role. It is further argued that the appearance of external genitalia—a physical consideration—first determined sex assignment in some of the cases studied; thus, determination of gender role predated socialization factors. Endogenous sex, moreover, cannot be ascertained on the basis of only one sexual characteristic. Detailed evidence from Money's own subjects is presented to suggest the impossibility of determining which endogenous sex was dominant and, therefore, whether the dominant sex was overridden by rearing. Specific cases from literature refuting Money and the Hampsons are also discussed. In these cases, either rearing was not successful in maintaining the assigned sex, or sex change without psychological damage was accomplished later in life than Money predicted the socialization factors would allow. It is concluded that the sex that asserts itself is the biological sex whose components prove dominant. (49 references)

Sociological Determinants

73
Almquist, Elizabeth M., and Angrist, Shirley S. Role model influence on college women's career aspirations. *Merrill-Palmer Quarterly,* 17:263-279, 1971.

Parental models. Sex-role perceptions. Career aspirations. College women.

This 4-year longitudinal study investigated role model and reference group influences on the career aspirations of one class (N=110) of college women. Data from these subjects were gathered with yearly questionnaires that queried adult role conceptions, occupational plans, work experience, academic achievement, school activities, social life, and marriage plans. Open-ended yearly interviews with some of the sample and senior-year interviews with the whole class probed these areas more fully and explored the processes of occupational choice. According to their questionnaire responses to three items on career orientation, 50 subjects were termed career salient—motivated to have both marriage and a career—and 60 subjects were designated as noncareer salient.

Data indicated that noncareer-oriented women tended more often to be sorority members, attached to a male, and have mothers active in leisure pursuits, and to feel that family or peers had influenced them about their future roles. Career-salient women had been exposed to occupational choices of male peers, had working mothers and a greater variety of work experience themselves, and felt influenced by faculty members and occupational role models in choosing an occupation. Career-salient subjects were only slightly less involved in dating than noncareer-salient subjects, but were more involved in faculty and work reference groups. While there was no marked difference in grades between the two sample groups, career-salient students perceived their professors as having a more positive evaluation of their academic ability. Both groups had parents who approved and encouraged their postcollege plans. (19 references)

74

Ban, Peggy L., and Lewis, Michael. *Mothers and fathers, girls and boys: Attachment behavior in the one-year-old.* Paper presented at meetings of the Eastern Psychological Association, New York, N.Y., 1971. 12 pp. (Mimeo.) Available from author.

Infant behavior. Parent-child relations. Distal and proximal behaviors.

This study investigated attachment behavior of 1-year-olds in relation to both fathers and mothers. The subjects were 10 male and 10 female infants of high SES parents. Each infant was observed twice, once with the mother and once with the father. Each observation lasted 15 minutes in a controlled situation, during which four attachment behaviors—proximity to parent, touching, looking, and vocalizing to parent—were recorded. These behaviors are termed "proximal" (touching and proximity) and "distal" (looking and vocalizing).

For the proximal mode, there were no infant sex differences or interactions. In general there was almost twice as much touching and proximity seeking displayed toward mothers as toward fathers. For the distal mode, the differences between behaviors toward mothers and fathers reached significance for vocalizing but not for looking. For looking, there was a significant sex-of-child/sex-of-parent interaction. Whereas girls looked equally at both parents, boys looked at fathers significantly more often than at mothers. Boys and girls also differed in the way and the extent to which they combined the four modes of behavior with one another. The boys showed a more highly integrated attachment pattern, with all behaviors correlating positively and significantly. The girls' attachment tended to utilize behaviors singularly and not in combinations. Estimates of amount of daily play fathers engaged in with their children did not correlate with attachment behaviors directed toward the father. (9 references)

75

Bandura, Albert; Ross, Dorothea; and Ross, Sheila A. Transmission of aggression through imitation of aggressive models. *Journal of Abnormal and Social Psychology,* 63(3):575-582, 1961.

Aggression. Imitation. Preschool children.

The major hypothesis of this study was that children exposed to aggressive adult models would reproduce aggressive acts resembling those of their models. They would differ in this respect from children observing nonaggressive models and from those not exposed to any models (the control group). Children observing nonaggressive models were expected to show even less aggressive behavior than the control group. Children were expected to imitate same-sex models more than opposite-sex models. It was predicted that boys would be more likely to imitate aggressive behavior than girls, especially when performed by a male model. The sample of 36 male and 36 female nursery school students, ages 37 to 69 months, was divided into three groups: One group observed an aggressive adult model in a play situation; a second group observed a nonaggressive model in the same situation; a third group had no prior exposure to the models. Half the subjects in the experimental conditions observed same-sex models, and half, opposite-sex models. Each subject was then observed alone in a setting with toys similar to those provided in the models.

Subject groups exposed to aggressive models displayed significantly more physical and verbal imitative, partially imitative, and non-imitative aggressive behavior than the nonaggressive or control groups, which did not differ from each other. Approximately one-third of the subjects observing the aggressive model also repeated the model's nonaggressive remarks. Subjects who observed nonaggressive models spent more than twice as much time as subjects in the aggressive situation sitting quietly and not playing with any of the materials provided. Boys showed more aggression than girls following exposure to male models, particularly on highly masculine-typed behavior. Subjects exposed to nonaggressive male models showed significantly less aggression than control subjects in several forms of play. (16 references)

76
Bandura, Albert; Ross, Dorothea; and Ross, Sheila A. A comparative test of the status envy, social power, and secondary reinforcement theories of identificatory learning. *Journal of Abnormal and Social Psychology.* 67(6):527-534, 1963.

Preschool children. Role models. Imitation. Sex-role identification.

Predictions derived from three theories of identificatory learning were tested in three-person groups representing prototypes of the nuclear family. Subjects were 36 boys and 36 girls, 37 to 69 months old, enrolled in a nursery school. In one treatment condition, one adult assumed the role of controller of rewarding resources and another adult was the consumer of these resources, while the child, a participant observer in the triad, was essentially ignored. In a second condition, one adult similarly controlled the rewarding resources; however, the child was the consumer, and the other adult was ignored.

For half the boys and girls in each condition, a male model controlled and dispersed the rewarding resources, simulating the husband-dominant family; for the remaining children, a female model mediated the resources, as in the wife-dominant family. Twenty-four children participated in each condition; an additional 24 were controls. Following the experimental interactions, the two models exhibited divergent patterns of behavior in the child's presence, and a measure was obtained of the degree to which the child subsequently imitated the models. All subjects participated in this procedure.

Children of both sexes tended to imitate the model who possessed rewarding power rather than the competitor model. Thus, the social power theory rather than the status envy theory was supported. Contrary to the secondary reinforcement theory, the condition in which the child, as consumer, was the recipient of positive reinforcements did not yield the highest imitation of the model controlling and dispersing the rewards. This finding was attributed to the tendency of the boys to sympathize with and later imitate the ignored male adult rather than the female controller. More girls than boys imitated the cross-sex controller model. Although the children adopted many of the characteristics of the model possessing rewarding power, they also reproduced some of the elements of behavior exhibited by the model occupying the subordinate position. It was concluded that children's behavior is the result of more than one imitation source. (21 references)

77

Barclay, A., and Cusumano, D. R. Father absence, cross-sex identity and field-dependent behavior in male adolescents. *Child Development,* 38:243-250, 1961.

Cross-sex identity. Father absence. Adolescent males. Role models.

It was hypothesized that the perceptual behavior of father-absent adolescent boys on field dependency tests would reflect a covert role orientation hampered by lack of appropriate male models. However, the overt self-reported behavior of father-absent boys would be at least as masculine as that of father-present boys. Subjects were 40 male freshman and sophomore high school students. The experimental group included 20 boys (10 white and 10 Negro) who had been without fathers since age 5, with a control group of 20 (10 white and 10 Negro) who had fathers present. The two groups were matched on age, grade point average, IQ, and socioeconomic status. Overt role identification was measured by the Gough Femininity Scale and by a semantic differential scale, which also was used to assess cross-sex identification. Field dependency was measured by the Rod and Frame Test as another means of indicating cross-sex identification.

Father-absent males were more field dependent than father-present males. Although Negro males were more field dependent than white males, the interaction between the race and father variables was insignificant. Identification measures indicated that father-absent boys manifested the same overt masculine identification as father-present boys. It was contended that father-absent boys, starting from an initially lower level of masculinity, show a compensatory adjustment in equaling the masculine orientation of father-present boys. If prevalence of the dominant Negro matriarch is assumed, the greater field dependency of both father-absent and father-present Negro males might suggest that a male child who identifies with instrumental and male-appropriate characteristics of his mother will be no better adjusted in his subsequent role identification than any other boy lacking a male model. (20 references)

78
Baruch, Grace K. Maternal influences upon college women's attitudes toward women and work. *Developmental Psychology,* 6(1):32-37, 1972.

Parental influence. College women. Working mothers. Sexual discrimination. Career attitudes.

This study assessed alternate hypotheses concerning the tendency of women to devalue feminine professional competence. According to one hypothesis, devaluations are the products of out-group self-prejudice. That is, women who devalue feminine competence have negative attitudes toward the career role and associate it with negative personal and social consequences. The alternate hypothesis is that the devaluations are products of a traditional feminine sex-role standard learned from a nonworking mother.

First-stage subjects were 110 upper middle-class females enrolled at Swarthmore, a college selected for this study because of its rigorous intellectual standards. Tendency to devalue feminine professional competence was measured by a test of reactions to written articles ascribed to male or female authors; attitudes toward the dual role pattern were measured by an attitude scale; and extent of maternal employment was indicated on a personal data sheet. In the second stage, 86 subjects selected for high or low tendency to devalue feminine professional competence were individually interviewed and rated on variables relevant to maternal influences on the subject's view of career commitment.

Results supported the competence model hypothesis that tendency to devalue is associated with having a nonworking mother. Daughters of working mothers evaluated women's competence highly, regardless of any negative personal consequences of working experienced by their mothers. Maternal employment per se did not, however, influence subjects' attitudes toward the dual role pattern. Whether a subject favors this pattern depends on whether her mother endorses it and whether her working mother has successfully integrated the two roles. The implications of these findings are discussed in relation to changing the status and attitudes of women. (6 references)

79

Berens, Anne. Socialization of need for achievement in boys and girls. In: *Proceedings, 80th Annual Convention, APA, 1972.* Washington, D.C.: American Psychological Association, 1972. pp. 273-274.

Achievement motivation. Parental influence. Elementary school students.

This study was undertaken to compare the socialization practices directed at boys and girls as related to differences in levels of need for achievement (n Ach). Subjects were 21 boys, 21 girls, and their mothers. The children were randomly selected from all fifth-graders in a working-class area public school. Mothers and children were administered the standard Thematic Apperception Test to determine levels of n Ach. The Endler Anxiety Scale and a child-raising practices questionnaire were given to mothers; the Mandler-Sarason Test Anxiety Scale to measure fear of failure and a questionnaire on patterns of mother-child interaction and control were given to children.

On the projective measure, boys and girls low in n Ach showed no significant differences on either n Ach or fear of failure. However, high n Ach boys showed a somewhat higher mean level of n Ach and a significantly lower fear of failure than did high n Ach girls. Children's n Ach and fear of failure were not significantly correlated with those of their mothers, perhaps owing to the small number of subjects.

However, different patterns emerged for boys than for girls. Results showed that the patterns of demands by mothers on boys and girls who were high and low in n Ach were opposite, suggesting that there may be a critical range of ages for optimal development of high n Ach. Results from the child-raising practices questionnaire showed significant differences between high and low n Ach subjects within each sex, and between boys and girls low in n Ach, but not between boys and girls high in n Ach. Results from the children's questionnaire responses paralleled the mastery demands reported by mothers in their questionnaire. Generally, it appears that, for both boys and girls, a balance of interaction and support combined with moderate controls and with expectations and achievement demands made at an appropriate age is much more effective in producing high n Ach than is the mother's own level of n Ach. (3 references)

80
Biller, Henry B. *Father, Child and Sex Role: Paternal Determinants of Personality Development.* Lexington, Mass.: D.C. Health, 1971. 193 pp.

Paternal behavior. Sex-role development. Psychological adjustment. Father absence.

This book draws extensively on empirical and theoretical sources in psychological and sociocultural literature to explore the effects of paternal factors in the child's sex-role development. A major concern involves the investigation of the difficulties in sex-role and personality development encountered by the paternally deprived child. Specific chapters deal with the effects of father-absence and father-presence on masculine development, sociocultural and constitutional aspects of paternal influence, paternal influence and general personality functioning, the mother-son relationship, fathering and female personality development, and a consideration of methodological issues and directions for further research. (474 references)

81
Biller, Henry B. The mother-child relationship and the father-absent boy's personality development. *Merrill-Palmer Quarterly,* 17(3):227-241, 1971.

Mother-son relations. Psychological adjustment. Father-absence.

Available data concerning the mother's influence on the personality development of the father-absent boy are reviewed, and indirectly relevant data from studies of children's personality development in father-present homes are presented. Many untested hypotheses and speculations are presented to stimulate further research on this subject.

Findings suggest that the mother-son relationship can have either a positive or negative effect on the father-absent boy's sex-role and personality development. Research relating to matriarchal families, maternal overprotection, and maternal rejection indicates that mothers in father-absent homes or in homes where the father is relatively ineffectual can undermine their son's feelings of masculine adequacy and ability to function interpersonally. Sociocultural factors, the intensity of the mother-child relationship, and various aspects of "positive mothering" are discussed. The importance of the mother's attitudes toward the absent father and of her expectations and encouragement of masculine behavior in her son is discussed. It is noted that future studies should consider such factors as sociocultural background, peer group interaction, and length and timing of father-absence. (65 references)

82

Biller, Henry B., and Borstelmann, Lloyd J. Masculine development: An integrative review. *Merrill-Palmer Quarterly,* 13(4):253-294, 1967.

Male role. Sex-role development.

This review presents a comprehensive conception of masculine development, drawn from an extensive examination of the theoretical and empirical literature. The primary purpose of the discussion is to suggest avenues for further research. Focus is on the preschool years and the process of learning behaviors appropriate for males in a particular society. Constitutional and sociocultural influences are briefly considered. Variables explored in depth are the degree to which the father is available, masculine, nurturant, and the setter of limits, and the degree to which the mother encourages masculine behavior. These factors do not appear to be simply additive, although interactions between them, as discussed, may have important effects.

In conceptualizing the impact of such factors, sex role is differentiated into three aspects: Sex-role orientation, sex-role preference, and sex-role adoption. Sex-role orientation, one basic facet of self-perception, is dependent on discrimination between the specific sex-role models of mother and father. Sex-role preference reflects the individual's desire to adhere to the culturally defined guidelines of the sex role. Sex-role adoption is the masculinity and femininity of the individual's publicly observable behavior. Possible antecedents of various patternings of these three aspects of sex-role are specified. (171 references)

83
Biller, Henry B., and Weiss, Stephan D. The father-daughter relationship and the personality development of the female. *The Journal of Genetic Psychology,* 116:79-93, 1970.

Father-daughter relations. Psychological adjustment. Paternal behavior.

A review of theoretical and empirical literature concerns the influence of the father-daughter relationship on the process of feminine identification and personality adjustment of the female. Various interpretations of paternal identification and role modeling are considered as they pertain to father-daughter relations. The father's personal characteristics and behavior appear to affect the daughter both directly, in his interaction with her, and indirectly, through his relationship with and attitudes toward his wife and family. The positive or detrimental developmental effects of paternal childrearing practices, discipline, social attitudes, and personality are discussed. Father absence and inadequate or inappropriate fathering have been linked to a number of social and emotional disorders in children of both sexes. Although studies in the field of father-daughter relations are numerous, there is a need for studies offering more representative subject and control group selection for more precise definitions of variables. There is also a need for studies of the influence of sociocultural, temperamental, and cognitive factors. (71 references)

84
Bing, Elizabeth. Effect of childrearing practices on development of differential cognitive abilities. *Child Development,* 34:631-648, 1963.

Parental influence. Elementary school students. Verbal ability. Mathematical ability. Spatial perception.

Investigations covering the early and present-day childrearing practices of mothers were made to test several hypotheses concerning differences in children's cognitive development. Subjects were 60 mothers whose fifth-grade children had similar total IQ's and had either high or low verbal ability (with compensating spatial or numerical abilities). The comparison of high and low verbal group mothers was based on results from a semistructured interview, a factual questionnaire, and a structured mother-child interaction session.

Results revealed significant differences in behavior between mothers of high and low verbal children. Findings concerning these patterns of specific maternal behaviors generally supported the hypotheses. It was concluded that a high degree of interaction between mother and child fosters the child's verbal ability. The marked pattern of help seeking and help giving which characterizes this close relationship of the high-verbal child and mother interferes, however, with the development of the independence and self-reliance required for nonverbal abilities. Interaction with the physical rather than the interpersonal environment provides the freedom to experiment, which develops a child's number and spatial ability. (24 references)

85
Bragg, Barry W. E. Academic primogeniture and sex-role contrast of the second-born. *Journal of Individual Psychology,* 26(2):196-199, 1970.

Sibling influence. Academic achievement. Role models.

This study explored the combined effects of sex, birth order, and sex of sibling on academic motivation as indicated by college attendance. A birth-order survey was administered to approximately 1,000 introductory psychology students at a university. From this group a sample was selected consisting of 59 males and 82 females from two-sibling families in which the siblings were 4 years or less apart.

Compared with the numbers of first borns, second borns with an opposite-sex older sibling were found to be underrepresented, whereas those with the same-sex older sibling were overrepresented. Sex-role contrast and sex-role modeling theories are offered to explain these findings. According to earlier studies, it is highly probable that a second born will find himself or herself in a family situation in which the older sibling is academically oriented. It is suggested here that, when the older sibling is of the opposite sex, the second born will consider academic behavior sex-role inappropriate for himself or herself. Thus, a second-born male will avoid academics as a feminine pursuit if his older sibling is a girl. A first-born male, on the other hand, will be seen as a fit model for a second-born male in all activities, including schoolwork. The academic predominance of first borns may therefore be a result of sex-role contrast by the second-born. (8 references)

86
Burton, Roger V. Cross-sex identity in Barbados. *Developmental Psychology,* 6(3):365-374, 1972.

Cross-sex identity. Father absence. Sex-role identification. Barbados.

Hypotheses derived from the status-envy theory of identification were tested by investigating cross-sex identity conflict in a society in which father absence is common and acceptable. Theoretically, a person's identity results from his or her envy of people who control desirable resources. Applied to sex identity, this hypothesis predicts that exclusive maternal control of important resources leads to an infant's primary feminine identification.

Subjects were 37 boys and 45 girls, ages 8 to 15, attending school in Barbados. The children were primarily from nonwhite families of semiskilled, service, and migratory agricultural workers. The Draw-a-Person Test assessed the child's preferred sex identity. School personnel supplied information on the academic and family background of each child, including father presence or absence in the household. Father presence or absence was intercorrelated with sex of first drawing, size of drawings, and certain control variables.

Findings supported the hypotheses derived from the status-envy theory. Father presence was positively related for boys to sex of first drawing, size of male drawings, and differential size of drawings. Alternative interpretations of father absence which assert that the extent to which children lack male role models determines sex identification were not consistently supported. Controlling for age, ordinal position, achievement in school, and for sex, age, and number of siblings did not affect the findings. Comparisons of discrete and continuous measures of father absence supported a critical period hypothesis for absence during the first 2 years of infancy. These data indicate that the social structure of Caribbean culture may lead to both sex conflict and consistent cross-sex identity in father-absent boys. (27 references)

87
Burton, Roger V., and Whiting, John W. M. The absent father and cross-sex identity. *Merrill-Palmer Quarterly*, 7(2):85-95, 1961.

Father absence. Cultural differences. Cross-sex identity. Sex-role identification.

The status envy hypothesis of identification and sex identity development was examined in a cross-cultural study and brief review of recent research on the effect of father absence in the household. According to this hypothesis, identification consists of learning a role by rehearsal in fantasy or play rather than by actual performance; the rehearsal, in turn, is motivated by envy of the model's privileged status. Three kinds of identity are distinguished: Attributed (a status assigned by others); subjective (a status the person sees himself as occupying); and optative (a status the person wishes to occupy). Thus, the optative identity is an envied status, and the aim of socialization in any society is said to be an adult whose attributed, subjective, and optative identities converge.

According to the status envy hypothesis, mother-infant sleeping arrangements in a culture where the father sleeps elsewhere should lead to a feminine (cross-sex) primary optative identity in the male infant. However, in a culture where both parents sleep in a room with the child, an adult primary optative identity (not characterized as to sex) should emerge. Marital residence pattern (patrilocal, matrilocal, or equilocal) should determine which sex is seen as the privileged status later in childhood, when the secondary optative identification is formed. Of six possible combinations of primary and secondary identities, two are examined. Exclusive mother-infant sleeping arrangements with patrilocal residence, which should yield maximum conflict between primary and secondary optative identities; and exclusive mother-child sleeping arrangements with matrilocal residence, which should yield maximum feminine optative identity, or cross-sex identity for boys. The index selected to represent maximum identity conflict was male initiation rites at puberty, seen as a cultural means of resolving sex identity conflicts. The index chosen for maximum feminine identity was couvade, which represents a means of symbolically acting out the female role in later life.

Results strongly supported a status envy interpretation of the development of optative sex identity. In the sample of 64 societies examined, 13 have elaborate male initiation ceremonies. Of these, all have exclusive mother-child sleeping arrangements, and all but one have patrilocal residence. Of the 12 societies which practice couvade, 10 have exclusive mother-child sleeping arrangements and nine have matrilocal residence. Several studies of boys in "delinquency cultures" in the United States and of father absence in the United States and Norway are reviewed. The findings from these studies are generally consistent with the status envy hypothesis. (14 references)

88
Carlsmith, Lyn. Effect of early father absence on scholastic aptitude. *Harvard Educational Review,* 34(1):3-21, 1964.

Father absence. Verbal ability. Mathematical ability. Cognitive styles.

This study investigated the effects of temporary father absence on scholastic aptitude in males. Both length of absence and child's age at onset of absence were considered. Subjects were 881 Harvard freshmen in the class of 1963, 307 freshmen in the class of 1964, and 137 male and 135 female seniors at three Massachusetts public high schools in 1961. All subjects were born during the war years, 1941-45, were from intact families, and had taken the college entrance Scholastic Aptitude Test. According to questionnaire data from the college students and the parents of the high school students, approximately one-third of the subjects' fathers had served overseas during the war from 3 months to 5 years. To control for subjects' general level of ability, the difference between each subject's mathematical and verbal scores was taken as the indicator of aptitude. An additional analysis of the effects of father absence versus father presence was made for a Harvard class of 1964 subsample, matched on age, ordinal position in family, private or public education, parents' age, and father's education and occupation.

For all three samples, early and long separation from the father resulted in relatively greater ability in verbal areas than in mathematics, and no separation produced relatively greater ability in mathematics. A late and brief separation appeared to produce an extreme elevation in mathematical ability relative to verbal ability. In relating these findings to sex-identification theory, it was suggested that the relative superiority of math or verbal attitude is a single measure of conceptual style or approach to problem solving. Development of a masculine analytic approach, as opposed to a feminine global approach, is apparently associated with a boy's relationship with his father during certain early periods of his life. The possibility that aptitude differences in father-present and father-absent boys could result from such variables as anxiety is also discussed. (31 references)

89
Cohen, Mabel Blake. Personal identity and sexual identity. *Psychiatry,* 29(1):1-14, 1966.

Sex-role development. Socialization variables.

The thesis of this discussion is that considerable incompatibility exists between society's traditional definition of sexual role and the optimal development of an individual's personal assets. Supportive evidence is provided by research on early infancy, longitudinal studies of child development, and psychological data on pregnant women and their husbands.

Most children are socialized to regard the male as independent and dominant and the female as dependent and passive. Infant studies have demonstrated innate behavioral and maturational differences in boys and girls. However, these differences are increased by parents' differential handling of male and female infants from birth on: For example, parents tend to talk more to girls and to hold and attend to boys more.

Longitudinal studies show that boys who were most active in childhood become strongly masculine, sexually active, but weaker in intellectual striving in adulthood. Boys nurtured by their mothers give up passivity and dependency under societal pressure in adulthood, but replace these behaviors with social anxiety, sedentary and intellectual careers, and low levels of sexual activity. Cultural pressures on girls to be traditionally feminine cause withdrawal from challenging tasks and decreasing interest in intellectual development. Inborn tendencies toward activity and passivity in boys and girls are not reversed, but are repressed, resulting in anxieties about not being considered appropriately masculine or feminine.

Results of childhood developmental processes are seen in the behavior of pregnant women and their husbands. The caretaking responsibilities and division of labor necessary for parenthood often intensify conflicts about masculine and feminine roles. These conflicts involve insecurity about one's worth as a sexual being and a person, as well as dependency imbalances between spouses. It is concluded that neither activity-passivity nor independency-dependency are valid indexes of masculine-feminine development. The cultural prevalence of these standards only serves to promote female incompetency, male hypermasculinization, and insecurity and lack of individual fulfillment in both sexes. (14 references)

90

Crandall, Vaughn J.; Preston, Anne; and Rabson, Alice. Maternal reactions and the development of independence and achievement behavior in young children. *Child Development,* 31:243-251, 1960.

Preschool children. Dependency. Achievement. Play behavior. Parental influence.

This study investigated the relationship between children's independence and achievement behaviors, the generality of these behaviors from home to nursery school, and maternal reactions to these behaviors as potential determinants of children's achievement development. The sample, taken from a larger, longitudinal study, consisted of 19 male and 11 female 3-, 4-, and 5-year-olds and their mothers. Subjects' parents were middle class and were better educated and scored higher on tested intelligence than national averages. The children were observed daily in free play for 3 weeks at the Fels Institute Experimental Nursery School and in interaction with their mothers at home. Children were rated at home and at school on frequency and persistence of achievement efforts and on amounts of help seeking, emotional support seeking, and approval seeking from adults. Mothers were rated on amount of general affection shown and on rewards granted for each behavior.

No marked sex differentiation was found in free-play achievement or in dependent behaviors, apparently because of the young age of the subjects. High-achieving children were less dependent on adults for help and emotional support than were low-achieving children. Children's behaviors were moderately consistent from home to nursery school, with the exception of emotional support seeking behavior. Mothers who frequently rewarded achievement efforts were less accepting of overtures for help and emotional support, but were no less affectionate than mothers less prone to reward achievement efforts. Neither maternal affection nor independence training was predictive of children's achievement behavior, whereas direct maternal rewards and approval seeking were predictive. (8 references)

91
Crandall, Vaughn; Dewey, Rachel; Katkovsky, Walter; and Preston, Anne. Parents' attitudes and behaviors and grade-school children's academic achievements. *Journal of Genetic Psychology,* 104:53-66, 1964.

Elementary school students. Academic achievement. Parental influence.

The relationship between parents' attitudes and behaviors and children's academic performance was investigated as part of a larger study. Subjects were 20 boys and 20 girls in the second, third, and fourth grades, and their parents. The sample was representative of all but the lowest social class. The children's intellectual abilities were assessed by the Stanford-Binet Intelligence Test, and academic performance was measured by the California Achievement Test. Parents were interviewed individually regarding general parental behaviors (affection, rejection, nurturance) and specific attitudes and reactions to their child's everyday achievement efforts.

Correlations between IQ and achievement scores were of the same magnitude generally found in research on children's intelligence and achievement. The only general parental behaviors that significantly predicted academic performance pertained to mothers and daughters: Mothers of academically competent girls were less affectionate and less nurturant toward their daughters than mothers of less proficient girls. Neither mothers' nor fathers' expressed values for their child's intellectual experiences were positively associated with the child's academic achievement. The mother's evaluation of and satisfaction with the child's general intellectual competence were positively related to the child's actual academic performance, whereas those of the father were not. Parental instigation of and participation in children's intellectual activities, when correlations were significant, were negatively associated with the children's academic performance. Fathers of the most academically proficient girls tended to praise rather than criticize their everyday intellectual achievement attempts. The greater number of significant correlations between parents' attitudes and behaviors and daughters' academic proficiency suggests that grade school boys may be less susceptible to adult influence than grade school girls. (9 references)

92
Crites, John O. Parental identification in relation to vocational interest development. *Journal of Educational Psychology,* 53(6):262-270, 1962.

College men. Parental models. Career aspirations.

This study of the relationships between parental identification and vocational interest development tested three hypotheses: Degree of identification with father and mother correlates with vocational interest pattern; the kind of identification with father and mother varies with vocational interest pattern; and the pattern of identification is associated with masculinity-femininity of interests. The original and replication samples each consisted of 100 male clients seen at the vocational-educational counseling service of the University of Iowa during 1 year. The generalization sample included 150 nonclients of comparable age and intelligence from the same university. The Semantic Differential Test measured perceived similarity of subject to parents, and the Strong Vocational Interest Blank assessed interests.

In all three samples, sons identifying closely with their fathers tended to have primary interests in business occupations, whereas those with mixed or cross-sex parental identification tended to have primary interests in verbal-linguistic fields. No significant correlation was found between degree of identification with mother and vocational interest pattern. Identification with either or both parents correlated with the development of a defined interest pattern. Pattern of parental identification was associated with masculinity-femininity of interests only in the generalization sample. Close like-sex parental identifications produced masculine interests; close mixed-sex identifications resulted in a combination of masculine and feminine interests; and both close cross-sex identification and negligible identification with both sexes yielded feminine interests. It was concluded that, for males, identification with both parents influences the formation of vocational interest patterns, but identification with the father is most important. (29 references)

93
DeVore, Irven. Male dominance and mating behavior in baboons. In: Beach, Frank A., ed. *Sex and Behavior.* New York: Wiley, 1965. pp. 266-289.

Sexual behavior. Primates. Social 'dominance. Social structure.

A report based on findings from over 1,200 hours of observation of free-ranging baboon troops in African national parks illustrates the effects of social setting on mating behavior in savannah baboons. Primary data came from two troops of baboons. One was a relatively small troop of 28 individuals with a higher than usual proportion of large adult males and a relatively low proportion of adult females (S.R. troop). The other was a larger, more typical troop consisting of 40 individuals with a wider range of physical size among adult males and a 2 to 1 ratio of adult females to adult males (S.V. troop).

The S.V. troop revealed the usual baboon pattern of mating behavior. Juveniles, subadult males, and less dominant males mounted an estrous female only early in her tumescent period; during the time when she was most tumescent, maximally receptive, and most fertile, one adult male formed a stable consort pair with her. This pair remained together constantly, but engaged in sexual activity relatively infrequently. In the S.R. troop, with its continual shortage of sexually receptive females, there was more tension and far more agonistic behavior (threat, attack, appeasement, subordination, etc.). Fighting over estrous females and harassment of a copulating pair by other males occurred frequently; as a result, there was less continuity of consort pairs over time. Duration of consort pairing could be measured in hours, as compared with a more typical duration of days. Sexual activity on the part of adult male troop members was far more frequent in the S.R. troop, but was also more often incomplete because of interference by other males.

It was found that, in contrast to the "linear" or "straight-line" dominance hierarchy described for other species, the dominance order in any baboon troop containing more than three males is most efficiently analyzed by employing the concept of "central hierarchy." Two or more males, not necessarily the two most dominant individually, tend to form a coalition which makes them jointly more dominant than any of the others in the troop. An adult male's relative dominance tended to be reflected in mating success—participation in consort pairs in the S.V. troop or the number of times he was able to copulate successfully in the S.R. troop. But mating success could not be predicted solely on the basis of a male's dominance status. Observation revealed that, partly due to the "central hierarchy" type of dominance pattern, the males which were most active in protecting the group and policing it internally were also the most effective breeders, despite the fact that they might be subordinate as individuals to other males in the troop. (12 references)

94

Fagot, Beverly I., and Patterson, Gerald R. An *in vivo* analysis of reinforcing contingencies for sex-role behaviors in the preschool child. *Developmental Psychology,* 1(5):563-568, 1969.

Play behavior. Teacher influence. Preschool children. Peer influence. Sex-typed behavior.

This study tested three hypotheses: Sex differences in play behavior are present in 3-year-olds, female teachers reinforce feminine behavior, and peers reinforce like-sex peers. The sample consisted of 18 female and 18 male 3-year-olds from upper middle-class homes in Eugene, Oreg., and their four female nursery school teachers. Free play behaviors were observed and recorded intermittently throughout the year.

Sex-appropriate behaviors were present at the beginning of the year and remained stable over time. Boys were more inclined to play with blocks and transportation toys, and girls were more likely to engage in painting and art work. Eighty-three percent of sex-preferred behaviors that the teachers positively reinforced by initiating, commenting favorably upon, or joining were feminine behaviors. When neutral behaviors were included, teachers reinforced both sexes about equally. The reinforcement of feminine behaviors did not affect the boys' preference for masculine behavior. Evidently, reinforcement from peers and family counters the teachers' reinforcement and maintains the masculine behavior exhibited by boys. Through interactive play, subjects were found to reinforce same-sex peers significantly more than opposite-sex peers. (16 references)

95

Fling, Sheila, and Manosevitz, Martin. Sex typing in nursery school children's play interests. *Developmental Psychology,* 7(2):146-152, 1972.

Preschool children. Sex-role preference. Play behavior. Parental influence.

This study investigated different components of sex typing in play interests of nursery school children, a potential masculine bias in the It Scale for Children (a projective test of sex-role preference), and selected social learning concepts of parental influence on sex-role development. It was hypothesized that parents exert more pressure on boys than on girls to conform to sex-role stereotypes.

The subjects were 32 predominantly upper middle-class 4-year-olds enrolled in a university nursery school in Texas. Fifty-six parents of the children were interviewed. Children were given an "imaginary it" and a "you" version of the It Scale for Children and they were scored at home on play interests to measure sex-role orientation, preference, and adoption. Parental responses on a modified It test and the interview were scored for differential reinforcement and modeling of sex-typed interests.

The prediction concerning potential bias in the It Scale—that both sexes would label the standard It more frequently as a boy, but would more frequently imagine a same-sex child on a blank card—was confirmed. On all measures of sex typing, boys were not significantly more sex typed than girls. The sex-role orientation and preference scores were positively correlated, but subjects were more sex typed on preference. However, correlations between parental influence measures and their children's sex-typing scores failed to support social learning concepts of sex typing.

As hypothesized, parents discouraged cross-sexed interests in boys more than in girls. Further, same-sex parents reported more encouragement of sex typing in their children than did opposite-sex parents. (14 references)

96
Forslund, Morris A., and Hull, Ronald E. Sex-role identification and achievement at preadolescence. *Rocky Mountain Social Science Journal*, 9(1):105-110, 1972.

Academic achievement. Elementary school students. Role models. Teacher influence.

This investigation tested the assertion that preadolescent children will perceive greater social-psychological rewards and experience a higher level of achievement under the direction of male rather than female teachers. Cluster samples of 47 male and 48 female teachers and their students (1,322 boys and 1,350 girls) were gathered from sixth-grade classrooms in the Albuquerque, N. Mex., public school system. The Teacher-Pupil Relationship Inventory was administered to measure students' perceptions of their relationship with their teacher in terms of teacher's feelings and actions toward them. The Science Research Associates Achievement Test and the Lorge-Thorndike Intelligence Test scores were obtained from school files.

Both boys and girls perceived male teachers as being significantly more rewarding than female teachers. Boys tended to identify less with female than with male teachers, but girls tended to identify with teachers of either sex more strongly than did boys. There was no significant difference between boys' and girls' achievement scores under the direction of male or female teachers. Intelligence was more highly correlated with achievement than was perceived relationship with teacher. Overall findings suggested that male models in the upper elementary grades are primarily valuable in teaching children their appropriate sex role in relation to the masculine role. Additionally, because male teachers increase preadolescent males' enjoyment of the school experience, their presence in the school system might help lower the dropout rate. (9 references)

97

Greenstein, Jules M. Father characteristics and sex typing. *Journal of Personality and Social Psychology*, 3(3):171-277, 1966.

Sex-role identification. Homosexuality. Father-son relations.

This study examined the effects of father absence, closeness, and dominance upon the son to test two theories of sex typing—developmental identification and differential reinforcement. Subjects were 25 father-absent and 50 father-present delinquent boys, ages 13 to 18, at the New Jersey Diagnostic Center. Data on father closeness and dominance were obtained from several interviews with the parents of the father-present subjects. Three aspects of sex typing were considered: Homosexual tendencies, fantasy identification, and masculinity-femininity. The Wheeler Rorschach Indices and an embedded figure preference test measured latent homosexuality. A psychiatric interview conducted with the subject under sodium amytal provided data on overt homosexual activity. Fantasy identification was measured by the degree to which the subject's stories involved a male or female hero. Three masculinity-femininity scales were administered.

Father-absence, father-presence, and paternal dominance were not significantly related to any of the indexes of sex typing. Father closeness, contrary to the developmental identification theory, was found to have a significant correlation with overt homosexuality. Whereas the three subjects with warmest father-son relations reported engaging in frequent homosexual acts, none of the four boys with distinctly cold relations with their fathers reported homosexual experiences. These findings are discussed in terms of a differential reinforcement theory of sex typing. Although anecdotal evidence suggests that a child's sex typing tends to be acquired through the expectations of significant adults, both male and female, rather than solely through modeling, it is emphasized that further experimental confirmation is necessary. (26 references)

98
Hampson, John L. Determinants of psychosexual orientation. In: Beach, Frank A., ed. *Sex and Behavior.* New York: Wiley, 1965. pp. 108-132.

Hermaphroditism. Sex-role development. Socialization variables.

Previous clinical research on the sex assignment and subsequent psychological health of 113 hermaphrodites is presented in an examination of the possible determinants of gender role. The hermaphrodites represented a variety of ambisexual incongruities between predominant external genital appearance and sex chromatin pattern, gonads, hormones, or internal reproductive structures, either singly or in combination. All subjects were exposed to rearing practices that were contradictory to at least one of these biological sex variables. Gender role data on these individuals were gathered by extensive interviews with them and their relatives, psychological tests, and observation of behavior.

The majority of hermaphrodites had attained an unambivalent gender role. These findings indicate that psychologic maleness or female-ness is not attributable to any one single physical sex variable. The individual's psychology is apparently sexually neutral at birth and becomes differentiated as masculine or feminine in the course of growing up. Physiology affects gender development in that an individual's appearance and sexual development determine the extent to which he or she can identify with a sex. It is suggested that critical periods in gender-role establishment and identification with role models may exist. Data on individuals who have had a change of sex at different ages indicate that a significant degree of gender-role development coincides with the development of language at 18 months to 2 years old. (5 references)

99
Harrington, Charles C. *Errors in Sex-Role Behavior in Teen-Age Boys.* New York: Teachers College Press, 1970, 109 pp.

Sex-role identification. Adolescent males. Cross-sex identity. Parental models.

This book reports a study which examined the link between sex identity and the two principal types of error in sex-role behavior among adolescent boys: Uncontrolled or exaggeratedly masculine behavior and inappropriate sex-role, or feminine, behavior. Subjects were 133 boys, ages 13 to 19, who had asked for help from any of five mental health agencies in upstate New York during a period of several months.

Data were obtained from interviews with and observation of subjects' families and from agency records and standard psychological tests. Instruments included measures of father absence and household composition, household task sharing, social class ranking (Hollingshead's Two Factor Index of Social Position), primary unconscious sex identity (Franck Drawing Completion Test), attitudes and interests (Gough's Brief Femininity Scale), secondary sex identity (modified Strong Vocational Interest Blank M-F Scale), and physique and constitution. Subjects were classified by their predominant behaviors: Exaggeratedly male (E), inappropriate to the male role (I), or control—deviant but unrelated to sex role (C).

Four hypotheses were tested: Boys labeled E and I will have greater primary cross-sex identity than C boys; boys labeled I will have greater cross-sex identity than either E or C boys; I boys will come from families marked by father absence, and E boys will have early father absence but later male influence; and E boys will share more household tasks with their fathers, and I boys will share more with their mothers.

The hypotheses were confirmed. An identifiable link was found between primary and secondary sex identity and sex-role behaviors. Sex-identity predicts behavior even when social class and physical constitution are controlled. The I boys shared more tasks with their mothers, whereas the E boys shared more with their fathers. Boys with E behaviors had not failed to learn the male role, but seemed to overcompensate for an initially feminine identity. The I boys, however, evidenced impaired learning and performance of the male role.

The book also includes an introductory review of psychological theories of identification and development of sex identity and anthropological studies of sex-role differentiation. (127 references)

100
Heilbrun, Alfred B., Jr. Sex-role identity in adolescent females: A theoretical paradox. *Adolescence,* 3(9):79-88, 1968.

Adolescent females. Femininity. Father-daughter relations. Parental models.

A review of selected studies of identification, sex-role identity, and adjustment in the adolescent female focuses on the father's role in developing the daughter's femininity. Three conclusions are drawn: That masculine fathers model appropriate feminine behavior for their daughters by manifesting feminine-expressive behavior toward them; that daughters modeling after masculine fathers are capable of acting both expressively and instrumentally; and that the dual capacity for feminine-expressive and masculine-instrumental behavior facilitates the adjustment of girls—at least in a college environment. These conclusions lead to the proposal that a feminine identity will be facilitated when the primary identification model is either a feminine mother whose behavior contrasts with that of a masculine father, or a masculine father whose daughter-directed feminine behavior contrasts with his own masculinity. Both models offer the potential for expressive behavior, but only the father model provides the additional potential for instrumental behavior. While father-identified girls have a more assertive goal orientation what might make them appear masculine on standard measures of masculinity-femininity, such identification still mediates a health adjustment. (17 references)

101

Heilbrun, Alfred B., Jr. Parental identification and the patterning of vocational interests in college males and females. *Journal of Counseling Psychology,* 16(4):342-347, 1969.

Parental models. Career aspirations. College students.

This study investigated whether the relationship between tested vocational interests and parental identification choice can be modified by the masculinity or femininity of the chosen identification model.

Students at Emory University (47 males, 33 females) were administered several scales as part of an intake battery for vocational-educational counseling. Measures obtained were: Child's perceived similarity between himself and each of his parents, indicating type and degree of parental identification; masculinity-femininity of the parental model, measured by subject's attribution to mother or father of nine traits previously shown to be sex-typed for similar samples; and the Strong Vocational Interest Blank.

Results showed the following relationships: Father-identified males had more primary occupational interests than mother-identified males. Males identified with masculine models (mother or father) showed more rejection scores (fewer occupational interests) and more high- or low-interest patterns. Females identified with a masculine mother or feminine father had more primary occupational interests than females identified with sex-role-appropriate parents, and a higher proportion of positive interests relative to total patterned interests. Females with a feminine sex-role model (either parent) had a higher number of rejection scores. A feminine-mother identification was associated with the most limited positive career interest development for both sexes. (21 references)

102
Hetherington, E. Mavis. A developmental study of the effects of sex of the dominant parent on sex-role preference, identification, and imitation in children. *Journal of Personality and Social Psychology*, 2(2):188-194, 1965.

Parental dominance. Sex-role preference. Parental models. Imitation. Elementary school students.

The effects of sex of the dominant parent on sex-role preferences, parent-child similarity, and the child's imitation of the parents were investigated in three age groups. The study was based on theories which emphasize the importance of parental power in the development of identification. Dependent variables were sex-role preference, parent-child trait similarity, and parent imitation in 36 boys and 36 girls ages 4-5, 6-8, and 9-11, in a public school system. Half of the boys and girls in each age group came from mother-dominant homes, half, from father-dominant homes. Parental dominance was determined by observation of discussions carried on by each set of parents. The dependent variables were obtained from the It Scale for Children, a projective test of sex-role preference, parent-child similarity measures based on personality ratings of parents by friends compared with ratings of the child by teachers, and an imitation task involving parent and child.

Parent-child similarities on non-sex-typed traits, which have fewer extrafamilial social sanctions bearing on them, were more directly and consistently related to actual parental behavior than were similarities on sex-typed traits. Parent-child similarities on sex-typed behaviors were increasingly related to parental dominance with increasing age, but the expected reverse pattern for non-sex-typed behaviors did not occur. Girls were slower and less consistent in developing appropriate sex-role preferences than the boys. Development of normal sex-role preferences was facilitated by identification with the same-sex parent, but was retarded when the dominant parent was of the opposite sex. (10 references)

103
Hetherington, E. Mavis. Effects of paternal absence on sex-typed behaviors in Negro and white preadolescent males. *Journal of Personality and Social Psychology*, 4(1):87-91, 1966.

Father absence. Racial differences. Parental models. Sex-typed behavior.

This study investigates the effects of race, father absence, and time of departure of the father on sex-typed behaviors of preadolescent males. Sex-typed behaviors include sex-role preferences, dependency, aggression, and recreational activities.

It was hypothesized that permanent departure of the father after the establishment of identification with the masculine role model would have either no effect or a compensatory strengthening effect on masculine sex-typed behaviors, whereas father departure before this time would tend to disrupt or inhibit development. Two hypotheses regarding special effects on Negro boys were suggested, based on an assumption that the Negro family structure is matriarchial: Father absence might be expected to have a less disruptive effect on boys' sex-typed behaviors in such a family; and Negro boys would score lower in overt social aggression than white boys, but would show a marked preference for aggressive, competitive play activities.

First-born boys (32 Negro and 32 white) ages 9-12, attending a recreation center, were evenly divided into two subgroups—both parents present and father absent. For half of the father-absent subjects for each race, separation had occurred at age 4 or earlier; for the other half, after age 6. Except for illegitimacy in the early-separation group, there were no differences between groups in causes of separation. Subjects were rated on seven-point scales by two male recreation directors at the centers. The measures used were dependence on adults, dependence on peers, independence, aggression, and observed recreational activity preferences. The It Scale for Children, a projective test of sex-role preference, was administered to all subjects.

Results indicated that absence of the father after age 5 has little effect on the sex-typed behaviors of boys. The only measure on which late-loss subjects differed significantly from father-present subjects was in greater dependence on peers, which occurred for all father-absent boys. Boys who lost their fathers early showed considerable deviation in sex-typed traits. The only racial difference found was the predicted higher participation of Negroes in competitive activities involving contact. (15 references)

104
Hetherington, E. Mavis. The effects of familial variables on sex typing, on parent-child similarity, and on imitation in children. *Minnesota Symposia on Child Psychology,* 1:82-107, 1967.

Parental dominance. Sex-role identification. Parent-child relations. Imitation.

Three studies that relate a number of childrearing variables and parental characteristics to sex-role typing, parent-child similarity, and the child's imitation of parents are described. Data were obtained from interviews with parents, structured play situations, and measures of parental imitation and sex-role preference.

Study I investigated the effects of parental dominance on identification. Subjects were three groups of 36 boys and 36 girls, ages 4-5, 6-8, and 9-11, and their parents. Parental dominance did not significantly affect sex typing in girls, but maternal dominance impeded the development of masculine sex-role preferences in boys at all ages. Preschool boys had already developed a preference for the masculine role; girls showed a sudden increase in appropriate sex-role preferences at ages 9 to 11. Maternal dominance inhibited father-child similarity for both sexes. Paternal dominance facilitated cross-sex identification, and children of both sexes imitated the dominant parent.

Study II investigated the effects of parental dominance, warmth, and conflict on the child's imitation of the parent. Subjects were 80 male and 80 female nursery school children and their parents. The children tended to imitate a warm parent more than a hostile one. Both boys and girls imitated dominant mothers; with paternal dominance, boys imitated the father; girls, the mother. In high-conflict families, the dominant parent was likely to be imitated.

Study III investigated a broader range of parental characteristics and practices as related to the child's identification. Subjects were 50 boys and 54 girls, ages 3-6, and their parents. Fathers who were masculine and dominant in their marriages tended to have feminine daughters. Maternal dominance disrupted sex typing in boys. The lack of relationship between childrearing variables and sex typing suggests that sex typing in boys, more than in girls, is influenced by factors outside the home.

It was concluded from these three studies that paternal dominance for boys and maternal warmth for girls are critical in the identification process. The three main theories of sex typing—identification based on power, on positive reinforcement and warmth, and on aggression—were all partially supported. (34 references)

105
Hetherington, E. Mavis. Effects of father absence on personality development in adolescent daughters. *Developmental Psychology,* 7(3):313-326, 1972.

Adolescent females. Father absence. Psychological adjustment.

This study explored how the causes and timing of father absence affect the behavior of adolescent girls. Subjects were three groups of 24 lower and lower middle-class first-born, brotherless, adolescent girls ranging in age from 13 to 17 years. The first group came from intact families with both parents at home; the second, from families where the father was absent owing to divorce; and the third, from families where the father had died. Observation of each girl's behavior at a community recreation center, measures of nonverbal interaction with a male or female interviewer, separate interviews with the daughters and with the mothers, and four indicators of personality (the California Personality Inventory Femininity Scale, the Internal-External Control Scale, the Manifest Anxiety Scale, and the Draw-a-Person Test) provided data.

Few deviations in traditional measures of sex-role typing were obtained; however, disruptions in interactions with males occurred. While daughters of widows were restrained and inhibited around males, daughters of divorcees sought male proximity and attention, engaged in early heterosexual relations, and communicated nonverbally in an open and responsive way. Early separation from fathers had more severe effects than late separation. Differences among divorcees, widows, and mothers of intact families on personality measures, on childrearing attitudes, and on relations with their daughters were also investigated. (27 references)

106
Hoffman, Lois Wladis. Early childhood experiences and women's achievement motives. *Journal of Social Issues,* 28(2):129-155, 1972.

Achievement motivation. Parental influence.

A critical review of child development literature of the last three decades examines women's achievement motives and behavior. Limitations of research on child development, such as lack of standardization of terminology, generalization of results from one population, and ambiguity in conceptualization, affect empirical data in this field. The examination of research on independence and autonomy training of young children, early mother-infant interaction, and sex differences in achievement motivation provide support for the theory proposed to explain female underachievement: Female children are not given enough parental encouragement in early strivings for independence. Consequently, female children do not develop the confidence and sense of independence needed to cope with their environments. They develop neither adequate skills nor confidence, but continue to be dependent upon others. Their achievement behaviors are motivated by a desire to please. Moreover, the females' high need for affiliation often blocks their achievement motives, and their performance is either sacrificed or achieved at the cost of high levels of anxiety.

It is concluded that further research is needed to provide insight into the processes that create differences between the sexes in achievement orientation. (98 references)

107

Jensen, Gordon D.; Bobbitt, Ruth A.; and Gordon, Betty N. Sex differences in the development of independence of infant monkeys. *Behaviour,* 30:1-14, 1967.

Primates. Mother-child relations. Dependency.

The major hypotheses tested were that the relationship between a mother monkey and her son differs from that of mother and daughter, even in the early weeks after birth, and that there is greater and earlier mutual independence between mothers and sons. Analysis centered on the first 15 weeks of life for five female and five male pigtailed monkeys and their mothers in caged, controlled environments. Variables of mother-child contact, infant's activity, mother's retaining and punitive manipulations, and mother's and child's orientation toward the environment were recorded by quantitative observational methods and analyzed in terms of mean occurrence and developmental trends.

Male monkeys and their mothers showed a rapidly accelerating change to greater mutual independence than that exhibited by females and their mothers. However, contrary to expectations, it was the mother rather than the male infant who actively instigated the male's independence. Although the infant monkeys did not actively initiate the change in mother-child relations, males responded to their new independence by interacting with the environment more than females. Behavioral and biological hypotheses are offered as possible explanations of the mothers' differential treatment of infants. (12 references)

108

Johnson, Miriam M. Sex role learning in the nuclear family. *Child Development,* 34(2):319-333, 1963.

Parent-child relations. Parental models. Sex-role development.

This theoretical proposal suggests that identification with the father, in the sense of internalizing a reciprocal role relationship with the father, produces appropriate sex-role orientation in both males and females. Modifications of Freudian and post-Freudian identification theory are offered, based on a review of empirical sociological and psychological literature.

The instrumental-expressive distinction applied to parental roles is central to the argument. The mother is the expressive role figure, oriented toward relationships within the family. She deals with love reciprocity and care of individual family members. The father is the instrumental figure, primarily responsible for providing for the family as a unit in the environment. A child's primary superego develops through a sexual infantile dependency on its mother's love. After this stage, the girl must learn more mature expressive behavior in transferring love reciprocity to an adult male; the boy must strive for corresponding expressive maturity and at the same time learn instrumental behavior. Male socialization, having an extra component, requires special encouragement. While the female learns expressiveness from the father's appreciation of her femininity, the male learns instrumentalness from the father's demands upon his masculinity. Unlike the father, the mother does not differentiate her behavior toward sons and daughters and remains expressive to both. (30 references)

109
Laosa, Luis M., and Brophy, Jere E. Effects of sex and birth order on sex-role development and intelligence among kindergarten children. *Developmental Psychology,* 6(3):409-415, 1972.

Birth order. Parental influence. Sex-role development.

A study of young children explored the hypothesis that, since first borns tend to be more socialized than later borns and parental expectations differ by sex of child, a sex-by-birth-order interaction should occur on sex-typed variables. This replication of an earlier study involved 47 boys and 46 girls, ages 5 to 7, from middle-class urban families. Instruments used to measure sex-role orientation, adoption, and preference included the It Scale for Children, Draw-a-Person, and two toy-preference measures; measures of sex typing in game, occupational, and peer preferences; teacher ratings of sex-role adoption; and sociometric play observations. Each child was also administered a questionnaire on perceived parental dominance and power.

Results failed to support the sex-by-birth-order interaction hypothesis on direct measures of sex typing, since the expected birth-order effects were not observed. Data from measures of variables showing sex differences provided partial support for the hypothesis, however, including some replicated findings. These consistent sex differences occurred for certain covert variables (attitudes, motives, and cognitive and expressive styles) and overt behaviors (independence, dependence, and solitary play), which are not rigidly sex typed but tend to be shaped by interaction with parents. (15 references)

110

Leland, Carole A., and Lozoff, Marjorie M. *College Influences on the Role Development of Female Undergraduates.* Stanford, Calif.: Institute for the Study of Human Problems, 1969. 90 pp.

College women. Autonomy. Lifestyle.

This report, prepared for the HEW Office of Education, reflects part of a two-part research program on the psychosocial factors affecting the educational and occupational development of women undergraduates with emphasis on manifestations and determinants of autonomy. Two decades of research literature regarding the educational, occupational, and sociopsychological development of undergraduate and adult women are surveyed. Portions of a 4-year longitudinal study of male and female members of the class of 1965 at Stanford University and the University of California at Berkeley are analyzed.

Test measures included the Omnibus Personality Inventory and the Scholastic Aptitude Test taken prior to college entrance. Eight interviews each were held with 49 Stanford women; tests at the freshman and senior year and questionnaires at the senior year were also administered. Questionnaire data concerned academic life; career choice; sexual development; attitudes toward marriage and family; relationship with parents; perception of self, change, and development; and personal values. Additional material was obtained from friends of the 49 Stanford women on their perceptions of change in subject's personality, behavior, and values during college. Analysis of the interview data led to the ordering of the female students on a continuum of degrees of autonomy. This ordering was corroborated by analysis of test and questionnaire data.

It was found that differences in the degree of autonomy achieved by these women were related to such background factors as parental upbringing. Autonomy was prognostic of different life-styles in and after college. Variations in female responses to pressures to follow specific role and career patterns are described. A typology is presented based on subjects' perception of feminine role and the degree of their achieved autonomy. For each of the typology's four subgroups, recommendations are made for course programs, counseling, and milieu modifications. An appendix contains senior questionnaire answers showing significant differences in attitudes and experiences between male and female students at Stanford and Berkeley (N=534 males and 451 females). (115 references)

111
Lewis, Michael. Parents and children: Sex-role development. *The School Review,* 80(2):229-240, 1972.

Socialization. Parent-child relations. Proximal and distal behaviors.

This inquiry examines socialization processes that produce observable sex differences in humans. The discussion of parental attitudes and behaviors as a function of the infant's sex and of some adult social patterns is based on several mother-infant studies.

Parental attachment behavior reflects an important socialization process and can be classified as either proximal (touching) or distal (actions, such as talking or looking, performed at a distance). Observational studies indicate that, after the age of 6 months, girl infants receive significantly more proximal behavior than boys. It appears that, in American culture, boys are socialized earlier and more emphatically from proximal to distal behavior. For males in adult society, touching is generally restricted to the opposite sex and is primarily sexual in its function. Observation of Jewish, Italian, and Greek subcultures supports the idea that proximal behavior toward boy infants is culture-specific. (12 references)

112
Lynn, David B. Sex-role and parental identification. *Child Development,* 33:555-564, 1962.

Parental models. Sex-role development. Cognitive styles.

Research is reviewed and cited to support a theory postulating basic sex differences in the nature of sex-role and parental identification, as well as basic differences in the process of achieving such identification. Sex-role identification refers to the internalization of the role of a given sex, and parental identification refers specifically to the internalization of personality characteristics of the same-sex parent.

The theory advanced follows an earlier hypothesis by this investigator that males tend to identify with a cultural stereotype of the masculine role, whereas females tend to identify with aspects of their own mother's role. From these separate sexual identification processes, it is postulated that girls acquire a general learning method primarily involving a personal relationship and imitation, whereas boys generally learn by defining a goal, restructuring the field, and abstracting principles. The suggested "lesson copying" versus "problem-solving" learning modes form the basis for five hypotheses that differentiate by sex the learning of tasks: Females demonstrate greater need for affiliation; females depend more on the external context of a perceptual situation and hesitate to deviate from the given; males generally surpass females in problem-solving skills; males tend to be more concerned with internalized moral standards; and females tend to be more receptive to the standards of others. Although these hypotheses are not presumed to account completely for the diverse findings of the research on sex differences, they are found to be in general agreement with the research reviewed. (36 references)

113
Lynn, David B. Divergent feedback and sex-role identification in boys and men. *Merrill-Palmer Quarterly,* 10(1):17-24, 1964.

Sex-role development. Cross-sex identity. Negative reinforcement.

This theoretical discussion integrates a number of existing sex-role identification studies into a framework of four hypotheses: Because males must shift from initial identification with the mother to masculine role identification, often with little interaction with male models, they have greater difficulty in achieving sex-role identification than females. Males are not told how they should act, but how they should not act (divergent feedback); consequently, they are more anxious regarding their sex-role identification than females. Because female behavior in young males leads to punishment and because activities for which one is punished become disliked, males tend to have stronger hostile feelings toward females than females toward males. Finally, from theories postulating that punished behavior is suppressed but not unlearned, and that the male role involves prestige and privileges not accorded the female, it is predicted that, where a discrepancy exists between sex-role preference and sex-role identification, males tend to show same-sex role preference with underlying opposite-sex role identification. Females, however, tend to show opposite-sex role preference with underlying same-sex role identification.

Although the relevant findings in general support the hypotheses, they indicate that more research and theoretical clarification in comparing males and females are needed in the areas of anxiety over sex-role identification and hostility toward the opposite sex. (19 references)

114
McCord, Joan; McCord, William; and Thurber, Emily. Some effects of paternal absence on male children. *Journal of Abnormal and Social Psychology*, 64(5):361-369, 1962.

Father absence. Psychological adjustment. Parental influence. Elementary school boys.

In a new analysis of data collected in a 1939-45 longitudinal study, hypotheses are advanced relating paternal absence to several areas of personality development in boys: Development of a feminine self-image, extent and type of anxiety experienced, and probability of engaging in antisocial behavior. The primarily lower class sample of 205 boys was divided into two groups: Those from permanently broken homes and those from intact homes. Each boy from a broken home was matched with a boy similar in other background variables whose parents were living together. The broken-homes group was subdivided by cause of father's absence, age of boy at time father left, and affectional relationship and stability of mother. The intact-homes group was rated on overt conflict versus relative tranquility between parents.

Trained social workers observed the subjects at home, work, and play, and recorded observations on each boy for 5 years (ages 5-10). Ten years later, trained researchers read each case record and rated each boy and his parents on a number of variables, ranging from occupation and religion to affectional interaction. Court records for each subject were also obtained as one measure of adult antisocial behavior. A series of hypotheses was proposed regarding the relative amount and kind of feminization, anxiety, and antisocial behavior expected of boys from broken homes as compared with those from intact homes.

The detailed report of results reflects the impact of paternal absence, parental conflict, reason for father's absence, child's age at the beginning of the absence, and the nature of the mother-child relationship. Conflict and general instability in the home, rejection, and deviance (alcoholism, criminality, or promiscuity) of the mother, rather than paternal absence alone, were found to be responsible for developmental problems. (34 references)

115
Minuchin, Patricia. Sex-role concepts and sex typing in childhood as a function of school and home environments. *Child Development*, 36(4):1033-1048, 1965.

Socialization   variables.   Sex-role   preference.   Sex-typed   behavior.
Elementary school students.

This study was designed to determine whether children of otherwise
comparable backgrounds develop different sex-role concepts and
sex-typed behavior as a function of differences in attitudes and
models offered by their schools and homes. Data were extracted from
a broad multiple-purpose study. It was predicted that traditionally
educated and reared children would hold more conventional sex-role
attitudes and demonstrate more conventional sex typing than children
from more modern backgrounds.

Subjects were 48 female and 57 male middle-class, urban children
drawn from several fourth-grade classrooms. Half the subjects were
attending   schools   categorized   as   "traditional";   half,   "modern"
schools. Each subject's family was assigned a Modern-Traditional
Orientation (MTO) rating, based on questionnaires and interviews
with the mother. Data used for the present study came from an
interview, the Stick Figure Scale, a play session, and the Children's
Picture Story Test. The interview and Stick Figure Scale assessed
conscious, expressed attitudes about sex-role advantages and social
sex images.

The findings showed a group trend toward stated preference for one's
own sex and toward conventional role imagery, but this trend was
more consistently characteristic of children from traditional backgrounds. More open attitudes were associated, as predicted, with
more modern backgrounds. An open stance toward sex-role preferences was more characteristic of the girls than the boys, and
particularly of the girls from modern schools and homes and from
families of higher socioeconomic status. A clearly stated preference
for opposite-sex roles was rare and was not systematically related to
either modern or traditional backgrounds.

The projective data on sex typing in play and fantasy yielded
somewhat different results. There was a substantial group trend
toward sex-typical reactions and concerns, but this trend was more
characteristic of children from traditional backgrounds. Less sex-
typical reactions were associated, as predicted, with more modern
backgrounds. The direction of association was consistent on all
measures, although the order of magnitude was not generally high.
Girls from modern backgrounds particularly tended to depart from
sex-typed expectations. Higher aggression in boys and stronger family
orientation and dependence in girls were associated with more
traditional backgrounds. In these projective data, the influence of
family orientation was more evident than that of the school. (16
references)

116
Mitchell, Gary D. Attachment differences in male and female infant monkeys. *Child Development,* 39(2):611-620, 1968.

Primates. Mother-child relations. Sex-role development.

Three mother-infant laboratory experiments on the rhesus monkey are reviewed to compare mother-infant relations in the first and second 90 days of life. The interactions of the mothers with male and female infants are also compared. Behaviors for the 32 mother-infant pairs (16 male and 16 female infants) were measured by a standardized system of defining, observing, and scoring.

The frequency and form of mother-infant contacts were found to depend on the behavior of the mother and on the age and sex of the infant. Mothers apparently promote different amounts of independence in the two sexes. Mothers restrained female infants more and had more physical contact with them. Although less frequent, physical contact between male infants and their mothers was quite intense. Mothers of male infants withdrew from, vigorously played with, and presented to their infants more often than did the mothers of females. Male infants bit their mothers more often than did females. Most infant-directed behaviors decreased from the first 90-day period to the second, with the exception of punishment and rejection behaviors.

These data suggest that experiential variables influence the sex-role development of the monkey, as in humans. Although the primate mother's relations with male and female infants are generally similar, the differences that exist may be crucial to the long-term development of the primate along a male-female continuum of behavior. (13 references)

117
Money, John. Differentiation of gender identity and gender role. *Psychiatric Annals,* 1(4):371-377, 1971.

Genetic determinants. Sex hormones. Prenatal influences. Socialization variables. Sex-role development.

This discussion explores the biological and psychological development of gender. The succession of differentiation—from sex chromosomes to embryonic gonads which, in turn, determine whether fetal masculinizing androgen is secreted to external genitalia—is examined both in sexually normal individuals and in clinical hermaphrodites. Prenatal androgenization of genetic and gonadal females and nonandrogenization of genetic and gonadal males result in a variety of abnormal behavioral effects. After birth, gender differentiation continues psychologically through society's responses to the individual's assigned sex. Studies of oppositely reared hermaphrodites show the importance of environment on psychosexual differentiation.

As the child develops its sexual identity through identification with one sex and complementation with the other, parents' lack of ambiguity in reinforcement, approval, and disapproval of gender-role behaviors is necessary. The existence of two systems of gender-identity in each individual's brain, one coded positively and the other negatively, and duality and unitarianism in personality are discussed relative to normal- and contragender-role behaviors. (11 references)

118

Moss, Howard A. Sex, age, and state as determinants of mother-infant interaction. *Merrill-Palmer Quarterly,* 13(1):19-36, 1967. Also excerpted in: Bardwick, Judith M., ed. *Readings on the Psychology of Women.* New York: Harper & Row, 1972. pp. 22-29.

Mother-child relations. Maternal behavior. Infant behavior.

This longitudinal study investigated maternal and infant behaviors to determine how the infant's experience affects potential learning patterns. A sample of 30 first-born children and their mothers was observed in the home for an 8-hour period during each infant's third week of life. At age 3 months, 26 of these infants and their mothers were again observed for 8 hours. The infant behavioral states examined were crying, fussing, sleeping, smiling, vocalizing, and being passively or actively awake. Maternal variables included attending, stimulating, imitating, and making affectionate contact with the infant. Mothers of 23 of the infants had been interviewed 2 years prior to the infant's birth, providing a measure of acceptance of the nurturant role and degree to which infants are seen in positive ways.

Sex differences were most pronounced at 3 weeks for both maternal and infant variables. Mothers held 3-week old males 27 minutes more per 8 hours than females. At 3 months, males were held 14 minutes longer. At 3 weeks, female infants slept an hour longer than males; at 3 months, they slept 41 minutes longer. During the test periods, infants slept from 25 to 75 percent of the time, and thus the amounts of time available for learning experiences varied. From 3 weeks to 3 months, maternal feeding and close physical behaviors significantly decreased, while those involving stimulation and social interaction (imitation, smiling, and talking) increased. At 3 months, infants spent significantly more time smiling, vocalizing, and looking at the mother. While the difference in maternal behaviors toward males and females was considerably less at 3 months than at 3 weeks, the trend persisted for males to have higher mean scores on elicited maternal behavior. When the infant's state was controlled for, most of the sex differences were no longer significant; probably because boys cried in general more and slept less, mothers interacted more with them than with females. However, maternal stimulation scores were nevertheless higher for boys and imitation scores higher for girls, suggesting that mothers reinforce verbal behaviors on the basis of sex of child. Positive correlations were found between maternal responsiveness and mother's previous acceptance of the nurturant role and positive attitudes toward infants in general. Thus, the psychological status of the mothers, as well as the infant's stimulus and reinforcing conditions, predicts maternal behavior. This behavior in turn influences future social learning. A discussion of the effects of stimulation on the child's development draws on a number of other infant studies. (27 references)

119
Moulton, Robert W.; Burnstein, Eugene; Liberty, Paul G., Jr.; and Altucher, Nathan. Patterning of parental affection and disciplinary dominance as a determinant of guilt and sex typing. *Journal of Personality and Social Psychology*, 4(4):356-363, 1966.

Parental dominance. Parental models. College men. Sex-role development.

It was hypothesized that both degree of guilt—an indicator of internalization of parental standards—and sex typing of young males could be predicted by the patterning of parental affection and discipline. Questionnaire data from 161 male university students from intact homes included self-reports on frequency and ease of arousal of guilt and parental affection and discipline. A modified Gough scale measured sex typing. Based on responses to the discipline items, 42 subjects were classified as mother dominated and 101 as father dominated.

Regardless of which parent was dominant, the affection level of the dominant disciplinarian was significantly related to the son's guilt, but the affection level of the nondominant disciplinarian was not. The more affectionate the dominant parent, the greater the likelihood of guilt feelings in the child. Disciplinary dominance alone was not a significant predictor of guilt. Low level of guilt occurred frequently when both parents were low in affection. The frequency of high guilt among subjects with two affectionate parents was somewhat less than among those with one affectionate parent who was also the dominant disciplinarian. This finding suggested that turning to the nondominant disciplinarian for affection was a possible alternative to conforming to the demands of the affectionate but dominant parent. There was a strong tendency for sex typing to correspond to the sex of the dominant disciplinarian, but only when that parent was also high in affection. Alternative sources of affection and discipline are discussed in relation to father absence and aggression. (30 references)

120
Mussen, Paul H., and Parker, Ann L. Mother nurturance and girls' incidental imitative learning. *Journal of Personality and Social Psychology,* 2(1):94-97, 1965.

Mother-daughter relations. Preschool children. Imitation. Parental models.

This study tested the hypothesis that parents who are generally warm and nurturant facilitate their children's imitation of parental behavior, even without specific instruction or reward for such imitation. It was specifically hypothesized that girls with highly nurturant mothers would show greater tendencies to imitate their mothers' incidental, task-irrelevant behavior than girls with relatively nonnurturant mothers. Subjects were 30 kindergarten girls, 5 to 6 years old, in a middle-class school. Each girl spent two sessions with the experimenter. In the first session, the Porteus Maze Test was administered as a game. In the second session 3 to 4 weeks later, each mother solved the maze, making certain irrelevant comments according to instructions from the investigator, while the daughter watched. The daughter then worked on the maze herself. Between the first and second sessions, each mother was interviewed to obtain data on nurturance and fostering dependency. The child's dependency was further assessed by teacher ratings.

Results showed that daughters of nurturing and nonnurturing mothers imitated task-relevant responses (maze solutions) to about the same degree, but task-irrelevant behaviors to different degrees. Daughters of highly nurturant mothers imitated task-irrelevant behaviors significantly more often than the daughters of nonnurturant mothers. Results were not related to higher dependency in the first group; in fact, both interview data and teacher ratings showed the highly nurtured girls to be less dependent than the others. The data are interpreted to support the idea that the identification process, including the child's acquisition of appropriate sex-typed behaviors, may result from incidental imitation learning. (10 references)

121
Nash, John. The father in contemporary culture and current
psychological literature. *Child Development,* 36:261-297, 1965.

Childrearing practices. Father-son relations. Parental models. Psychological adjustment. Paternal behavior.

This review examines the study and opinions of a number of
sociologists and psychologists on the childrearing practices of Western
industrial society. Primary consideration is given to father-son
interaction. The examination reveals that, to many sociologists,
Western Society appears matricentric in its childrearing philosophy.
Unlike societies with primitive family cooperative economies, Western
industrialized countries assign sole economic support of the family to
the father and child care to the mother. Adopting this cultural
philosophy, psychologists have assumed that the seemingly predominant system is both the only and the most desirable method of
childrearing. Consequently, insufficient attention is given to the
father's role, and studies of father-child relationships are scarce.

Clinical studies and investigations of delinquents suggest that
father-son relationships may be of considerable etiological importance
to both social and psychological abnormality. Psychosexual difficulties, such as homosexuality, apparently result when a child's major
identification is with the opposite-sex parent. When reared predominantly by women, boys may acquire feminine patterns that are in
conflict with cultural norms for males. Identification of the child
with the same-sex parent is therefore important in sex-role and
psychosexual development. The warm, affectionate relationship and
prolonged associations emphasized in learning theory, rather than the
veiled hostility of the oedipal theory, appear to be most necessary for
successful identification. Studies of the effects of paternal deprivation
on sons suggest that the preschool period is critical in establishing
this kind of relationship with the father. The role of the peer culture
in influencing sex-role development is also discussed. (110 references)

122
Padan-Eisenstark, D. Career women in Israel: Their birth order and
their sibling groups' sex composition. *Journal of Marriage and the
Family,* 34(3):552-556, 1972.

Birth order. Sibling influence. Career predictors. Professional women.
Israel.

The influences of birth order and sex of siblings on high-status Israeli
career women were investigated. As part of a wider study on

women's intergenerational occupational mobility, questionnaires were sent to eminent women in seven occupational fields. Data were collected on demographic and occupational characteristics of 184 respondents, their parents, husbands, siblings, and children.

Findings supported the main expectation that youngest daughters would be significantly overrepresented among women in high-status positions, although this held true only for large sibling groups. Eldest daughters were overrepresented only in smaller sibling groups, although at a nonsignificant level. As expected, middle-born daughters were either proportionally represented or underrepresented, but not significantly. Contrary to expectation, sex composition of sibling groups was unrelated to career status. Moreover, all-female sibling groups of all sizes were underrepresented among the career women, although not significantly so. It is noted that youngest daughters and youngest sons advance under similar favorable conditions, but that eldest daughters have a less favorable position than eldest sons. (16 references)

123

Propper, Alice Marcella. The relationship of maternal employment to adolescent roles, activities, and parental relationships. *Journal of Marriage and the Family,* 34(3):417-421, 1972.

Working mothers. Adolescents. Mother-child relations. Canada.

Hypotheses concerning the relationship between maternal employment and the roles, activities, and attitudes of adolescents were tested. Questionnaire data were collected from 229 Toronto high school students with intact families and employed fathers. The final sample was restricted to the 72 girls and 44 boys whose mothers had worked full time at least 7 years since their birth, and to the 65 girls and 48 boys whose mothers had never worked outside the home. Subjects with working and nonworking mothers were similar in age, religion, and socioeconomic status; families with nonworking mothers tended, however, to be larger. Questionnaires included checklists of household chores and leisure activities and questions about areas of disagreement with parents and about their relationship with each parent.

Findings indicated that adolescents have only slightly more household responsibilities when the mother is employed, and that they do not differ consistently from subjects with nonworking mothers in degree of social participation. Although parent-child disagreements are more common when the mother is employed, perceptions of parental interest, help with school and personal problems, and degree of closeness to parents are similar to those of children with nonworking mothers. The finding that fewer sons of working women choose their father as an adult ideal than sons of nonworking mothers requires further investigation in studies that include middle-class and upper class respondents and that examine the father-child relationship. Sex differences, although not the focus of this study, are reported. (7 references)

124
Rapoport, Rhona, and Rapoport, Robert N. Early and later experiences as determinants of adult behavior: Married women's family and career patterns. *British Journal of Sociology*, 22(1):16-30, 1971.

Working wives. Career patterns. Career predictors. Great Britain.

This study examined the effects of early life experiences and current influences on various patterns of married women's participation in the labor force. From mailed questionnaire data obtained in a larger study of British wives and husbands 8 years after the wives' university graduation, 298 women with children were typed as nonworkers, noncontinuous workers, or continuous workers. They were subtyped within these divisions according to their values and satisfaction concerning their present roles and their future work intentions. Early possible determinants of adult role behavior examined were birth-order position, father's and mother's occupations, and family relationships. Later possible influences examined were perceptions of husband's commitment to the idea of careers for women, marital happiness, and combinations of early and later variables.

Women who combined work with family life tended to have fathers who were manual workers, mothers who enjoyed working or disliked not working, and/or tense relations with their mothers but warm relations with their fathers. In their adult social environment, the women whose attitudes and work intentions indicated they were the most career committed had supportive relationships with husbands and friends. These later influences appeared to be the most effective determinants of work patterns. However, findings indicated that early and later influences combine in more complex ways than generally recognized. Two types of variable interaction—simple interaction and metamorphosis—are discussed. (15 references)

125
Rheingold, Harriet L. *Maternal Behavior in Mammals.* New York: Wiley, 1963. 349 pp.

Parental influence. Maternal behavior.

This book contains 10 research reports by various investigators of maternal behavior in nonhuman mammals. Maternal behavior—in the sense of the behavior of the mother or her surrogates in the presence of the young—is described for laboratory rats, the genus *Peromyscus* (deermice and others), rabbits, cats, dogs, sheep and goats, moose and elk, rhesus monkeys, langurs, and free-ranging baboons.

The research reflects the disciplines of genetics, physiology, psychology, zoology, anthropology, and medicine. Methods of study vary from naturalistic field observation to experimental laboratory manipulation. The research focuses primarily on how maternal behavior affects the behavior of the young. Maternal behavior is viewed as the main source of the infant's early physical and social experience, influencing the animal's later behavior as an adult, a member of a social group, and a member of the species.

Overall the book aims to contribute to the formulation of general principles about the genesis of social behavior, the formation of the family, and the organization of social groups. The study of nonhuman maternal behavior is seen as contributing objectivity to the study of human maternal care. (4-69 references per chapter)

126
Romney, A. Kimball. Variations in household structure as determinants of sex-typed behavior. In: Beach, Frank A., ed. *Sex and Behavior.* New York: Wiley, 1965. pp. 208-220.

Cultural differences. Family structure. Sex-typed behavior.

Cross-cultural findings are used to consider the effect of household structure on socialization of sex-typed behavior. Major variables of household structure related to sex-typed behavior are household size, patterns of authority, polygyny, degree of internal coherency, dispersion of sibling groups, and continuity of mother-daughter relationships. These variables derive from residential arrangements and rules governing succession of authority.

The strength of the male authority figure is greatest in nuclear families, where the father is present and unchallenged in authority. His authority is weaker in extended bilateral households, where he is one of several authority figures, and in extended lineal households, where he is subject to the authority of an older male. Studies of households without male figures suggest that the effect of father absence on children varies with the timing and length of separation.

Research on sibling order indicates that first-born children identify most closely with parental values and display less aggressive play than younger siblings.

Economic factors and patterns of subsistence are also related to family organization and socialization. Large sex differences in socialization are associated with economies that emphasize male strength and motor skills, and with customs giving rise to large family groups with high cooperative interaction. Because societies with high accumulation of food resources require males to spend large amounts of time in care of fields and herds, females predominate in childrearing. These societies tend to emphasize the female virtues of obedience and responsibility. Conversely, low-accumulation societies emphasize achievement, self-reliance, and independence, especially in males. (11 references)

127
Rosenberg, B. G., and Sutton-Smith, B. Family interaction effects on masculinity-femininity. *Journal of Personality and Social Psychology,* 8(2):117-120, 1968.

Family structure. Sex-role development. Sibling influence.

Masculinity-femininity responses of all members of two-child nuclear families were compared to explore the hypothesis that sex-role attributes are influenced by family interactional structures as well as by simple identification with the same-sex parent. The Gough Scale of Psychological Femininity was administered to 160 female college sophomores from two-child families, their siblings, and their mothers and fathers. Analysis of variance, multiple *t* tests, and correlational techniques were used in the analysis of results.

Sex of sibling was a significant influence of subjects' femininity scores: Girls with sisters scored significantly higher than girls with brothers. Fathers with a daughter and a son scored significantly higher on femininity than fathers with two daughters. Birth order was not a significant source of variance in subjects' scores. Families with two girls showed distinctly different patterns of intercorrelation among family members' scores than families with girl-boy dyads. In two-girl families, scores of all females (children and mother) tended to be intercorrelated, with the father's score isolated. In girl-boy families, the scores of mother, father, and boy tended to intercorrelate, and the girl's score was isolated except for some correlation with her mother's score. The conclusion is drawn that sex-role learning involves sibling-sibling and child-parent effects as well as parent-child effects. (25 references)

128

Rothbart, Mary K., and Maccoby, Eleanor E. Parents' differential reactions to sons and daughters. *Journal of Personality and Social Psychology,* 4(3):237-243, 1966.

Sex-role perceptions. Parental influence. Dependency. Aggression. Preschool children.

This study examined parental behavior as a function of sex of parent and sex of child. It was hypothesized that both parents would consistently reinforce dependency more strongly in girls and aggression more strongly in boys. Subjects were 98 mothers and 32 fathers of nursery school children. The sample came from several socioeconomic status levels, with a concentration of upper middle-class families. Using as a stimulus a sexually ambiguous child's voice, experimenters told one group of mothers and one group of fathers that they were hearing a four-year-old boy's voice and told two other parent groups that they were hearing a girl's voice. Subjects wrote what they would do or say in response to the imaginary son's or daughter's statements in a fictional situation. Most of the subjects also completed questionnaires on the extent to which they believed that boys and girls do and should differ on selected characteristics.

A pattern of results emerged, with fathers showing generally greater permissiveness toward girls than boys for both dependency and aggression against parent, and mothers showing a similar pattern of permissiveness toward boys over girls. Parents' sex-role differentiation scores derived from the questionnaires were found to be related to responses to the child's voice, with high-differentiation parents showing greater differences in their reactions than low-differentiation parents. However, contrary to expectations, these differences were in the direction of the sample as a whole (fathers more permissive to imaginary daughters and mothers to sons). Parents showing high sexual differentiation expectations did not tend more than other parents to promote assertiveness in the imaginary son or dependency in the imaginary daughter. (13 references)

129

Rushing, William A. Adolescent-parent relationship and mobility aspirations. *Social Forces,* 43:157-166, 1964.

Parent-child relations. Adolescents. Social aspirations.

The influence of parents as rewarding-depriving agents, independent of their role as norm senders, on children's social mobility aspirations was investigated empirically. Specifically, the hypothesis tested was that children with high mobility aspirations are more likely than nonaspirants to perceive their family milieu and the relationship with each parent as depriving. The effect of social class was also analyzed.

All juniors and seniors (124 females, 137 males) in a high school near Cape Canaveral, Fla., were the subjects of the investigation. Subjects were classified as mobility aspirants or nonaspirants according to their response to the question, "In the years ahead, do you hope to achieve a higher social position than your parents?" Subjects' perceptions of deprivation or satisfaction in their family milieu were assessed in two ways: Three questions were asked about happiness with the family in general, in comparison to peers' families, and in comparison to siblings; and 15 questions dealing with specific aspects of the parent-child relationship were asked in reference to each parent. Respondent's socioeconomic status was classified by father's occupation as manual or nonmanual labor.

Perceived deprivation in the family milieu was significantly associated with mobility aspirations for females, but not for males. Mobility aspirations were associated with deprivation in the father-daughter relationship, but not with the mother-daughter relationship or with either parental relationship with sons. More sons of manual workers were aspirants, but father's occupation was not related to female mobility aspirations. Father's occupation was not related to feelings of family deprivation for either sex. (29 references)

130
Rutherford, Eldred E. A note on the relation of parental dominance as a decision maker in the home to children's ability to make sex-role discriminations. *Journal of Genetic Psychology,* 114:185-191, 1969.

Parental dominance. Elementary school students. Sex-role perceptions.

Hypotheses were tested relating paternal and maternal dominance to children's ability to make masculine and feminine sex-role discriminations. Subjects were 39 boys and 37 girls from three third-grade classes. Questionnaires from 25 sets of subjects' parents provided data regarding which parent dominated in household decisions. Children's masculine and feminine discrimination scores were based on their ability to associate highly masculine boys and low feminine girls with highly masculine games, and highly feminine girls and low masculine boys with highly feminine games. High and low feminine girls and high and low masculine boys had been rated as such by their classmates.

Paternal dominance in decisionmaking in the home was significantly related to the children's ability to associate masculine games with highly masculine boys and with low feminine girls. Children from father-dominated homes were also able to associate feminine games with low masculine boys. There was no significant relation between maternal dominance and children's ability to make feminine discriminations. Results are discussed in terms of two alternative possibilities: That paternal dominance is more important than maternal dominance as a basis for modeling by young children, and that sex-role cues provided by the mother are less generalized to the school situation than those furnished by the father. (8 references)

131

Rychlak, Joseph F., and Legerski, Anne T. A sociocultural theory of appropriate sexual role identification and level of personal adjustment. *Journal of Personality,* 35(1):31-49, 1967.

Parental models. Psychological adjustment. High school students. Sex-typed behavior.

Two studies tested the theory that cross-sex parental identification is associated with personal maladjustment only when the resultant behavioral pattern does not allow an offspring to fulfill his or her sexual role. Masculine and feminine sexual roles were defined by their respective association with ascendant-dominant (A-D) and retiring-passive (R-P) behaviors. A projective instrument was developed requiring subjects to make two forced choices of 24 descriptive statements. Subjects made like-self versus unlike-self choices at one session; and a week later, made like-mother versus like-father choices.

The sample for study I consisted of 119 boys from the four grades of a St. Louis secondary school. Subjects ranged in age from 14 to 18, were volunteers, and came from intact, upper middle-class and upper-class families. In addition to the sex-role identification instrument, subjects were administered intelligence tests and the Cattell High School Personality Questionnaire (HSPQ). Sophomore through senior groups (N=89) also completed the Minnesota Multiphasic Personality Inventory (MMPI). Findings revealed that only 20 boys considered themselves passive in personality; 15 of these boys attributed the same passive-retiring characteristics to their mothers. These 15 boys had the highest mean scores on the MMPI depression, psychasthenia, and schizophrenia scales and the lowest scores on the Cattell's super ego strength and warmly sociable variables.

Study II subjects were 35 delinquent girls residing in a detention home and 26 nondelinquent female high school student volunteers of comparable age (16 to 18), socioeconomic status (upper lower- and lower middle-class), and religion (varied). The delinquent girls were administered the MMPI and the HSPQ measures; the controls, the HSPQ. The sex-role identification instrument was also administered. The most frequent identification category (37 percent) for the delinquents was A-D father, whereas 31 percent of the nondelinquent were R-P mother identifiers. The three delinquent girls who manifested a projected R-P mother pattern of identification were highest on the MMPI hypomania scale and the lowest on Cattell scales related to good personal adjustment, interpersonal relations, and living by a code. The three nondelinquent girls who identified with the perceived A-D characteristics of their fathers were more guilt prone and excitable than members of the other identification grouping. Thus, it was concluded from the normal populations of both studies that R-P boys who identify with their mothers and A-D girls who identify with their fathers suffer in personal adjustment. Other normals who identify across sex are found to be as well-adjusted on personality tests as those who make sex-appropriate parental identification. (15 references)

132
Santrock, John W. Relation of type and onset of father absence to cognitive development. *Child Development,* 43:455-469, 1972.

Father absence. Cognitive ability.

It was hypothesized that the effect of father absence on a child's cognitive development varies with the type of absence and the child's age at onset of the absence. A sample of 286 father-absent, lower-class junior high and high school students provided information on whether their fathers were absent owing to death or marital breakup, whether a stepfather was present, and their own age at onset of absence. School files provided third- and sixth-grade IQ and achievement test scores. The scores of father-absent subjects were compared with those of a random sample of 57 father-present students of the same age and social class as the test sample.

Father-absent subjects scored consistently lower than father-present subjects on the cognitive measures. Father absence due to divorce, desertion, or separation in the initial 2 years of life had the most negative influence on the cognitive measures for boys and girls; father absence due to death was most detrimental when it occurred in the 6-to-9-year period of the boy's life. No significant differences were found for any of the comparisons of girls whose fathers died at different times in their lives. Father-absent boys consistently performed less well than father-absent girls and father-present boys. It was expected that, when the father departed in the 3-to-5-year period, girls would be more negatively affected than boys owing to their oedipal attachment to their fathers during this period. No conclusive support for this proposition was found. Remarriage of mothers who were divorced from, deserted by, or separated from their previous husbands in the initial 5 years of their children's lives had a positive influence on sons' cognitive development, but not on daughters'. (15 references)

133
Sears, Robert R. Development of gender role. In: Beach, Frank A., ed. *Sex and Behavior.* New York: Wiley, 1965. pp. 133-163.

Parental influence. Sex-role development. Childrearing practices.

Research on the childrearing antecedents of children's adoption of gender roles is reviewed, with a discussion of the problems of defining gender roles. Styles of aggression exhibited in doll play by 3-year-olds suggest that gender-role differentiation has started by that age. Girls' aggression is primarily verbal and prosocial (emphasizing discipline and order), and boys' aggression is physical and initially antisocial. By age 4, measures of nonaggressive manifestations of gender role (observation of activity in sex-typed play areas and tests of preferred activities and toys) indicate sex-oriented development of other aspects of personality.

Studies of childrearing practices associated with high development of appropriate gender role show that father's sex anxiety and mother's punitiveness toward aggression, high levels of physical punishment and ridicule, high demands for table manners, and severe weaning and toilet training all contribute to feminizing children of both sexes. The affectionate participation of the father in the girl's upbringing tends to masculinize her. It is emphasized that, because of imprecise definitions, gender-role concepts and childrearing variables should be reduced to operational definitions permitting more exact measurement of various role components. Specific childrearing variables should be viewed in reference to which parent displays them. (23 references)

134
Shaw, Merville C., and White, Donald L. The relationship between child-parent identification and academic underachievement. *Journal of Clinical Psychology,* 21:10-13, 1965.

Parental models. Academic achievement. High school students.

This study investigated the relationship between child-parent identification and academic performance. The sample consisted of 66 male and 48 female 10th- and 11th-grade students and some of their parents (89 mothers and 73 fathers). These students came from a high school serving a large and economically varied area and had IQ's of at least 110 on the California Test of Mental Maturity. The subjects defined as achievers had 3.0 or higher grade point averages, and the underachievers had averages of 2.7 or below. The Adjective Check List, administered to all subjects, measured degree of relationship (identification) between children and parents. Each parent completed checklists on self-perception and perception of his or her child. Each child completed checklists on self-perception, perception of mother, and perception of father.

For achieving males, significant correlations were found between self-perception and perception of father and between self-perception and perception of father's self-perception. Similarly, there was a significant correlation between self-ratings of female achievers and their mothers. A significant negative correlation was found between self-ratings of the mothers of underachievers and their ratings for their daughters. Male achievers identified much more closely with their fathers than with their mothers, but female achievers identified more closely with their mothers. No such distinctions could be made in underachiever groups of either sex. Overall, there was considerable agreement between members of achiever families in their self-perceptions and the perceptions of them reported by their parents. This agreement was lacking in underachiever families. Although agreement was found on ratings of their child by the mother and father of both achievement groups, more parents of achievers than underachievers ascribed the characteristics of success to their children. (7 references)

135

Sherman, Richard C., and Smith, Frances. Sex differences in cue-dependency as a function of socialization environment. *Perceptual and Motor Skills*, 24(2):599-602, 1967.

Cognitive styles. Sex-role identification. Role models. Adolescents.

The hypothesis that sex differences in cue-dependency are the result of differential sex-identification modes was tested. Subjects were parochial school students with a mean age of 12 years, 9 months. Twelve males and 7 females lived with their families, and 13 males and 7 females were living in a Catholic orphanage. Subjects learned to identify a geometric figure and were then tested for their ability to select the figure from among similar shapes. It was predicted that males from normal family situations would be less cue-dependent than females from normal families. This hypothesis derived from the theory that girls learn cue-dependency from direct mother identification, whereas boys see less of their fathers and learn abstraction and cue-independence from the less imitative mode of role imitation, rather than father imitation. The findings were expected to show that orphaned females, lacking a consistent model to imitate, would be less cue-dependent than normally raised females; and that orphaned subjects would show no significant sex differences in cue-dependency and would be less cue-dependent than subjects from normal families.

Results indicated that females from normal family situations were significantly more cue-dependent than males from normal family situations. Orphaned females were significantly less cue-dependent than females from normal families. However, orphaned males were significantly more cue-dependent than normal males and orphaned females. It was suggested that the nuns who care for the orphaned girls are less imitable (and thus elicit less cue-dependency) than the full-time male counselors who care for the male orphans. (7 references)

136

Siegel, Alberta Engvall, and Curtis, Elizabeth Ann. Familial correlates of orientation toward future employment among college women. *Journal of Educational Psychology,* 54(1):33-37, 1963.

College women. Career aspirations. Parental influence.

This study explored the relationships between college women's employment orientation and five family characteristics: Socio-economic status, parents' educational levels, mother's work orientation, parents' views on purpose of college, and parents' attitudes toward importance of education for the daughter. Individual open-ended interviews with 43 female university sophomores provided data.

According to five of the six criteria measuring work orientation, 70 percent or more of the subjects were oriented toward future employment. The majority intended to both marry and work. Of all family variables, only mother's work orientation was found to be significantly correlated with the subject's work orientation. While this finding confirmed the general view of the continuity of the generations through role modeling within the family, several factors affected confidence in the study's outcome. The homogeneity of the sample may have operated to depress the observed correlations. It is suggested that future studies replace the work-orientation index with one variable of expectation of employment and one of aspiration of achievement in employment, and that information on the subject's parents be obtained independently. (3 references)

137
Tangri, Sandra Schwartz. Determinants of occupational role innovation among college women. *Journal of Social Issues,* 28(2):177-199, 1972.

Career aspirations. College women. Achievement motivation. Parental models.

This study investigated the relationships between non-sex-typical occupational choices and background, personality, and college experience. Subjects were 200 female University of Michigan seniors randomly selected from a larger longitudinal study of 1963 entering students. Data were derived from a questionnaire administered to the total sample in their senior year. In addition, projective measures of need achievement (nAch) and motive to avoid success (M_{-s}) for 118 of these subjects were also available. Subjects were classified as role innovators, moderates, or traditionals on the basis of chosen occupations indicated in the senior questionnaire.

Role innovators were found to be more autonomous, individualistic, and motivated by self-imposed demands to perform to capacity. The ambiguous social meaning and difficult standards of performance of their occupations were reflected in doubts about identity and ability to succeed. The role innovators' career commitments were greater, but they had as many romantic and platonic relationships with men as did traditionals. Faculty in their major field and female college friends provided role support, but a supportive boy friend appeared to be quite important at this stage. There is some evidence that higher educated mothers were used as role models. A four-part typology is suggested in which role modeling and the type of maternal model available are related to the subject's occupational choice and motivational patterns. (32 references)

138
Tiller, Per Olav. Parental role division and the child's personality development. In: Dahlström, Edmund, ed. *The Changing Roles of Men and Women.* Boston: Beacon Press, 1971. pp. 79-104.

Working mothers. Parental models. Psychological adjustment. Parent-child relations.

This review of child development studies considers ways in which men's and women's participation in working life can influence their roles as childrearers and their positions within the family. It is contended that whether the mother is working outside the home or is a full-time traditional housewife does not solely determine the child's development and personality adjustment. The decisive factor appears to be whether the child in early developmental stages experiences sufficient maternal contact to gain a fundamental confidence in itself and its surroundings.

Different forms of paternal and maternal absence and cross-cultural parent-child relations are examined in terms of primary and secondary sexual identification and such developmental phenomena as compensatory masculinity and juvenile delinquency. A discussion of parental authority and identity seeks to explain further how the child identifies with the person perceived as controlling the means to satisfy its needs. It is concluded that too much contact with a mother in the traditional homemaker role, rather than too little, may pose the greater risk of harming the child's chances for self-sufficiency. (23 references)

139

Vogel, Susan R.; Broverman, Inge K.; Broverman, Donald M.; Clarkson, Frank E.; and Rosenkrantz, Paul S. Maternal employment and perception of sex roles among college students. *Developmental Psychology,* 3(3):384-391, 1970.

Sex-role perceptions. College students. Working mothers.

Sex-role perceptions held by male and female college students were examined in relation to the employment history of the students' mothers. It was hypothesized that individuals whose mothers have been employed would perceive less difference between the masculine and feminine roles than those with homemaker mothers. A sample of 120 college students (59 males, 61 females) rated men in general, women in general, and themselves on an inventory of bipolar phrases describing characteristics relevant to sex roles.

Results indicated that both men and women with employed mothers perceive significantly fewer differences between masculine and feminine roles than men and women with homemaker mothers. Women's perceptions of sex roles were more strongly influenced by the mother's employment than were men's. Maternal employment also tended to raise the estimation of one's own sex with respect to characteristics that are seen as socially desirable for the opposite sex: male-valued competency items and female-valued warmth-expressiveness items. Additional conclusions drawn are that sex-role perceptions are affected by actual parental role behaviors and that the traditional conceptions of sex roles are not immutable. (15 references)

140
Vroegh, Karen. The relationship of birth order and sex of siblings to gender role identity. *Developmental Psychology,* 4(3):407-411, 1971.

Birth order. Sibling influence. Sex-role development.

The effects of birth order and sex of siblings on gender role identity were examined. Three groups of subjects included children from suburban, middle-class homes. Two preschool groups included 66 boys and 68 girls and 67 boys and 70 girls, respectively, and a third group included 183 boys and 185 girls from grades two to eight. Preschool subjects were selected on the basis of teacher rankings of most or least masculine boys and feminine girls. Rank order scores of gender role identity for the third group were derived from teacher and peer ratings. School records provided data on birth order and sex of siblings.

Gender role identity of all subjects in all groups was not consistently affected by sex of younger siblings or sex of siblings without regard to birth order. The presence of like-sex siblings, whether older or younger, did not show any predictable effect upon masculinity or femininity as ranked by teachers or peers. The only evidence that same-sex siblings have a positive effect upon gender identity was that girls in grades seven and eight with sisters only were considered more feminine by teachers than girls with brothers only. However, they were not more feminine than girls with both brothers and sisters. In grades two and three, girls with both brothers and sisters were judged more feminine by teachers and peers than other girls. In those grades, oldest siblings were ranked more feminine by teachers than other girls. The only significant difference shown was for the sex of older sibling variable, and this does not support the idea that the presence of older like-sex siblings reinforces appropriate gender role identity. It was suggested that future measures of gender identity and role modeling consider variations in appropriateness of gender identity within sex rather than between sexes. (14 references)

141
Ward, William D. Sex-role preference and parental imitation within groups of middle-class whites and lower-class blacks. *Psychological Reports,* 30:651-654, 1972.

Parental models. Sex-role preference. Elementary school students. Racial differences. Socioeconomic differences.

The generalization that there is a dominant female influence in sex-role development among lower class black children and a dominant masculine influence among middle-class white children and was tested empirically. It was predicted that, when same-sex role preference and parental imitation were assessed, middle-class white boys would have a higher masculine sex-role preference than the counterpart feminine preference of the female group; that the feminine sex-role preference of the black girls would be higher than the counterpart masculine preference of the black boys; that the white boys would score higher on a measure of father imitation than the white girls would score on mother imitation; and that the lower-class black girls' mother-imitation score would be higher than the father-imitation score of the lower-class black boys.

Subjects were 32 second-grade children, eight in each sex/race category, attending the Campus School of the State University College, Brockport, N.Y. Socioeconomic class of each racial group was based on the makeup of the communities from which the school draws its population. A modification of the It Scale for Children was used to assess sex-role preference. An imitation schedule which utilized projective doll play assessed preferences in parent imitation. For white middle-class children, boys scored more masculine than girls did feminine on the preference measure, but there was no significant sex difference on the imitation measure. For black lower-class children, girls scored more feminine than boys did masculine on the imitation measure, but there was no significant sex difference on the preference measure. In cases where there were no significant sex differences, each sex scored in the sex-appropriate direction. (10 references)

142
Werner, Emmy E. Sex differences in correlations between children's IQs and measures of parental ability, and environmental ratings. *Developmental Psychology,* 1(3):280-285, 1969.

Intelligence. Parental influence.

Correlations of son's and daughter's IQ's with measures of parental ability and environmental ratings are reported in an investigation of sex differences in parent-child relationships. The hypothesis tested was that intellectual performance of boys is more responsive to environmental events, whereas that of girls has a larger component of genetic control. The 485 subjects (231 boys, 254 girls) were participants in a longitudinal study of all children born in Kauai, Hawaii, in 1955. One or both of their parents had attended school on the island and taken group intelligence tests there between the ages of 10 and 15 years. The Cattell Infant Intelligence Test was administered to the children at about 20 months of age, and the SRA Primary Mental Ability Tests (PMA) were administered at about 10 years of age, yielding a total PMA IQ and five factor scores for each child. Parents' IQ scores were collected from their school records; most had taken the California Test of Mental Maturity, which yields a verbal, a nonverbal, and a full IQ score. Ratings of the home environment evaluated socioeconomic status (SES), educational stimulation, and emotional support, based on reports of home interviews with the mothers.

Children's IQ's at 20 months were correlated with each parent's partial and total IQ scores and education, and with SES and father's occupation. Of these 10 correlations, 8 were significant for girls, 3 for boys. Girls' scores showed higher relations with the parental measures than did boys' scores for 7 of the 10 correlations. The children's IQ's at age 10 were correlated with each parent's partial and total IQ scores and education and with each of the three environmental ratings—educational stimulation, SES, and emotional support. All correlations for girls and all but one for boys were significant. Girls' IQ's had a higher relationship with parent and environmental measures than boys' scores did for 7 out of the 11 correlations. Significantly higher correlations of IQ with all three environmental ratings were obtained for girls than for boys. Higher correlations were found for both sexes between children's IQ's at age 10 and educational stimulation in the home than between measures of parental ability and children's IQ's. Findings point to sex differences in the rate of intellectual maturation favoring girls and, contrary to the hypothesis, to a greater responsiveness of girls to achievement demands and educational stimulation in the home during middle childhood. (17 references)

143
Weston, Peter J., and Mednick, Martha T. Race, social class, and the motive to avoid success in women. *Journal of Cross-Cultural Psychology, 1(3):284-291, 1970.* Also in: Bardwick, Judith M., ed. *Readings on the Psychology of Women.* New York: Harper & Row, 1972, pp. 68-71.

Achievement motivation. Racial differences. Socioeconomic differences. College women.

Black and white college women were compared on their fantasy responses to fictional situations suggesting male-female competition. It was hypothesized that black college women would exhibit fewer motive-to-avoid-success responses (M-s) than white college women, and that lower class black women would have fewer M-s responses than middle-class black women. Subjects were 50 black and 13 white undergraduate women enrolled at Bluefield State College, and 11 black and 11 white undergraduate women enrolled at American

University. Social class was determined by questionnaire data on parents' occupation and education. All subjects wrote 5-minute stories in response to each of four verbal Thematic Apperception Test cues. Two cues were neutral and two were designed to elicit images of female success in masculine fields. M-s scores for the stories were computed on the basis of concern about negative consequences of such success.

For both cues eliciting success imagery, significantly fewer black women at both schools exhibited M-s responses in their stories than did white women. It is suggested that the traditional dominance of black females causes successful women to be regarded as economic assets rather than threats to black manhood. Another possibility suggested is that black women are unable to project themselves into high aspiration careers and thus do not identify with or fear social rejection due to success at that level. Within the Bluefield State sample (the only group large enough for social class comparisons), class differences among blacks were not significant in predicting M-s responses. (13 references)

144
Whiting, Beatrice B., ed. *Six Cultures: Studies of Child Rearing.* New York: John Wiley and Sons, 1963. 1017 pp.

Socialization variables. Cultural differences.

This book reports on a cross-cultural study relating socialization patterns to adult psychology in six societies: A Gusii community in Kenya; the Rājpūt caste in Khalapur, India; the village of Taira, Okinawa; the Mixtecans of Juxtlahuaca, Mexico; an Ilocos barrio in the Philippines; and a New England town in the United States. Teams of two social scientists each spent from 6 to 14 months with the society they were investigating. Hypothesized individual and cultural personality differences concerned nine behavioral systems: Succorance, nurturance, self-reliance, achievement, responsibility, obedience, dominance, sociability, and aggression.

Each culture is discussed first in terms of the ecology, economics, and social and political organization that determine adult behavior and roles, and then in terms of childrearing observed in 24 families with children between the ages of 3 and 10. Also considered are reward and punishment techniques, socialization agents, and a child's identification with each of its parents and the relationship with the nature and strength of internal controls. The varied treatment of boys and girls in each culture and possible universal age and sex differences in behavior are examined. (1-23 references per chapter)

145
Whiting, Beatrice B. Sex identity conflict and physical violence: A comparative study. *American Anthropologist,* 67(6-Part 2): 123-140, 1965.

Cultural differences. Socialization variables. Sex-role conflict. Aggression. Delinquency.

This analysis compares the frequencies of assault and homicide in six societies and considers the differences in light of the protest-masculinity concept and the status-envy hypothesis of identification. It was predicted that, in societies where the male child develops a cross-sex identification from frequent maternal contact and little or no paternal contact and is later confronted with a male dominated adult world, he will experience sex-role conflict. In seeking to reject his underlying female identity and achieve male status, the young male will engage in violent and aggressive behavior (protest masculinity), resulting in a greater number of assaults and homicides than are found in societies not engendering sex-role conflict.

Societies studied were communities within the towns of Taira, Okinawa (60 families); Orchard Town, New England (24 families); a Mixtecan barrio (population 600) in Juxtlahuaca, Mexico; the barrio of Tarong (population 309) in Luzon, Philippines; Rājpūt caste members (N=602) in Khalapur, India; and the Nyansongo (18 contiguous homesteads) in Kenya. Twelve girls and 12 boys between the ages of 3 and 10 were selected from each society. The behavior of children was observed, and both they and their mothers were interviewed. Field teams also observed leisure activities and incidents of personal and group conflict in each community. Interviews with community members yielded cases of assault and homicide involving persons known to them.

More cases of assault and homicide were reported in Nyansongo and Khalapur than in the other four societies. In these two societies, especially the polygamous Nyansongo, the small child sees his father infrequently. Adult men and women eat together, share leisure activities, and work together considerably less than in Taira, Tarong, Juxtlahuaca, or Orchard Town. Rājpūt and Nyansongo children observe separation of the sexes and the inferior status of women. In Juxtlahuaca, the male has greater status than the female, but adequate adult male visibility during early childhood prevents the child's initial identification with the mother and subsequent sex-role conflict. From these findings, four hypotheses relative to primitive law are proposed: In societies whose social structure engenders sex-identity conflict and consequent hypermasculinity, more forms of violence will be considered lawful than in other societies; more conflict will arise in the resolution of trouble because it is considered unmanly to admit guilt; more formalized legal codes and procedures and more litigation will be necessary; and punishment for deviant behavior will be more severe and will be characterized by desire for revenge. (40 references)

146
Woods, Merilyn B. The unsupervised child of the working mother. *Developmental Psychology,* 6(1):14-25, 1972.

Working mothers. Elementary school students. Psychological adjustments. Mother-child relations.

Maternal absence due to employment and the consequent substitute supervision arranged were studied in relation to children's academic achievement, intelligence, personal and social adjustment, health, family relationships, and school and community behavior. A sample of 47 female and 61 male fifth-graders from the North Philadelphia lower-class black community were classified into four groups according to reported extent of mature supervision. All subjects were administered the California Test of Personality, the California Short Form Test of Mental Maturity, the Iowa Test of Basic Skills, and the Parent Behavior Inventory. Other data on the variables under investigation were provided by teachers' Gough Adjective Check List ratings of each student and by school, hospital, and police records. In addition, 38 mothers of 40 of the children were interviewed concerning their personal background, maternal and work-role attitudes, and child care functions.

Findings indicated significant differences between supervised and unsupervised girls. Unsupervised girls exhibited verbal and language deficits on the Mental Maturity Test; capitalization, language, and arithmetic deficits on the Basic Skills Test; and difficulties in school relations, indicated by the personality test. Unsupervised girls perceived their mothers as significantly less controlling and intrusive than did supervised girls. More girls than boys reported a lack of supervision. There were no significant differences between supervised and unsupervised children in teacher descriptions, police records, hospital emergency room visits, school absences or tardiness, and number of psychological referrals. Full-time maternal employment, compared with work at home and part-time work, was a positive influence on a child's social adjustment and intelligence. Maternal quality, mother-child relationships, and maternal attitudes toward employment were positive correlates of cognitive and personal development. It was concluded that, because full-time employment is an economic necessity rather than a personal choice for these lower-class mothers, it produces less maternal role conflict for the mother and less feeling of maternal rejection for the child than in middle-class and upper middle-class families where the mother works. (6 references)

147
Wright, Benjamin, and Tuska, Shirley. The nature and origin of feeling feminine. *British Journal of Social and Clinical Psychology*, 5:140-149, 1966.

Femininity. College women. Parent-child relations.

This study investigated the nature of young women's feelings of "femininity" or "masculinity" and the origins of these feelings based on recollections of parent-child relationships. A sample of 2,650 middle-class college and university women rated themselves on a 26 word-pair semantic differential. Of these, 1,892 rated themselves very feminine on the feminine-masculine item and were identified as the feminine group; 210 rated themselves slightly feminine or masculine and were identified as the masculine group. The nature of feeling feminine was examined by comparing self-descriptions of the feminine group with those of the masculine group on 25 word pairs. Possible origins of these feelings were examined by comparing the two groups on which parent was designated the more important in 19 parent-child relationships.

Feminine women rated themselves significantly more narcissistic, confident, and comfortable than masculine women. Masculine women rated themselves more forceful, intelligent, and responsive. Recollections of an emotionally satisfying mother and a successful father characterized the feminine group. Recollections of an emotionally satisfying father and a frustrating, unsympathetic mother characterized the masculine group. Masculine women felt less well understood in general. It is suggested that a more influential relationship with the father exists for masculine women, but that a more favorable image of the father in his masculine (successful) role is perceived by feminine women. (28 references)

Attitudes Toward Sex-Roles

148
Arkoff, Abe; Meredith, Gerald; and Iwahara, Shinkuro. Male-dominant and equalitarian attitudes in Japanese, Japanese-American,

and Caucasian-American students. *Journal of Social Psychology,* 64:225-229, 1964.

Marital dominance. Cultural differences. College students. Japan.

This study investigated the marriage-role attitudes of Japanese college students and compared these attitudes with those of comparable Japanese-American and Caucasian-American students. Subjects were 48 male and 97 female Japanese students from Nara Gakugei University and Yokohama National University, and 26 male and 49 female third-generation Japanese-Americans and 30 male and 30 female Caucasian-Americans from the University of Hawaii. A 28-item scale measured male-dominant and equalitarian attitudes toward marriage.

Japanese-American males held the most male-dominant attitudes of the subgroups, although no significant differences were found between them and males of the other two groups. Japanese females were the most equalitarian in their marriage attitudes, but not significantly more equalitarian than the Caucasian-American females. Japanese-American females were significantly less equalitarian than other females. No significant difference was found in the marriage-role attitudes of male and female Caucasian-Americans, but the Japanese and Japanese-American groups showed significant sex differences, the males being more male-dominant and the females more equalitarian. (15 references)

149
Brun-Gulbrandsen, Sverre. Sex roles and the socialization process. In: Dahlström, Edmund, ed. *The Changing Roles of Men and Women.* Boston: Beacon Press, 1971. pp. 59-78.

Socialization. Sex-typed behavior. Sex-role perceptions. Parental influence.

A theoretical explanation of the process of child socialization, focusing especially on sex-based variations, is illustrated by data from selected studies of child and parent attitudes toward sex roles. This discussion addresses the extent to which actual sex differences in behavior and attitudes are environmentally determined. Observations are limited to Scandinavian and American urban middle-class cultures.

Findings in various studies reflect a conflict between an apparent cultural ideology of sexual equality and in underlying unwillingness to accept the full consequences of this ideology. Certain aspects of the process and content of role distribution between the sexes are examined. Extensive evidence of stereotyped sex-role images among children supports hypotheses concerning the process by which sex-role patterns become internalized behavior: In general, behavior which best demonstrates possession of a trait included in the sex ideal is the one most strongly ascribed to the sex role.

The advantages and disadvantages of each sex role are considered in relation to the perceptions of children of varying ages and the perceptions of their mothers, as well as in relation to stated sex preference and adult patterns of deviant social behavior. Questions of whether sex should continue as an important differentiating criterion in socialization and whether attempts should be made to hasten social change in this area are addressed. (8 references)

150

Dahlerup, Pil. The lack of awareness of attitudes by a literature critic. [Omedvetna attityder hos en recensent.] In: Westman-Berg, Karin, ed. *Konsdiskriminering forr och nu.* Stockholm: PRISM, pp. 37-46, 1972.

Artistic activities. Sexual discrimination. Denmark.

This discussion concerns two literary reviews written by the same critic on two poetry collections published by the same Danish poet. In the first newspaper review, the reviewer considers the poet a man; by the time of the second review, he has learned that the poet is a woman. The two reviews are compared to demonstrate unconscious sex discrimination in the reviewer's selection and usage of words in describing the two collections. Both reviews are reprinted in their entirety.

The reviews are both complimentary and rather similar at first sight. However, a word-by-word examination of the articles shows specific language devices that distinguish the poet as a female from the poet as a male. The adjective "little" appears frequently in the second review, whereas in the "male" review it is not once used. Such adjectives as "bright," "rich," "enthusiastic," and "splendid" are used for the male poet; the female's writing is "nice," "beautiful," "healthy," and "down to earth." Linguists generally agree that adjectives are static and immobile and verbs are dynamic. This distinction is reflected in a comparison of the two reviews: The male review has 46 verbs and 14 adjectives, whereas the female review has 45 verbs and 36 adjectives. There are also differences among the verbs used. The male poet's creative process is described by such active verbs as "can" and "will." Use of the passive tense suggests that the female writer is acted upon, rather than the actor. The same pattern is found in the use of nouns. The author as female is often described by metaphors, but no such allusions are used to describe the author as male.

It is concluded that, although the critic says nothing explicit about the superiority of the male writer over the female, this sentiment is implicitly expressed through separate descriptive modes. (5 references)

151
Dorn, Dean S. Idealized sex roles among young people. *Journal of Human Relations,* 18(1):789-797, 1970.

College students. Sex-role perceptions. Female role.

This study tested the hypothesis that the female career role of the 1960's has become increasingly accepted as the norm, at least among college students. Forty male and 30 female college juniors and seniors completed an open-ended questionnaire on the double standard of male-female behavior, male-female relationships, the ideal role of the American woman, and whether most other college students would agree with their views on the female role. Fifteen of the male students were interviewed in depth on the reasons for their answers.

Sixty percent of the females and 70 percent of the males thought that the double standard had declined, particularly in the areas of employment, education, sexual behavior, the military, and political involvement. Fifty percent of the females and 70 percent of the males indicated their belief that women were increasingly having egalitarian relationships with men. Both males and females listed as characteristics of the ideal female role an egalitarian relationship with males, a companion-complementary marriage with mutually agreed upon decisions, and a lifestyle allowing the female to develop her capabilities to the fullest. Despite this general consensus, males reported difficulty in acknowledging this ideal in their own behavior. However, perceiving no alternative to accepting female freedom, the males were attempting to overcome both the traditional female stereotypes and traditional male stereotypes of dominance and insensitivity. Subjects thought college students of both sexes would agree with their views on women's role. (12 references)

152
Droppleman, Leo F., and Schaefer, Earl S. Boys' and girls' reports of maternal and paternal behavior. *Journal of Abnormal and Social Psychology,* 67(6):648-654, 1963.

Maternal behavior. Paternal behavior. Parent-child relations. Junior high school students. High school students.

This paper reports on two studies investigating the differences between maternal and paternal behavior as reported by children and differences between boys and girls in their description of each parent. The subjects of the first study, 85 male and 80 female seventh-grade students from a suburban Catholic school, were administered behavior inventories about nurturance and control for each parent.

Both boys and girls reported mothers to be significantly higher than fathers in expression of affection, emotional support, and child-centeredness. Boys reported fathers and girls reported mothers as higher in negative behavior—irritability and nagging. Girls reported fathers significantly higher than mothers in detached negative behavior (rejection, neglect, and ignoring), while boys reported fathers only slightly higher than mothers on such behaviors. Both sexes reported that mothers use covert, indirect methods of control more frequently than fathers. Both boys and girls reported the opposite-sex parent as granting more autonomy. Girls reported significantly more affectionate treatment from both parents than boys, and boys reported more hostile treatment and control.

The second study attempted to replicate these findings using a different sample. Subjects were 36 boys and 34 girls from the 11th grade of an urban, predominantly Protestant public school. Their social class, as indicated by parents' educational level, was lower than that of the first sample. Each subject completed paternal and maternal behavior inventories.

In general, the results of differences between mothers and fathers as reported by both boys and girls were consistent with the first study. Eleven of the 12 behavior cluster comparisons were essentially similar. However, the differences between boys and girls in their reports on each parent were completely unlike the first study. The only significant difference between the sexes for either parent was that girls reported receiving more covert, indirect control from mothers than did boys. These variations in boys' and girls' reports between the two studies suggest that there may be an interaction between two or more of several variables: Sex of parent, sex of child, age of child, social class, and religion. (31 references)

153
Elman, Judith; Press, Alan; and Rosenkrantz, Paul. *Sex-Role Self-Concepts: Real and Ideal.* Paper presented at the annual meeting of the American Psychological Association, Miami Beach, Fla., 1970. 9 pp.

Self-concept. Idealized roles. Stereotypes. College students.

How men and women conceptualize ideal males and females was studied in relation to their perceptions of typical males and females and their perceptions of themselves. The effects of sex-role stereotypes and sex-role ideals on individual self-concept were also investigated.

Subjects were 52 male and 52 female students at a 2-year community college. A 60-item, bipolar stereotype questionnaire was developed from the longer stereotype questionnaire used in earlier studies. Respondents indicated traits of the typical male and female, the ideal male and female, and their own real and ideal selves on scales consisting of stereotypic differentiating, and non-differentiating male- or female-valued items.

Male and female responses on ideal male and female traits were more similar than their responses on typical male and female traits. Ideal males and ideal females were seen as possessing similar socially desirable adult traits. The real self-images were more like the perceived stereotypes than like the ideal sex roles, and the ideal self-images more closely resembled the sex-role ideals than they resembled the stereotypes. Both males and females perceived ideal men and women as possessing many of the traits presently valued for the opposite sex. Findings suggest a shift by individuals toward more flexible sex typing. (7 references)

154

Emmerich, Walter. Family role concepts of children ages six to ten. *Child Development,* 32:609-624, 1961.

Elementary school students. Role perceptions. Family structure.

This study examined the development of children's conceptions of sex and age roles within the family. A middle-class sample of 111 girls and 114 boys, ages 6 to 10, was divided into 12 subgroups on the basis of sex and age. Paired figure comparisons (mother-girl, father-boy, mother-father, and girl-boy) provided data on the children's perceptions of relative power of the figures in each interaction and on the positive or negative attitude of each figure toward each interaction.

There was much greater consensus on the power dimension of parent roles than on the attitude dimension. Children discriminated age roles by assigning high power actions to the adult and low power actions to the child. With increasing age of subject, there was an increasing tendency to discriminate male but not female age roles by power. Some age-role relationships were more differentiated by power than others. It was suggested that children type love-oriented interactions by age more than object-oriented interactions. All subjects assigned more high-power actions to the father than to the mother. A curvilinear relation was found between the child's age and the extent to which the father's sex role was perceived as more powerful than the mother's. The amount of power attributed to the father increased between the sixth and eighth years, suggesting that this period is important in the development of father-role concepts. Differentiation of the sex- and age-role components of the father role appeared to begin between the 8th and 10th year. Positive correlations among the measures of parent sex- and age-role discrimination by power suggested that use of the power dimension generalizes across role situations. Girls discriminated child sex roles by assigning positive actions to the girl and negative actions to the boy figure. Boys varied in their attitude discrimination of child sex roles according to the specific interaction. (26 references)

155
Entwisle, Doris R., and Greenberger, Ellen. Adolescents' views of women's work role. *American Journal of Orthopsychiatry,* 42(4):648-656, 1972.

Adolescents. Female role. Career attitudes.

The effects of adolescents' sex, race, IQ, social class, and residential locus on their attitudes toward women's work role were explored. The sample of 270 male and 305 female ninth graders were attending six Maryland schools described as black inner-city, white inner-city, black blue-collar, white blue-collar, white rural, and white middle-class. Subjects answered three forced-choice questions on women's role included in a large test battery. The questions, followed by indexes of how strongly the subject felt about each opinion, concerned whether women should work, what kinds of jobs they should hold, and whether they are intellectually curious.

Data indicated a marked difference between boys and girls about women's role, with boys consistently holding more conservative opinions. Both sexes disapproved of women holding "men's" jobs. Black students were less opposed to women working than were white students, but they were just as negative toward their doing the same work as men. Both black and white inner-city students were generally willing for women to work. Blue-collar girls were more conservative than inner-city girls on women's role. The greatest differences between girls' and boys' views were found among the middle-class white sample. Although subjects of high IQ generally held liberal views, high-IQ middle-class boys were least liberal. High-IQ blue-collar students of both sexes were the most liberal. These findings are discussed briefly in relation to adolescent sex-role behavior, occupational aspirations and peer pressure, education, and women's role in American society. (5 references)

156

Epstein, Gilda F., and Bronzaft, Arline L. Female freshmen view their roles as women. *Journal of Marriage and the Family,* 34(4):671-672, 1972.

College women. Career aspirations. Marriage aspirations.

Marriage, family, and career plans of women entering a tuition-free public university under an open admissions policy were examined. The College Student Questionnaire (CSQ), consisting of 200 questions on background, attitudes, and future plans, was administered to a sample of 1,063 women freshmen at Lehman College (City University of New York—CUNY) in 1970. Subjects came from predominantly lower middle-class and working-class backgrounds. Their responses to one question on the CSQ presenting five options concerning marriage, family, and career plans for the next 15 years were compared with the 1965 responses of a national sample of 677 freshman women.

A plurality of 48 percent of CUNY women in 1970 anticipated having a career, marriage, and children within 15 years, compared with 42 percent of the national sample in 1965. In the 1970 CUNY sample, 28 percent planned to become housewives with one or more children, but none chose to become a housewife without children. Very small percentages chose to become either unmarried career women or married career women without children.

If interpreted from an overall lifetime perspective, the percentages of women choosing the housewife-with-children option are inflated, since direct data were not obtained for the long-term sequence or combination of roles. The findings of this study show a trend away from the traditional role of women among lower middle-class and working-class students. (7 references)

157

Freedman, Mervin B. The role of the educated woman: An empirical study of the attitudes of a group of college women. *Journal of College Student Personnel,* 6(2):145-155, 1965.

College women. Career aspirations. Marriage aspirations. Female role.

This study presents the results of an empirical investigation of the attitudes of college women toward women's role. Forty-nine students at an Eastern college were interviewed several times a year during their 4 college years concerning personal experiences and views on woman's role, career and marriage, women in America, and the feminist movement. Most members of the three college classes, including the class from which the interview sample was drawn, took two personality inventories, an attitude inventory, and the Authoritarianism and Ethnocentrism Scales in their freshman and senior years. Freshmen classes averaged around 400 students and senior classes under 300.

Most students were not inclined to value conventional feminine characteristics or behavior. Almost every student indicated she would like to marry, and over half the seniors said they desired careers. Career-oriented interviewees foresaw various amounts of conflict between the two aspirations. Personality test differences suggested that students planning a career were somewhat more intellectual, unconventional, independent and flexible in their outlook, and more alienated socially. Results from the Ethnocentrism Scale showed that women having traditional views on women's role also had stereotyped racial views. Both interview and test data indicated that most subjects were content with the current status of the educated woman in American society. Although they recognized the existence of discrimination, they considered it surmountable. The findings of this study and other literature on the subject are discussed in relation to the practicality of college women's expectations, reasons for the revival of primacy of home and family, and future social and economic conditions. (48 references)

158
Goldberg, Philip. Are women prejudiced against women? *TransAction,* 5(5):28-30, 1968.

Sexual discrimination. College women. Professional women.

An experimental study was designed to investigate whether there is real prejudice by women against women; i.e., whether perception itself is distorted by sex discrimination. Two hypotheses were tested: That even when the work is identical, women will value the professional work of men more highly than that of women; and that this tendency will be greatly diminished or reserved when the professional field happens to be one traditionally reserved for women.

Subjects were 140 randomly selected college women, of whom 100 were used for pretesting and 40 in the experiment proper. In pretesting, the 100 subjects were given a list of 50 occupations and asked to rate the degree to which they associated the profession with men or with women. The two occupations most associated with men, the two most associated with women, and two neutrals were selected. Six articles from the professional literature representing the six occupations were combined into booklets. Each article was attributed to a male author in half the booklets and to a female author in the other half. Each booklet had three male and three female authors' names. In a group session, the subjects read the articles and evaluated each one on a set of nine questions. No mention was made of the sex of the author in the instructions.

Results clearly supported the first hypothesis: Of 54 possible comparisons of male and female authors, 3 were tied, 7 favored female authors, and 44 favored male authors. The pronounced tendency for subjects to evaluate more highly articles attributed to male authors held not only for the two "male" professions, but for all six. Thus, the second hypothesis was not supported. Results showed a general bias by women against women across professions and for nine different aspects of competence as a professional. (No references)

159

Hall, Marjorie, and Keith, Robert A. Sex-role preference among children of upper and lower social class. *Journal of Social Psychology,* 62:101-110, 1964.

Sex-role preference. Socioeconomic differences. Elementary school students.

This study investigated the relationship between sex-role preference and social class and the differences in sex-role preference patterns of boys and girls. Subjects were 44 girls and 44 boys from the third and fourth grades in two public schools. Twenty-two girls and 22 boys were from upper-class families as determined by the residential area and father's occupation, and 22 girls and 22 boys were from lower-class families. Upper- and lower-class subjects were matched on California Mental Maturity IQ scores. The It Scale, a projective test involving sex-typed item and activity choices for a sexually ambiguous figure, measured sex-role preference. Two additional measures were obtained by asking the subject to choose a male or female parental role for It, plus a male or female name.

As expected, boys of lower socioeconomic class demonstrated a more distinct masculine sex-role preference than upper-class boys. There was an unexpected trend for upper-class girls to demonstrate a more feminine preference than lower-class girls, but the difference was not as great as that between the boys. Boys of both classes showed a more distinctly masculine sex-role preference than girls showed a feminine sex-role preference. Girls viewing the It figure as a father or calling It by a male name had scores toward the masculine end of the scale, whereas girls selecting a feminine role and name had scores toward the feminine end. Sex-role preference patterns among girls are apparently more diffuse than among boys, the result in part of girls' broader sex-role socialization and the greater prestige attached to the male role. The difference in sex-role preference between upper- and lower-class boys was seen as a reflection of the more patriarchal environment of the lower-class family. (16 references)

160
Hartley, Ruth E. Sex-roles and urban youth: Some developmental perspectives. *The Bulletin on Family Development,* 2(1):1-12, 1961.

Sex-role perceptions. Sex-typed behavior. Elementary school students.

The development of women's social roles was examined in terms of children's perceptions of adult sex-role activity. A sample of 91 girls and 40 boys, ages 8 and 11, from upper middle-class and lower middle-class, intact, nonminority urban homes was subgrouped by sex, age, and mother's working status. Two structured pictorial techniques—Role Distribution: Adult Series and Role Situations—were used to establish the children's classifications of activities by sex and their feelings toward a number of adult activities. All the girls' mothers and 25 percent of their fathers were interviewed.

In the Role Distribution test—how children perceive activities by sex of the performer—the subjects assigned 57 activities to men and only 44 to females, despite the attempted inclusion of an equal number of items for each sex within the test. Few differences in the assignment of sex were shown by subgroup, with the greatest variation occurring for the working-mother group. The Role Situations test—children's impressions of how people feel about what they do—was given to the girls only. The results varied significantly by subgroup, but the girls' responses indicated considerable contentment with female role activities and little desire to perform traditional male activities. More 11- than 8-year-olds tended to see women as disliking their activities. Daughters of nonworking mothers were more positive toward some domestic items. The working-mother subgroup indicated more positive feelings toward becoming a doctor, judge, or butcher. The greatest differences in perceived attitudes, however, were between socio-economic classes, with upper middle-class girls less in favor of low-prestige female occupations and useful activities in general than the lower middle-class girls. (9 references)

161

Hartley, Ruth E. A developmental view of female sex-role definition and identification. *Merrill-Palmer Quarterly of Behavior and Development,* 10(1):3-16, 1964.

Sex-role development. Female role.

In this discussion of female sex roles in childhood, sex role refers both to perceptions of what females do and to attributed expectations, such as what females like to do. Sex-role definitions also involve age-role definitions. A lack of empirical data in the literature for ages below 3 years is noted.

One point of view about sex-role specification holds that some of the related behaviors are developed as integral personality functions without awareness of the part of the subject of their sex-status connection. An earlier survey of sex-typing techniques during ages 1 to 5 revealed several kinds of handling by which this generalized molding takes place, such as canalization, application of sex-appropriate verbal appellations, sex-typing indoctrination devices, and concentrated exposure to women's traditional activities. The gradual nature of the development of limitation and specification in toy preferences by female children is discussed.

Continuity and change in sex-differentiating cognitions and implementations in 8-to-11 year old girls are discussed, based on data from earlier studies. These data report two types of sex-role information: cognitions and preferences. Rejection of femininity during ages 8 to 11 is not found. Differences resulting from different socioeconomic classes do not, on the whole, appear in age-appropriate, sex-role cognitions, but do appear in preferences—largely as a rejection of work roles by upper middle-class girls—and in cognitions of adult female roles. (30 references)

162

Hartley, Ruth E. Children's perceptions of sex preference in four culture groups. *Journal of Marriage and the Family,* 31(2):380-388, 1969.

Cultural differences. Sex-role perceptions. Preschool children. Elementary school students.

To test earlier findings that young children do not perceive culturally determined male sex favoritism or general cross-sex preference on the part of adults, this study sampled 5- and 8-year-old boys and girls of four different culture groups. A total of 408 subjects were selected from lower middle- and working-class families of Caucasian and Japanese Hawaiians and of Caucasian and Maori New Zealanders. In individual interviews, subjects supplied endings to an illustrated story involving adult choices of a boy or girl for adoption. They also predicted their own parents' choice in a similar hypothetical situation, giving reasons for their responses.

Children in the four culture groups sampled perceive adults as having parallel sex preferences. Despite the actual male dominance within each culture represented, children from all except Caucasian Hawaiian cultures (three of the four) saw females as more frequently preferred than males in story situations requiring parental agreement on sex preference. Reasons supplied by the children portray the girl as prettier, less troublesome, useful around the house, and someone for the father to play with and the mother to enjoy looking after. The 5-year-olds, more than the 8-year-olds, displayed sex centrism and a tendency to see women as preferring girls and men preferring boys. This finding suggests that sex-role concepts are functions of basic, developmental modes of cognitive organization rather than the internalization of social norms.

Implications are that the more sex separated culture offers the boy insufficient opportunity to feel wanted and worthwhile until he is old enough to assume his adult—and culturally superior—male role. (4 references)

163
Hartley, Ruth E., and Hardesty, Frances P. Children's perceptions of sex roles in childhood. *The Journal of Genetic Psychology,* 105:43-51, 1964.

Sex-role perceptions. Elementary school students.

This study investigated the effects of age, sex, class, and mother's working status on children's perceptions of peer-age sex roles. Data were collected from 91 girls and 40 boys, ages 8 and 11, from upper middle-class and lower middle-class intact, nonminority urban homes. Instruments used were the Role Distribution: Children's Series, a structured pictorial test of the sex assignment of a number of activities and toys, and an open-ended question on what the subject would tell a Martian visitor about earth's boys and girls. Differences in distribution of answers on sex assignment were evaluated. Responses of "both," "either," or "neither" were considered egalitarian, in contrast to sex-typing distinctions.

Data indicated that children distinguish between boys' and girls' sex-role activities and that toys are definite indicators of sex roles. Female childhood sex-role activities, more than male activities paralleled their traditional adult counterparts. Of the variables tested, sex of subject proved most important in influencing role perception. Each sex tended to claim more participation in certain activities than was attributed to them by the other sex. The greater consensus on sex typing of girls' toys and the more definite awareness of girls' sex roles by boys suggest that the negative directive operates in the development of male sex identity. (3 references)

164

Hartup, Willard W., and Zook, Elsie A. Sex-role preferences in three- and four-year-old children. *Journal of Counseling Psychology,* 24(5):420-426, 1960.

Preschool children. Sex-role preference.

This study investigated the sex-role preferences of 3- and 4-year-old children and examined the effects of verbal instructions on these preferences. Subjects were 65 three-year-olds and 96 four-year-olds from four Iowa nursery schools, including 78 girls and 83 boys of lower- and middle-class backgrounds. Verbal instructions stressed similarities between the subjects and the figure used in the projective test of sex-role preference. Group A subjects were individually administered the It Scale of sex-role preference and told that they were making choices for a child named "It." In group B, boys were told It was a boy; girls, that It was a girl. Subjects in group C were told that It had the same name as they did.

It Scale scores indicated distinct sex differences among children of both ages. Girls at 4 years had significantly more feminine scores than 3-year-old girls. Four-year-old boys indicated more masculine preferences than 3-year-old boys, but at the borderline level of significance. Girls responded with scores more toward the feminine end of the scale when the figure was called a "little girl" than when the figure was called "It." Boys had scores that were more masculine when the figure was called by the subject's name than when the figure was called "It." Neither birth order nor social class significantly affected the findings. (11 references)

165

Hartup, Willard W.; Moore, Shirley G.; and Sager, Glen. Avoidance of inappropriate sex-typing by young children. *Journal of Consulting Psychology,* 27(6):467-473, 1963.

Sex-typed behavior. Preschool children. Elementary school students. Sex-role preference.

This study proposed to measure young children's avoidance of inappropriate sex typing unbiased by sex-appropriate preferences. It was hypothesized that, in children between the ages of 3 and 8, avoidance of inappropriate-sex objects would increase with age; this avoidance would be greater when an adult was present; and the relationship between avoidance of inappropriate-sex objects and It Scale scores of appropriateness of sex typing would be positive.

A sample of 69 males and 78 female upper middle-class nursery and elementary school students was administered the It Scale for Children, a projective test of sex-role preference. The subjects were also observed individually playing in a room with attractive sex-inappropriate and unattractive sexually neutral toys. It was assumed that preference for the unattractive neutral toys would reflect deliberate avoidance of the attractive sex-inappropriate toys. For half of the subjects, a female adult was present during the play period. The amount of time elapsing before the subject looked at, approached, or played with the sex-inappropriate toys (latency score) and the percentage of time actually looking at, approaching, or playing with such toys (percent inappropriate scores) were recorded.

166
Hawley, Peggy. Perceptions of male models of femininity related to career choice. *Journal of Counseling Psychology,* 19(4):308-313, 1972.

Sex-role perceptions. Idealized roles. Career aspirations. College women.

This investigation replicated a previous finding that women's career choices were differentially related to their perceptions of men's views of the feminine ideal. The sample of 136 female San Diego State College students consisted of education, math or science, and counseling majors. Subjects were divided into married and nonmarried categories. Thirty-five written statements to be agreed or disagreed with, according to what "significant men in my life think," were used to rate the importance of woman as a partner, ingenue, homemaker, competitor, and knower. To determine if different perceptions of men's views on women could be related to factors others than career choice, eight covariates of personal data were considered in addition to marital status and career plans.

Those preparing for careers in the male-dominated areas of math and science believed men made little differentiation in male-female work roles and related behaviors and attitudes. Subjects preparing for the more traditionally feminine career of teaching thought that men divided work, behavior, and attitudes into male and female categories. Counselors-in-preparation, although expected to score similarly to teachers-in-preparation because of the "helping" nature of their profession, instead scored closer to the math-science group. The feminine model held by the math-science group allowed the widest range of career choices without violation of sexual identity. This group and the counselors-to-be were more concerned with having good relationships with and providing support for men than were the women who were planning to become teachers. (16 references)

167

Hewer, Vivian H., and Neubeck, Gerhard. Attitudes of college students toward employment among married women. *The Personnel and Guidance Journal,* 42(6):587-592, 1964.

College students. Sex-role perceptions. Working wives.

In the context of educators' concern with determining the optimal nature and timing of professional training for women for purposes of recruitment, this study was designed to measure college freshman attitudes toward the motivations of women for seeking employment after marriage. As part of a larger study, 4,283 students of both sexes—94 percent of the entering freshman class at the University of Minnesota in 1959—completed a questionnaire which included 18 items dealing with possible motivations for women to work. For each reason given, subjects were asked to respond in three ways: Whether they would accept that reason for married women's working, whether most men and women would accept it, and whether it should be a reason.

Subjects in most instances accepted the traditional and nurturant role for women; the more the reason under consideration was related to this traditional role, the more acceptable it was to the students. They also indicated belief that the husband is responsible for the financial support of the family, although women were less accepting of this belief than were men. When the relationship between the students' own attitudes and those they attributed to others was assessed, there was significant agreement for almost all items and for both sexes. There is little evidence from the responses of these entering freshmen that a cultural change is occurring in values regarding married women working outside the home. In fact, the results reflect a denial of such a trend. (3 references)

168

Kammeyer, Kenneth. The feminine role: An analysis of attitude consistency. *Journal of Marriage and the Family,* 26(3):295-305, 1964.

Sex-role perceptions. Female role. College women.

Ordinal scales were developed to distinguish between "traditional" and "modern" attitudes toward two aspects of the feminine sex role—female personality traits and feminine role behavior. It was hypothesized that these two role aspects would be highly related. Subjects in a random sample of 209 unmarried university women were classified as traditional or modern with respect to feminine role behavior using a five-item Guttman scale. An eight-item summed rating scale measured beliefs about female personality traits. Both scales were developed by means of a structured questionnaire administered to all subjects.

Analysis of test results showed that attitudes toward role behavior and toward personality traits were related, but not as highly as expected. Variables bearing a positive relationship to attitude were the number of college friends and, to a lesser degree, frequency of dating and amount of parental contact. It is speculated that social interaction and communication feedback alert the girl to inconsistencies in her attitudes toward these two aspects of the feminine role, and that she modifies her position accordingly. (5 references)

169
Kammeyer, Kenneth. Birth order and the feminine sex role among college women. *American Sociological Review,* 31(4):508-515, 1966.

College women. Sex-role perceptions. Female role. Birth order.

This study explored the influences of birth order on "traditional" and "modern" attitudes toward two aspects of the feminine sex role. Subjects in a 1961 random sample of 232 unmarried university women were classified on the basis of structured questionnaire results. A five-item Guttman scale measured orientation toward feminine role behavior, and an eight-item summed rating scale measured beliefs about female personality traits.

Although results on birth order and the sex-role behavior items showed only weak associations, the trend was toward a positive relationship, as hypothesized. Beliefs about female personality showed a stronger relationship to birth order. Analysis of results indicated that first-born girls are more traditional and more in agreement with their parents' perceived views of the feminine role and female personality than are later born girls. First borns are also more willing to choose marriage over graduation from college and are more likely to describe themselves as religious. Findings generally supported the hypothesis that first-born children tend to be "conservators of the traditional culture."

Since the college experience proved to diminish the influence of birth order, a similar study of the noncollege female population is recommended. Possible relationships between birth order and social change also merit further exploration. (22 references)

170
Komarovsky, Mirra. Cultural contradictions and sex-roles: The masculine case. *American Journal of Sociology,* 78(4):873-884, 1973.

College men. Sex-role perceptions. Idealized roles. Working wives.

The intellectual relations of men with their female friends and male attitudes toward working wives are discussed in this report extracted from a larger study of masculine role strain in a variety of status relationships. A random sample of 62 seniors at an Ivy League men's college was administered five schedules, the California Personality Inventory, and the Gough Adjective Check List. Subjects were interviewed in depth on actual role performance, ideal role expectations and limits of tolerance, personal preferences, perception of role partner's ideal expectations, and relevant attitudes of significant others. Extensive quasi-projective tests and some direct questions on role strain were used.

Nearly one-third of the sample confirmed the hypothesis that men would experience anxiety over perceived failure to meet a norm of masculine intellectual superiority. This group was characterized by two modes of role strain: Scarcity of resources for role performance and ambivalence. A changed role definition, in which an ideal of intellectual companionship between male-female equals is increasingly accepted, appears to explain the absence of strain in the majority of subjects. Ambivalence and inconsistencies largely characterized attitudes toward working wives and future marital roles. Despite weakening ideological supports for traditional sex roles in marriage, emotional allegiance to a modified traditional pattern was still strong. Such inconsistencies were not highly stressful, however, because of their current low emotional salience and their continuing congruence with self-interest. (8 references)

171
Lansky, Leonard M., and McKay, Gerald. Sex role preferences of kindergarten boys and girls: Some contradictory results. *Psychological Reports,* 13:415-421, 1963.

Sex-role preference. Preschool children. Methodological issues.

As part of a larger sex-role study, this investigation tested the hypothesis that modern middle-class boys have greater preference for the feminine role than girls have for the masculine role. Cultural factors supporting this thesis are discussed. A corollary hypothesis tested was that most children see the It stick figure in the It Scale for Children (a projective test of sex-role preference) as a male. Twenty male and 16 female middle-class Boston kindergarteners took the It Scale twice—once with the figure concealed and once with a concluding question as to the figure's sex.

Although boys' scores were generally rated as more masculine and girls' as more feminine, boys were more variable in their choices. The major hypothesis was confirmed in that several boys had preference scores near the feminine end of the scale; no girls had scores near the masculine end. There was no significant tendency for either boys or girls to see the It figure as a male figure. Boys were more likely to guess It was a girl than were girls likely to say It was a boy. For boys, there was a definite association between perceiving It as a boy and getting relatively masculine preference scores, or saying It was a girl and getting relatively feminine scores. (15 references)

172
MacKay, Ann; Wilding, Paul; and George, Vic. Stereotypes of male and female roles and their influence on people's attitudes to one parent families. *Sociological Review*, 20(1):79-92, 1972.

Stereotypes. Great Britain. Family Structure. Sex-role perceptions.

This British survey is concerned with stereotypes of male and female roles as reflected in attitudes toward both motherless and fatherless one-parent families. A sample of 359 adults of varying social class and education was interviewed in Nottingham; of these, 38 percent were men and 62 percent were women.

A comparison of replies on father's and mother's working revealed that 75 percent thought the man should work but the woman should stay home. Of the subjects who felt that the mother should work, 42 percent suggested part-time employment. Ninety percent said a mother who left her husband with young children should contribute financially to the support of the children. Only 43 percent thought the wife should also support the husband; the remainder said it was odd or degrading for a man to be supported by a woman.

Seventy-eight percent of the sample thought a widowed or divorced father with preschool children should work, and 96 percent thought the same of a father with school age children. The higher the social class or education level of the subject, the more likely he or she was to support the view that fathers with preschool children should work.

However, women were less likely than men to support this view. The most frequent reasons given for fathers going to work were that work was man's place in society and good for his morale, and that men should not "sponge off the state." But 88 percent agreed that government stipends to supplement wages from part-time work were good for both the father and the children. Both men and women felt that a financially secure mother on her own could provide more adequately for her children than a father in the same situation. Those saying a father could not manage stressed the emotional needs of the children; those doubting the mother's abilities emphasized the father's role in discipline. However, two-thirds of the sample felt that either the mother or the father could provide for all the needs of the family if financially secure. The lower the subject's social class, the more likely he or she was to think a lone parent of either sex could manage. More subjects in the upper classes mentioned the ill effects of lack of mother's love than lower-class subjects. Overall findings suggest that male and female roles in relation to work and child care are seen as fundamentally different. (10 references)

173
Matthews, Esther, and Tiedeman, David V. Attitudes toward career and marriage and the development of life style in young women. *Journal of Counseling Psychology,* 11(4):375-384, 1964.

Lifestyle. Career attitudes. Marriage attitudes. Adolescent females. Young adult women.

A cross-sectional study explored the effect of three developmental stages on young women's attitudes toward career and marriage in relation to the lifestyle they choose. Subjects were 1,237 girls and women who had attended a junior high school in Newton, Mass., during the period 1943-58. The sample was divided into three age groups: 432 junior high girls, ages 11-14; 282 senior high girls, ages 15-18; and 523 young adult women, ages 19-26. A career-history questionnaire and a set of attitude scales were administered at school for the junior high girls and by mail for the other subjects. Data were gathered on age, education, high school curriculum, occupation, marital status, academic subject preferences, career preferences, and life plans in 2, 4, 6, 8, and 10 years. Attitudes toward marriage and career were assessed by 14 scales derived from the questionnaire and by four separate items on preferred school subject and career. Lifestyle was evaluated from the high school curriculum chosen and the 10-year life plan in regard to marital and career status.

Results showed that the lifestyles of young women are related to their attitudes toward career and marriage and that this relationship is modified by age. The majority of subjects at each developmental stage hoped to be married and not involved in a career 10 years later, with the percentage increasing sharply from junior high to senior high, then declining to an intermediate level for young adults. Attitudes toward career and marriage differed according to the curriculum choice: College-bound women accepted the "feminine lot" rather extensively, but reported having parents who displayed a more relaxed attitude toward the time of dating and marriage than parents of noncollege-bound subjects. Attitudes also differed according to life plans, which were differentiated primarily by attitude toward marriage and attitude toward feminine careers versus homemaking. The pattern of attitudes changed with increasing age, particularly in the move away from belief in one's inferiority to men. (6 references)

174
Meyer, John W., and Sobieszek, Barbara I. Effect of a child's sex on adult interpretations of its behavior. *Developmental Psychology,* 6(1):42-48, 1972.

Sex-role perceptions. Sex-typed behavior. Preschool children.

This study investigated how the ascribed sex of a child affects adults' interpretations of his or her behavior. A sample of 44 male and 41 female middle-class and upper middle-class adults were shown two videotapes, each portraying a 17-month-old child in a play situation. Both children in the videotapes (one male, one female) were sexually ambiguous in appearance; each was sexually identified to the subjects correctly in half the group viewings and incorrectly in the other half. Questionnaires required subjects to rate each child's behavior on 24 sex-linked and non-sex-linked attributes and to provide certain background information on themselves. Ratings for a child specified as male were compared with ratings for the same child specified as female.

Overall, subjects showed no tendency to attribute more masculine qualities to a child specified as male, but subjects of both sexes having little contact with small children were slightly more likely to respond to the children's behavior in terms of sex-role stereotypes. Female subjects, especially those reporting high contact with children, rated the children lower on characteristics of their ascribed sex. There was a significant tendency for both male and female subjects to attribute a greater number of qualities, apart from sex-linked characteristics, to children of their own sex. This finding suggests that adults are able to define and respond more meaningfully to behavior of same-sex children. (5 references)

175

Putnam, Barbara A., and Hansen, James C. Relationship of self-concept and feminine role concept to vocational maturity in young women. *Journal of Counseling Psychology,* 19(5):436-440, 1972.

Adolescent females. Self-concept. Sex-role perceptions. Career aspirations.

The relationship of feminine role concepts and self-concepts to vocational maturity was investigated. A socioeconomically stratified sample of 375 girls, primarily middle class, was drawn from all 16-year-old girls in urban, suburban, and rural-suburban schools in Buffalo, N.Y. Instruments used were a feminine role rating inventory, a self-concept scale, a vocational development inventory, and a personal data form. Data were analyzed by stepwise multiple-regression and analysis of covariance techniques.

The self-concept was shown to be significantly associated with vocational maturity, in accordance with vocational development theory. Self-concept and feminine role concept of own self were useful in predicting vocational maturity, although accounting for only 10 percent of individual variation in vocational maturity. The more liberal a girl's view of her own feminine role concept, the higher her level of vocational maturity. Feminine role concepts of the ideal woman and of man's ideal woman were not useful predictors. Girls tended to be somewhat vocationally immature in comparison with boys and to have had a lower self-concept than the average individual. The feminine role concept which each girl selects appears to be consistent with her self-concept, and her occupational choice appears to implement her self-concept. (9 references)

176

Rappaport, Alan F.; Payne, David; and Steinmann, Anne. Perceptual differences between married and single college women for the concepts of self, ideal woman, and man's ideal woman. *Journal of Marriage and the Family,* 32(3):441-442, 1970.

Female role. Self-concept. College women.

A study was conducted to compare perceptions of married and single college women of the female sex role. Childless, full-time college students, 45 single and 45 married, at the University of Connecticut, completed the 34-item Inventory of Female Values. Each subject filled out three forms of the Inventory, responding first, as herself;

second, as her ideal woman; and third, as she perceived man's ideal woman. Scores on the Inventory represent the relative strength of the subjects' intrafamilial (domestic and familial) and extrafamilial (active and self-achieving) orientations.

The married college women perceived themselves as significantly more self-achieving than did the single women. Married subjects also perceived their ideal woman to be significantly more self-achieving than did single women. Both married and single subjects perceived man's ideal woman as having a strongly intrafamilial orientation. Whereas married students perceived their ideal woman as more self-achieving than themselves, single women perceived their ideal woman as more family oriented than themselves. Thus, married and single college women differed in their perceptions of themselves and the ideal woman, but had similar perceptions of man's ideal woman, which in both groups differed from their self-perceptions. (2 references)

177
Rosenberg, B. G., and Sutton-Smith, B. Ordinal position and sex-role identification. *Genetic Psychology Monographs,* 70(2):297-328, 1964.

Birth-order. Family size. Elementary school students. Sex-role identification. Anxiety.

This study was undertaken to measure whether ordinal position affects personality in preadolescent youth to the extent it affects 6-year-olds, as determined in an earlier study. The study also examined findings for families of various sizes. Sex role identification of first-born and later born children, 9- to 12-years-old, was compared in one-, two-, and three-child families. The view of ordinal position as an ecological variable and the principles of reinforcement theory comprise the theoretical framework of the study.

A total of 900 children in the fourth through sixth grades in 14 schools in northwestern Ohio were administered a test booklet containing the Children's Manifest Anxiety Scale, the Impulsivity Scale, and the Play and Game Scale. A form to record sex, age, and ordinal position was included in the booklet. Protocols were analyzed for only children (N=19), children in two-child families (N=134), and three-child families (N=199).

The principal finding was that family size is an important variable in evaluating the effects of ordinal position on sex-role identification. Moreover, relationships between the variables of family size, sex, age of siblings, and anxiety were demonstrated. It is concluded that the complex effects of ordinal position indicate that comparisons of first-born with all later born children without reference to family size may conceal more information than they reveal. (42 references)

178

Rosenkrantz, Paul; Vogel, Susan; Bee, Helen; Broverman, Donald M.; and Broverman, Inge. Sex-role stereotypes and self-concepts in college students. *Journal of Consulting and Clinical Psychology,* 32(3):287-295, 1968.

College students. Sex-role perceptions. Stereotypes. Self-concept.

A questionnaire administered to college students probed the extent to which sex-role stereotypes, with their associated social values, influence the self-concepts of men and women. The 74 male and 80 female students were asked to characterize the behaviors, attitudes, and personality traits of typical adult males, adult females, and themselves, by means of 122 bipolar items.

In contrast to expected results, self-concepts did not differ from stereotypic concepts of masculinity and femininity as a function of the social desirability of the stereotype. Results indicated strong agreement between sexes about differences between men and women, corresponding differences between the self-concepts of the sexes, and more frequent high valuation of stereotypically masculine characteristics by both sexes. Women seemed to hold negative values of their worth relative to men, indicating the influence of the factors that create this sex stereotyped self-concept. A cultural lag may account for the persistence of sex-role stereotypes despite contemporary changes in the prescribed sex-role behavior in this society. It is also noted that older or married subjects or subjects of other educational and social class levels might produce different patterns of responses. (25 references)

179

Ross, Dorothea M., and Ross, Sheila A. Resistance by preschool boys to sex-inappropriate behavior. *Journal of Educational Psychology,* 63(4):342-346, 1972.

Preschool children. Sex-typed behavior.

Three hypotheses were proposed for this experimental study of resistance by preschool boys to sex-inappropriate behavior: Most preschool boys would resist an esteemed woman teacher's advocacy of a sex-inappropriate toy choice; boys would more often exhibit techniques of resistance than girls; and both boys and girls would select toys appropriate for boys more often than for girls. Subjects were 30 male and 30 female middle-class nursery school students, ages 42 to 63 months. Twenty boys and 20 girls were in the experimental group, and 10 boys and 10 girls were in the control group. In the experimental procedure, each child chose a toy to keep and stated a toy preference for a child of the opposite sex. The female teacher then advocated a sex-inappropriate toy choice. The child was free to resist the teacher's choice and to attempt to gain support for his or her decision through interaction with the teacher or with the experimenter. After making a final toy choice, the subject chose one of 12 books, each of which had a sex-typed toy on the cover, and advised a same-sex child on a toy choice. The procedure for the control group was the same except that no important adult advocated a different choice.

In the experimental group, 14 boys maintained their original sex-appropriate toy choice, one shifted to a different sex-appropriate toy, and five changed their original sex-appropriate choice to the sex-inappropriate toy advocated by the teacher. All boys in the control group chose sex-appropriate toys for themselves. Although the same number of girls as boys resisted change, boys more often argued with the teacher about her choice, derogated her in her absence, and sought support for their original choice by eliciting the experimenter's agreement, by persuading the same-sex peer to make the same choice, or by selecting a book with their toy choice on the cover. All 60 subjects picked sex-appropriate toys for boys, but picked sex-inappropriate toys for girls far more often than appropriate ones. (12 references)

180
Roussel, Louis. Attitudes of several cohorts toward marriage, the family, and divorce in France. [L'attitude des diverses générations and a l'égard du mariage, de la famille et du divorce en France.] *Population,* 26:101-142, 1971.

France. Sexual behavior. Marital roles. Public opinion.

In this study, several cohorts of newlyweds—half married before 1961, half after that date—were asked their opinions on items related to sexual mores, marriage, and the family. A total of nearly 2,500 individuals completed a written questionnaire. Results indicated that later cohorts were in favor of emancipation at an early age and greater sexual liberty before marriage, but less freedom after marriage. More women than men approved of changes that have occurred in marital life in the last generation. Earlier cohorts seemed to be more sensitive to changes in comfort and security, whereas later cohorts put more emphasis on changes in human relationships within the family. Overall, differences in attitudes resulted more often from geographical location of subjects, date of marriage, and religious practices. (8 references)

181

Seward, G. H., and Larson, W. R. Adolescent concepts of social sex roles in the United States and the two Germanies. *Human Development*, 11(4):217-248, 1968.

Sex-role perceptions. Adolescents. National differences. Self-concept.

This cross-national study was designed to compare concepts of adult social sex roles held by adolescents. The total sample consisted of 396 males and 457 females, 16 to 19 years old, from the United States, the German Federal Republic, and the German Democratic Republic. The semantic differential technique was the principal research tool.

The findings showed consistent cross-national differences reflected in the subjects' views of men, women, father, mother, and self. Specifically, American subjects rated men as more competitive and courageous and women as less brave than did subjects from East and West Germany. American subjects rated father and self as less active than did German subjects. East German subjects rated men as braver, women as more active, and the father as less of a leader than did American or West German subjects. All subjects, regardless of sex or nationality, showed a tendency to adopt new models that differ from the old in terms of placing emphasis on action, leadership, cooperation, and wisdom. Differences at the national level among subjects were more prominent than differences among subjects within ethnic and social class subcultures. (33 references)

182

Stein, Aletha Huston. The effects of sex-role standards for achievement and sex-role preference on three determinants of achievement motivation. *Developmental Psychology*, 4(2):219-231, 1971.

Sex-role perceptions. Achievement motivation. Academic achievement. Elementary school students. Junior high school students.

The central hypothesis in this investigation was that children's sex-role standards for mechanical, athletic, mathematical, reading, and artistic achievements and for social skills are related to three aspects of their achievement motivation. Attainment values, expectancies, and performance standards. Data were collected from 235 sixth- and ninth-grade students in Ithaca, N.Y., public schools using a number of tests. Some were devised specifically for this study and others had been used in previous research. For all analyses, groups were divided by sex, grade, and high and low socioeconomic status (SES).

Sex differences were greatest on mechanical and artistic skills; these areas were also the most clearly sex typed. Findings were consistent with the theory that sex-role standards preceded differences in motivation, but not necessarily in a causal relationship.

Also as expected, the effects of age and SES differed for the three measures relating to achievement: Ninth-grade attainment values were more influenced by sex typing than sixth-grade; and lower SES children, especially boys, were more affected by sex typing in their standards and expectancies than higher SES subjects. There were no age or SES differences in sex-role standards, but individual variations in sex-role standards were correlated with motivation scores. Sex-role preferences were not related to the pattern of motivation scores. (16 references)

183
Stein, Aletha Huston, and Smithells, Jancis. Age and sex differences in children's sex-role standards about achievement. *Developmental Psychology,* 1(3):252-259, 1969.

Sex-role perceptions. Academic achievement. Elementary school students. High school students.

This study is the second in a series of investigations of children's sex-role standards for achievement in the areas of athletic, spatial and mechanical, arithmetic, reading, artistic, and social skills. Sex-role standards were defined as an individual's conception of the behaviors and attributes appropriate to each sex. Subjects were 120 middle-class boys and girls from the 2nd, 6th, and 12th grades of Ithaca, N.Y., public schools. They were asked in an interview to make forced choices and to rank order sex-role judgments on activities reflecting the above skills. The two measures allowed achievement areas to be rated separately for masculinity and femininity as well as on a masculine-feminine continuum.

Despite age and sex differences, the sample as a whole considered artistic, social, and reading skills to be most feminine, and athletic, spatial and mechanical, and arithmetic skills to be most masculine. As expected, older subjects generally had more definite and extreme sex-role standards. Girls tended to view more activities as feminine than did boys, especially in athletic and reading skills, but sex differences decreased with age. Twelfth graders showed an awareness of both adolescent and adult standards. Significant age-sex interactions in some skill areas suggest that the change in sex-role standards from 2nd to 12th grade is primarily concerned with learning what is inappropriate for one's own sex, rather than what is appropriate. (7 references)

184

Steinmann, Anne. A study of the concept of the feminine role of 51 middle-class American families. *Genetic Psychology Monographs,* 67:275-352, 1963.

Female role. Idealized roles. Self-concept.

This study investigated the concepts of the feminine role held by middle-class father, mother, and college-age daughter and the degrees of agreement and disagreement of these concepts. Subjects were 51 female Hofstra College undergraduates and their parents. The students ranged in age from 17 to 22 and resided with their parents in New York City suburbs. All subjects completed a feminine role-rating inventory that measured degrees of traditional other-orientation and liberal self-orientation regarding the feminine role. Daughters responded to the inventory statements for own self, ideal self, average woman, men's ideal woman, and as they believed their mothers and fathers would prefer them to respond. Mothers responded for own self, ideal self, average woman, and men's ideal woman. Fathers responded for average woman and men's ideal woman. Eleven families, taken from the extremes and the middle of the inventory continuum of daughter's own-self scores, were interviewed to further explore the attitudes under investigation. All subjects completed personal data forms on background variables and attitudes on family relations.

Comparison of the concept of feminine role of daughters, mothers, and fathers indicated that the daughters' concept of the average woman was significantly more other-oriented than either their mothers' or fathers'. Mothers' concept of the average woman was significantly more other-oriented than was the fathers'. Daughters' concept of men's ideal woman was significantly more other-oriented than was the fathers' concept of their ideal woman. Daughters' concept of their mother's expectations for them was close to their mothers' own-self concept and ideal-self concept. Daughters', mothers', and fathers' concepts of the feminine role are also considered individually. Subjects' feminine-role concepts are additionally presented in terms of closeness of family relationships, daughters' perception of parental dominance, subjects' ordinal position in family of origin, religion, mothers' work status, and daughters' work aspirations. (105 references)

185
Steinmann, Anne; Fox, David J.; and Levi Joseph. Shared values about woman's role within and across cultures in the United States, Peru, and Argentina. *International Understanding,* 2(1):13-17, 1964.

Cultural differences. Sex-role perceptions. Female role. Idealized roles.

This paper comprises part of a larger, worldwide study hypothesizing that women share values about their role despite differences in nationality, education, social class, and occupational status. Subjects were 150 American, 158 Peruvian, and 157 Argentine women, from 20 to 50 years old. Three populations were represented in each of the three samples: College women, nonprofessional working women, and housewives who had at least completed high school. All subjects completed the 34-item Inventory of Feminine Values in two forms, one indicating self-perceptions of woman's role and another indicating how they thought men want their ideal woman to respond.

Although the Peruvian sample had significantly more active self-perceptions of woman's role than the American and Argentine samples, all three samples had self-perceptions with large components of active (emphasis on personal and creative satisfaction) and passive (family orientation and self-sacrifice) elements. In contrast, all three samples perceived the male ideal of the female role to be primarily passive. For self-perceptions of woman's role, 60 percent or more of the American women were in agreement on 19 of the 34 items. Twenty-one items were shared by at least 60 percent of the Peruvian sample; and 20 items, by the majority of the Argentine sample. On man's ideal woman, American women agreed on 19 items; Peruvian and Argentine women, on 25 each. Cross-culturally, the subjects almost unanimously agreed on preferring to marry a man they could look up to and on desiring the man's affection more than his fame. There was similar agreement on six other items concerning woman's role. Peruvian and Argentine women consider it primarily their responsibility to make the marriage a success, whereas American women do not. The three samples had the same response patterns on 26 of the 34 man's ideal items. (No references)

186
Steinmann, Anne, and Fox, David J. Male-female perceptions of the female role in the United States. *Journal of Psychology,* 64:265-276, 1966.

Sex-role perceptions. Female role. Idealized roles. Role conflict. Self-concept.

This study tested the hypotheses that American women share a perceived conflict between the level of activity and independence they prefer and the much lower level of activity they believe men prefer them to have; that this shared perception prevails despite differences in socioeconomic class, ethnic or racial background, level of education, or occupational status; and that American men, however, say that their desired level of activity for women is not different from that desired by women.

Data were gathered on 10 cluster samples totaling 837 women and 6 cluster samples totaling 423 men. Subjects were New York City residents, ranging in age from the late teens to the seventies, including college undergraduates, physicians, lawyers, artists, working women and their husbands, nurses, and Negro professional men and women. All subjects had at least a high school education. Female subjects responded to the Inventory of Feminine Values in terms of how they perceive themselves, how they perceive their ideal woman, and how they perceive men's ideal woman. Male subjects responded as their ideal woman would. Inventory items involved value judgments related to women's activities and satisfactions.

The average response pattern of the self-perceptions of the female samples was relatively balanced between strivings of self-realization and intrafamily nurturing. Women's ideal woman was also balanced between self-achieving and other-achieving striving, but was slightly more active than their self-perceptions. Women's view of men's ideal woman, however, was significantly more family-oriented and personally subordinate than their own self-perceptions. On the other hand, all six samples of men delineated an ideal woman as relatively balanced on the continuum between self- and other-oriented elements. Particularly, men responded positively to general items of a woman being active outside the home to fulfill herself. On more specific statements of marriage and children in the lives of women, men were less certain and often contradicted their more general opinions. Despite their general agreement on men's ideal women, women as a group gave bimodal responses on several items. It was suggested that women's uncertainty about what men want in women reflects in part the contradictory cues they receive from men. (2 references)

187
Vener, Arthur M., and Snyder, Clinton A. The preschool child's awareness and anticipation of adult sex-roles. *Sociometry*, 29:159-168, 1966.

Preschool children. Sex-role perceptions. Sex-role preference.

This study examined the relationship between a child's age and sex and its awareness of and preference for clothes, household tools, and equipment linked with sex roles. These items were chosen by adults and were validated for appropriate sex linkage by 50 children ages 7 to 11. The subjects in the study were 60 girls and 60 boys between the ages of 2½ and 5, who were asked to identify the sex linkage of 44 items presented to them.

The total group of children was able to clearly distinguish the sex linkage of the items. Even the 30-to-40 month old subjects showed sex perception similar to that of the 7-to-11 year olds. Maternal influence on preschool children was evident, in that more female than male sex-linked articles were accurately identified by both boys and girls at all ages. Also, a majority of the girls' preferences were same-sex choices at all ages, whereas the boys did not choose a majority of same-sex items until the age of 51-to-60 months. The high consensus between the adult and preadolescent perceptions of sex-role linkages, plus the preschoolers' awareness of these linkages, indicated a high intergenerational stability of sex-role definition. (33 references)

188
Ward, William D. Process of sex-role development. *Developmental Psychology*, 9(2):163-168, 1969.

Sex-role development. Sex-role identification. Sex-role preference. Preschool children. Elementary school students.

This study experimentally investigated the timing and sequence of sex-role development and the degree of interrelatedness or independence of three aspects of role development—role preference, role adoption, and role identification. Hypotheses were that preferences would be established for both sexes by age 5; that girls would demonstrate identification earlier than boys; that preference would precede adoption of both sexes; that adoption would precede identification for both sexes; and that there would be low but positive correlations among the measures of preference, adoption, and identification.

Subjects were 16 boys and 16 girls randomly selected from the kindergarten and first and second grades from a Brockport, N.Y., elementary school. The independent variable was age rather than grade. Sex-role preference was measured by a Toy Preference Test, in which each child is presented a series of paired pictures of toys which have previously been sex-typed and is asked to select the preferred toy. Sex-role adoption was measured by the Pointer Game, which requires the child to choose between imitating a man or a woman, one of whom administers reinforcement during the game. Sex-role identification was determined by a Polar Adjectives Test, in which each child described himself or herself as similar to the father and/or mother on a set of 14 pairs of polar adjectives.

The first three hypotheses relating to timing and sequence of sex-role development were supported; the fourth was supported for boys, but not for girls; and the fifth hypothesis, that the three aspects would be moderately related, was not supported. On the Toy Preference Test, boys and girls clearly preferred their own-sex toys. No age effect was evident, nor was there any interaction of sex with age. On the Pointer Game, boys imitated the man, and girls imitated the woman; but this effect was much stronger for the older children. On the Polar Adjectives Test, younger children showed no self-perceived similarity to either parent, but both older boys and older girls saw themselves as similar to the mother significantly more often than to the father. Correlations among the three different measures of sex-role development were significant. (6 references)

189

Williamson, R. C., and Seward, Georgene H. Concepts of social sex roles among Chilean adolescents. *Human Development,* 14(3):184-194, 1971.

Sex-role perceptions. National differences. Adolescents. Self-concept. Idealized roles.

This study proposed that there would be greater differences between Chilean male and female adolescents' conceptions of sex roles (actual and ideal) than between males and females previously studied in the United States and East and West Germany. Subjects were 166 males and 94 females, ages 16 to 19, from two private and two public Santiago secondary schools. One-third were from upper- and upper middle-class homes, and two-thirds were from lower middle-class homes. Subjects rated mother, father, men, women, the ideal man, the ideal woman, and self on 12 characteristic semantic differential scales.

Chilean boys perceived men as less sensitive, less friendly, and less physically attractive, but braver, stronger, wiser, more competitive, and having higher leadership capability than women. Girls differentiated more between the sexes than did boys, generally giving males less favorable ratings than females. They viewed women as more sensitive and less excitable than boys did, but also as less beautiful. Girls saw their fathers as more excitable and their mothers as braver, less passive, and stronger than boys did. Both sexes tended to idealize their parents as compared with men and women in general. For both sexes, the ideal man was strong, handsome, somewhat sensitive, very wise, and brave. The ideal woman was attractive, wise, and brave. Both boys and girls considered themselves below the ideal for their sex. The girls judged their mothers to be closer to the ideal and their fathers farther from the ideal than did the boys.

These differences in ratings for male and female traits were similar to those for the American and German samples. However, there was a greater tendency for the Chileans to idealize their parents and to fall short of what they considered the ideal for their sex, possibly a reflection of their slightly lower age compared with the other samples. (14 references)

SPECIALIZED SEX ROLES IN INSTITUTIONAL SETTINGS

Family and Social Networks

190

Andrieux, Cecile. The association of some sociocultural variables with characteristics of the role of mother. [Association de quelques variables socio-culturelles avec la représentation du rôle de la mére.] *Psychologie Francaise,* **6(2):126-136, 1961.**

Working mothers. France. Childrearing attitudes.

This article is based on research from a larger study dealing with sociological effects on perceptions of motherhood and the role of wife in France. Women's opinions about the importance of mothers exclusively rearing their own children were solicited in interviews with 216 professionally employed women and 184 women staying at home. All subjects represented professional and managerial backgrounds. Major independent variables were restriction of family size, access to higher education, professional status, and influence exerted by lay and religious ideologies. The first three variables appeared to be negatively related to the attitude that a mother must rear her own child exclusively. Ideological influence appeared to have an opposite effect. Data collected from the interviews also indicated some differences among nonworking mothers in attitudes toward exclusive childrearing. For example, Catholic women indicated that they felt a particularly strong pressure to raise their own children. (2 references)

191

Arnott, Catherine C. Husbands' attitude and wives' commitment to employment. *Journal of Marriage and the Family,* **34(4):673-684, 1972.**

Working wives. Marital roles. Female role. Work commitment.

Two hypotheses were tested: That a married woman seeks congruency among her role preference, her actual role, and her perception of her husband's preference for her role; and that a married woman's attitude toward female autonomy affects her expectations of which partner should adjust when there is conflict over the wife's role. Questionnaires on personal data and a 10-item inventory on attitudes toward women's autonomy were administered to 235 members of southern California suburban women's groups and to three-fourths of their husbands. The women also answered items on their comparative involvement in home activities and employment and on whether this involvement was congruent with their role preferences and husbands' preferences for the wife's role. Husbands' statements were used mainly to ascertain the reality orientation of the wives' perception of their preferences.

When wives approved of their present roles and perceived that their husbands also approved, they tended to plan to continue in these roles. Similarly, when husbands and wives shared a preference for a different role for the wife, the wife planned an eventual role change. When husbands and wives differed on their preference for the wife's role, women with higher female autonomy scores were slightly more likely to select their preferred role over their husband's than were women with lower scores, especially when preference differences were minimal. It is suggested that even women high in female autonomy attitude scores prefer not to risk major differences with their husbands on their roles. When wives were in roles incongruent with their own preferences, significantly more husband-wife tension was reported than in situations where the husbands' preferences were overruled. Regarding conflict resolution, the more autonomous women expected their husbands to make adjustments, whereas less autonomous women tended to make the adjustments themselves. (23 references)

192
Axelson, Leland J. The working wife: Differences in perception among Negro and white males. *Journal of Marriage and the Family,* 32(3):457-464, 1970.

Working wives. Racial differences. Marital roles. Sex-role perceptions.

This study investigated the hypotheses that Negro and white males differ significantly in their perceptions of the working wife's relationship to her husband, and that the Negro male has greater uncertainty in his evaluation of the working wife. Subjects were 565 white and 67 Negro male adults residing in a Florida community of mainly skilled and semiskilled blue-collar, immigrant workers. Individual structured interviews were conducted to ascertain circumstances under which a wife should work, her financial earnings, control of family income, and relationships with husband and children.

A detailed discussion of Negro-white differences indicates that the Negro male is somewhat more accepting of working wives and mothers, but that he does show inconsistencies in his evaluations of their role. Test variables of socioeconomic status and age did not materially change patterns of differences between the races. It is speculated that the Negro male's apparent indecisiveness in evaluating the working wife results from intrusion of the dominant white culture into his own role experiences in the Negro subculture. (22 references)

193
Babchuk, Nicholas; Marsey, Ruth; and Gordon, C. Wayne. Men and women in community agencies: A note on power and prestige. *American Sociological Review,* 25:399-403, 1960.

Civic participation. Sex differences. Community agencies.

This study tested the hypotheses that, the more vital the function of an agency to the welfare of a community, the higher is the rank of the agency board and the status of its members; and the more highly ranked and instrumental an agency and the larger its budget, the more likely is its board to be male dominated. Seven civic leaders from a large northeastern city ranked 73 agencies according to how vital they were to the city. These agencies were classified as instrumental, expressive, or instrumental-expressive. Instrumental agencies provide services or products (for example, a hospital); expressive agencies provide their participants with immediately gratifying service (as in a settlement house); and instrumental-expressive agencies perform both functions. Agency records supplied data on sex of board members and on budget size. Status of individual board members was based on club memberships, social register listings, and occupation or, for female members, husband's occupation.

Of the 38 instrumental agencies, 33 were directed by boards having a majority of male members, six of which were entirely male. The five instrumental agencies with majorities of women board members provided services for children and young people. Of the 16 instrumental-expressive agencies, 14 had boards with substantial male majorities. More women were found on the boards of expressive agencies (39 percent of the membership), although the boards were still predominantly male. Of the most vital agencies, 89 percent of the board members were men. Only 61 percent of the board members of the least vital agencies were male. All eight agencies ranked most vital were instrumental. Two random samples of 25 board members each were selected from the total board membership of the eight agencies ranked as most vital and the eight ranked as least vital. Eighteen of the 25 board members from the most vital agencies, as opposed to three from the least vital agencies, were company or bank officers. Persons with high occupational status and those of social prominence were most likely to be members of highly ranked boards. Of the 25 board members of the most vital agencies, one was a woman. In contrast, 13 of the 25 board members of the least vital agencies were women. (8 references)

194
Babchuk, Nicholas, and Bates, Alan P. The primary relations of middle-class couples: A study in male dominance. *American Sociological Review,* 28(3):377-384, 1963.

Marital dominance. Friendships.

A study of the close friendships of middle-class couples explored the hypothesis that, of the primary friendships shared by the couple, those initiated by the husband would be more numerous than wife-initiated friendships, would be characterized by more frequent visiting and by a stronger positive affect, and would involve a wider range of activities in which both he and his wife participated. The sample consisted of 39 college educated couples, 20 to 40 years old, living in Nebraska. Each spouse was interviewed separately, with no opportunity for joint discussion. The pretested, structured interview schedule asked each respondent to list the initials of persons regarded as very close mutual friends by both spouses, excluding relatives, with no limit on the number to be listed.

Results showed less consensus between spouses in their independent identification of mutual friends than was expected. There was consistent support for the hypothesis that husbands initiated more mutual friendships for the couples than wives. Very close friends of the husband in the period prior to marriage were more likely to become close mutual friends after marriage than were the wife's prior close friends. The male was also more likely to initiate mutual lasting friendships following marriage. However, frequency of contact between friends was approximately the same regardless of origin of the friendship.

Three measures were used to represent the degree of positive affect in friendships: Sharing of intimate confidences, readiness to borrow money, and designation as one of three closest friends by either spouse. Both husbands and wives felt freer to borrow money from friends initially known through the husband, and responses indicated greater willingness to borrow money than to confide in close friends. Wives showed a tendency to identify the husband's male friends as among their own three closest friends, and neither spouse was as likely to identify with women as with men. The range of activities, whether between couples or between husband and wife and a single friend, was similar for all friendships. The overall conclusion drawn is that middle-class couples give the appearance of being equalitarian, but in the sphere of friendships, the male predominates. (9 references)

195

Bailyn, Lotte. Career and family orientations of husbands and wives in relation to marital happiness. *Human Relations,* 23(2):97-113, 1970. Also in: Theodore, Athena, ed. *The Professional Woman.* Cambridge, Mass.: Schenkman, 1971. pp. 545-567.

Marital satisfaction. Career attitudes. Great Britain.

This study explored the orientations of husbands and their wives to combinations of family and career patterns. Each combination pattern was evaluated by the degree of marital happiness associated with it. It was hypothesized that the married women's resolution of the career-family dilemma would depend on the way her husband fits his work and family into his life. Women graduates (N=223) from British universities in 1960 and their husbands completed mailed questionnaires on personal background, first and second greatest sources of satisfaction in life, general attitude toward married women having careers, and degree of marital happiness.

Of the 210 husbands who mentioned career or family as major sources of satisfaction, 140 were termed family oriented and 70 career oriented. The women in the sample were classified into three categories: Integrated—favoring careers for women and listing career as a source of satisfaction; traditional—not favoring careers for married women and not deriving satisfaction from work outside the family; and mixed—favoring careers for women but not themselves deriving satisfaction from work. The ratio of traditional to career-integrated women was 2 to 1.

Very few combinations of career-oriented husbands with a career-integrated wife termed their marriage "very happy." The other possible combinations of husband-wife orientation were very similar in degree of marital happiness, with one-half to two-thirds seeing their marriages as "happy." Two patterns—traditional wives married to career-oriented husbands (conventional) and career-integrated wives married to family-oriented husbands (coordinated)—were examined in terms of the effect of the following variables on marital satisfaction: Number of children, spouses' occupational situations, husband's income, work status of spouses' mothers, attitudes of couple's social circle, and division of household labor.

Marital happiness in the conventional pattern was associated with number of children, husband's job satisfaction, overlap of spouses' fields of work, income and ambition of husband, the husband's mother having worked during his childhood, and attitudes of social circle. In the coordinated pattern, marital happiness was associated with wife's having household help, husband's income and ambition, and mother's work history. It is concluded that the husband's career-family orientation is a vital determinant to marital happiness when a married woman has a career. (19 references)

196
Bell, Robert R. The related importance of mother and wife roles among black lower-class women. In: Staples, Robert, ed. *The Black Family: Essays and Studies.* Belmont, Calif.: Wadsworth, 1971, pp. 248-255.

Maternal behavior. Marital satisfaction. Racial differences. Socio-economic differences.

This examination of patterns related to black lower-class family life includes a review of research findings and a report on two interview studies of marital and parental attitudes. Subjects of the first study were 75 lower-class (low-status) and 122 upper lower-class (middle-status) black mothers. The subjects lived in Philadelphia and had at least two children, one of whom was in nursery school or kindergarten. The second study sample consisted of 100 black and 100 white female college graduates.

Sixty percent of the low-status sample and 40 percent of the middle-status sample responded "nothing" when asked what they liked best about marriage. Interaction between husband and wife—of great importance to middle-class marriages—was mentioned by only one-third of the middle-status and one-fourth of the low-status black women. In rating their marriages, 43 percent of the low-status black women, 50 percent of the middle-status black women, 51 percent of the black college graduates, and 80 percent of the white college graduates replied, "very good" or "good." However, if they had to choose between being a wife or mother, 74 percent of the white college women, 50 percent of the black college women, 24 percent of the middle-status women, and 16 percent of the low-status women would choose to be a wife. Seventy-two percent of the low-status and 78 percent of the middle-status black women responded to why they liked being mothers: "to love and help my children." Although their husband's role in child care was minimal, few of these lower class mothers said he should do more.

It was concluded from the literature review and from these studies that, for the lower-class black male, both marriage and parental roles are frequently of minimal importance. The lower-class black female, however, views the parental role as highly significant. For her, marriage is associated with the possibility that a husband may drain off the limited economic and personal resources needed for the care of her children. (18 references)

197

Benson, Leonard. *Fatherhood: A Sociological Perspective,* New York: Random House, 1968. 371 pp.

Paternal behavior. Parental models. Family structure.

This book surveys research and theory from sociology, anthropology, and social psychology on the role of the father in family and community life. The purpose of this wide-ranging survey is to provide a framework for the consolidation of various data relevant to fatherhood, the family, and the interaction of paternal and familial factors in society. Specific core topics are fatherhood in the perspective of social organization, the man as parent, the bread-winner, and fatherhood and the emerging family. Within this framework, the discussion includes the relationship between marriage and parenthood, trends in paternal authority, the problems of identification with fathers, father-child conflict and the effects of fatherlessness, the changing implications of the breadwinner ethic, and the future of the father role in the modern family. (700 references)

198

Blood, Robert O., Jr., and Wolfe, Donald M. Negro-white differences in blue-collar marriages in a northern metropolis. *Social Forces,* 48:59-64, 1969.

Marital dominance. Household tasks. Marital satisfaction. Racial differences. Working-class families.

Differences in marriage patterns for Negro and for white blue-collar families were studied, controlling for husband's employment in a high or low blue-collar job. Subjects were 354 white and 110 Negro wives in intact blue-collar families. The high blue-collar work category included foremen and skilled workers; the low blue-collar category included unskilled laborers and service personnel. The wives were interviewed about family power structure, division of labor, companionship, and marital satisfaction.

At both high and low blue-collar levels, more Negro families than white were wife-dominant in family decisionmaking. In general, there was little equalitarianism in low blue-collar family decisionmaking; decisions not made unilaterally by the wife were made unilaterally by the husband. The division of labor in Negro homes involved less sharing and flexibility than in white homes, despite a slightly higher proportion of Negro working wives. Negro wives emphasized their own contributions to family welfare rather than the husband's mobility prospects. Negro low blue-collar wives said that they seldom told their troubles to their husbands after a hard day, whereas white low blue-collar wives said that they always did. Negro high and low blue-collar husbands and wives also discussed the husband's day at work less often than white blue-collar couples. White blue-collar wives were on the average highly satisfied with their marriages; Negro blue-collar wives were only moderately satisfied. It was suggested that this relative dissatisfaction resulted from the nonsupportive role played by Negro blue-collar husbands in making family decisions, sharing household duties, and providing companionship for their wives. (8 references)

199
Booth, Alan. Sex and social participation. *American Sociological Review,* 37(2):183-192, 1972.

Friendships. Social interaction. Kinship relations.

Male and female social participation were compared by type, extent, and quality in friendship dyads, voluntary associations, and kin relations. Semistructured interview data were collected from 800 men and women in Lincoln and Omaha, Nebr. Subjects were 45 years or older and were from a variety of occupational and ethnic backgrounds. Variables of class, labor force membership, marital status, age, health, and residential and occupational mobility were examined.

A detailed discussion of findings shows that sex-related behavior modes accounted for only a few sex differences in social participation patterns. No support was found for claims of stronger and more stable male bonds, and women showed greater affiliative stability over time. These sex differences are expected to diminish as cultural sex-role distinctions decline.

Males and females in almost all categories reported equal numbers of close friends; only healthy, white-collar married men and unmarried women had more close friends than either men or women in the other categories. Female friendships manifested more spontaneity and sharing of confidences. Voluntary association participation was similar to friendship participation patterns: Males belonged to more organizations, but only when early and adult socialization had favored such participation. Men tended to belong to more "instrumental" groups, and women to "expressive" groups. Women devoted more time to voluntary organizations and took more leadership roles in expressive groups. Females and males were equally affiliated with sexually exclusive organizations. Among people with diminished kinship contacts, women reported more close kinship ties than men. Whereas males with many kinship resources tended to have more extensive interpersonal associations in general, females with many kin developed fewer but more affective friendship ties. There was no support for the thesis that male bonds are stronger than women's. Moreover, extensive friendship ties for males were linked to early socialization rather than to any biological tendency to aggress. (35 references)

200

Britton, Joseph H., and Britton, Jean O. Children's perceptions of their parents: A comparison of Finnish and American children. *Journal of Marriage and the Family,* 33(1):214-218, 1971.

Parent-child relations. National differences. Elementary school students.

In this study, cross-cultural and cross-sexual comparisons were made of Finnish and American boys' and girls' perceptions of their parents and of perceptions of the parent of the opposite sex by younger and older children.

The subjects were 394 American children (201 boys, 193 girls) and 421 Finnish children (202 boys, 219 girls), 9 to 11 years old, drawn from elementary school populations in two cities in central Pennsylvania and central Finland. Subjects completed five-item questionnaires on how they view their parents in terms of punitiveness and/or support.

The findings indicate considerable similarity and few differences between the national groups, between boys and girls, and between age levels, in the ways parents are viewed. The subjects tended to view the mother rather than the father as a source of understanding and comfort and tended to view the father rather than the mother as dominating, punitive, and fear-provoking. The proposition that older children tend to view the parent of the same sex less positively than younger children was not supported. (7 references)

201
Burr, Wesley R. An expansion and test of a role theory of marital satisfaction. *Journal of Marriage and the Family,* 33(2):368-372, 1971.

Marital satisfaction. Role conflict.

The proposition that discrepancies between role expectations and role behavior influence marital satisfaction is expanded by further proposing that this relationship is mediated by the subjectively perceived importance of these discrepancies.

The data in this study were gathered as part of a larger project by interviewing 116 middle-class married couples in a large midwestern city. An area-probability sample of intact couples in a group of census tracts was selected to eliminate lower socioeconomic strata. All stages of the family life cycle were represented. The mean age was 47.5 years for men and 45.6 years for women. The mean years of education were 13.5 for men and 12.7 for women. The sample had experienced marriage stability; only six were remarriages. The data regarding role discrepancy were obtained from role expectation and role-behavior questionnaires. The importance of role discrepancies was derived from the role-expectation questionnaire. A questionnaire was also used to measure marital satisfaction. Husbands and wives responded to the questionnaires separately.

The findings supported earlier findings that role discrepancies show a high negative correlation with marital satisfaction. Two tests were used to determine whether the importance attached to these discrepancies affects the variance in marital satisfaction. The correlational test indicated that the use of the importance variable does not account for additional variance in marital satisfaction. However, use of the importance variable helps to identify the role discrepancies that account for major differences in marital satisfaction. Some secondary data also indicate that degree of importance may influence the effect of role discrepancies on satisfaction in a curvilinear manner, and that this curve may differ for men and women. (18 references)

202
Clarkson, Frank E.; Vogel, Susan R.; Broverman, Inge K.; Broverman, Donald M.; and Rosenkrantz, Paul S. Family size and sex-role stereotypes. *Science,* 167(1):390-392, 1970.

Family size. Self-concept. Stereotypes.

Factors affecting family size were investigated, with emphasis on the relationship between completed family size and self-concepts of women with respect to alternative sex roles. Ninety-six Catholic mothers of male college students completed a bipolar, 122-item, sex-role stereotype questionnaire three ways: Describing adult men, adult women, and self. Male and female poles of each item were defined by majority opinion of the mothers. Items with very high consensus were termed "stereotypic." The positive poles of 45 male-valued stereotypic items comprised a competency cluster. The positive poles of 12 femaie-valued stereotypic items comprised a warmth-and-expressiveness cluster. Two self-concept scores were computed for each mother, based on self-responses to the competency and to the warmth-and-expressiveness clusters. Background information on family size, education, and work experience was also gathered.

The responses of 60 mothers between the ages of 45 and 59 who were living with their husbands and who had two or more children were selected for the analysis. Subjects were divided into two groups based on a median split of the self-concept scores from the competency cluster. Statistical analysis showed that mothers with high competency self-concept scores had significantly fewer children than did mothers with low competency self-concept scores. There was a nonsignificant, negative relationship between the number of years worked and the number of children. Number of years worked tended to be more related to family size for women with low competency self-concepts than for women with above-median self-concepts. Similar analyses performed with self-concept scores on warmth-expressiveness did not yield significant results.

Thus, women whose self-concepts included more socially desirable traits stereotypically associated with the male role had fewer children than women who perceived themselves as more stereotypically feminine on these traits. The incorporation of male-valued stereotypic traits into the female self-concept involved a rejection of the negatively valued, but not the positively valued, aspects of the feminine stereotype. A longitudinal study would be required to determine the developmental sequence of these findings. (10 references)

203
Emmerich, Walter, and Smoller, Faye. The role patterning of parental norms. *Sociometry,* 27:382-390, 1964.

Social interaction. Preschool children. Parental expectations.

This study investigated how middle-class parental norms for a child's interpersonal behavior vary according to the parent's sex, child's sex, and status attributes of certain individuals with whom the child interacts. Subjects were 40 couples with children enrolled in a nursery school; half were parents of girls and half parents of boys. The administered questionnaire included five positive and five negative interpersonal norms and six individuals (mother, father, sister, brother, teacher, friend) with whom the child was likely to interact. Positive attributes were assertiveness, friendliness, independence, obedience, and trustingness; negative attributes were aggression, avoidance, dependency, overfriendliness, and submissiveness. Each parent indicated how important it was for the child to exhibit each attribute in interaction with each of the six individuals.

For both the positive and negative norm sets, results revealed no connection between parent's expectations of behavior and sex of parent, of child, or of the specified individuals. Generalized patterns of child roles were evident, with trust and friendliness most favored and aggression and avoidance most disapproved of in young children. There was a stronger pattern of emphasis on a child's positive behavior obligation toward adults than toward other children. However, negative behavior was discouraged about equally in all the child's interactions. In general, parents encourage young children to trust and obey adults and to be assertive and independent toward other children. Expectations of behavior toward parents and teachers are compared, as are expectations of behavior toward siblings and friends. Results indicate that greater autonomy is expected of the child in nonfamilial than in familial interactions. (14 references)

204
Garland, T. Neal. The better half? The male in the dual profession family. In: Constantina, Safilios-Rothchild, ed. *Toward a Sociology of Women.* Lexington, Mass.: Xerox College Publishing, 1972. pp. 199-215.

Dual-career families. Professional women. Working wives. Marital roles.

Data were collected to test the validity of the idea, prevalent in popular and some research literature, that a wife employed in a high-status, high-paid professional position threatens her husband's self-image and status as breadwinner and head of household.

A total of 53 couples comprised the sample of dual-profession families. The couples were selected on the basis of the wife's profession—lawyer, physician, or college professor—and no attempt was made to control for the husband's occupation. The couples represented all stages of the career cycle, from near completion of professional training to 30 or more years of professional practice. A typology of family structure emerged from an evaluation of interview responses of wives and husbands. Of the 53 couples interviewed, 20 were classified as traditional, 27 as neotraditional, five as matriarchal, and one as egalitarian.

Three aspects were examined to determine the existence and extent of any sense of threat among the husbands: Whether the couple discussed the wife's career before marriage, husband's feelings about marrying a professional woman, and husband's present feelings about wife's career.

The findings are that the majority of the husbands defined their wives' careers in positive terms. The 20 traditional husbands valued their wives' professional interests; the 27 neotraditional husbands viewed their wive's professions as having significance in family decisionmaking. The one factor that appeared to have a negative effect on the quality of the marital life was income, when the wife earned more than the husband. (30 references)

205
Gavron, Hannah. *The Captive Wife: Conflicts of Housebound Mothers.* London: Routledge & Kegan Paul, 1966. 176 pp.

Family structure. Marital roles. Socioeconomic differences. Working mothers. Great Britain.

This study of young British women with preschool children investigates patterns of family life in the working class and the middle class. A general review of the literature on the social and historical background of current British family structures and role patterns is included. Data for the study were provided by interviews with 48 working-class and 48 middle-class wives born in or after 1930. Interview data involved factual information and opinions on subject's and husband's backgrounds, marriage, children, the running of the home, social contacts, leisure, and subject's work status.

None of the working-class mothers engaged in the kind of street life or extended family contacts traditionally associated with working-class urban living. They, more than the middle-class mothers, reported concern about play areas for their children and neighborhood social contacts for themselves. Thirty-five percent of the working-class subjects and 21 percent of the middle-class subjects felt they had married too young. Over half of the wives of both classes felt their relationship with their husband was more egalitarian than that between their parents. For the middle class, equality meant independence; and for the working-class, it meant closeness. Sixty-two percent of the working-class husbands shared the care of the children, compared with 44 percent of the middle-class husbands. All middle-class mothers were in favor of education for their children. Of the working-class, 37 percent did not consider education important, and 19 percent said it was important for boys but less so for girls. Forty percent of the middle-class sample said that mothers should be with their young children all the time.

In the running of the household, middle-class subjects were more likely to have joint authority in making financial decisions, but less likely to have their husbands help with the housework than the working-class subjects. Considerably more middle-class (67 percent) than working-class (27 percent) wives went out once a week with their husbands. Thirty-seven percent of the middle-class mothers and 29 percent of the working-class mothers were currently working. Ninety percent of the middle-class wives had some clearly defined occupation by the time they became mothers, and 77 percent intended to return to work when the children were older; 87 percent of the working-class mothers intended to return to work, chiefly to unskilled jobs. A concluding essay suggests methods of reintegrating mothers of young children into society. (124 references)

206

González, Nancie L. Toward a definition of matrifocality. In: Whitten, Norman E., Jr., and Szwed, John F. *Afro-American Anthropology.* New York: The Free Press, 1970. pp. 231-244.

Social structure. Family structure. Matrifocality.

The concept of matrifocality is discussed in structural and functional terms to define its features and forms more explicitly than has been done in the literature. Anthropologists and sociologists use this term to refer to female role dominance in such social structures as families, households, neighborhoods, communities, and voluntary associations.

The degree to which women make decisions without calling upon a male authority figure varies among societies and sectors of a society. It is possible to have matrifocal family organization without having matrifocal societal organization. In fact, no known society formally delegates the woman as primary representative at the highest levels of jural affairs. Matrifocality seems to be directly related to the increasing complexity of society and is an organizing principle in the domestic and supradomestic domains, rather than in the jural domain. The development of industrialization involves increasing separation of the domestic and jural domains and the emergence of the supradomestic domain (i.e., schools, public health, etc.). Males in complex modern societies can less easily predominate in all areas at once, and matrifocality serves to maintain individual household units and to create supradomestic structures which enhance community solidarity.

The validity and utility of several kinds of social factors thought to induce or coincide with matrifocality cross-culturally are examined. These structures, institutions, and circumstances include African origin and/or slavery, unstable marriages, consanguineal households, bilateral kinship systems, shortage or absence of males, and lower-class status in an industrial society. (35 references)

207
Gover, David A. Socio-economic differential in the relationship between marital adjustment and wife's employment status. *Marriage and Family Living,* 25(4):452-458, 1963.

Marital satisfaction. Working wives. Socioeconomic differences.

This study retested the hypothesis that working-class employed wives experience less marital satisfaction than middle-class employed wives because of the less desirable nature of their occupations. A random sample of 361 Greensboro, N.C., wives completed the General Evaluation of Marriage Scale and a questionnaire on personal background, employment, and sex-role attitudes. Subjects were grouped according to husband's occupation (middle or working class), degree of marital adjustment (high, medium, or low), and work status. Findings are discussed in relation to earlier studies by other investigators. Comments on this study by those investigators are included.

Both the middle-class and working-class nonemployed wives had a higher average marital adjustment score than employed wives, with a greater difference appearing in the working class than in the middle class. However, no significant differences were found for either class between employed wives' marital adjustment and having a low-prestige job, working over 30 hours a week, earning less than $50 a week, or not having help with the housework. Thus, the hypothesis on marital dissatisfaction and unfavorable conditions associated with work situations was not supported. Thirty-one percent of the subjects expressed complete agreement with the statement, "the woman's place is in the home," and 62 percent expressed some degree of agreement. Consequently, an alternative interpretation is proposed: Nonemployed wives' higher average marital adjustment scores may reflect aspects of conforming behavior; the more conservative the community from which the sample is drawn, the more a married woman's employment is regarded as nonconformist. Therefore, it is recommended that research use samples from less conservative communities. (22 references)

208
Hall, Douglas T. A model of coping with role conflict: The role behavior of college educated women. *Administrative Science Quarterly,* 17(4):471-486, 1972.

Role conflict. Coping behavior.

The types of conflict faced by married women as the result of multiple-role performance, strategies used for coping with these conflicts, and the varying degrees of satisfaction gained from different strategies were investigated empirically. A model of role-conflict coping behavior based on a three-component concept of role is presented. The three types of coping behavior identified are: Alteration of externally imposed expectations of others, or structural role redefinition (type I); changing one's own concept of role demands, or personal role redefinition (type II); and reactive role behavior with no attempt to restructure role demands (type III).

The pilot sample consisted of over 100 college-educated women in New Haven, Conn., who attended talks on women's roles. The main sample consisted of the 170 respondents to a mailed questionnaire who reported role conflict. The questionnaire queried roles performed in current life, conflicts experienced between roles, strategies used for dealing with these conflicts, and satisfaction with one's overall way of dealing with life roles. Sixteen strategies for coping with role conflicts were identified from pilot group responses and categorized by the three major types of coping behavior. The relationship between coping style and satisfaction was explored with data from both samples.

Type I strategies were positively related to satisfaction in dealing with life roles. Type II strategies were not significantly related to satisfaction, though a weak positive relationship was found in some analyses. Type III strategies showed a strong negative relationship to satisfaction. When combinations of various strategies were examined, use of type I with no type III was significantly related to high satisfaction. Separate analyses of various occupational groups within the sample yielded similar, though slightly weaker, results. Analysis of the effect of the number of type I or II strategies used revealed that the critical difference for satisfaction is between having at least one coping strategy and having none. Reinterpretation of type III behaviors as methods of defense rather than coping mechanisms reinforced this conclusion. Functional interrelationships among different coping strategies, the effect of early socialization on methods of coping with role conflict, and degree of psychological success or failure as an intervening variable are discussed. (27 references)

209
Hass, Paula H. Maternal role incompatibility and fertility in urban Latin America. *Journal of Social Issues,* 28(2):111-127, 1972.

Working wives. Role conflict. Family size. Latin America.

Based on fertility surveys conducted in seven Latin American cities, this study examines the proposition that the crucial variable determining the relationship between maternal employment and fertility rates may be the extent of incompatibility in performing simultaneously the roles of mother and worker. Specifically, it was hypothesized that wives employed outside the home, employed full time, or employed in white-collar occupations have lower fertility rates than those unemployed, employed part-time, or in other than white-collar occupations.

The sample consisted on native-born women, 20 to 50 years of age, married and living with native-born spouses for at least 5 years, and classified as probably fecund. Questions were also asked about education and attitudes toward women's role.

There was no consistent relationship between role incompatibility and fertility; in most cities, employment outside the home and white-collar employment were negatively related to fertility rates, whereas the number of hours employed outside the home was usually unrelated. Many of the relationships can be attributed to more education and greater approval of nondomestic activities among employed wives. The wife's motivation for employment, her education, and her preferred role seem to exert greater influence on fertility than her actual role of employee or homemaker. Employment histories, general domestic and nondomestic activities, and reproductive histories are important variables influencing fertility rates. However, individual cities with their unique environmental conditions are also important variables. (16 references)

210
Heiss, Jerold, ed. *Family Roles and Interaction: An Anthology.* Chicago: Rand McNally, 1968. 569 pp.

Social interaction. Family structure. Role theories.

This book is a collection of sociological papers relating role theory to family interaction. Although Meadian conceptualizations emphasizing social-psychological processes and Lintonian theories stressing content and structure are both noted as relevant to the study of the family, most of the articles included are empirical tests or theoretical discussions based on the Meadian conceptual scheme. Of primary concern is the importance of social interaction in human development, particularly in the areas of language, self-concept, role-taking ability, and other social skills. An introductory essay discusses these elements of role theory in relation to the process of social interaction. The studies and discussions in the book are grouped according to the family life-cycle and concern premarital interaction, family interaction, marital roles, sex-role conflicts, fertility, children's personality development, postparental roles, and family dissolution. Introductions and postscripts to the selections clarify their relation to role theory and attempt to resolve conflicts between their findings and other research in the field. A concluding essay suggests implications for future research testing Meadian role theory. (0-25 references per article)

211
Hoffman, Lois Wladis. Parental power relations and the division of household tasks. *Marriage and Family Living,* 22:27-35, 1960. Also in: Nye, F. Ivan, and Hoffman, Lois W., eds. *The Employed Mother in America.* Chicago: Rand McNally, 1963. pp. 215-230.

Working mothers. Marital dominance. Household tasks.

The effects of the mother's employment on task participation, routine decisionmaking, and power structure in the family were investigated. The total sample included 324 intact Detroit families with at least one child in the third through sixth grade. As the primary test group, a subsample of 89 working and 89 nonworking women was matched on husband's occupation, number of subteen children, age of oldest child, and agreement of ideologies about sex roles and male dominance. Measures of each parent's task participation and routine decisionmaking were obtained from the children's responses to interview questions. Family power was determined by the extent to which the child's responses on task participation and household decisionmaking favored one parent over the other. The mothers completed mailed questionnaires on employment and ideology.

As expected, even when ideology was held constant, working mothers participated less than nonworking mothers in household tasks, and their husbands participated more. Working mothers made fewer decisions about routine household matters than nonworking mothers, and their husbands made more. There was no difference in husband-wife power in either of the matched samples, although in the total sample working women had more power than nonworking women. The analysis suggested that controls on husband's occupation and on age and number of children resulted in the lack of relationships in the matched subgroups. Further analysis of both the total sample and the subsample showed a positive relationship between employment and power for women who endorsed the male dominance ideology and for those who consistently rejected it. However, a negative relationship between employment and power within the family was found for women who showed a reserved rejection of the ideology. It was concluded that women's employment does not affect family power structure directly, except in interaction with the preexisting ideologies and personalities of the women and their husbands. (5 references)

212
Holm, Lennart. Sex roles in community planning. [Könsroller i glas och betong.] In: *Könsroller.* Falköping, Sweden: Prisma, 1965. pp. 185-191.

City planning. Sexual discrimination. Sweden.

This discussion is concerned with the lag between the theory of a new society and the creation of a new society by city planners. Just as socially desegregated city plans were not realized until the traditional class society had been politically destroyed, it is suggested that city and community developments will continue to reflect conventional patterns for the roles of men and women for some time.

The author, who participated in a jury that examined an architect's plans for a large new community development in Sweden, uses these plans to describe the influences of traditional, unconscious sex discrimination in community planning. The architect's plans for single-family housing indicate an expected traditional distribution of responsibilities within the family: The wife at home in a well-designed, congenial worksite; the husband away at his equally well-designed, congenial worksite. The planned balance between private and community property also reflects traditional family roles, in that the absence of child care centers, playgrounds, community centers, etc., assumes that every household is self-sufficient and does not require such communal services.

An alternative to traditional housing and communities is the incorporation of the "servicehouse" in community planning. Servicehouses include a common dining room, child care center, laundry room, and various activity rooms, and could provide services for families in which both parents work. However, there are very few such houses and they generally are linked to specific populations, such as students, nurses, and old people. Reasons why the servicehouses have not become more prevalent in the new society are discussed. It is concluded that improved mass communications are needed to combat isolation of women and children in suburban areas. (No references)

213
Hutner, Frances Cornwall. Mother's education and working: Effect on the school child. *Journal of Psychology,* 82:27-37, 1972.

Parental influence. Working mothers. Academic ability. Academic achievement.

Data from an official study of pupils and parents in the Princeton, N.J., school systems were analyzed in this study of the influences of maternal education and employment on children's academic ability and performance. School records supplied IQ, achievement, and aptitude scores at selected grade levels for 3,583 elementary and high school children. Parent questionnaires supplied information on maternal educational attainment and labor force participation. Information on teachers' expectations and parents' expectations and aspirations for the children were also collected. Mean scores for all tests were compared for students grouped by seven maternal education levels (from eighth grade or less to graduate training) and by three maternal employment categories (full time, part time, and not working).

A significant relationship was found between maternal educational attainment and the child's IQ, aptitude, and achievement. Educational level of the mother was also significantly related to parental and teacher expectations and aspirations for the child. Working was typically associated with significantly lowered parental and teacher expectations and aspirations. Maternal labor force participation was not, however, significantly related to child's ability and performance in four-fifths of the comparisons made. The few instances of significant negative relationships between maternal employment and children's scores affected achievement rather than aptitude and were found among children whose mothers had completed only high school, and among children in elementary school. (16 references)

214
Hyman, Herbert H., and Reed, John Shelton. "Black matriarchy" reconsidered: Evidence from secondary analysis of sample surveys. *Public Opinion Quarterly,* 33:347-354, 1969.

Parental dominance. Racial differences. Matriarchy.

A secondary analysis of three surveys examined the concept of a culturally linked Negro-white difference in family organization. After a brief review of the statistical evidence for the theory that more Negro than white families are mother headed, the major question considered was whether the mother was dominant even in intact Negro families.

A 1951 Gallup Poll asked 1,400 adults, 80 of them Negro, which parent had been most influential during their childhood. In 1961 the National Opinion Research Center interviewed approximately 900 white and 100 Negro adults. All subjects were asked who had made certain decisions in their families of origin. Married subjects were asked whether they or their spouses made certain decisions. To test parental influence on political preferences, questionnaire data from a 1965 national survey were analyzed for 2,350 white and 150 Negro high school seniors from intact families with parents of different party loyalties.

Results gave little evidence of any social-psychological pattern of matriarchy in America that is peculiar to the Negro family. In all aspects of these studies, racial differences were small and inconsistent. In both races, women's influence exceeded that of men in a number of instances, including politics where male dominance has long been assumed. (25 references)

215
Jackson, Jacqueline J. But where are the men? *Black Scholar,* 3(4):30-41, 1971.

Family structure. Racial differences.

Statistical evidence is presented in support of the thesis that the smaller proportion of males in the black population prevents black females from conforming to traditional white American patterns of sex, marriage, and family living. The large proportion of black female-headed households, it is argued, results from this demographic insufficiency rather than from black females' matriarchal or emasculating personalities. Census data for this century provide sex ratios and other information disputing the contention that black females are more advantaged than black males in their educational, occupational, employment, and income levels.

Although black women exceed black men in median years of formal education, the difference is insignificant and gives women no advantage in the labor force. Since 1900, black males have outnumbered black females in the labor market, and unemployment rates generally have been higher for black females than for the males. Rather than directly competing with black males, black females have been largely restricted to such fields as domestic work or teaching, nursing, and social work. Black females of all educational levels earn less than comparably educated black males.

Females have outnumbered males in the black population since at least 1850 and in the white population only since 1950. Comparison of black and white male-female ratios in relation to illegitimacy rates and proportions of female-headed households shows that recent trends among whites are paralleling earlier trends among blacks. In 1900, for persons aged 15 or older, there were no significant differences in marital status by race or by sex between black and white males and females. However, as the black sex ratio decreased during the century, the proportion of female-headed households among blacks increased. Although present illegitimacy rates and proportions of female-headed households are still higher among blacks than among whites, as white sex ratios have decreased, whites have also experienced rises in illegitimacy and deviant family patterns since 1950. Further evidence of the effect of the sex ratio on marital patterns is that States such as Hawaii with more black males than females also have lower proportions of black female-headed households. Two suggestions are offered in light of this unequal geographic distribution: That black females be encouraged by educational and occupational opportunities to migrate to States having more black males, and that alternative familial forms such as polygyny be legally recognized. (21 references)

216
Kandel, Denise B. Race, maternal authority, and adolescent aspiration. *American Journal of Sociology,* 76(6):999-1020, 1971.

Parental dominance. Parental models. Racial differences. Matriarchy. High school students. Educational aspirations.

Two hypotheses were tested in this study: That the matriarchal character of black families is associated primarily with father absence, and that a matriarchal family structure has detrimental educational consequences for black males. The sample, taken from a larger study, included working-class urban high school students and their mothers. The school's 1,683-member student body was 20 percent black. Questionnaires were administered to students and mailed to mothers in comparable black and white, intact and mother-headed families. Data were derived on parental authority and support, parent-child communication, affection, and identification, as well as on the educational consequences of the two family patterns. School records and self-reports provided indicators of educational interests and performance.

Within the limitations imposed by the small number of certain subgroups in the sample (e.g., middle-class blacks), the results led to a tentative rejection of both hypotheses. Among blacks, maternal authoritarianism was more prevalent in intact than in broken homes. Black males were closer to their mothers, were more likely to turn to their mothers for advice, and were less likely to model after their fathers than were white males. The differences in parental relations by race were less between girls than boys, but white females showed greater involvement with and desire to be like their fathers than did black females. Maternal authority in the household and identification with a female role model did not appear to have negative consequences on educational aspirations and high school performance of black males. Black mothers and children at all socioeconomic levels had educational aspirations similar to or higher than those of whites. Thus, the lower educational attainment of blacks cannot be attributed to lower educational aspirations in the matriarchal family structure. (33 references)

217
Kohn, Melvin L., and Carroll, Eleanor E. Social class and the allocation of parental responsibilities. *Sociometry,* 23(4):372-392, 1960.

Childrearing practices. Socioeconomic differences.

This study examined the effects of middle-class and working-class parents' ideologies of childrearing on the division of parental responsibilities for the support and constraint (limiting behavior) of the children. Previous studies of class differences in attitudes regarding children's behavior had indicated that middle-class parents tend to emphasize support for children's feelings, and working-class parents tend to emphasize constraint of their actions. A representative sample included 200 middle-class and 200 working-class families with fifth-grade children in Washington, D.C. All mothers and every fourth father and child were interviewed. Parents were queried on how supportive and constraintive responsibilities should be allocated, and both parents and children were asked how such responsibilities were actually allocated.

The findings confirm the class differences in emphasis on supportive or constraintive parental childrearing ideologies. The findings also indicate sex differences within each class in the allocation of responsibilities. These sex differences not only apply to the parents—which parent has the responsibility for which behavior—but to the sex of the child as well—which parent has the responsibility for which behavior toward which child. Findings are briefly discussed in relation to traditional theories of personality and of supportive-constraintive family differentiation. (14 references)

218
Lamousé, Annette. Family roles of women: A German example. *Journal of Marriage and the Family,* 31(1):145-152, 1969.

Marital dominance. Household tasks. German Federal Republic.

This study investigated factors affecting two dimensions of family structure: division of labor and power allocation. Subjects were a random sample of 245 wives and 264 husbands (couples excluded) from Munster, West Germany. Interviews covered family income, husband's occupation. wife's work experience, and the husband's and wife's education. Subjects also indicated which spouse performed each of 14 household tasks (division of labor), which spouse made each of the 10 family decisions (power allocation), and their attitudes on husband-wife roles in division of labor and decisionmaking.

Division of labor followed generally traditional lines. In 42 percent of the families, the husband performed external and traditionally male tasks, such as bill paying and putting out the garbage, but rarely participated in other household tasks. In an additional 16 percent, this pattern of separate tasks was even more clearly defined. An increased degree of mixed role allocation was found in families where the wife worked. Working wives had more progressive attitudes toward task roles than housewives, but husbands in both groups were more progressive than the wives. Although all subjects tended to favor male dominance in the allocation of power, there was more equal participation in decisionmaking than in the division of labor. The wife's influence in decisionmaking varied with the social status of the husband and the external role experiences of the wife: Wives from lower social strata had more influence than others, although they were more conservative in their attitudes. In all social strata, the husband's authority decreased when the wife was working. However, working and formerly working wives who favored unrestricted male authority had less decisionmaking influence than full-time housewives with more progressive attitudes. (19 references)

219
Lansky, Leonard M. The family structure also affects the model: Sex-role identification in parents of preschool children. *Merrill-Palmer Quarterly,* 10(1):39-50, 1963.

Sex-role identification. Family structure. Parental models. Preschool children.

This study investigated the relationships among family structure, parental sex-role identification, and age of the preschool child. Subjects were middle-class and upper middle-class Boston parents of 58 male and 41 female preschool and kindergarten students. Questionnaires mailed to each parent provided scores on the Gough Femininity Scale (manifest sexual attitudes) and the Franck Drawing Completion Test (latent sexual identification), plus data on the age and sex of each family member. Families were categorized according to family structure—preschool girl or boy; number and sex of sibling(s) of the preschool child.

Analysis of the parents' Gough scores and their preschool child's age showed several significant correlations. For boys with at least one sister, the older the preschool boy, the more feminine were the father's attitudes and interests. In families with boys only, the older the preschool son, the more masculine the father or the more feminine the mother, or both. Similarly, in families with girls only, the older the preschool girl, the more feminine the mother or the more masculine the father, or both. There was no correlation found between the Gough tests of mothers and fathers for any of the groups. For girls with brothers, the older the preschool girl, the more feminine the father. In families with either boys or girls, the older the preschooler, the more feminine the mother. In families with children of both sexes, the older preschoolers, whether boys or girls, had fathers who were more feminine than fathers of younger preschoolers. From these partial findings, it was suggested that older and younger preschoolers who come from different family structures had different models. (26 references)

220
Lupri, Eugen. Contemporary authority patterns in the West German family: A study in cross-national validation. *Journal of Marriage and the Family,* 31(1):134-144, 1969.

Marital dominance. German Federal Republic. Urban-rural differences.

Contemporary West German urban and rural families were studied to test the cross-national validity of the family resource theory of conjugal power. In particular, three hypotheses derived from the theory that decisionmaking power stems from the resources that an individual brings to the marriage were tested. The effects of the husband's social status, the wife's employment status, and the comparative contributions of husband and wife on the family's balance of power were also examined. A farm husband's mean power score was computed from an interview survey of 812 farm wives, which covered six decisionmaking areas. An urban husband's mean power score was developed from several items on a lengthy interview schedule administered to 682 urban mothers as part of a larger study.

In general, theoretical expectations were borne out; in both farm and urban families, the West German husband's power is positively related to his social status. The working wife has much more power than the nonworking wife, but her gain in power decreases with increasing social status. When the husband's income, occupation, and social class are controlled, the wife's working status is still significantly associated with her power position. The husband's authority is significantly weakened by the wife's comparatively equal or greater economic contribution. It is concluded that the partner's comparative participation in the external system determines his or her power position in the internal system. The West German data are consistent with recent cross-national data indicating an inverse relationship between national economic development and extent of paternal authority. (25 references)

221
McIntire, Walter G.; Nass, Gilbert D.; and Dreyer, Albert S. A cross-cultural comparison of adolescent perception of parental roles. *Journal of Marriage and the Family,* 34(4):735-740, 1972.

Parent-child relations. Adolescents. Cultural differences.

Two instrumental-expressive role differentiation models of family structure were evaluated, using American, Ghanaian, and Israeli samples. The Parsons-Bales model states that both boys and girls perceive the father to be typically functioning in the instrumental role in relation to the family unit, with the mother in the expressive role. The Breznitz-Kugelmass model agrees, but adds that, in relation to themselves, boys continue to perceive the father as instrumental and the mother as expressive, whereas girls see the roles as becoming reversed. Subjects were high school students: 59 female and 181 male Ghanaians, and 149 female and 137 male Americans from a Connecticut suburb. Data from these samples were compared with data from a study of Israeli students. Comparisons were based on eight questionnaire items on perceptions of each parent's role in the family and relationship with the subject.

Ghanaian, U.S., and Israeli girls supported the Breznitz-Kugelmass model by perceiving their mothers as more instrumental toward them. However, Ghanaian and Israeli girls saw their mothers as more expressive than their fathers, thus supporting the Parsons-Bales model. U.S. girls perceived their fathers and mothers as equally expressive. Overall, the Breznitz-Kugelmass model provided a better prediction for parental instrumentality. Also, this model was a better predictor of parental expressiveness for U.S. girls. From overall findings, however, it was concluded that there are significant limitations in instrumental-expressive explanations of family interaction. (8 references)

222

Michaelson, Evalyn Jacobson, and Goldschmidt, Walter. Female roles and male dominance among peasants. *Southwestern Journal of Anthropology*, 27(1):330-352, 1971.

Patriarchy. Marital roles. Agricultural societies.

This analysis draws on a broad range of anthropological studies covering the past 40 years to explore the economic setting of peasant androcentrism and how this masculine bias affects relations between women and men in peasant households. Peasants are defined as agricultural producers who have rights to the land they cultivate, who produce primarily for their own subsistence needs but also for exchange, and who are part of a state-organized political system.

In 35 of the 46 peasant communities studied, sex roles and statuses are clearly demarcated, with social and economic dominance assigned to the male. Fathers tend to be dominant and mothers indulgent. Communities with strong male dominance tend to have social segregation of the sexes and sexual division of labor. In 26 cases land is inherited in the male line, and in 20 cases it is inherited bilaterally. In patricentric patrilineal families, marriage is usually by arrangement, with weak affective ties between spouses and a strong bond between mother and son which increases her power in later years and results in strained relations with daughters-in-law. Filiocentric patrilineal groups appear to have a similar pattern, except that the son's wife takes charge of the household and suppression of affection between spouses is less evident. Both groups stress the female's reproductive role. In bilateral families, the increased economic power of women tends to produce brother-sister rivalry and, where male authoritarian roles are expected, appears to create a machismo syndrome. Overall, the degree of internal consistency in the patterned social relationships of these community types suggests a close connection between social structure and the organization of interpersonal sentiment. (49 references)

223

Michel, Andrée. Roles and structure of the family. [Fonctions et structure de la famille.] *Cahiers Internationaux de Sociologie,* 29:113-135, 1960.

Marital dominance. Working class families. National differences.

This article compares the family in history with present working-class industrial families. Most radical of the changes seen in the family is the status of women and children. The modern industrial family is seen as less patriarchal than the family of the past. Overall, the working-class French woman has a higher status in relation to her husband than women in any other class. In a working-class family, the husband usually gives his salary to his wife, who is then in charge of shopping. She also makes most of the decisions concerning the children. This is in contrast to sociological studies in the United States showing greater patriarchy in working-class families than in the middle class. Closer examination of the U.S. data shows, however, that the opposite trend prevails in working-class families of second and third generation American citizenship. (34 references)

224

Michel, Andrée. Masculine and feminine family roles: An examination of classic theory. [Rôles masculins et féminins dans la famille: Examen de la théorie classique.] *Information sur les Sciences Sociales,* 10(1):113-135, 1971.

Marital dominance. Household tasks. Marital satisfaction. France.

The study examines decisionmaking and role differentiation within the family and their effects on marital satisfaction. Parisian married women (N=450) under 60 years of age were interviewed. These women constituted a probability sample drawn by the National Institute of Statistics and Economic Studies. The sample was stratified by socioeconomic status. The study tested four hypotheses proposed by Parsons, Bales, and Zelditch, based on classic theoretical concepts of the family—sexual differentiation, sex-determined decisionmaking, and managerial roles in the functioning of the family system. The four hypotheses stated that women achieve greater marital satisfaction and couples are more harmonious, communicate more successfully, and achieve family goals more readily if: (1) The husband exercises decisionmaking power; (2) the decisionmaking areas are clearly defined as the responsibility of the husband or the wife; (3) the wife's exclusive role is to perform household tasks; (4) the specific tasks are clearly defined as the responsibility of the husband or the wife.

None of the hypotheses was supported. Of all the factors involved, differentiation of decisionmaking roles to the husband's advantage was most damaging to family integration and functioning, followed by the specialization of domestic task performance and the differentiation of authority roles to the husband's advantage. It was concluded that maximum family integration, satisfaction, and communication are attained where there is a minimum of traditional differentiation and specialization of sex roles. (23 references)

225

Mulligan, Linda W. Wives, women, and wife role behavior: An alternative cross-cultural perspective. *International Journal of Comparative Sociology,* 13(1):36-47, 1972.

Family structure. Role theories. Marital roles.

This analysis is intended to establish some theoretical propositions regarding marital dyad interaction in professional upper class and upper middle-class life. An exploratory examination of historical and contemporary marital and nonmarital dyad interactional patterns in Western and non-Western cultures provides empirical documentation of commonalities and differences supporting these propositions. Sources include anthropological and sociological literature.

Central to the discussion is the concept of structurally extant polygyny, a situation in which two or more women perform wife-role tasks which involve physical care of the home, husband, and children; the sexual and procreative role; being a companion to the husband and socializer of the children; and serving as an affective-expressive and cultural leader inside and outside the family. It is suggested that the historical shift in American marriage patterns from institution to companionship has led to a rise in divorce. Once remarried, a man remains structurally/psychologically dependent on his former wife for the care of the children and on his present wife for companionship and the other wife-role functions. Another variant of structural polygyny involves the secretary. Owing to the complexities and technicalities of his occupation, a man can no longer depend on his wife for assistance in his work. Furthermore, as the professional man rises in the corporate structure, his wife assumes an entertainment-sociability-decorative role, delegating her other household functions to domestic employees. Each of these women (former wife, wife, secretary, domestic) is in effect a wife, in that she performs nurturant, supportive tasks. (52 references)

226

Nye, F. Ivan. Marital interaction. In: Nye, F. I., and Hoffman, L. W., eds. *The Employed Mother in America.* Chicago: Rand McNally, 1963. pp. 263-281.

Marital satisfaction. Working mothers.

The relationship between maternal employment and marital success was analyzed for the effects of socioeconomic status, age and number of children, duration of employment, contingent conditions of marital status, and attitude of husband and wife toward wife's employment. Completed mailed questionnaires covering these areas were received from 1,993 mothers from three towns in Washington State as part of a larger study of the employment status of mothers. Following analysis of marital success in terms of self-reports on marital conflict, permanence, happiness, and satisfaction, a single-dimension marital adjustment scale was developed.

Findings supported the hypothesis that more marital conflict exists in families with an employed mother. The data on marital permanence were ambiguous and not statistically significant. Although socio-economic status had no significant effect on the relationships between employment status and marital adjustment, the smallest differences in degree of marital adjustment were among higher socioeconomic families. Family size, age of children, and length of maternal employment had insignificant effects on the relation of employment to marital adjustment. Even though dissatisfaction with the wife's occupational role felt by either spouse was related to poor marital adjustment in this study, the sequence involved is unclear. The significant effects of maternal employment on marital adjust-ment found in original-marriage families did not appear in the marital adjustment of women in remarriages. (11 references)

227
Osofsky, Joy D., and O'Connell, Edward J. Parent-child interaction: Daughters' effects upon mothers' and fathers' behaviors. *Developmental Psychology*, 7(2):157-168, 1972.

Parent-child relations. Preschool girls. Elementary school girls. Dependency.

This is an investigation of the effects of dependent and independent behavior of daughters on both parents' behavior toward the child. Fathers were included in the sample to focus on possible differential parent responses. Both observational and interview methods were used to evaluate discrepancies among the findings of earlier studies that had used different modes of investigation. Mothers, fathers, and their 4- to 6-year-old daughters from 42 middle-class Ithaca, N.Y., families participated in structured and unstructured play situations which were observed and videotaped. Interactions were scored for the child's independent or dependent behavior and the parental responses to these behaviors. Each parent was observed alone with the child in each type of situation and was also interviewed separately concerning child-related attitudes and behaviors.

Results indicated that structured laboratory tasks can effectively produce differential dependent and independent child behaviors, and that the general amount of such behavior displayed is not related to the sex of the participating parent. Differential child behaviors resulted in differential parent behaviors: Under the dependent condition, both parents interacted more with the child, both verbally and physically, and displayed more controlling behaviors. Significant differences were found between the child's behavior to mother and to father and between the two parents' behavior in each experimental condition. In general, the child appeared to exhibit more task specificity with her father and more interpersonal interaction with her mother. The father was more likely to help the child physically or to become detached, whereas the mother was more likely to encourage independence and to explain, comment, or question the child. A major implication for future socialization research is the need to study children's effects on both mothers and fathers, as well as parents' effects on children. (21 references)

228
Orden, Susan R., and Bradburn, Norman M. Working wives and marriage happiness. *American Journal of Sociology,* 74(4):392-407, 1968.

Working wives. Marital satisfaction.

This empirical study of the effects of women's work status on their marriages was designed to fill in some neglected areas of inquiry: Husbands' opinions, perceived financial need to work contrasted with need determined by external standards, and measurement of the positive as well as the negative side of marital adjustment. Subjects were 748 husbands and 903 wives, representing 1,651 couples, who reported the husband as the chief wage earner in the household. The sample was drawn from probability samples of large metropolitan areas in the United States. Subjects were divided into three groups: Those from marriages where the wife worked outside the home because of perceived economic necessity; those where she was in the labor market by choice; and those where she worked in the home by choice. Subjects filled out two checklists—one of recent pleasurable experiences in the marriage and another on disagreements. Four measures of marital happiness were derived from these checklists—two indexes of satisfaction (companionship and sociability), a single index of tension, and a score of the difference between these two dimensions called the Marriage Adjustment Balance Scale (MABS). The individual's own direct assessment of his or her marriage was obtained in a personal interview. The satisfaction and tension indexes were found to be uncorrelated in the marriages sampled. Approximately one-third of the women participated in the labor market; this proportion increased with the woman's educational level and the age of her children, but declined as the husband's level of education and the number of children increased. Over half of the women in the labor market reported that they would work even if they did not need the money. For both husbands and wives and for all social levels and stages in the life cycle, marital adjustment was significantly better when the wife was free to choose between the labor market and the home than when she was in the labor market out of economic necessity. Part-time employment was more favorable to marriage adjustment than either the home choice or full-time employment. Both husbands and wives were significantly higher on the MABS index if the wife chose to participate in the labor market than if she chose the home, but there was no difference between these two groups in their own assessment of their marital happiness in interview statements. (21 references)

229
Papanek, Miriam L. Authority and sex roles in the family. *Journal of Marriage and the Family,* 31(1):88-96, 1969.

Marital dominance. Adolescents. Sex-role perceptions. Parent-child relations.

Adolescent concepts of authority and sex role were examined in relation to the marital authority patterns of their parents. The study was based on questionnaire results from 219 boys and 267 girls and individual interview data from 201 parents. Questions probed each family member's perceptions of how the husband and wife divide decisionmaking authority and which spouse holds greater authority in household affairs, social activities, economic functions, and child-rearing. Subject families are lower middle and upper middle class and are categorized by degree and type of differentiation in marital authority roles.

Study results supported the hypothesis that boy and girl roles are more sharply differentiated if the authority roles of husband and wife are highly differentiated. Unlike wives and children, husbands tend to emphasize sex-role differentiation in children regardless of the degree of marital role differentiation. Girls stress sex-role differentiation less than boys do. Parent-child roles and some childrearing practices also vary according to marital authority patterns. Contrary to hypotheses, parents reportedly exert more control over a child of the same sex as the dominant parent, rather than reinforcing that child's dominance. In general, parents exercise more control over their daughters than their sons, but in a more democratic manner and with more open affection by the father. Father-daughter relations tend to be distant or strained in families with highly differentiated roles. (16 references)

230

Rapoport, Rhona, and Rapoport, Robert N. The dual career family: A variant pattern and social change. *Human Relations,* 22(1):3-30, 1969.

Dual-career families. Role conflict. Great Britain.

This study examined the dual career family, concentrating on the stresses associated with it in its present social context. A series of joint and individual interviews were conducted with the upper middle-class husbands and wives of 13 British families in which both spouses had careers and of three families in which the wife had currently given up her career at least temporarily. All couples had at least one child.

Five major areas of stress and a variety of methods of dealing with these stresses were identified: Role overload, dilemmas between personal norms and social norms, dilemmas of identity, social network dilemmas, and role cycling dilemmas. Role overload was affected by the importance of children and family life to the couple, standard of living, the degree to which conjugal roles could be rearranged, and how household duties were delegated. Remedies for overload included deliberate provision of leisure time and assignment of nonpersonal domestic chores to outsiders. Dilemmas arising from the discrepancy between personal norms and the expectations of society varied according to family stages and occupational cycles. Birth of the first child was frequently a time of stress for career-committed mothers. Dilemmas of personal identity occurred as husbands and wives attempted to maintain individual identities while pursuing personal development through the same role channel (a career). Rivalries and resulting difficulties in marital relations were dealt with by consciously separating spheres of work and family and by establishing tacit limits to competition within the work sphere. Although the dual career subjects had less active involvement with kin and friends than other professional middle-class families, social network dilemmas did arise concerning time given to these relationships. Role cycling dilemmas resulted from conflict among different stages in the husband's career, wife's career, and family life. Sacrifices had to be made in each area at different stages, but always for the purpose of continuing all three role systems (two careers and the family). (50 references)

231
Reed, Julia. Marriage and fertility in black female teachers. *Black Scholar,* 1(3-4):22-28, 1970.

Racial differences. Female teachers.

An examination of 1960 U.S. census data was undertaken to test the hypothesis that black female primary and secondary school teachers are more middle class than their white counterparts in characteristics reflecting individual initiative, and less middle class in areas where personal endeavor may be undermined by other persons and/or the social system. This contradiction of status was expected to interfere with their adjustment of some areas of marital and family life.

Black female teachers were found to be more likely to marry than white female teachers and more likely to be divorced, especially if they had children. However, black female teachers were less likely to have children than were their white counterparts. Black female teachers who had children were more likely to continue work after the birth of their children and tended to stop working later in their marriage than white female teachers. Although black female teachers had completed more years of school than white female teachers, there was a discrepancy in income received and income expected on the basis of educational attainment. Black female teachers were more likely to marry blue-collar workers than were their white counterparts; black male teachers were considerably less likely to do so. Consequently, the family incomes of black and white male teachers were more comparable than were those of black and white females.

Despite their middle-class outlook and behavior in years of schooling, propensity for marriage, and patterns of fertility, the black female teachers appeared to experience less satisfaction than the traditional middle class regarding family income, spouse's occupational status, and marital stability. (8 references)

232
Safilios-Rothschild, Constantina. Family sociology or wives' family sociology? A cross-cultural examination of decision-making. *Journal of Marriage and the Family,* 31(2):290-301, 1969.

Marital dominance. Cultural differences. Methodological issues.

This study examined wives' and husbands' perceived decisionmaking patterns in two cultures representing different levels of technical development and family ideology. This study was designed to test the assumption that the viewpoint of the wife is sufficient for a study of familial decisionmaking. Interview data from two earlier studies, one of 160 matched couples in Detroit and another of 250 randomly sampled Athenian husbands and wives, were used to determine whether the husband, the wife, or both made certain family decisions.

It was concluded that perceptions of one spouse only are invalid in testing decisionmaking in the family. Findings from both cultures indicated that there are significant discrepancies between husbands' and wives' views of the familial power structure. Some of the trends in perceived decisionmaking were similar in Athens and Detroit, despite social, economic, and cultural differences. Within the Detroit sample, for which more data were available, there was no consistent pattern differentiating agreement or disagreement according to sociopsychological characteristics of husbands and wives. Data also showed possible inadequacies in the usual method of calculating the overall decisionmaking score. To remedy this, several methodological procedures are suggested regarding decisions to be used in future cross-cultural family studies and in the analysis of data on decisionmaking. (17 references)

233
Safilios-Rothschild, Constantina. The influence of the wife's degree of work commitment upon some aspects of family organization and dynamics. *Journal of Marriage and the Family,* **32**(4):681-691, 1970.

Working wives. Work commitment. Marital dominance. Marital satisfaction. Household tasks. Greece.

The variable of work commitment was used to specifically define the effects of married women's working status on marital satisfaction, family decisionmaking, division of household labor, and degree of husband's permissiveness regarding the wife's various activities. A sample of Athenian married women—549 nonworking subjects stratified by social class and 347 working subjects stratified by occupational category—was interviewed on work attitudes and on the four family variables. The work commitment (WC) variable was obtained from questions eliciting the subjects' willingness to give priority to work obligations over familial obligations.

Working women with a high work commitment (HWC) reported more satisfaction with their marriages than did nonworking women. Working women perceived themselves as generally prevailing in decisionmaking, as giving in less often in disagreements with their husbands, and as having more freedom of behavior in and outside the home. Women with low work commitment (LWC) perceived a more egalitarian model of family dynamics, tending to compromise with their husbands in disagreements and to share family decisionmaking. But LWC women had a restricted amount of personal freedom in or outside the home. While the degree of WC was closely related to a woman's level of education and type of occupation, the relationship was by no means perfect; some women in low prestige jobs had HWC. Full-time workers with children up to 18 years old tended to have higher WC than those in the same family cycle stages who worked part time. (21 references)

234
Safilios-Rothschild, Constantina, and Georgiopoulos, John. A comparative study of parental and filial role definitions. *Journal of Marriage and the Family*, 32(3):381-389, 1970.

Family structure. Cultural differences. Racial differences. Parent-child relations. Greece.

This study compares parental and filial role definitions held by parents in two cultures—American and Greek—to test the Parsonian conceptualization of instrumental and expressive roles among parents and spouses. The American sample consisted of 178 black couples, all of whom were parents of children 6 years old or younger. The Greek sample consisted of 250 randomly selected couples living in Athens; in 133 cases, wives were interviewed, and in 117 cases, husbands were interviewed. Parents in the Detroit study (American sample) were asked to rate eight parental duties and six items of filial duties in order of importance to provide comparability with the Greek study.

The definitions of parental roles given by both samples did not support the Parsonian typology of instrumental and expressive roles. Rather, parents of both sexes regardless of culture tended to include both components in their definitions of parental roles. Further, all the Greek couples and the particularly well-educated couples from both samples tended to be less constrained by sex stereotypes in defining parental and filial roles. The Detroit data corroborated existing data on white families, indicating the lack of significant differences in parental and filial role definitions between black and white American parents. The data from the Greek sample provided additional evidence that family modernization may be more advanced in Greece than in the United States, since the Greek sample seemed less constrained by category or stereotype. (19 references)

235
Schneider, David M., and Smith, Raymond T. *Class Differences and Sex Roles in American Kinship and Family Structure.* Englewood Cliffs, N.J.: Prentice-Hall, 1973, 132 pp.

Family structure. Socioeconomic differences. Cultural differences.

This book is a sociological and anthropological investigation of differences in family structure and kinship behavior in the middle and lower classes of American society. A primary theoretical concern is the relationships among culture, social system, and social action. The analysis of lower-class kinship is based on interview and field observation data on approximately 59 Afro-American, southern white, and Spanish-American families living in Chicago. These data include subjects' spontaneous ideas about kinship and occupational and status domains, personal histories of the subjects, and factual information on their kin. Comparable data on middle-class kinship were derived from previous studies.

The analysis of differences in middle-class and lower class kinship and family form indicates that family and kinship roles are actually compound roles comprised of kinship elements, sex-role elements, and elements derived from the system of status and class differentiation. Variations between middle-class and lower-class kinship and family norms are due primarily to variations in the sex-role component of the norms. The discussion of sex role involves cultural definitions of sex and sex roles and an analysis of the interactions between sex roles and social behavior in the two classes under examination. This analysis, combined with a discussion of occupational and ethnic factors, the family, household composition, and childrearing, challenges the assumption that all deviations from the middle-class nuclear family structure are the result of disorganization, deprivation, or poverty. (89 references)

236
Schulz, David A. Variations in the father role in complete families of the Negro lower class. *Social Science Quarterly,* 49:651-659, 1968. Also in: Staples, Robert, ed. *The Black Family: Essays and Studies.* Belmont, Calif.: Wadsworth, 1971, pp. 213-221.

Family structure. Paternal behavior. Parental models. Racial differences.

An exploratory investigation was undertaken to document variations in the father role in lower-class Negro families. Subjects were household members and family members of five complete and five fatherless Negro families living in a public housing project in a midwestern city. Only the complete families are considered in this report. The age of the parents ranged from 33 to 55. Family size varied from 6 to 18 persons and the number of people living in the household (family members and relatives) ranged from 5 to 18.

Overall sample size varied during the study, but about 88 persons lived in the households over this period. Data were collected by participant observation and open-ended interviews over 250 ten-hour days. Supplemental information came from the files of the Housing Authority, schools, and the police. Variables considered were the strength of the conjugal bond, support given by the father to his family, and the relationship of the father to the children.

Three types of fathers were found: the indiscreet free-man, the discreet free-man, and the monogamous father. The relations of the two indiscreet free-man fathers with their wives and children were strained owing to the undisguised split in the husband's allegiance between his legitimate family and one or more illegitimate families. These men had little justification for authority within the family on the basis of expressive ability, and none as models for traditional respectable behavior. Their only instrumental contribution to the family was financial support. The extramarital activities of the two discreet free-man fathers were known to their wives and family but did not impair their relatively comfortable family relationships. These fathers legitimated their authority within the household on the basis of being warm and loving to their children and expressive companions to their more instrumentally oriented wives. Discreet free-men tended to be able to muster their children's respect for their ability to cope with the environment by means of such manipulative strategies as gambling and circumspect affairs. The one monogamous father in the sample legitimated his paternal authority on the basis of his example for respectable behavior, his desire to be an adequate supporter, and his warm family relations. It was concluded that these fathers, particularly the discreet free-men, offered successful models for effective coping in a harsh environment. (22 references)

237
Siegel, Alberta E., and Haas, Miriam B. The working mother: A review of research. *Child Development,* 34(3):513-542, 1963.

Working mothers. Methodological issues.

Empirical studies of maternal employment and its correlates among working mothers in the United States are reviewed, excluding studies that are purely demographic or that focus on the impact of maternal employment on children. Some general observations are made regarding problems of conceptualization and definition and on methodological problems of comparison, representativeness, subjects' defensiveness, data-collection techniques, and formation of research hypotheses. Research findings are reported in the areas of social attitudes toward working mothers; reasons mothers work; maternal employment and certain family functions—family size, husband-wife relations, and performance of household tasks; and maternal employment and childbearing. It is suggested that few of the individual results reviewed are sufficiently well-based methologically to be accepted without question. Insofar as the results reviewed are meaningful, they indicate that maternal employment per se is not a particularly relevant variable. However, the mother's reasons for working or not working and the meaning she attributes to work, homemaking, and motherhood do appear to be important and should receive greater attention in future research. (76 references)

238
Stolz, Lois Meek. Effects of maternal employment on children: Evidence from research. *Child Development,* 31:749-782, 1960.

Working mothers. Parental influence. Historical trends.

This review of published and forthcoming research on the effects of maternal employment on children includes studies from 1914 to 1960. Historical trends in maternal employment and in attitudes and approaches toward it are reviewed. The effects of maternal employment on school achievement, personal adjustment, and attitude development are discussed.

In each area of inquiry, a number of different and opposing findings appeared. This divergency is attributed to lack of control of pertinent variables, such as socioeconomic status and intactness and size of family, and to the broad range of time of data collection. When only well-controlled studies based on data collected since 1946 were considered, the findings, though sparse, were less divergent. In such studies, no statistically significant relationships were found between maternal employment and delinquency, adolescent adjustment, school marks in high school, or dependent-independent behavior of 5-year-olds. A study which attempted to take into account different attitudes of mothers toward their work indicated that underlying characteristics of the mother may influence her attitude toward both her work and her child, with consequent effects on the child's behavior.

Data regarding effects of maternal employment on sons and daughters are discussed, though the studies reviewed yielded relatively little information. An overall conclusion is drawn: The outside employment of married women with children is a social phenomenon which invites investigation, but research will obtain conclusive results only insofar as it takes into account variations in the nature of maternal employment and the complex interpersonal relations in the family. It is suggested that future research further explore the definition of maternal employment and nonemployment, maternal occupations in relation to the family, the characteristics of the mother, and actual behavior of children. (52 references)

239
Stuckert, Robert P. Role perception and marital satisfaction—A configurational approach. *Marriage and Family Living,* 25(4):415-419, 1963.

Marital satisfaction. Marital roles. Role perception.

The hypothesis that marital satisfaction is a function of the mutual interaction of several significant components of role perception and expectation was explored. Individual interviews with members of 50 newly married couples, ages 19 through 26, probed the relative importance of 10 personality factors in the husband and wife roles. Each subject rank ordered the factors by their importance in marriage in general, in one's own marriage, and from the spouse's point of view. Marital satisfaction scores, based on responses to a questionnaire, were correlated with these interview data to categorize the sample by configurational marital types.

Data supported the thesis that the husband's role definitions and expectations are more important to early success of marriage than the wife's. The dominant factor associated with marital satisfaction for wives was the extent to which their perceptions of their husbands' expectations correlated with the husbands' actual expectations. For husbands, the actual similarity between their role concepts and expectations and those of their wives was the most important factor. Other conclusions drawn were: Accurate perception may perhaps lessen marital satisfaction if the partners have widely differing expectations of the roles of husband and wife. Inaccurate perception may not cause dissatisfaction if a person defines the marriage as typical of marriages in general. Family adjustment may be greatly affected by the extent to which both husband and wife are oriented toward actual and potential role changes. (9 references)

240
Tharp, Roland G. Dimensions of marriage roles. *Marriage and Family Living,* 25(4):389-400, 1963.

Marital roles. Role perceptions.

This study provides a description of marriage roles based on empirical data to suggest the structure of marriage roles and to provide a scheme for measuring the role patterns of marriages. The sample consisted of couples drawn from the subject pool of a longitudinal marriage study initiated 18 years earlier. Couples were selected on the basis of having remained married to each other since the earlier study, having at least one living child, and having completed all questionnaire items. The 128 to 141 subjects (the number varied for various portions of the data analysis) had a mean age of 45 for men and 43 for women at the time of the study.

The subjects responded to a battery of questionnaire items dealing with role expectations ar.d role enactment. The results on 50 variables for the former and 48 for the latter were factor analyzed for men and women separately and for the sexes combined. The analysis showed a number of discrete factors yielding roughly 12 dimensions of marital roles for each sex or for the sexes combined. There were many instances in which the role dimensions were not the same for the two sexes, and in some cases the dimensions of role enactments differed from those of role expectations. Implications of these results for marital counseling and for future research are discussed. (9 references)

241

Williamson, Robert C. Marriage roles, American style. In: Seward, Georgene H., and Williamson, Robert C., eds. *Sex Roles in Changing Society.* New York: Random House, 1970. pp. 150-176.

Marital roles. Marital satisfaction.

This extensive review of research on marital role behavior in America emphasizes sex differences. The current societal redefinition of marriage and family roles and basic changes in the marriage relationship are discussed. A discussion of the nature of roles focuses on conflicts in the feminine role, specifically, the ambiguity of role expectancies of women with respect to career, marriage, and children. Role expectancies and behaviors are said to be determined by both the socialization of the individual and the immediate situational need. The theoretical distinction between instrumental and expressive roles is described, but is said to have only limited relevance when applied to marital interaction.

Homogamy, the ideal mate concept, and the theory of complementary needs are examined as factors in the selection process of marriage. Problems presented by sex adjustments and by in-laws are outlined, as are a number of factors that have reduced problems in these areas in recent years. Several interrelated mechanisms that become established early in a marriage and tend to sustain the relationship are suggested: Identification, differentiation of marital roles, emulation, idealization, enhancement, and interhabituation, along with the functions of perception, consensus, and communication.

Five types of marriages are identified: Conflict-habituated, devitalized, passive-congenial, vital, and total. Marriage roles are also discussed in terms of the decisionmaking and power structure of the relationship. Decisionmaking undergoes an almost continuous alternation of egocentricity and altruism over time. Marriage can be conceptualized as an exchange of powers, with marital interaction as the bargaining process. Marital role conflict is discussed in relation to the life cycle. Several studies dealing with the disenchantment process are reviewed, along with several studies documenting the frequency of increasing marital dissatisfaction in the later years of marriage. (98 references)

242
Wortis, Rochelle Paul. The acceptance of the concept of the maternal role by behavioral scientists: Its effect on women. *American Journal of Orthopsychiatry,* 41(5):733-746, 1971.

Maternal behavior. Mother-child relations. Parental influence.

This review of the literature on maternal role critically examines the concept of "mothering" and its function in behavioral science assumptions. These assumptions are seen as culturally determined and scientifically inadequate. Certain contradictions in the culture's system of childrearing are discussed in terms of their negative effects on women and children. Studies of mother-infant attachment and separation, theories of maternal instinct, and evidence of the social needs of mothers and children have failed to prove the biological necessity of the single mothering figure. However, behavioral scientists and clinicians encourage acceptance of the model in which the biological mother must provide most of the stimulation, conditioning, and emotional satisfaction considered essential for normal development of the child.

It is asserted that, since so few studies have explored the effects of male-infant or father-infant interaction on subsequent child development, it is scientifically unacceptable to advocate the natural superiority of women as childrearers. Quality day care and alternatives to the nuclear family are discussed as possible means of achieving a more democratic, egalitarian society for children and for adults. (46 references)

243
Yarrow, Leon J. Maternal deprivation: Toward an empirical and conceptual re-evaluation. *Psychological Bulletin,* 58(6):459-490, 1961.

Maternal behavior. Parental influence. Mother-child relations.

This review of research and theoretical literature investigates variables and concepts associated with maternal deprivation. Three major kinds of deviation from the hypothetical norm of maternal care are considered: Institutionalization; separation from a mother or mother-substitute; and multiple mothering, in which no one person performs mothering functions in a continuous fashion. These deviant conditions are discussed in terms of the specific environmental factors facilitating or inhibiting developmental progress, the reversibility of the effects of childhood events, and the extent to which age at time of experience and length of deprivation determine the effect on the child. Maternal deprivation conditions are discussed in terms of developmental theory. It is concluded that institutional environments can best be analyzed in terms of sensory, social, and emotional deprivation; and maternal separation and multiple mothering, in terms of stress consequent to change or inconsistency. Included are tables of major studies on this topic. (100 references)

244
Yarrow, Marian R.; Scott, Phyllis; de Leeuw, Louise; and Heinig, Christine. Child-rearing in families of working and nonworking mothers. *Sociometry,* 25(2):122-140, 1962.

Working mothers. Childrearing practices. Mother-child relations.

This study examined childrearing practices of working and non-working mothers. It was hypothesized that maternal performance is affected by gratifications and frustrations in the woman's other roles. Subjects were 50 working and 50 nonworking mothers from middle-class, upper middle-class, and upper working-class intact families living in Washington, D.C. All subjects had at least one child between the ages of 4 and 11. Interviews were concerned with childrearing discipline and control; sex-role and dependency-independency training; and the mother's emotional satisfaction and involvement with the child, sensitivity toward the child, and confidence in her role as mother. These variables were analyzed and compared with additional interview data on subject's current employment status, role motivation, social class, and educational level. Prior to analysis, a model of good maternal practices and philosophy was constructed to provide adequacy-of-mothering ratings.

Mother's employment status was found to be independently significant on only one childrearing variable: More working mothers than nonworking mothers expressed lack of confidence about their success in the mother role. However, working and nonworking subjects did not differ in their adequacy-of-mothering scores. Additional significant findings appeared, however, when motivation and education were considered with work status. More nonworking mothers who are dissatisfied with their employment status reported difficulties in the areas of control, emotional satisfaction in relations with their children, and confidence in the mother role. They also had the lowest adequacy-of-mothering ratings. There were few group differences in childrearing practices between working mothers who preferred to work and those who did not, suggesting that dissatisfied working mothers achieve certain valued family goals through their employment. In the high school educated group, children were more firmly controlled, given greater responsibility, and more strictly disciplined by the father in families where the mother worked than where she did not. In the college educated group, these differences did not appear. However, more college educated working mothers reported that they and their husbands plan and spend time in shared activities with their children than did nonworking college mothers. (6 references)

Educational Institutions

245
Anastasiow, Nicholas J. Success in school and boys' sex-role patterns. *Child Development,* 36(4):1053-1066, 1965.

Sex-typed behavior. Academic achievement. Preschool boys. Elementary school boys.

This study tested the hypothesis that 5- and 6-year-old boys who make consistent sex-typed toy preferences show higher achievement test scores and are rated as more successful in school by their teachers than those who make inconsistent choices. Consistent choices were considered indicative of sex-role adoption, whether culturally appropriate or not. Subjects were 98 lower and upper middle-class boys selected from a kindergarten and first grade sample on the basis of their choices on the Group-Toy-Preference Test. Twenty-nine subjects were rated masculine, 39 feminine, and 30 median (inconsistent). Each subject was individually administered the

Picture-Preference Test (a measure of masculine versus feminine and adult versus child role preferences), the Toy-Preference Test, and the Franky Fable (a story completion test measuring resolution of oedipal stage castration anxiety). The entire sample was administered the California Achievement Test and was rated by teachers on eight dimensions of achievement.

Results of the Toy- and Picture-Preference tests yielded essentially the same ratings as the Group-Toy-Preference Test. On the Franky Fable, significantly more of the boys rated as feminine on the group test gave answers associated with castration fears. Achievement test scores of masculine boys were significantly superior to median boys in reading, but not in arithmetic. Masculine boys were rated higher than median boys by kindergarten teachers on readiness for first grade, constructive play, maturity, physical ability, and social virtues. In first grade, masculine boys were rated significantly higher than feminine boys on social virtues, physical ability, and outdoor versus indoor play. Masculine boys were not significantly higher than median boys on social virtues, but median boys were significantly higher than feminine boys. It was concluded that, in kindergarten, teachers differentiate boys on the basis of sex-role adoption; and in first grade, on the cultural appropriateness of the sex role adopted. (14 references)

246

Angrist, Shirley S. Variations in women's adult aspirations during college. *Journal of Marriage and the Family,* 34(3):465-468, 1972.

College women. Career aspirations. Marriage aspirations. Lifestyle.

This longitudinal study examined patterns of change and consistency in women's aspirations during college. Of 188 female freshmen at a private, coeducational university, 58 percent graduated 4 years later. Class members completed questionnaires each fall on the previous year's experiences and their attitudes toward education, work, family life, and future plans and aspirations. Interviews were conducted with each subject once in the first 3 years of college and once in the spring of the senior year. A lifestyle index was constructed from questionnaire items measuring career- versus noncareer-oriented lifestyle aspirations. Since all the women aspired to family life, career aspirations were defined as the desire to pursue an occupation in addition to family roles.

Five student types were derived from the 87 students who completed the 4 years in phase: Careerists, 18 percent; noncareerists, 33 percent; converts, 22 percent; defectors, 13 percent; and shifters, 14 percent.

The careerists and noncareerists remained relatively constant in their lifestyle aspirations all 4 years, whereas the converts, defectors, and shifters did not.

The careerist typically majors in the humanities, chooses a male-dominated occupation, and does not join a sorority. She is influenced by the example of a working mother, but does not try to fit her parents' ideas about success. Careerists view domesticity and child care as matters to be delegated to others, if necessary. The noncareerist intends to center her life totally on her family and to work only in case of financial need; she typically becomes engaged during her senior year. The convert is slow to develop academic competence and gradually acquires her career interests. The defector is most likely to be a home economics major rather than a physical or social science major; she is a poor student, but often ends up in teaching. Defectors want to marry young and focus their energies on home and children. The shifter tends to be a social science major and a top student. Her goals change, but her ideas of husband-wife responsibilities remain traditional. (16 references)

247
Bayer, Alan E. Marriage plans and educational aspirations. *American Journal of Sociology,* 75(2):239-244, 1969.

High school students. Educational aspirations. Marriage aspirations.

To determine whether marital plans, independent of socioeconomic status and academic aptitude, exert a strong influence on educational aspirations, a random subsample of 2,000 male and 2,000 female 12th-graders was drawn from the Project TALENT national research sample. Multiple-regression and path analyses were performed on data from a 2-day battery of tests and inventories. Academic aptitude was a composite score derived from over 750 items in the test battery; the socioeconomic index was a composite based on nine items in the battery; the marriage plans variable was based on a question concerning the age at which the participant expects to get married; and educational aspirations were measured by the stated amount of education the participant expects to receive.

Each independent variable was found to affect the educational aspirations of both males and females. The independent influence of marriage plans was substantial, with the direct effect especially marked for girls. However, the large unexplained variance in the dependent variable indicates either that educational aspirations are largely unpredictable, or that additional variables need to be introduced into the prediction system. (9 references)

248
Bayer, Alan E. College impact on marriage. *Journal of Marriage and the Family,* 34(4):600-609, 1972.

Married students. College attendance.

A series of stepwise multiple-regression analyses and supplemental tabulations was undertaken to assess the impact of personal and institutional variables on students marrying during their college years and the relationship of marriage to attrition among college students. A random subsample of 2,091 married (857 men, 1,234 women) and 2,124 single (851 men, 1,273 women) college students was drawn from a nationally representative longitudinal study sample.

The 61 student characteristics and the 60 institutional variables yielded modest relationships with getting married during college. Actually asking the student to estimate his or her chances of marrying while in college was by far the single best predictor of actual later marriage in college. Some additional variables that produced significant relationships were: Students of both sexes were more likely to marry during college if they came from lower socioeconomic homes. The more academically able students, those with graduate education aspirations, Roman Catholics, Jewish males, and students from the Middle Atlantic States were less apt to marry as undergraduates. Neither enrollment at a co-ed institution nor at one emphasizing social life was shown to increase the probability of early marriage. Students at academically selective, Roman Catholic, or metropolitan schools and women at predominantly black institutions or at institutions rated high on verbal aggressiveness of its students were less likely to be married by their senior year. Enrollment at colleges in the west and, for males, at schools rated low on the regularity of sleeping habits among students was positively related to early marriage. As married students are more likely than single students to drop out of college, recommendations are offered concerning institutional means of curbing attrition among married students. (25 references)

249
Coates, Thomas J., and Southern, Mara L. Differential educational aspiration levels of men and women undergraduate students. *Journal of Psychology,* 81:125-128, 1972.

Educational aspirations. College students. Professional women.

This study examines the reasons for the underrepresentation of women in academic professions, specifically psychology. Male and female college student aspiration levels and intellectual abilities were considered. Data on 198 male and 166 female undergraduates enrolled in an upper division psychology course at San Jose State College were provided by questionnaires eliciting highest degree aspirations and demographic information. In addition, three predictors of academic success were also considered: Four psychology course examinations converted into a summation score, the Concept Mastery Test of verbal facility, and the Wechsler Adult Intelligence Scale.

Findings showed that women set lower educational goals for themselves than men, despite their apparent equal intellectual capabilities for pursuing graduate education. It is concluded that not only discrimination, but also the aspiration levels of women account for their small numbers in the academic professions. (11 references)

250
Ellis, Joseph R., and Peterson, Joan L. Effects of same sex class organization on junior high school students' academic achievement, self-discipline, self-concept, sex role identification, and attitude toward school. *Journal of Educational Research,* 64(10):455-464, 1971.

Junior high school students. Coeducation. School performance. School attitudes. Self-concept. Sex-role identification.

In an empirical study, the effects of sex-segregated class organization on five developmental variables of junior high school students were investigated. Five null hypotheses predicted no change for each variable—academic achievement, self-discipline, self-concept, sex-role identification, and attitude toward school. Subjects were 300 seventh- and eighth-grade students randomly selected in two junior high schools in northern Illinois. For 1 academic year, subjects spent approximately five-sixths of the schoolday in same-sex classes. Pretests and posttests were administered at the beginning and end of the school year. The Iowa Test of Basic Skills, Metropolitan Achievement Tests, Standard Achievement Test, California Test of Personality, and the Ellis-Many-Frey Report of Self-Concept Scale measured the variables under study. Additional data were gathered by interviews and teacher reports.

Each of the five null hypotheses was tested using analyses of covariance, and no significant differences were found which were attributable to same-sex grouping. Several general observations were made apart from the hypotheses being tested. Girls tended to receive higher marks from teachers, to achieve higher scores on standardized achievement tests, to report more favorable attitudes toward social groups and institutions, and to respond more negatively to the sex-segregated school experience than did boys. The attitudes of students and teachers toward the same-sex grouping became more negative as the year progressed. (11 references)

251
Feldman, Saul D. Impediment or stimulant: Marital status and graduate education. *American Journal of Sociology*, 78(4):982-994, 1973.

Married students. Graduate education. Role conflict.

Data on how the spouse role affects both men and women in graduate education were examined, with special attention to the effects of divorce. Mailed questionnaires were completed by 32,963 students at 158 graduate schools in 1969. Data from this nationwide sample were weighted to represent over 1 million graduate and professional school students. Part-time and noncitizen students were excluded from the findings reported here.

The effects of sex and marital status are discussed in relation to demographic characteristics, educational motivation, professional attainment, future plans, and finances. Conflict is consistently observed between the roles of wife and full-time graduate student. Married women students, compared with all other students, face greater pressures to drop out, have fewer informal socialization experiences of graduate student life, and encounter more limited mobility and job alternatives.

The greatest adherence to a career-primacy model in graduate school is found among married men and divorced women students. The data suggest that male graduate students lose a supportive relationship in divorce, whereas females lose a source of great role conflict. In general, the data on all variables show large differences between divorced men and women in graduate school. (20 references)

252
Fichter, Joseph H. Career expectations of Negro women graduates. *Monthly Labor Review*, 90(11):36-42, 1967. Also in: Theodore, Athena, ed. *The Professional Woman*. Cambridge, Mass.: Schenkman, 1971, pp. 427-440.

Career aspirations. Racial differences. College educated women.

Career expectations of female Negro college graduates were compared with those of female southern white graduates and female non-southern graduates. Three distinct student populations were examined: The primary population was represented by 2,265 women at 50 predominantly Negro institutions in the South; the comparison population was represented by 2,079 predominantly southern white women from the National Opinion Research Center's (NORC) nationwide study of the 1964 senior class; and the third was represented by 10,968 nonsouthern women comprising "all other" subjects in the NORC study (excluding predominantly Negro institutions in the South).

Women graduates of predominantly Negro southern colleges were more likely than the white subjects to be gainfully employed. Findings indicated that the Negro women preferred and expected to combine marriage, children, and gainful employment. The Negro sample was about one-half as likely as the southern white and "other" women graduates to view marriage and family as interfering with postgraduate study. Only 4 percent of the Negro women estimated marriage would make it difficult to have a career. Forty-two percent of the Negro women, compared with 23 percent of the southern whites and 18 percent of the "others," said their men prefer them to work at some point during their married life.

More than half in each of the three sample groups were planning careers in education. However, a higher proportion of Negro women planned to go into social work. Despite their higher aspirations, fewer Negro females than whites were found in graduate school or had made a definite job commitment a year after graduation. Socio-economic class differences among Negro graduates did not emerge in their orientation toward marriage and career, with the exception of type of occupational field chosen. Elementary and secondary teaching attracted more women from the least educated families; the upper class women tended to have less confidence in their personality qualifications for the job. (2 references)

253
Fredriksson, Ingrid. Sex roles and education in Sweden. *New York University Education Quarterly*, 3(2):17-24, 1972.

Sweden. Social equality. Education.

This description of recent Swedish national policy on sexual equality shows how the country is moving deliberately toward career, home, and political roles that are undifferentiated by sex. The educational system is a key target for official policy in accordance with the new standard.

Under the present voluntary system of preschools, financing is insufficient to meet the needs of increasing numbers of working mothers, and standards of care sometimes suffer. Compulsory preschools accommodating the schedules of working mothers and stressing sex role equality will be set up by local authorities. Sweden has moved away from tracking in the first 9 years of school, and boys and girls receive the same instructional opportunities, including domestic science, infant care, and industrial arts. Since sex continues to be a factor in choosing electives, however, additional steps might be taken, such as requiring technical science courses in the early grades and encouraging girls to enter science and technology tracks.

Efforts to place the same social expectations on both sexes and to overcome sex typing are being made in vocational education, universities, professional schools, and adult education. Preschool and adult education are likely, in the next several years, to become the two sectors of greatest expansion and public expenditure in Swedish education. (19 references)

254

Ginzberg, Eli; Berg, Ivar E.; Brown, Carol A.; Herma, John L.; Yohalem, Alice M.; and Gorelick, Sherry. *Life Styles of Educated Women.* New York: Columbia University Press, 1966. 224 pp.

Lifestyle. Professional women.

This exploratory investigation probed the changing role of work in the lives of educated women. Subjects were 311 women who had pursued graduate studies at Columbia University between 1945 and 1951. Seventy-three women completed questionnaires for a larger study of talented men and women. An additional 238 women answered a revised version of the original questionnaire. All subjects had won fellowships, stood high in their class, and/or had been elected to honor societies. Questionnaires included open-ended inquiries on education; occupational, domestic, and community activities; family background; present home life, and general influences on personal outlook.

Findings from this study are presented under the following topic headings: Development and education, options and decisions (regarding career and/or family), family and community, work and careers, occupational achievement, accommodation (between career and family life), satisfaction and fulfillments (from various roles), and lifestyles. A discussion of the broader findings and interpretations concerning work in the lives of women compares and contrasts subjects' occupational choice and career development with those of educated men. Three stages of life are considered: Adolescence, young adulthood in college and graduate school, and the early years after the completion of education. A final chapter includes suggestions for specific private and public action permitting women of talent and training to make the best use of their skills. (51 references)

255
Horner, Matina S. Toward an understanding of achievement-related conflicts in women. *Journal of Social Issues,* 28(2):157-175, 1972.

Achievement motivation. Sex-role perceptions. Stereotypes. Self-concept.

A series of achievement-motivation studies conducted over a 7-year period is reviewed in detail within the framework of an expectancy-value theory of motivation. The individual female is said to develop an expectancy that success in achievement-related situations will be followed by negative external and/or internal consequences, as a result of a widely held societal stereotype. This stereotype views competence, independence, competitiveness, and intellectual achievement as basically inconsistent with femininity, even though positively related to masculinity and mental health. It is hypothesized that a motive to avoid success is thereby aroused in otherwise achievement-motivated women and inhibits their performance and levels of aspiration.

Male and female college students, female junior high and high school students, and female administrative secretaries in a large corporation were administered the standard Thematic Apperception Test for the achievement motive, using verbal rather than pictorial cues. A verbal cue connoting a high level of accomplishment in a mixed-sex competitive achievement situation was added. A simple present-absent system was used for scoring fear of success imagery. Some subjects also responded to a questionnaire and had intensive interviews which explored the behavioral impact of the motive to avoid success. Fear of success was investigated as a function of age, sex, educational and ability levels, general positive achievement motivation, and social environment.

Fear of success was found more often among females than among males and increased with age, educational level, and ability (i.e., probability of achieving success) for the females. This fear was most often exhibited by females in mixed-sex competitive situations, rather than in noncompetitive but achievement-oriented ones. It is concluded that highly competent and otherwise achievement-motivated young women, when faced with a conflict between their feminine image and development or expression of competence, adjust their behaviors to an internalized sex-role stereotype. Impairment of the educational and interpersonal functioning of those high in fear of success was found. Some possible causative mechanisms and possible consequences of the motive for both the individual and society are discussed. (19 references)

256
Houts, Peter S., and Entwisle, Doris R. Academic achievement effort among females: Achievement attitudes and sex-role orientation. *Journal of Counseling Psychology,* 15(3):284-286, 1968.

Sex-role perceptions. Achievement motivation. Academic achievement. High school girls.

The relationship of academic performance to achievement motivation was investigated, with special attention to the modifying effect of sex-role orientation—perception of achievement goals as acceptable or nonacceptable within the female role. It was hypothesized that, if masculine competitive behavior were seen as appropriate for the female role, there would be a relationship between achievement attitudes and school grades (with verbal ability held constant), but not otherwise.

Subjects were 405 tenth-grade girls from a wide range of socioeconomic backgrounds. A questionnaire measured need for achievement. The three questions on achievement attitudes dealt with the importance of getting high grades and with competition for grades with boys and with other girls. The questionnaire also included items on attitudes toward women's role. Sex-role orientation was measured on a 10-point scale based on preference expressed between two contrasting descriptions of "what women should be like." Verbal ability scores and grades in English and social science were also obtained. Subjects were grouped by verbal ability, sex-role orientation, and achievement attitudes.

A statistically significant interaction was found between sex-role orientation and achievement attitudes for the "competition with boys" and the "importance of high grades" questions. Grade-point differences between subjects with high and low achievement attitudes were significant on only the "competition with boys" question and for only the masculine sex-role orientation group. The achievement-related attitudes that seem crucial to actual achievement for the masculine-oriented group and those possibly relevant for the traditional group are discussed. (17 references)

257

Levitin, Teresa, A., and Chananie, J. D. Responses of female primary school teachers to sex-typed behaviors in male and female children. *Child Development,* 43:1309-1316, 1972.

Teacher influence. Sex-typed behavior. Aggression. Dependency. Achievement. Elementary school students. Female teachers.

An experiment was designed to test two alternative hypotheses about primary school teachers: That teachers fundamentally evaluate behaviors of young children on their effect rather than on their sex-appropriateness, or that teachers expect, encourage, and reward traditional sex-typed behaviors. Assertiveness/aggressiveness in boys and dependency in girls were the sex-typed behaviors considered. Achievement behavior was also examined as an example of a non-sex-typed behavior.

Subjects were 40 female first- and second-grade teachers from nine suburban, middle-class schools in a large Midwestern public school system. A 10-minute, three-item questionnaire asked each teacher to rate two hypothetical children as if they were children in her classroom. The three questions dealt with approval of the behavior, liking for the child, and typicality of the child's behavior for his or her sex. Responses were made on a seven-point scale. Each hypothetical child had a specifically male or female name and was described as performing either a dependent, aggressive, or achievement behavior. Each teacher rated one of the four possible pairings of male or female with dependent or aggressive behavior, and one of the two possible pairings of male or female with achievement behavior. Achievement results were analyzed separately from dependency/aggression results.

Teachers approved of dependent behavior more than aggressive behavior regardless of the sex of the child. Dependent girls were liked significantly more than aggressive girls, but there was no significant difference in liking between dependent boys and aggressive boys. In neither condition was there a significant difference in ratings when sex alone was considered. Achievement behaviors were liked and approved of more than either dependent or aggressive behaviors. The achieving girl was more liked, but not more approved of, than the achieving boy. Results, which partially supported both hypotheses, are tentatively attributed to a distinction between personal and professional orientations in the teachers' evaluations under different instructions (liking or approval). (11 references)

258
Liljeström, Rita. Sex roles in the mass media and books for the young. [Könsroller i ungdömsbocker och massmedia.] In: *Kynne eller Kon.* Stockholm: Raben o Sjögren, 1966. p. 73-95.

Children's books. Sweden.

Sex roles in the mass media in Sweden were investigated in relation to exposure to particular types of literature and how the central figure in girls' and boys' literature is presented. Swedish school children between the ages of 12 and 14 (N=456) were asked to give the title of a book they had read during the winter vacation and the titles of two other books they had read. The books were categorized by topic.

The findings showed that more adventure books were selected by both boys and girls. As their second choice, girls tended to read books about nurses, stewardesses, and other popular, glamorized occupations. No classical books were chosen by girls and all topics were related to the conventional female role in traditional occupations. The boys' most frequent second choices were six classic books representing a patriarchal world. In general, girls chose stories that took place in settings similar to their own surroundings, whereas boys preferred wilderness or fictional settings.

A sample of five adventure books and 20 others was selected for examination of the presentation of the central figure and the verbal expressions used by the protagonist. Verbal expressions were categorized as positive phrases, neutral and initiating phrases, neutral questions, and negative phrases. They were further distinguished by the person spoken to: Equals of the same sex, a mixed group including older people, equals of the opposite sex, and remaining groups. In girls' books, the central figure expressed more verbal emotions, with the exception of aggression, than in books for boys. The protagonist in books for girls also had significantly more interactions with persons of the opposite sex and adults. In representation of the central figure, the female role in boy's literature differs conspicuously from the male role and also from the female role as presented in girls' literature. The male role, however, is similarly presented in both kinds of books.

Role expectation derives from learning patterns of behavior as related to personal appearance and achievements. The analysis showed that the books chosen by girls deal largely with clothing and appearance, whereas the boys' books give only limited descriptions of these aspects. (6 references)

202 SEX ROLES: A RESEARCH BIBLIOGRAPHY

259
Slee, F. W. The feminine image factor in girls' attitudes to school subjects. *British Journal of Educational Psychology,* 38:212-214, 1968.

Sex-role perceptions. Junior high school students. Academic interests. Great Britain.

Analysis of boys' and girls' attitudes toward secondary school subjects was expected to reveal sex differences in the structure of their attitudes resulting from differing role perceptions. The 265 male and 248 female students, ages 12 to 14, were a representative sample of secondary modern schools in Lancashire County, England. Subjects were stratified by age and size of school. To yield 16 variables in addition to child's age, a test battery measured general attitude toward school, attitudes toward 11 school subjects, practical and academic interests, and two aspects of personality. The 11 school subjects included handicraft and technical drawing for boys only, and housecraft and needlework for girls only.

Factorial analysis showed the boys' responses to school subjects to be based on subject content, whereas the girls' attitudes appeared to be strongly influenced by their perceptions of their future role, i.e., the "feminine image" factor. Age was a factor in increasing mechanical scientific interests for boys and in housecraft, art, and music pursuits for girls. Boys' conceptions of their sex role were apparently more generalized, and a masculine image factor was not readily identifiable. (5 references)

260
Thagaard Sem, Tove. Sex roles and motivation for higher education. [Kjönnsroller og studiemotivering.] Norges Almenvitenskapelige Forskningeråd. Oslo: Utredningsavdelningen, 1967. 131 pp.

College attendance. Norway.

The relationship between sex roles and motivation for higher education in Norway was investigated, both separately and in connection with students' social, geographic, and educational backgrounds. The main hypotheses were that motivation for academic studies would be correlated with high ability, having parents with high socioeconomic status, and being brought up in urbanized, central areas.

Only about 20 percent of the sample population of students were women, although the percentage of women increased from 17 to 24 percent in the period studied (1946-58). However, the distribution of women's choice of subjects to study did not change significantly over time. The dropout rates from institutions of higher education were greater for women than for men; only 33 percent of the female students graduated, compared with 75 percent of the male students. There were considerably better results for the limited-entry schools than for open universities—80 percent of the women and 93 percent of the men graduated.

The probability of entering and graduating from institutions of higher education increased with the increase in gymnasium grades for both sexes. The gymnasium grades seemed to be more important for women's than for men's motivation for higher education.

The socioeconomic status of parents was an important factor in determining whether students entered institutions of higher education. It was more important for women than for men; about 60 percent of the female students and about 40 percent of the male students came from higher socioeconomic strata. There was also a tendency for more female students coming from higher strata to graduate than those from a lower strata. This was not the case among men. Neither degree of urbanization nor geographic location influenced the probability for graduation.

The differences in higher education between men and women can to a large extent be explained by the sex roles of the society. First, the man will probably be more motivated to graduate than the woman because this will enable him to fulfill his prescribed duty of supporting a family, whereas good education is of little use to the woman in her duty as a mother. Second, the attitudes and behavior necessary to complete higher studies might be in conflict with those we expect from women. Third, the women from higher socioeconomic strata may achieve more success in higher education because of the less traditional roles for women in these classes than in lower strata. (68 references)

261
Weitzman, Lenore J.; Eifler, Deborah; Hokada, Elizabeth; and Ross, Catherine. Sex-role socialization in picture books for preschool children. *American Journal of Sociology,* 77(6):1125-1150, 1972.

Children's books. Stereotypes.

The treatment of sex roles in illustrated children's books was examined on the premise that picture books play a large part in socializing the child at an early age, in teaching "appropriate" behavior. Portrayal of females in roughly half of the pictures would indicate a lack of bias in the books, since women comprise 51 percent of our population. The study focused on a content analysis of all Caldecott Medal-winning books since 1938 and a more intensive analysis of the 18 winners and runners-up for the past 5 years. Additional reading of several hundred picture books and an investigation of other types of children's books were undertaken to ensure the representativeness of the sample.

Results showed that women were greatly underrepresented in the titles, central roles, and illustrations. The sample of 18 prize-winning books illustrated 11 males for every one female. Where women did appear, their characterizations reinforced traditional sex role stereotypes: Boys are active, girls are passive; boys lead and rescue others, girls follow and serve others. Adult men and women were also sex typed: Men engage in a wide variety of occupations, but women are wives and mothers. Results of the large-scale investigation indicated that the average book for children is even more sex stereotyped than the Caldecott winners. (41 references)

World of Work

262
Angrist, Shirley S. Leisure and the educated woman. *American Association of University Women Journal,* 60(1):10-12, 1966.

College educated women. Lifestyle. Leisure.

As part of a research project on the role outlook of educated women, this study examines how the life situations of college educated women affect their leisure pursuits. The 318 respondents to mailed survey questionnaires were alumnae from the classes of 1949, 1950, 1959, and 1960, and ranged in age from 24 to 40. Most respondents had majored in business studies or home economics, although other college majors were represented. Of the nonmarried women, 95.5 percent were working at least 20 hours a week, as were 75 percent of those who were married but childless.

Only 10.7 percent of the mothers were gainfully employed, although another 29 percent expected to be working within 5 years.

An inventory of 38 leisure activities was categorized into three basic areas: Community welfare, self-enrichment, and recreation. An analysis of questionnaire responses showed that the subjects were only moderately active in leisure pursuits. Educational factors such as undergraduate major and grades did not appear to differentiate the subsequent leisure patterns of alumnae.

Specific combinations of conditions, however, did characterize women who are more active or less active in leisure pursuits. Greatest participation in leisure activities is by married women in their late thirties with school-age children and without outside employment. Least participation is found in homes with preschoolers. Women tend to increase their leisure activity as children reach school age, even in homes with domestic help. Women with only lower school age children far exceed the other women in community welfare activities; women with preschoolers tend to spend more time in recreational activities; single alumnae and childless married women engage primarily in nonorganizational, self-enrichment activities. (No references)

263
Astin, Helen S. Factors associated with the participation of women doctorates in the labor force. *Personnel and Guidance Journal,* 46(3):240-246, 1967.

Professional women. Career predictors. Graduate education.

This study of the employment status and career commitment of women doctorates focuses on the personal and environmental factors associated with their labor force participation. The final study sample was 1,547 women, comprising 80.1 percent of the population of women who earned their doctorates in 1957 and 1958. Subjects were mailed a 41-item, structured questionnaire on work experience, marital status, awards and achievements, publications, domestic and community activities, career development problems, and other personal data. A stepwise multiple regression analysis was used to investigate the effects of 28 personal variables and 19 environmental variables on employment outcomes.

Ninety-one percent of the women were found in the labor force 7 to 8 years after completion of the doctorate; 81 percent were working full time. Being married and having preschool children were the major reasons stated for nonparticipation in the labor force. Women who married after the doctorate, rather than during or before graduate school, were less likely to be working full time. The married woman doctorate who persisted in her career had shown an early career interest, as measured by such activities as being a graduate assistant while in training, or a postdoctoral fellow, or having had a full-time job immediately after completion of the doctorate. The husband's income and occupation also affected employment patterns. The influences of other personal and environmental factors and of certain job and professional characteristics are also examined and discussed. (5 references)

264
Astin, Helen S. *The Woman Doctorate in America: Origins, Career, and Family.* New York: Russell Sage Foundation, 1969, 196 pp.

Professional women. Career patterns. Lifestyle. Career predictors.

This book reports on an intensive investigation of the familial and academic backgrounds and the career development of professional women. Primary concerns are influences on career choice, work patterns, and occupational achievements, and the interaction between family and career. Subjects were 1,653 women who had received doctorates from 108 American educational institutions in 1957 and 1958. Of these women, 1,547 completed a mailed questionnaire on work experiences, marital status, awards and achievements, publications, domestic and community activities, problems during career development, and other personal data; 106 women completed a shorter form of the questionnaire. Six of the women doctorates in the sample provided autobiographical sketches emphasizing events and forces that influenced their educational and occupational development. High school data on aptitude and achievement and other data collected at the time of doctoral graduation were also obtained to provide a base for longitudinal consideration of several factors.

At the time of the survey, 91 percent of the women who had received their doctorates in 1957 and 1958 were employed. Almost half had stayed with the same employer, and an additional 30 percent had changed jobs only once since receiving their degree. Less than one-fifth of the fully employed had ever interrupted their postdoctoral careers. These interruptions were primarily for childbearing and childrearing and averaged about 14 months. A little over half the sample had married, over half of them to men of comparable educational attainment. Over half the subjects were full or associate professors in a variety of academic disciplines.

The most prevalent obstacles to their career development were the scarcity of domestic help and employer discrimination. Based on these findings, a number of implications for action by guidance counselors, educational institutions, social service planners, and employers are suggested. Implications for future research are also included. (37 references)

265

Astin, Helen S.; Suniewick, Nancy; and Dweck, Susan. *Women: A Bibliography on their Education and Careers.* Washington, D.C.: Human Service Press, 1971. 243 pp.

Female role. Employment. Education. Sex-role development. Sexual discrimination.

This bibliography contains abstracts of the research literature concerning the educational and occupational status of women. The majority of the articles, monographs, and books included were written since 1960. However, some especially pertinent literature from the fifties is also included. References are classified according to the following topics: Determinants of career choice; marital and familial status of working women; women in the world of work; developmental studies on sex roles, identification, and socialization; history and economics of women at work; commentaries and policy papers; and women's continuing education. Material is also indexed by author and subject. Key subject headings preface each abstract. The two introductory essays consider trends in research and implications for future study and discuss some of the ideologies reflected in the research on women. (352 references)

266

Bachtold, Louise M., and Werner, Emmy E. Personality characteristics of women scientists. *Psychological Reports,* 31:391-396, 1972.

Professional women. Scientists. Personality differences.

The personality characteristics of women prominent in the chemical and biological sciences were assessed and compared with those of women in general and those of eminent men scientists. All women listed as biologists, microbiologists, chemists, and biochemists in *Who's Who in America* and *Who's Who of American Women* were asked to complete the Sixteen Personality Factor Questionnaire (16PF) and a checklist regarding employer, position, and age. Of the 267 women contacted, 146 responded.

The successful women in biology and chemistry differed markedly from women in the general population on 9 of the 16 traits studied. As a group, the scientists tended to be more serious, less sensitive, more confident, more dominant, bolder, more intelligent, more aloof, more radical, and less group-dependent than women in general. On the other hand, their composite profile was strikingly similar to that of the men in biology and physics. They did not, however, show the variance in personality profiles according to professional functions and field of employment which the men scientists showed. Results indicated a generalized "scientist" personality profile across sexes which is different from that of either men or women in the general population. (14 references)

267
Bäcklander, Cecilia, and Powell-Frith, Ella. *Women and work.* [*Kvinnor och arbete.*] Stockholm: TRU, 1971, 70 pp.

Female role. Sweden. Social equality. Female employment.

This book was written to accompany and supplement a 1972 Swedish Broadcasting Corporation radio series on women's role in society. Two ideologies are represented in the debate about a housewife's life choices. The moderate ideology accepts the dual role of women and tries to find the best and easiest ways to combine the roles. This view holds that a woman's life is divided into three parts. The first is when she first enters the labor market; the second, her childbearing and childrearing period; and the third, when she returns to the labor market. The goal for moderates is that every woman be given a free choice as to when she wants to start the third period. The radical ideology aims at equality between men and women. Women should be socially and economically independent of men. To reach this independence, they must have equal levels of education and training for the labor market. Equality also has to be achieved within the family. The radical ideology rejects the dual-role concept and argues for one role for both men and women—that of human beings. In this role, the responsibility for upbringing of children is shared.

Some statistical evidence is introduced to support both views. In a study of housewives desiring employment outside their homes, about 50 percent wanted to work because it would improve their contacts with other people. The second most common reason was to earn their own money (35 percent). Another study on the mental health of housewives showed that the use of tranquilizers and sleeping pills was much less frequent among women with full-time jobs than among housewives with older children. During the last decade, the demand for adult education has grown and there has been a constantly increasing demand for women in the labor market. However, women get lower incomes than men, and women are the first to be laid off in periods of unemployment. Low-income work is often dull, heavy, dirty, and noisy; offers a minimum of social benefits; and is usually subject to dictatorial supervision. The low-income worker's opportunities to make decisions and plan his or her work are limited, leading to feelings of alienation and dissatisfaction. Recommendations are made for working women to improve their status. (34 references)

268

Baruch, Rhoda. The achievement motive in women: Implications for career development. *Journal of Personality and Social Psychology*, 5(3):260-267, 1967.

Achievement motivation. College educated women. Career patterns.

Two hypotheses were tested: That there is a temporal cycle in the level of achievement motive (n Ach) associated with a woman's age and family situation, and that high n Ach is associated with return to paid employment. Subjects were 137 Radcliffe alumnae living in the Boston area who had graduated 5, 10, 15, 20, or 25 years previously. Scores of n Ach for each Radcliffe subject were provided by stories written in response to pictures evoking achievement imagery. The mailed test materials also included inquiries on marital status, number of children, and employment status.

The group 5 years out of college had a disproportionate number of women with high n Ach scores, but the sample 10 years after graduation showed a lower level of achievement motive. Compared with the 10-year sample, the 15-year sample showed a recovery of n Ach. The association between n Ach as measured by stories of the female pictures and career pattern was high for women 20 and 25 years out of college. In these groups, subjects with high scores tended to have careers, whereas those with low and medium scores tended not be employed. There was no significant relationship between career pattern and n Ach scores for the 15-year group. However, a developmental sequence suggests a timelag between increased achievement motive and increased participation in employment, due to childrearing. Family data indicated that the number of children reaches a peak for the group 15 years after graduation.

The hypotheses were tested in a nationwide sample of 763 women. Neither hypothesis was confirmed in the nationwide sample, although in a subsample of college educated women the temporal pattern of n Ach resembled that of the Radcliffe sample. (27 references)

269

Bass, Bernard M.; Krusell, Judith; and Alexander, Ralph A. Male managers' attitudes toward working women. *American Behavioral Scientist*, 15(2):221-236, 1971.

Female employment. Male managers. Stereotypes.

Male managers' attitudes toward working women were studied in relation to the managers' age, experience, and level in organization. The sample was 174 Rochester, N.Y., males, ages 21 to 66, who held full-time management and staff positions and were attending graduate management classes. Subjects completed a 56-item opinion questionnaire on current stereotypes, attributes, and issues about women in the labor force. Only 40 unfavorable items were considered in the factor analysis.

Managers as a whole agreed that there should be societal norms and etiquette defining interaction between men and women. They were most in accord with negative statements concerning women's dependability and supervisory potential. They agreed less with unfavorable statements regarding women's capabilities, emotionality, lifestyle, and alleged lack of career orientation. Age was not significant in determining their willingness to accept women as work equals, but married subjects were more likely to regard women as lacking career orientation. High-level managers tended to regard women as undependable employees. Men who did not work with women had more positive regard for them than men who did.

Possible explanations for and implications of this last finding are explored. (12 references)

270
Bastide, Henri. Women's work in the country. [La tâche des femmes a la campagne.] *Ésprit,* 295:938-945, 1961.

France. Urban-rural differences. Household tasks.

This study of the comparative conditions of urban and rural French women is based on data collected by the National Institute of Demographic Studies in 1958. A sample of 1,650 rural women, drawn from diverse social milieu, recorded how they utilized their time within a given 24 hours. They recorded the nature and duration of all of their activities in diary form. A similar study was performed on a sample of urban women in the same year.

Both rural and urban women spend a high proportion of their time working, and in both cases the amount of working time increases with the number of children. However, the fertility rate is higher in the country than in the city, and the working conditions for women are more difficult there with respect to housing quality, household appliances, domestic help, and isolation.

The farmwife can only escape these conditions by migrating to the city. If the urban migration of women is to be controlled, rural living conditions will have to be raised to the level of urban standards, so that rural residents can also profit from technical progress and escape from their isolation. It is concluded that it may be desirable to revitalize the countryside by consolidating communities to establish social, medical, scholarly, cultural, and commercial institutions to improve rural living conditions. (No references)

271

Baude, Annika. Employers and women. [Arbetsgivarna och Kvin-norna.] *Könsroller, en Debatt om Jämställdhet.* Stockholm: Prisma, 1965. pp. 58-79.

Sweden. Female employment. Employee behavior.

This analysis concerns Swedish employers' attitudes toward the employment of women. In a comparison of two studies of employers' attitudes, one in the late thirties and one in the mid-sixties, the same arguments against female employment were found. Each of the major reasons given for not employing women is evaluated on the basis of statistics compiled by the Central Bureau of Statistics.

Women are assumed to have a short duration of employment. A study on the mobility of white-collar workers in 1962 showed that the female stability rate was only 8 percent lower than the male. However, this lower percentage is explained by the younger age of the female labor force—in industry, the average age of the female worker is 25 years and the average age of the male is 40. Age is also a factor in women's higher absenteeism rate; Absenteeism is directly correlated with age, remuneration, and working status. Women workers tend to be young, underpaid, and employed in unskilled jobs. Women also are the family member chosen to stay home to care for sick children. Women themselves are often sick over longer periods of time than men, possibly due to their double burden of work and household duties. Also, men, as primary supporters of the family, can less easily afford to be absent.

The general assumption that industry requires physical strength has led many unemployed women to avoid factory work. Classification of each factory position according to its physical strength requirements could increase the number of women applying for many positions. This method was highly successful at one large factory, increasing its female force from 6 to 25 percent. There is considerable reluctance to employ women with young children because it is assumed that they will be frequently absent and unwilling to work overtime. More day care centers and opportunities to work part time would facilitate the employment of women with small children. (11 references)

272
Bowers, John Z. Women in medicine: An international study. *New England Journal of Medicine,* 275:362-365, 1966.

Professional women. Medicine. National differences.

Educational statistics and personal impressions provided by physicians from Europe, Australia, Asia, sub-Saharan Africa, Latin America, and the United States are reported to assess international trends for women entering the medical profession. The highest proportions of women M.D.'s were found in Eastern Europe—30 to 85 percent of all M.D.'s. Western Europe, Latin America, and Asia came next, with several countries in the 20-to-35 percent range. The figures are 6 to 13 percent in Spain, Brazil, Guatemala, Iran, Pakistan, Japan, and Taiwan. In Thailand, admission rates for women had reached 44 percent in 1949, but were then intentionally limited to 25 percent. In several East Asian countries, particularly where the Chinese influence has been strong, there are powerful cultural traditions which favor women's entering medicine. But in Latin America, the trend is definitely upward even without such influences. In sub-Saharan Africa, the low percentages found (7.7 percent in Nigeria and Uganda) appear to be the result of shortages of premed teachers and of secondary-school facilities for girls, rather than the traditional woman's role.

There is a worldwide increase in the number of women preparing for medical careers. The United States, though participating in this trend, has one of the lowest figures (9.1 percent) of any of the countries surveyed. More women in the United States are interested in medical and other scientific careers, but the inflexibility and duration of medical training and an antifeminine attitude in the medical establishment tend to discourage female students from pursuing a medical career. Women's greater control over their reproductive functions should make such careers more feasible, as would greater flexibility in medical education and provision of high-quality child care for children of physician mothers. It is noted that women could be of particular value in medical specialities that do not attract adequate numbers of men, such as pediatrics, child psychiatry, and preventive medicine and public health. (6 references)

273
Brown, Judith K. A note on the division of labor by sex. *American Anthropologist,* 72(5):1074-1078, 1970.

Sex-typed occupations. Subsistence activities. Child care.

A critical reassessment of the scant theoretical literature and of some ethnographic data dealing with the division of labor by sex suggests the need for a reinterpretation of women's economic role. Earlier explanations of sex typing of labor theorized physiological, psychological, and cultural causes. However, this new interpretation states that the degree of women's participation in subsistence activities depends upon their compatibility with simultaneous child care responsibilities.

Nowhere in the world is childrearing primarily a male responsibility, yet only a few societies exempt women from subsistence activities. The range of economic pursuits substantially involving women remains universally narrow, however, despite proven female proficiency at certain tasks involving great strength and endurance. If the economic role of women is to be maximized, either their responsibilities in child care must be reduced or the economic activity must be receptive, interruptible, not dangerous, and close to home. (28 references)

274
Cartwright, Lillian Kaufman. Conscious factors entering into decisions of women to study medicine. *Journal of Social Issues,* 28(2):201-215, 1972.

Medical students. Career aspirations.

The conscious motivations of female medical students for attending medical school were explored and compared with those of male medical students. Subjects in this study were 58 female students, ages 22-37, attending the University of California School of Medicine. Unstructured interviews were conducted with subjects from the 1964-67 entering classes, and the psychological test scores of 102 students from incoming 1960-67 classes were used. These tests included the Adjective Check List (ACL), the California Psychological Inventory (CPI), and the Strong Vocational Inventory Blank (SVIB).

External supports and internal needs are discussed in an inductive analysis of the total 173 reasons supplied by the subjects. No single motive was endorsed by all subjects, but encouragement from others was most frequently mentioned. Other conscious reasons often cited included longstanding interest, self-development motives, and altruism.

A review of earlier studies indicates that men and women share certain key motives for entering medical school. However, self-discovery and self-expression via work may be more significant goals for women than men, since more women tend to have life options other than working. Entering women medics also scored significantly higher than men on the Achievement via Independence scale of the CPI, which suggests their greater self-sufficiency and inner-directedness. Economic and prestige factors, as well as the unreachability of other occupations, were seldom mentioned by women, in contrast to male responses. (29 references)

275
Collver, Andrew, and Langlois, Eleanor. The female labor force in metropolitan areas: An international comparison. *Economic Development and Cultural Change,* 10(4):367-385, 1962.

Female employment. National differences. Economic development. Employment trends.

This cross-national study examines trends in modern woman's labor forces participation, effects of this development, and sources of resistance to it. Analysis centers on women's work-participation rates and the composition of the female labor force in the metropolitan populations of 38 countries of varying levels of economic development. These countries are distributed as follows: 16 in Middle and South America, 7 in Africa and Asia, 3 in North America, 2 in Oceania, and 10 in Western and Southern Europe. A three level classification of economic development was made on the basis of per capita energy consumption and percentage of male labor force employed in non-agricultural pursuits.

Women's work-participation rates, in contrast to male rates, manifest a remarkably high variability. This variability is discussed in relation to variations in economic organization and prevailing family system. The mean female work-participation rate in countries of the top economic class (39 percent of the work-age metropolitan population) was found to be only eight points above the next economic class, suggesting that overall female participation rates do not increase with economic development. Economic development appears to produce a decline in certain occupations and an increase in others; private domestic service is an example of an occupation which declines.

Four patterns of female work-participation associated with different social and economic contexts are outlined. When female labor force composition is placed in the context of the total labor force, statistics indicate that economic development is accompanied by increasing proportions of all workers in manufacturing, a decrease in the proportions of workers of each sex in services, and a replacement of male workers by females in commerce. Data examining the relationship between female work-participation rates and birth rates suggest that employment of women is particularly important in underdeveloped areas because of the positive contribution to economic production and the negative effect on fertility. (4 references)

276

Dahlström, Edmund, and Liljeström, Rita. The family and married women at work. In: Dahlström, Edmund, ed. *The Changing Roles of Men and Women.* Boston: Beacon Press, 1971. pp. 19-58.

Working wives. Family structure. Female employment.

This broad overview outlines variables in modern industrial society affecting married women's position in the home and in the labor force. Data are based on statistics and studies from Sweden and other industrialized countries. Low fertility rates among women of childbearing age, the decreasing average number of children per family, longer life expectancies, and higher divorce rates have increased the likelihood of employment for modern women. However, earlier marriage and motherhood have decreased women's vocational training opportunities. Factors that promote female work participation include rising family consumption and standards of living, increasing equal treatment of boys and girls in schools, and the current emphasis on quality rather than quantity of mother-child interaction. These factors are discussed in terms of their effect on the female employment rate and on the family structure.

Other considerations affecting employment involve role division norms within the family: Attitudes of relatives and social circle, ideology regarding child rearing, husband-wife role differentiation, and the social prestige of the housewife versus the working woman. Sex roles and socialization in the family tend to produce a passive role for women which is at variance with the independent achieving role of an occupational career.

Despite changes in the role and lifestyle of women and social climate conducive to wider personal interests, the current view of the family as an isolated and therapeutic unit apart from an anonymous society may continue to keep married women in the nurturant role within the home. (24 references)

277

DeJong, Peter Y.; Brawer, Milton J.; and Robin, Stanley S. Patterns of female intergenerational occupational mobility; A comparison with male patterns of intergenerational occupational mobility. *American Sociological Review,* 36(6):1033-1042, 1971.

Occupational mobility. Occupational inheritance. Mobility barriers. Sex differences.

Female intergenerational occupational mobility patterns were studied on a national basis. Findings were expected to show more restricted mobility for females than for males when compared with already known male occupational mobility patterns.

Data on 2,371 females over 21 who had been in the labor force at any time were obtained from six nationwide samples surveyed between 1955 and 1965. The comparison sample consisted of 20,700 noninstitutional civilian males, ages 20 to 64. Occupations of the female subjects and of their fathers were classified into 10 categories and ranked according to median income and education. The following aspects of mobility were examined: Occupational inheritance, direction and distance of mobility, concentrations of supply and recruitment, relative magnitudes of upward and downward mobility, and the nature of barriers to mobility. A theoretical model of perfect mobility defined by statistical independence of occupational origins and destinations provided a baseline of comparison.

Contrary to expectation, there were no major differences in the patterns for males and females. There was proportionately more upward than downward mobility for both sexes. Barriers to mobility between occupations indicated that having a father in a blue-collar occupation may be more of a handicap to entering a white-collar profession than being a female. It was suggested that role conflict of the female, status attributions of females, and the openness of the occupational system be reexamined in light of these findings. (17 references)

278
Denard-Toulent, Anne. The two ages of women. [Les deux âges de la femme.] *Ésprit*, 295:784-798, 1961.

France. Female employment. Physiological determinants.

A comparative study of the working capacity and output of French women according to age identifies relationships between certain working characteristics of women and their biological status. Detailed questionnaires were sent to working and nonworking women under 40, from 40 to 55, and from 55 to 80 years old. Primarily, the capacity for activity in young women was found to relate to good ovarian functioning and normal pregnancies. Older women who were professionally successful reported gynecologically healthy youths.

It is asserted that women's problems with respect to work are different from men's, physically and morally. Laws must be developed to favor and protect women's unique makeup. For example, a young woman should be able to care for her children without exhausting herself and without denying other options in life. After 40, she should be able to resume the use of skills she had as a young woman. Returning to work after 40 should be regarded as an ideal situation for women. (No references)

279
Dewey, Lucretia M. Women in labor unions. *Monthly Labor Review,* 94(2):42-48, 1971.

Labor unions.

This paper reports on the recent activities of American women as trade union members and union officers and discusses factors influencing female union participation. Data are provided by union statistics and surveys, U.S. Bureau of Labor Statistics studies, and information from discrimination cases brought before the Equal Employment Opportunity Commission.

From 1958 to 1968, the number of women union members increased, but did not keep pace with the increase in women entering the labor force. A major proportion of the total female membership consistently came from 21 unions, each with more than 50,000 women members. The increased number of women union members during the 1960's reflects a recent upsurge of union organization in government and a greater proportion of women union members at the local level.

Although union members generally earn more than nonunion workers in all comparable occupations studied, organized women receive lower wages than all men. As union officials, women have not attained the levels of responsibility and authority proportionate with their membership; women officeholders are concentrated in local unions. There are no female union presidents on a national level; the Executive Council of the AFL-CIO is exclusively male. Specific issues that concern female workers are equal opportunity for entering occupations, seniority rights, pay, promotional opportunities, and the need for day care centers and adequate maternity leave programs. Recently, labor union conventions have begun to take note of these issues. (9 references)

280
Dodge, Norton T. *Women in the Soviet Economy: Their Role in Economic, Scientific, and Technical Development*. Baltimore, Md.: Johns Hopkins Press, 1966, 331 pp.

U.S.S.R. Female employment. Professional women.

This book presents a broad survey of the role of women in the contemporary Soviet economy, particularly in the fields of science and technology. Extensive data are derived from Soviet publications; statistical and empirical studies of the Soviet Union; field observations; and interviews with Soviet officials, scientists, and training and employment experts. Specific topics covered are demographic, social, and economic factors affecting employment; family versus work; education and training; and female participation in the general labor force and in specific occupations and professions. The uses of labor resources of the U.S.S.R. and the United States are compared.

General conclusions are that Soviet policy toward women is complex and perhaps counterproductive, as with programs encouraging higher birth rates versus those encouraging greater female labor participation. Having access to many economic and social means not available to other forms of government, the Soviet Union is better able to rapidly achieve certain of its economic ends. However, despite differences in political mechanisms, it is suggested that other countries could benefit from a study of the Soviet emphasis on the training and utilization of women. (335 references)

281
Epstein, Cynthia Fuchs. *Woman's Place: Options and Limits in Professional Careers*. Berkeley, Calif.: University of California Press, 1970, 221 pp.

Professional women. Role conflict. Sexual discrimination.

This book draws on sociological data to identify the social factors hampering women's participation in prestigious occupational spheres. Areas of discussion and analysis include the cultural values and early socialization processes affecting career orientation as well as the varieties of role conflict faced by female professionals. Role conflict involves the sexual division of labor in marital and family life; the power, authority, and ranking structure of the social system; and institutional pressures encouraging middle-class women to be consumers rather than earners. Suggestions for the reconciliation of professional women's roles concern both personal decisions regarding the allotment of activities and social structures, such as shared husband-wife practices. Data from the author's studies of the legal and academic professions and research on other professions are used to describe the structure and the behavioral norms maintaining the homogeneity of these professions. Possibilities for changes relating to women's participation in professional fields are considered. (144 references)

282

Epstein, Cynthia Fuchs. Encountering the male establishment: Sex-status limits on women's careers in the professions. *American Journal of Sociology,* 75(6):965-982, 1970. Also in: Theodore, Athena, ed. *The Professional Woman.* Cambridge, Mass.: Schenkman, 1970. pp. 52-73.

Professional women. Sexual discrimination.

This broad discussion draws on existing research and census data to examine some of the difficulties experienced by women professionals in fulfilling their career potential. Also discussed are some factors that may mitigate these difficulties. Structured professional processes, such as the colleague system, sponsor-protege relationships, social interactions within organizations, and sex typing of occupations, cause the sex status of women to equal or surpass their occupational status. The dynamics of these processes result in a cultural definition of women as holding a status inappropriate for certain occupations. The practice of female self-exclusion and the role confusions in male-female professional interaction are discussed. Interviews with successful women professionals provide information on patterns of professional life which can prevent or minimize problems faced by women.

It is concluded that a woman is more likely to have a normal career if the environment filters out responses to her sex status which intrude on her professional role, and if she has perfected techniques for handling such responses. Despite recent challenges to the traditions of the professions and the renewed movement toward job equality, it appears that more radical changes are necessary to eliminate the problems of the professional woman. (34 references)

283

Epstein, Cynthia Fuchs. Positive effects of the multiple negative: Explaining the success of black professional women. *American Journal of Sociology,* 78(4):912-935, 1973.

Professional women. Racial differences. Lifestyle.

This study explores the career patterns of black professional women, who are seen as holding two immutable, negatively evaluated statuses.

Thirty-one successful black professional women were interviewed, and the results were analyzed in relation to official census data and prior research. Three major patterns of interaction between statuses which account for the subjects' success in prestigious, male-dominated professions were identified. Focusing on one of the negatively valued statuses may cancel the negative effect on the other. Two statuses in combination may create a new status which has no established bargaining value because it is unique. Because the individual in a unique status is outside the normal opportunity structure, she can choose (or may be forced to choose) an alternate lifestyle. This alternate lifestyle can then create selective barriers which insulate her from diversions from occupational success, thus strengthening ambition and motivation.

Findings are presented regarding access to professional sectors, cultural models of woman as doer, middle-class values in the family, West Indian blacks as a special case, self-confidence, education and its structure, professional schools, marriage, motherhood, and career choices and paths. The maintenance mechanisms of the present stratification system within the professions operate to keep the participation of certain persons low in spite of their possible intellectual contributions. For this small sample of black women, however, these mechanisms are seen to have reinforced their commitment to careers which would normally be closed to them and, by defining them as special cases, to have made it possible for some to rise within the professional structure. (59 references)

284
Eyde, Lorraine Dittrich. Work Values and Background Factors as Predictors of Women's Desire to Work. *Bureau of Business Research Monograph No. 108.* Columbus: Ohio State University, 1962. 88 pp.

Career attitudes. Work motivation. College women. College educated women.

This study investigated the relationships between work values, attitudinal items, background factors, and women's work motivation. Subjects were 60 Jackson College alumnae 5 years after graduation and 70 college seniors. The first questionnaire to the college seniors queried attitudes toward female roles, personal background data, and applicability of a number of work values. Factor analysis of the work-value items produced a general factor and six work-value factors: Dominance-recognition, economics, independence, interesting activity-variety, mastery-achievement, and social relations. These factors formed the basis for two work-value scales—a five-point rating and a ranked scale. The ranked-scale questionnaire was administered to 58 of the seniors; a questionnaire containing both scales plus the original attitudinal and background items was mailed to the alumnae. For both samples, the desire-to-work criterion was based on weighted self-estimations of work motivation under postulated conditions relating to marital status, family size, and income. Each sample was divided into upper and lower halves according to their desire to work, reflecting high or low motivation.

The overall work motivation of the two samples was not significantly different. However, proportionately more value variables predicted the work motivation of the alumnae than of the seniors, perhaps because of the alumnae's greater work experience, additional education, and greater understanding of the dual homemaker-career role. Desire for graduate education was associated with work motivation for seniors; attainment of a graduate degree, for alumnae.

The extent to which subjects believed compromises had to be made in the traditional homemaker role to allow outside employment was related to level of work motivation for both samples. Alumnae with high work motivation desired to have their children later in life and indicated relatively lower salaries as adequate for their husbands. High work motivation alumnae stressed the "masculine" values described in the ranked interesting-activity and mastery-achievement factors, whereas low work-motivation alumnae chose "feminine factors" emphasizing desire for independence and social work outside the home. For seniors, the ranked dominance-recognition and independence work values were related to high work motivation. By using the most valid predictors (work values) from one class and applying them to the other, it was possible to predict significantly the work motivation of members of that class. (49 references)

285
Fogarty, Michael P.; Allen, A.J.; Allen, Isobel; and Walters, Patricia A. *Women in Top Jobs: Four Studies in Achievement.* London: Allen and Unwin, 1971. 328 pp.

Professional women. Great Britain.

This book contains four studies from a larger project on British women's prospects in professional and managerial work and related aspects of family life. These occupational studies are concerned with women managers at two large companies, women directors in business, women in the British Broadcasting Corporation, and women in the administrative class of the Civil Service. The BBC and Civil Service studies include historical accounts of employment of female administrators in these organizations.

Because of the small numbers of professional women in these organizations, most analyses are of a qualitative nature. Data are based on interviews, questionnaires, and employment information. Primary emphasis was placed on young female management trainees and women and men in the 35 to 45 age range who had reached senior positions but were still young enough to be raising families. Senior managers and personnel officers were also consulted for an overall view of male and female career patterns and prospects. The analyses focused on high-level careers for women in terms of availability, recruitment, promotion, and job performance. Common factors in the performance of women and men were examined in relation to various modes of management. The feasibility of adapting careers to women's life cycles and economic advantages of planned approaches by employers to fully utilize highly qualified women are discussed. (0-23 references per study)

286
Fogarty, Michael P.; Rapoport, Rhona; and Rapoport, Robert N. *Sex, Career, and Family.* London: Allen and Unwin, 1971. 581 pp.

Professional women. Career patterns. Great Britain. National differences.

This book reports on an extensive study of factors relating to women's prospects for professional and managerial occupations in Britain. These factors are the conditions of individual, familial, and organizational experience which affect behavior and satisfaction at work, at home, and in other spheres of personal activity. An international review of empirical data on women's roles is included. National data were provided by questionnaire surveys of 2,000 secondary school seniors, 1,000 British university seniors, and British university graduates 8 years out (N=382 men, 483 women) and 209 spouses of the women graduates. Intensive case studies were made of 12 dual-career families and 3 families in which the wives had currently discontinued their careers. The career problems faced by women in contrast to men were explored in relation to the occupational and organizational environments of architects, the Administrative Civil Service, the BBC, women business directors, and women managers in two large companies. All of these substudies were exploratory in nature, although some used quantitative analysis of data.

The effects of differences in male and female work styles and performance are discussed, as well as possible adaptations of employment practices to women's life cycle. A variety of observable career patterns for educated women and their families are traced.

Certain positive steps are suggested to be taken by government and private agencies to increase the number of women in top jobs and to facilitate career and family roles for both sexes. The international review of women's roles includes recent developments in the role ideology and female employment policies of Eastern Europe compared with those of Western Europe, Israel, and the United States. (20-50 references per chapter)

287

Goldman, Nancy. The changing role of women in the Armed Forces. *American Journal of Sociology,* 78(4):892-911, 1973.

Military personnel.

Data on the position of women in the U.S. Armed Forces are discussed historically, focusing on the role strains, the effects of sexual symbolism and ideology, and the organizational resistance of the military in relation to the current women's liberation movement and push for occupational equality. Statistical and other background data were gathered from official documentary sources and military newspapers, Armed Forces personnel studies concerning an all-volunteer system, 34 interviews of women Naval line officers regarding their professional attitudes, and 30 interviews of military officials and personnel officers.

It is concluded that establishing an all-volunteer force will not dramatically increase or change the role of women in the military. A gradual increase in numbers and a slow but steady expansion of assignments are expected for women, although without increasing similarity between men's and women's tasks. Women are not likely to be trained and armed for direct combat, especially given the current military emphasis on deterrence. The Armed Forces will increasingly need to accommodate organizational strains produced by childrearing requirements and changing sexual symbolism, even though the most socially and ideologically militant young women will probably not join an all-volunteer military system. (23 references)

288

Goldstein, Mark L. Blue-collar women and American labor unions. *Industrial and Labor Relations Forum,* 7(3):1-35, 1971.

Labor unions. Female employment. Sexual discrimination. Historical trends.

The history of women in American blue-collar labor is traced from the introduction of the factory system in the early 19th century to the present. Data sources are historical tests, government statistics, studies and surveys of female workers and union members, labor legislation, and legal rulings. Part I involves blue-collar women's status from 1820 until the outbreak of World War I. Hampered by historical precedent, insufficient education and skills, and a lack of financial security and political power, female workers had to struggle against employers and male-dominated unions for decent wages and working conditions. Blue-collar women briefly allied with the middle-class woman suffragists after the Civil War, formed their own protective associations, and were gradually admitted in small numbers to male unions.

Part II concerns the 20th century controversy surrounding protective legislation and its capabilities to shelter or discriminate against women workers. Discussion of blue-collar women's present situation focuses on the Civil Rights Act of 1964 and the Equal Pay Act of 1963. Part III utilizes recent statistics and surveys to consider the actual policymaking power women exert within unions today. It is concluded that, until blue-collar women augment their legal equality with administrative control in both local and international unions, they will continue to face discrimination in work status. (43 references)

289
Goldstein, Rhoda L. Work—an emerging value for daughters of the Indian middle class. *International Journal of Sociology of the Family,* 1(2):186-196, 1971.

India. College educated women. Female employment.

The employment status and attitudes of middle-class women of Southern India were examined to assess changes in definitions of the female role and current trends in women's labor force participation. Subjects were 20 percent of all women who graduated from Bangalore University in 1965 and gave Bangalore home addresses. The 97 women represented bachelor's, master's, medical, and law degree recipients in proportion to the total graduates. Structured interview data on current employment status, attitudes about work, and attitudes of family members were gathered more than a year after graduation. Demographic information was also obtained.

A majority (N=53) of the sample either worked or would like to work. They reported that parents and other family members supported or tolerated this new role. Traditional proscriptions against the employment of middle-class women appear to be diminishing, perhaps in response to such changes as the later age of marriage, increased educational and job opportunities, and economic pressures on the family. The value that middle-class Indians place on education now appears to include daughters, and work has become an established pattern rather than the exception for the college-educated woman in Bangalore.

In line with tradition, however, the family defines what is considered suitable work, maintains strong control over its daughters, and expects them to contribute their salaries to the family as their brothers do. The jobs held by the employed respondents were limited in range, falling into main categories: 60 percent were teachers (at all levels) and 35 percent were employed in clerical positions. Subjects who were living at home and were not studying, employed, or seeking employment represented a somewhat higher income level and class status. However, 85 percent of all subjects responded that, even without financial necessity, they would rather work than stay at home. Almost three-fourths of those who expected to remain at home preferred employment. Although some husbands and in-laws will not allow a new bride to work, others value her economic contribution. When asked whether they think employment helps or hinders a girl in finding a "suitable partner," 37 percent responded that it helps; 23 percent, that it hinders. (17 references)

290
Gubbels, Robert. *The Economic Citizenship of Woman: Reflections on Women's Part-Time Work. [Le Citoyenneté Économique de la Femme: Réflexions sur le Travail Féminin à Temps Partiel.]* Brussels: Free University of Brussels Sociological Institute, 1966. 98 pp.

National differences. Female employment. Part-time employment.

This cross-national study of female employment is based on the premises that the status of women is changing, that women are trying to redefine themselves in relation to society, and that the driving force for both is women's increasing access to the world of work. Data used are from the 1961 Belgian Census, from two opinion polls conducted by the author in Charleroi and Gand, Belgium, and from other research efforts.

The results of the surveys in Charleroi (N=274 women) and Gand (N=252 women) are analyzed and used to describe woman's role in society. The questionnaire queried women's attitudes toward woman's place in society—her place in the home, her interest in politics and organized labor unions, the extent to which husbands should help with housework, etc. Characteristics of working women are discussed, including labor force participation; sex differences in educational level and absenteeism; and the size, composition, and changes in the age and occupations of the female labor force. The last four items were compared cross-nationally with the United States, Canada, and Japan, and with European and African countries. Part-time female workers in Sweden, France, England, and the United States are compared. It is concluded that, although part-time work is a useful step toward inducing women to enter the world of work, the real liberation of women must begin on the psychological level. (38 references)

291
Guilbert, Madeleine, and Isambert-Jamati, Vivianne. *Women Employed at Home. [Travail Féminin et Travail à Domicile.]* Paris: National Center for Scientific Research, 1956. 211 pp.

France. Female employment. Role conflict.

This study of women who work at home for the French clothing industry explores the relationship between working roles and family roles with the objective of identifying problems of working women in general. Interviews with 150 employers and with 2,123 women working for clothing factories were conducted in the metropolitan Paris area. The characteristics described for the sample included working conditions at home, nature of work performed, extra expenses incurred by the work, and regularity of work; attitudes of the women toward working at home; and the reasons for women working at home. The major variables were age, marital status, number of children, and place of birth. Women's psychological motivations for not working are also presented.

Findings suggest similarities between the reasons some women abstain from working at all and the reasons cited by women for working at home—child care, physical handicaps, independence, and ability to maintain the womanly role. Even women with no children or husbands see their vocation as being "women," and thus an inducement to work at home. This same ideological view was expressed across class lines and among women with very poor working conditions at home. These attitudes were especially prevalent among women in rural settings. It is concluded that the study of women working at home may suggest the point at which women's professional life is bound to a traditional conception of their role in society. (77 references)

292
Harmon, Lenore W. Anatomy of career commitment in women. *Journal of Counseling Psychology,* 16(1):77-80, 1970.

Work commitment. Career predictors. College educated women.

In a study of differences between women who are and are not career committed, 169 women who had entered the University of Minnesota from 10 to 14 years earlier were asked to complete a questionnaire on their postgraduate activities. The sample was selected on the basis of high scores on the social worker scale of the Strong Vocational Interest Blank at the time they entered college. The 94 women who reported having a usual occupation on the questionnaire were labeled career committed regardless of current employment status; the 75 women who did not report usual occupation were considered noncommitted. Biographical variables were examined in relation to career commitment.

Career-committed subjects attended college longer, worked more years after leaving college, married later in life, had fewer children, and bore them at more advanced ages than the noncommitted group. However, there were no significant differences between the two groups on measures of intellectual ability as measured by high school rank and the Minnesota Scholastic Aptitude Test. Retrospectively, career- and noncareer-committed subjects reported no differences in their career plans at age 18. The two groups were also similar in reported current levels of accomplishment by their husbands and levels of satisfaction from homemaking and volunteer activities. (5 references)

293
Harmon, Lenore W. The childhood and adolescent career plans of college women. *Journal of Vocational Behavior,* 1(1):45-56, 1971.

Career aspirations. Adolescent females. College women. Career predictors.

To provide information for counselors and others seeking a theory of vocational development in women, this study focuses on occupations ever considered by female college freshmen. The majority of the 1,188 subjects, entering freshman women at the University of Wisconsin-Milwaukee, were under the age of 20, although ages ranged from 16-44. They were asked to report, retrospectively, which of 135 occupational titles they had ever considered as careers. The list of occupations was primarily derived from the Strong Vocational Interest Blank for Women (Part I). The overall popularity of each occupation, the median age at which each occupation was first considered, and the persistence of various preferences were investigated.

The few occupations preferred early in life, such as actress, artist, and nurse, were typically feminine, popularized careers. Later preferences, although more varied, were still largely confined to typically feminine occupations. Housewife was the earliest, most popular, and most persistent vocational preference. Other persistent preferences were in educational and social service occupations. Least persistent preferences involved unusual talent, long training periods, or short, noncollege training courses. Medical, social service, and verbal fields were considered by most of the subjects, with business and clerical-secretarial occupations considered by the fewest.

A comparison of freshman women currently planning careers in social work or medical technology indicated that the two groups have different histories of vocational preferences. Findings in general suggest that the career choices of college women are not random, and that unusual occupational preferences of adolescent girls may be indicators of future vocational behavior. (8 references)

294
Helson, Ravenna. The changing image of the career woman. *Journal of Social Issues,* 28(2):33-46, 1972.

Professional women. Public opinion. Psychological research.

This discussion deals with social determinants of attitudes toward career women and how changes in these attitudes have been reflected in the design, interpretation, and visibility of psychological research. Relevant studies from the 1950's to the 1970's are considered in light of changing cultural trends.

After World War II, societal acceptance of the single or widowed working woman was enlarged to include the married woman, provided her career was financially required and came second to her family. This acceptance was facilitated by women's participation in men's work during the war; women's improved education and earlier completion of childbearing; and a labor shortage of teachers, nurses, and technicians. However, as psychological research from that period indicates, the career woman found less approval than the wife and mother. In psychological research, the variables tested and their interpretation portrayed the career woman as maladjusted and unfeminine. Studies showing career orientation in a favorable light received little attention.

In the 1960's, the deemphasis of women's reproductive role made possible by birth control, the greater number of divorcees and widows supporting their families, and the exposure of discrimination by anti-establishment ideology revised social attitudes. Current research gives a more differentiated and positive picture of career women regardless of their era and concentrates more on needed institutional change and revised sex role concepts to support a new level of women's professional participation. (50 references)

295

Holter, Harriet. Women's occupational situation in Scandinavia. *International Labour Review*, 93(4):383-400, 1966.

Scandinavia. Female employment. Employment trends.

The occupational status of women in Norway, Sweden, Denmark, and Finland is surveyed on the basis of census data and research findings, with special emphasis on Norway. The current public debate in Scandinavia regarding the proper occupational roles of men and women is outlined, and past employment trends for women are reviewed.

Considerable variations exist among the four countries in the percentage of economically active married women. Sweden, Denmark, and especially Finland have a fairly high proportion of employed married women. The proportion in Norway is one of the lowest in Europe, although it is increasing. The present trend is for women to move from basic industries and manufacturing into office work and service roles. The tendency among women to participate in occupational life is more pronounced for the younger, the unmarried, the highly educated, and/or the urban woman. Despite recent formal adoption of the principle of equal pay for equal work in these countries, women tend to hold the lesser status and lower paid positions. Their earnings are thus generally lower than men's, except in civil service and in highly professional and academic work. Men's and women's wages within various occupations are compared. In some occupational areas, women's subordinate positions reflect lower skill levels, but a clear discrepancy exists between women's level of skill and their actual position, especially in the middle-range occupations. Girls are encouraged less than boys to view economic activity as an important part of their lives. As the standard of living rises, more girls are receiving a general education, but tend to stop their education earlier than men do and are less inclined to take special or vocational training or to seek education outside traditionally feminine fields.

Whereas the women's emancipation movements are seen as quite vigorous, the governments follow fairly vague official ideologies of equality. Care is taken to secure sexual equality in new laws and administrative rules, but a few traditional legal inequalities remain. Labor unions have a long tradition of supporting women's causes, but the employers' organizations have little interest in women's occupational situations and have resisted giving equal pay. Proposed solutions to women's occupational problems are discussed, including high-quality child care institutions, more part-time work opportunities, encouragement of women to pursue more and different types of education, reeducation and vocational training, active vocational guidance for women, and the provision of new types of job openings for women. (5 references)

296
Isambert-Jamati, Vivianne. Female absenteeism in the Paris region. [Adaptation au travail et niveau de qualification des femmes salariées.] *Revue Francaise de Sociologie,* 1(1):45-60, 1960.

France. Female employment. Absenteeism.

This article describes a research effort that addressed absentee costs, specifically in the female work force. The study is primarily based on data from the Statistical Division of the General Administration of Labor and Manpower and on information furnished by heads of various companies. The average percentage of absences for salaried workers within 1 year was calculated, using a sample of 3,697 Parisian female workers. The findings show that conflicts between work and life outside work are particularly acute in the female work force. Widows and single women were absent less than any other group, and women with at least one child under 14 years were absent most often. Distance from place of work and length of work week were positively related to rate of absenteeism. (37 references)

297
Kosa, John, and Coker, Robert E., Jr. The female physician in public health: Conflict and reconciliation of the sex and professional roles. *Sociology and Social Research,* 49(3):294-305, 1965. Also in: Theodore, Athena, ed. *The Professional Woman.* Cambridge, Mass.: Schenkman, 1971. pp. 195-206.

Medicine. Professional women. Role conflict. Career patterns.

This study of the medical career patterns of physicians working in public health yielded data pertinent to females as the minority sex in medicine. Three main areas of conflict between the female sex role and the professional role of doctor were initially theorized: The professional role tends to impose limitations on full realization of the female role; the female role tends to limit full realization of the professional role; and female practitioners face particular difficulties in assuming professional duties which are incompatible with female tasks.

A nationwide sample of 481 male and 44 female physicians who have worked in public health showed sex differences on career pattern variables that are affected by sex roles. Factors related to sex role included marital status, full-time employment, income, attitudes toward the entrepreneurial role in medicine, development of specialized interests, attitudes toward public health, and general professional attitudes. Male and female respondents were similar in their socioeconomic origin, religion, age, and medical education.

Study results showed that early marriage or engagement is associated with quite different career patterns for men than for women. At the time of graduation from medical school, females are more likely than males to defer marriage. Entrepreneurial features of medical practice, such as self-employment, independence in work, money incentives, and competitiveness, are of less importance to women. In every comparable medical position, women work for a shorter time than men, and more accept part-time positions. (16 references)

298
Kreps, Juanita. *Sex in the Marketplace: American Women at Work.* Baltimore: Johns Hopkins Press, 1971. 117 pp.

Female employment.

This book surveys the literature on women and work. Specific chapters concern the effects on female employment of such variables as marital status and race, the demand for and supply of women workers, women in the academic professions, the value of women's work in the home and the labor force, home and work in women's life cycle, and legal aspects of sex discrimination in employment. The investigation centered on reasons for women's continuance in the same types of low-paying jobs. Suggestions for improving women's employment situation involve encouraging women to apply for jobs in more diversified "masculine" fields, retraining women to complete with men for these jobs, and paying women who remain at home for their nonmarket work. (142 references)

299
LeVine, Robert A. Sex roles and economic change in Africa. *Ethnology,* 5:186-193, 1966.

Africa. Female employment. Cultural differences. Marital roles.

This cross-cultural examination of two divergent patterns of change in the occupational roles of men and women in Africa was made to determine the resulting effects on husband and wife roles. A traditional ideal of male domination exists throughout the agricultural societies of sub-Saharan Africa. Customs such as polygyny and patrilocality reinforce the subordination of African women to their husbands. Although her occupation as cultivator or trader is generally less prestigious than that of her husband, the typical African woman plays an essential role in the labor force and her occupation is an important part of her self-image.

Differing patterns of economic development have magnified traditional differences between the Bantu agricultural peoples in Kenya and South Africa and certain Nigerian societies, despite their shared patrilineal traditions. In East and South African societies, the pattern of labor migration has enabled husbands to retain economic control while increasing the workload of their wives. Since the traditional ideal has not been challenged there, the overworked women show more aggression toward their children, but they do not feel deprived in terms of status in the society. In the Nigerian societies, economic development has allowed wives to expand their traditional marketing role and thus to attain independent incomes, sometimes exceeding those of their husbands. Men in these societies experience intense feelings of deprivation which result in cultural expressions of hostility to women, fears of sexual inadequacy, and envy of women. The degree of perceived deviation from the traditional ideal of male domination appears to produce the divergent outcomes in various African societies. (15 references)

300

Lopate, Carol. *Women in Medicine.* Baltimore, Md.: Johns Hopkins Press, 1968. 204 pp.

Medicine. Professional women.

This book is an analytic account of the problems faced by female physicians, with suggestions for increasing the proportion of women in American medicine. Data are provided by government statistics, surveys and studies of women doctors, and interviews with a variety of medical students, doctors, administrators, and counselors. Following a review of the history of American women in medicine, contemporary topics considered are: The reasons women do or do not enter medicine, the effect of counseling in high school, the premedical student, women in predominantly male medical schools, the medical school dropout, the female intern, specialization, residency, and practice. The problems involved in combining a medical career with marriage and motherhood are discussed in detail. Specific recommendations include increased financial aid to medical students, more flexible training schedules, and child care tax deductions. It is also emphasized that the solution for increasing the number of qualified female physicians does not lie in having a rigid female medical student quota, but in a social climate that is more conducive to women entering the traditionally male fields. Changes in socialization, education, and counseling are urged to encourage more young women to seriously consider medical careers. (8-30 references per chapter)

301

Márkus, Mária. Women and work (I): Feminine emancipation at an impasse. *Impact of Science on Society,* 20(1):61-72, 1970.

Female employment. National differences.

Women's employment problems are discussed with reference to relevant research and statistical evidence. Despite growing political and legal equality and increased female employment resulting from industrialization, women are still hampered by the burden of home and child care. Women's traditional commitment to the home maintains their status as low-paid, low-level members of the labor force. In the United States, the employment pattern for women involves gainful employment, ceasing at the birth of the first child, and resuming when the children are older. This pattern causes loss of skills and a narrowing of contacts outside of the family. Socialist countries finance child care services, but do little to ease the burden of other household duties. Because of the lower level of technological development in these countries, household chores consume more time than in the United States.

Employment patterns in some countries, such as Hungary, resemble the American pattern of interrupted employment, except that the state supports mothers who stay with their young children. Even in Socialist countries, childrearing is viewed as women's primary purpose. It is suggested that full female emancipation requires an extensive network of services to assume more of the household work to free women for fulfillment of their employment goals. In addition, making homemaking a legitimate, trained profession would allow women who prefer family work to care for several households while other women pursue outside careers. (5 references)

302

Martin, Walter T., and Poston, Dudley L., Jr. The occupational composition of white females: Sexism, racism and occupational differentiation. *Social Forces,* 50(3):349-355, 1972.

Female employment. Racial differences. Discrimination.

This analysis of 1960 U.S. Census data focuses on the degree of occupational differentiation for white females as compared with white males and nonwhite females. An index of dissimilarity measured differentiation among 11 broad occupational categories applied to official data from 66 Standard Metropolitan Statistical Areas (SMSA's). This index ranges from 0 to 100 and represents the percentage of occupational redistribution necessary for one subpopulation to achieve an occupational composition proportionately identical to the other subpopulation. Measures of occupational differentiation by sex, by color, and by sex and color were computed for nine age groups and for all ages combined.

Major variations among SMSA's were found in the degree of occupational differentiation involving white females, even though all measures ignored differences within occupational categories. Differences between white females and nonwhite females (suggesting racial discrimination) and differences between white females and white males (suggesting sexual discrimination) showed similar low and high degrees of occupational differentiation. Possible determinants and consequences of these patterns are discussed briefly. It is speculated that physiological factors will continue to differentiate occupations by sex, but not by color, despite an elimination of sexism. (17 references)

303
Mattfeld, Jacquelyn A., and Van Aken, Carol G., eds. *Women and the Scientific Professions: The MIT Symposium on American Women in Science and Engineering.* Cambridge, Mass.: Massachusetts Institute of Technology Press, 1965. 250 pp.

Professional women. Scientists. Engineers.

This volume consists of the papers and panel discussions presented at a 1964 Massachusetts Institute of Technology national Symposium on American Women in Science and Engineering. The symposium was designed to explore the personal, social, and economic factors affecting women's commitment to scientific professional careers; to report on the current status of women in industrial and academic settings; to examine the employment problems of women; and to analyze women's prospects in these fields. The 21 conference speakers included psychologists, sociologists, educators, employers, and scientists. Empirical and statistical data and a range of personal perspectives are presented on the major topics of: "The Commitment Required of a Woman Entering a Scientific Profession," "Who Wants Women in the Scientific Professions?" "The Case For and Against the Employment of Women," and "Closing the Gap." (0-52 references per chapter)

304

Matthews, Esther. Employment implications of psychological characteristics of men and women. In: Byham, William C., and Katzell, Mildred, eds. *Women in the Work Force: Confrontation with Change,* New York: Behavioral Publications, 1972.

Sex differences. Employment. Cognitive ability. Achievement motivation. Creativity. Stereotypes.

This address before the New York State Psychological Association reviews research on sex differences in such areas as vocational aptitudes, interests and values, cognitive abilities, problem-solving behavior, curiosity and creativity, and achievement motivation. The emphasis of the discussion is on the problems resulting from applying mass data on sex differences to the employment of men and women. Suggestions are made for evoking vocational potential from women accustomed to adjusting to external occupational stereotyping. The social, historical, and psychological contexts and applications of research on sex differences are discussed.

A review of studies of sex differences in cognitive abilities indicates that they have produced conflicting and inconclusive results, except for studies of field independence as a cognitive style, and even those results have been generalized far beyond what the data seem to justify. A discussion of vocational aptitudes and interests points out that aptitude tests in fact measure performance and the results of experience, and that score distributions for the two sexes on vocational aptitude tests show an extensive amount of overlap.

The existing literature on problem solving and risk taking is said to be too sparse to support any generalized conclusions regarding sex differences. Risk-taking studies as they are now constituted consistently show men as scoring higher, but it is quite likely that use of different types of tasks would yield different results. Curiosity and creativity, which can be key factors in adult employment, have been studied mainly in children. Noting that differences in expressed achievement motivation can be shown in the two sexes, the discussion focuses on the conflicts aroused in many women in responding to a need to achieve. The need for researchers to be more discriminating in interpreting research results is discussed. Overall, the discussion calls for a developmental applied psychology and for a form of reporting research results that would constantly direct attention toward human variability. (18 references)

305

Matthews, Margie R. The training and practice of women physicians: A case study. *Journal of Medical Education,* 45(12):1016-1024, 1970.

Medicine. Professional women.

This survey of the recruitment, training, and practice of women physicians focuses on students and house staff at Duke University and doctors in Orange and Durham Counties, N.C. Factors affecting recruitment of women include the small number of female science majors who apply to medical schools, lack of effort by the schools of medicine to recruit female undergraduates, and the financial and academic requirements. Female medical students surveyed considered financial aid and career counseling to be their greatest overall needs; seniors and house staff (interns, residents, and postdoctoral fellows) were most concerned about part-time schedules for training and child care centers.

Of the women doctors in Durham and Orange Counties, 95.7 percent were active professionally; however, few were in high-level hospital or teaching posts. Within an eight-State area, an earlier survey had found that 35 of the 46 inactive physicians under 55 who desired retraining were women. There are, however, few retraining programs in the country. Since it is recognized that the greatest number of women doctors with children drop out of medicine after their internship, several residency programs have been initiated featuring financial aid for child care and schedules which extend training over a longer time period. It was suggested that, despite these program innovations and the changing roles of women in America, female doctors and medical students as a group have not been active enough in pressing administrators and institutions for solutions to their problems. Countering the argument that women's professional training is an economic waste, studies have evidenced women's increasing longevity, long-term medical activity, and entry into such critical fields as pathology and teaching. (7 references)

306

Michel, Andrée. Needs and aspirations of married women workers in France. *International Labour Review,* 94(1):39-53, 1966.

France. Working wives. Working mothers.

French married women were surveyed to discover what actions should be taken to integrate them into the work force. Subjects were 450 women from the Paris area and 100 women from the Bordeaux area. Subjects were asked which measures they considered most likely to improve the position of working women, and whether they would prefer their daughters to learn an occupation and work after marriage or to rely entirely on the income of their future husbands. Replies were analyzed in terms of geographic region, number of children, family income, availability of domestic help, education, employment status and occupation, and whether the family home and furnishings were owned or leased.

For both the Paris and Bordeaux samples, provision of convenient nurseries, training for a well-paid occupation, and a shorter work week were given top priority. Second or third priority choices were shorter travel time to work, canteens and services providing cooked meals, and inexpensive laundries. Nurseries were top-priority choices for women with children, with smaller family incomes, without domestic help, or with lower levels of education. A shorter work week was most likely to be preferred by childless women and those with university education. Manual workers (paid by the hour) gave top priority to a well-paid occupation rather than a shorter work week. Women whose families lease their homes were most likely to emphasize the need for nurseries. A majority of subjects expressed preference for some vocational education allowing their daughters to work despite marriage and motherhood. However, nearly 40 percent of the Bordeaux women, compared with only a third of many Parisiennes, thought their daughters should rely entirely on their future husbands for support. It was concluded that the major obstacle to greater employment and promotion of French married women of all backgrounds is the lack of child care services. (9 references)

307
Noordhoek, Johannes, and Smith, Yrsa. Family and work. *Acta Sociologica,* 14(1-2):43-51, 1971.

Denmark. Working wives. Career patterns. Marital dominance. Household tasks.

This study is based on a survey of married women's employment in Denmark. Factors that influence employment are analyzed and some of the consequences of employment for women and their families are examined. Data were obtained from a representative sample of 2,610 women under 60 years old.

Married women follow five basic patterns of employment, withdrawal, and reentry. Factors influencing a married woman's employment include: Conditions of supply and demand of married women in the labor market, degree of urbanization of the place of residence, the woman's age and vocational training, social status of her family, and age of her youngest child. Vocational training and age of youngest child, respectively, were the most decisive positive and negative factors affecting employment.

The impact of married women's employment is discussed in terms of household duties, division of labor within the family, and family power structure. Two alternative theories of the family power structure are analyzed: That the balance of power between husband and wife depends on each spouse's individual economic, educational, and social resources; and that the husband's and wife's sex-role ideologies determine power within the family. Varied interpretations are offered regarding the effects of certain variables on economic decisionmaking in the family: Family's place of residence (urban, rural), wife's age, her attitude toward the role of housewife, and the relative income and education of husband and wife. It is suggested that the importance of relative resources between the spouses depends heavily on ideological context. (4 references)

308
Oppenheimer, Valerie Kincade. The Female Labor Force in the United States: Demographic and Economic Factors Governing its Growth and Changing Composition. *Population Monograph Series No. 5.* University of California, Berkeley: Institute of International Studies, 1970, 197 pp.

Female employment. Employment trends.

The primary aim of this study is to explain the increase in American female labor force participation during the 20th century. Two distinct trends are considered: The gradual rise from 1900 to 1940 and the unprecedented sharp rise in the work rates of some women after 1940. Analysis of this acceleration centers on demographic, economic, and sociologic variables and their effects on the total female work rate and the work rates of older women and married women. Statistical information is provided by census data, public opinion polls, and labor force studies.

It is concluded from analysis of various factors that the rise in the demand for female labor is the result of basic industrial and occupational shifts produced by postwar economic development. The most rapidly expanding industries offering such occupations as factory and clerical work have for some time been major employers of women. There is some evidence that the rise in the total female work rate resulted from the response of women as a group to the expansion of job opportunities. However, the number of unmarried women and women under 35 years old in the population decreased during the 1940-60 period. This shortage in the preferred female work force produced a broadening demand for older and married women, who were previously discriminated against. As a consequence of the rapid growth of the older and married female labor force, the female labor force as a whole has achieved a moderate growth in the postwar period. (91 references)

309
Oppenheimer, Valerie Kincade. The sex-labeling of jobs. *Industrial Relations,* 7(3):219-234, 1968.

Sex-typed occupations. Stereotypes.

This discussion draws on employment statistics and empirical studies to outline reasons for the development and persistence of "female" jobs in the United States. Historical and current factors that promote the attachment of the female sex labels to jobs and that make and keep many jobs predominantly male are examined. A preliminary consideration is the difficulty of determining the range of largely "female" jobs and the percentage of the female labor force actually concentrated in these jobs.

The combination of their lower cost and high availability has traditionally encouraged the use of women workers in many jobs. To substitute men in such skilled fields as teaching and secretarial work would require a raise in wages and/or a decline in labor quality. Both employers and employees appear tradition-bound in their concepts of certain jobs. Women have traditionally sewn, nursed, and kept house; consequently, they are textile workers, nurses, and domestics. Sex-linked characteristics, actual or imagined, have also contributed to sex labeling of jobs. Many employers assume that women are more manually dextrous and patient in performing routine tasks. A factor discouraging mixed work groups in many occupations is the widespread belief that women are not good supervisors. If men and women were used interchangeably in jobs in fair competition, more women might rise to supervisory positions.

Three factors tending to keep certain jobs predominantly male are career continuity, motivation, and geographic mobility. Career continuity and skills development are likely to be interrupted by women's family life cycle. Being secondary breadwinners and primary family caretakers, women are not expected to have the career motivation of men. Careers involving geographic mobility are closed to married women who give priority to their husbands' careers. Even when a woman has the necessary time, dedication, and mobility for a career in a male field, employers operate on stereotypic ideas about female behavior and are not willing to take long-term risks. (23 references)

310

Oppenheimer, Valerie Kincade. Demographic influence on female employment and the status of women. *American Journal of Sociology,* 78(4):946-961, 1973.

Female employment. Employment trends.

This discussion cites various statistical sources to argue that demographic factors required major changes in female labor-force participation to fulfill the demands of post-World War II American economic development. Prior to the war, there was considerable job discrimination against both older and married women. The decline in discrimination stemmed from a rising demand for female labor which exceeded the supply of traditionally preferred (young, unmarried) female workers. The major reason for the demand for female labor was that, by the early 20th century, women dominated the teaching and clerical occupations—fields that expanded with the country's industrial growth. Recent surveys show no decline in the concentration of women in these occupations.

During the period from 1940 to 1960, the pool of young and single employable women decreased because of the low Depression fertility rate, the high postwar fertility rate (involving more mothers with preschool children), a decline in age at marriage, the rising number of girls in college, and a decrease in the proportion of women remaining single. Employers then turned to married and older women. The greater availability of jobs and rising wages produced incentives for these women to supply the rising labor demands. It is predicted that, despite the postwar population boom, the trends toward increased schooling, controlled fertility, and early marriage will cause the supply of female labor to remain insufficient for the demands of the period 1960-2000. Young married women and mothers with young children will make use of their greater education and more recent training to augment family income. It is concluded that, as more women work for longer periods of their lives, there will be greater dissatisfaction with the lower pay scales and limited advancement of most female occupations. (17 references)

311
Parrish, John B. Women in medicine: What can international comparisons tell us? *The Woman Physician,* 26(7):352-361, 1971.

Medicine. Professional women. National differences. U.S.S.R.

International statistics, with an emphasis on the Soviet Union, are examined to determine why women in countries outside the United States are more highly utilized in the professions, particularly in medicine. The percentage of women physicians and dentists is strikingly lower in the United States than in almost any other country. The reasons why 65 percent of physicians in the Soviet Union are women, however, involve very special and probably temporary factors: The necessity of self-support by the large percentage of unmarried women in the population; the necessity of increasing the very low, real family income, and the desire of women to rise from the manual into the professional class by whatever limited means available to them. Yet medicine is the lowest paid Soviet profession, and less than 5 percent of top-level Soviet medical positions are held by women.

Since U.S.-Soviet comparisons are thus not very meaningful, more intensive study of our own situation is necessary to evaluate the role of the women in U.S. medicine. An alternative approach to utilizing women involves adapting and restructuring medical jobs. The accelerating paramedical movement in the United States is creating many new jobs to meet the demand for adequate health care. Paramedical jobs offer American women wishing to enter medicine shorter term training, flexibility, part-time positions, and an opportunity for continued study to advance to professional positions. (50 references)

312
Perrucci, Carolyn Cummings. Minority status and the pursuit of professional careers: Women in science and engineering. *Social Forces,* 49(2):245-259, 1970.

Professional women. Scientists. Engineers. Career patterns.

The sexual integration of the science and engineering professions was investigated, and selected social characteristics of career and non-career women and men who have similar training were compared. It is posited that careerist women adjust their marital and maternal roles to accommodate professional employment and to minimize the difficulties of their minority sex status in the labor force. Data were collected as part of a larger study of 3,289 male and 300 female post-World War II engineering and science graduates of a large Midwestern university. A mailed questionnaire probed precollege background and college and postcollege experience. Women graduates were classified into four groups: Young-old, length of time since highest degree, careerist-noncareerist, and amount of full-time occupational employment since graduation. Type of work place, principal function, level of technical and supervisory responsibility, and remuneration were compared for initial and current jobs for the B.S. degree recipients only. Family and career sequence patterns were analyzed for the two age groups of women.

Initial employment positions of male and female graduates were relatively similar in levels of technical and supervisory responsibilities, but were dissimilar in salary. This salary disparity favored men and became more pronounced over time. Moreover, current jobs of career women compared with those of men showed men more likely to hold higher levels of career responsibility. Even when amount of work experience, place of employment, and principal job function were comparable, career women earned less than men; this salary difference was twice as great among engineers as among scientists. Among working women and men of comparable education, women were less likely to hold positions in keeping with their employment goals. For these women, a full-time career was related to the temporal ordering of college graduation, employment, marriage, and childbearing.

Of the married women, three-fifths got married after or very near college graduation. Fifty-five percent of the married women were employed prior to marriage, and few married women had children prior to initial employment. Career women were more likely than the noncareerists to be childless. Over half of the mothers became parents prior to the completion of 3 years of marriage. These patterns are discussed by subgroups of age and career orientation as possible adaptations of women to their "deviant" sex status in the professions of science and engineering. (30 references)

313
Pichault, Geneviève. Repercussions on the family of the wife and mother who works. [Les répercussions familiales du travail professionel de la femme mariée et mere de famille.] *Population et Famille,* 22:1-20, 1970.

France. Working wives.

This article explores the French research literature on women's employment in terms of the effect on the family. Research suggests that most women work for financial reasons, although a substantial number are motivated by interest in their trade or by their own personal development; working women do as much housework as others; women who work generally maintain better organized households; although modern appliances make housework easier, they apparently do not make it less time consuming; professional employment enhances the family roles for some women, the determining factor being working conditions, not the fact of working or not; and childrearing continues to be a problem for working women.

The article also briefly reports findings from a survey in France of attitudes and opinions on married life and working wives. Professional aspirations and lifestyles of husbands and wives were compared, as well as their attitudes toward working wives. It is concluded that husbands of working wives tend to appreciate the financial benefits and the personal satisfaction that employment provides their wives. However, for the majority of husbands studied whose wives did not work, the negative aspects of having a working wife predominate. (2 references)

314
Psathas, George. Toward a theory of occupational choice for women. *Sociology and Social Research,* 52(2):253-268, 1968.

Female employment. Career aspirations. Career predictors.

Various approaches to a theory of occupational choice applicable to women are reviewed and analyzed in an effort to foster research on women's entry into occupations and the development of more general theories of occupational entry. The discussion does not attempt to develop a theory, but deals with factors which are particularly important for women and may not operate in the same fashion for men, as well as factors which are of importance for both sexes. Existing studies of occupational choice are also discussed. Various current theoretical formulations are reviewed. The one on which this study is based includes psychological, sociopsychological, historical, socioeconomic, and immediate situational factors. A major thesis of the discussion is that an understanding of the factors which influence the entry of women into occupational roles must begin with the relationship between sex role and occupational role. The explication of "settings" which engender predictable orientations to the occupational world is substituted for the concept of "choice."

Among the primary links between sex role and occupational entry are the intention to marry, time of marriage, reasons for marriage, and the husband's economic situation and attitude toward his wife's working. The pattern of occupational participation and the level at which the occupational system is entered are also strongly affected by the state of finances of the family of origin, since occupational roles vary in the length and expense involved in requisite training and in the immediacy of financial return to the trainee. The influence of social class on occupational entry is discussed in terms of education and occupation of parents; value-orientations shared by the family and members of their social class, including social-mobility aspirations; and the perceived relation between occupation and marital chances. (25 references)

315
Rossi, Alice S. Women in science: Why so few? *Science,* 148(3674):1196-1202, 1965. Also in: Safilios-Rothschild, Constantina, ed. *Toward a Sociology of Women.* Lexington, Mass.: Xerox College Publishing, 1972. pp. 141-153.

Scientists. Professional women. Career patterns. Role conflict.

This essay draws on official U.S. Census and empirical data to examine reasons for the paucity of women scientists and the problems women encounter in combining marriage with a scientific profession. Women employed in scientific and engineering fields in 1960 were less likely than men to have advanced degrees, particularly the Ph.D.; less likely to be employed in industry; and considerably less likely to be married. Women also earned less money and worked fewer hours per week than men. Although women questioned 3 years after college graduation chose as people they admired women prominent in scientific, scholastic, or artistic fields, their own primary choices were to be married to a prominent man and to have accomplished children.

Female respondents to a national study of career development expressed views on female employment that were more liberal than those of males. In terms of behavior, however, most women conformed to their husband's preferences for them: They gave up advanced training or employment for childbearing and rearing, returning to work in middle age. Unfortunately, the scientist's creative peak is reached in the late twenties and early thirties, the years most women tend to devote entirely to their families.

The characteristics typical of successful scientists of either sex are high spatial and mathematical abilities, intense channeling of energy in work, extreme independence, and low interest in social activities. These characteristics are not, however, normally associated with the verbal, dependent, interpersonal socialization of females. It is concluded that, to produce more female scientists, American society must educate both men and women to fulfill a variety of adult roles, counsel women to strive for high occupational roles, provide house-care service firms, and encourage men successfully married to professional women to articulate their experiences and attitudes. (26 references)

316
Roux, Claude. Recent trends in work patterns of women in France. [Tendances récentes de l'activité féminine en France.] *Population,* 25:179-194, 1970.

France. Female employment. Employment trends.

This article, based on census figures, analyzes trends in women's labor force participation in France. According to these figures, the percentage of women engaged in the labor force between 1921 and 1962 declined sharply, but evidence suggests that since 1968 the trend has shifted. Comparisons between working women in 1954 and 1968 are made according to age, marital status, and rural-versus-urban location. The article concludes with the view that the upward trend in the employment of women will continue, particularly in view of the availability of birth control and increased educational opportunities for women. (3 references)

317
Safilios-Rothschild, Constantina. The relationship between work commitment and fertility. *International Journal of Sociology of the Family,* 2(1):64-71, 1972.

Work commitment. Female employment. Fertility. Greece.

This study was designed to challenge the hypothesis that working women comprise an internally homogeneous group with respect to variables affecting family dynamics and level of fertility. Level of work commitment was selected as a variable likely to differentiate significantly among working women; level of fertility was chosen as the dependent variable. Nonworking women (N=550) from all social classes in Athens, Greece, and Athenian working women (N=346) in all occupational categories were interviewed. Subjects' degree of work commitment was measured by work continuity throughout adult life and by questionnaire responses. Their knowledge of, attitudes toward, and practice of birth control methods (KAP) were also assessed. Physiological and anatomical fecundity-infecundity were also investigated in the interviews as a possible modifying variable.

Results revealed the following relationships: (1) When work commitment was high, fertility was low, either because of effective birth control or because of total or partial infecundity; (2) when KAP was high, the degree of work commitment determined whether birth control was practiced for restricting fertility or for spacing; (3) when work commitment was low, KAP did not play an important role in determining the level of fertility—fertility of fecund working women with low work commitment was the same as that of fecund nonworking women regardless of birth control methods used; and (4) when KAP was low, only women who were totally or partially infecund had a high work commitment. Working women in this study did not form a homogeneous group in regard to work commitment or to knowledge of, attitudes toward, and practice of birth control. (23 references)

318

Sandlund, Maj-Britt. Labor market policy for both sexes. [Arbetsmarknadspolitik för båda könen.] *Könsroller, en dabatt om jämställdhet.* Stockholm: Prisma, 1965. pp. 80-94.

Sweden. Female employment. Sexual discrimination. Government policy.

This review of official Swedish Government policy relating to the labor market suggests that the policy discriminates against women. Official statistics show that unemployment is very low in Sweden; however, surveys on the availability of labor disclose very high underemployment among women. In comparison with other countries, women are less advanced on the labor market than would generally be expected. The employment of women varies from 58 to 28 percent in various cities. Many women indicate that they would enter the labor market if there were any suitable possibilities close to their residence.

The government departments have varying views on women's role in the labor market. Some are very conservative in their attitudes. The labor unions seem to be the most liberal. The inequity of the official policy on labor relations is accentuated by the activation of underemployed women during a boom in the economy when labor is scarce, only to have the women return to unemployment when no longer needed.

In spite of the fact that most unemployment exists among women, considerably more men visit the official employment agencies. This is particularly true for the larger urban areas. The distribution of positions among persons seeking employment shows a very marked sex bias. Most women found employment in domestic work, health services, and administrative work, whereas many of the men were placed in industry. In government retraining programs the distribution between the sexes is reasonably even, but men are generally trained for more highly skilled industrial operations and also take much longer courses than women do. Government support is given to those who are willing to move to a new area which offers better employment possibilities; but this opportunity is seldom used by women. Another form of help to the unemployed—emergency works—is given exclusively to men, since it generally consists of construction work. Because such emergency work is unavailable to women, they bear the brunt of structural unemployment resulting from economic shifts and reorganizations. (No references)

319
Sartin, Pierrette. *Women's Promotion. [La Promotion des Femmes.]* Paris:Hachette, 1964. 303 pp.

France. Female employment.

This book utilizes various statistics and other data to challenge several myths that have been advanced about working women in France and adjoining countries. Specific questions discussed relate to the type of work that women orient themselves toward: the conditions under which women work; and the physical, psychological, and intellectual capacity of women. There is also an attempt to question whether the roles of wife and mother are antagonistic to that of career women, and whether women are happy with employment roles. (72 references)

320
Segal, Bernard E. Male nurses: A case study in status contradiction and prestige loss. *Social Forces,* 41(1):31-38, 1962.

Medicine. Sex-typed occupations. Nurses.

The attitudes of male and female nurses regarding their intrahospital status and their status in society were compared. A sample of 22 male and 79 female nurses employed at a private Boston psychiatric hospital were interviewed concerning their attitudes toward nurses of the opposite sex, toward other staff members, and toward their own personal and occupational status inside and outside the hospital.

None of the female nurses but two-thirds of the male nurses questioned physicians' expertise or indicated regret that they were not physicians. Fifty percent of the males and 15 percent of the females indicated they believe that physicians think less highly of nurses than they should. Sixty percent of the male nurses and 20 percent of the female nurses said the public does not grant nurses the prestige they warrant. In general, the male nurses aspire to share the prestige of the male doctors and to maintain a clear differentiation between themselves and the male aides. When asked their view of men in nursing, male nurses indicated first that males and females were equally capable, but then noted that they would feel more comfortable if they were not so outnumbered. Over half the men and 10 percent of the women disliked being supervised by a nurse of the opposite sex. The lower class, less-educated female nurses were more likely to think male nurses effeminate or homosexual.

Male nurses' retrospective accounts of why they entered nursing emphasized the initial goal of a secure job above the manual, semiskilled level. Many male nurses regretted that their lack of education prohibited them from upward mobility into higher medical or administrative positions. Nearly three-fourths of the males and one-fourth of the females indicated that they had not made enough progress in achieving their important goals. In terms of self-placement, 40 percent of the men and 10 percent of the women considered themselves to be below middle class. It is concluded that the number of male nurses will not increase until society revises its negative attitudes about men who do traditionally women's work. (20 references)

321
Shuval, Judith T. Occupational interests and sex-role congruence. *Human Relations,* 16(2):171-182, 1963.

Career aspirations. Adolescent females. Sex-typed occupations. Israel.

The hypothesis of this study was that traditional female role patterns, represented in this case by orthodox Judaism, encourage interest in sex-linked occupations. The occupations specifically considered were nursing and elementary school teaching. Data were drawn from questionnaires on occupational interests and attitudes from a stratified sample of 1,266 Israeli-born and immigrant girls in the 10th, 11th, and 12th grades. Subjects were also asked to indicate the degree of religious tradition in their homes, which were then rated as extremely orthodox, moderately orthodox, or secular.

More girls raised in extremely orthodox families expressed a positive interest on the attitude toward nursing question than did girls from moderately orthodox or secularly oriented families. Girls from extremely orthodox homes were also more likely to select elementary school teaching as their first-choice occupation. An interest in nursing did not preclude selecting another first-choice occupation. The extremely orthodox girls further demonstrated orientation to traditional female role patterns in that they were less interested in work after marriage and had a greater tendency to identify with their mothers or other female figures. Interest in the nursing profession was higher among orthodox immigrants who were experiencing strain with their parents than among Israeli-born girls.

It is suggested that the nursing role, because of its high level of congruence with nurturant and diffuse relationship patterns, provides an acceptable alternative for an unmarried girl who wishes to leave home without deviating from the traditional female role. Teaching, with its more achievement-oriented components, appears to present a less acceptable alternative for these immigrant girls. On the other hand, Israeli-born girls appear to be better able to identify additional occupational alternatives and more willing to break with the orthodox role patterns of their families. (12 references)

322
Shuval, Judith T. Sex role differentiation in the professions: The case of Israeli dentists. *Journal of Health and Social Behavior,* 11(3):236-244, 1970.

Professional women. Dentists. Israel.

The effects of sex and age on professional role performance were explored in a sample of 522 dentists in three Israeli cities. The dentists, one-third of whom were women, were interviewed concerning setting and conditions of practice; factors influencing their decision to enter dentistry; professional interaction through journals, consultation, and conventions; and perceived composition of patient population.

There was evidence for traditional sex-role differentiation in several aspects of dentistry. Women dentists tended to treat more children and more less-educated and lower-class patients. They also tended to be more involved with general dental practice than with a combination of general and specialized practice. To the extent that professionals acquire prestige from the nature of their professional role and from the clientele they serve, women dentists appeared to have less status than men. The female subjects worked fewer hours than men, carried a lighter patient load, read fewer journals, and engaged in less professional interaction with colleagues. It was suggested that these differences reflect the family demands made upon women dentists rather than differences in values between men and women dentists. Men and women dentists tended to be quite similar in relative emphasis they placed on various characteristics of dentistry and on the qualities of the profession which attracted them. (12 references)

323

Stycos, J. Mayone, and Weller, Robert H. Female working roles and fertility. *Demography,* 4(1):210-217, 1967.

Working wives. Fertility. Turkey.

This survey investigated the relationship between female employment status and fertility in Turkey, a developing nation. The sample of 2,700 Turkish married couples was stratified by type of community (village, town, city, or large metropolitan area). Interviews concerned number of children, husband's and wife's education, husband's occupation, wife's employment status, age at marriage, and attitudes toward, knowledge about, and use of birth control.

Only 8 percent of the women surveyed (rural or urban) worked outside the home. Differential fertility was indicated, but not by labor force status. Rural women had more children than urban women, and urban women without schooling had more children than urban women with schooling. The intervening variables of age at marriage and birth control practice were also associated with residence and education but not with employment status. When residence was controlled, knowledge of birth control and attitudes toward family size and birth control showed no significant variation by employment status. Employed rural women were somewhat more favorable to a restricted family size than nonemployed rural women. A typology is presented predicting the relationship between fertility and employment status on the basis of the availability of birth control technology and the presence or absence of conflict between the roles of mother and worker. (15 references)

324

Theodore, Athena, ed. *The Professional Woman.* Cambridge, Mass.: Schenkman, 1971. 769 pp.

Professional women.

This collection of 53 articles reflects recent research on the socioeconomic role of the female professional in America. The majority of articles included are reprints from sociological and psychosociological literature sources as well as from journals representing specific professions. A few articles are previously unpublished papers presented at professional meetings. The selections are grouped into eight topic areas: Trends and prospects, the sexual

structure of professions, cultural definitions of the female professional, career-choice processes, adult socialization and career commitment, career patterns and marriage, the marginal professional, and
female professionalism and social change. (0-41 references per
chapter)

325
Thorsell, Siv. Employer attitudes to female employees. In: Dahlström,
Edmund, ed. *The Changing Roles of Men and Women.* Boston:
Beacon Press, 1971. pp. 135-169.

Sweden. Female employment. Sexual discrimination.

This discussion is based primarily on an investigation of possible
sexual discrimination in Swedish employers' recruitment and personnel policies. Sixty male high-level managers and administrators from
manufacturing fields, hotel and restaurant services, and banking and
insurance firms and about 10 male officials in the national
employment service and labor market organizations participated in
group discussions held during the course of a year. In addition,
interviews were conducted at 27 of the 41 firms investigated.

Men dominate the highly skilled and supervisory positions in the
firms studied; women occupy primarily unskilled or low-skilled
positions. Reasons given for the prevailing division of jobs according
to sex fall into three categories—cost, role conceptions, and physical
and mental differences. Company representatives claimed that women
were placed in routine, unskilled positions because these jobs are less
sensitive to high rates of absence and turnover. Skilled jobs require
training and long-term interest, which make offering them to women
an economic risk. Unskilled positions can be economically filled by
women because females are seen as being content with low wages, as
having less need or desire for promotion than men, and as being
psychologically suited for repetitive work.

Role conceptions included the assumptions that men, as family
supporters, deserve higher wages than women, and that the female's
family obligations could not be successfully combined with highly
skilled work. Jobs viewed as fitting for women are traditional tasks
such as cooking, sewing, or nursing. Women were deemed unfit for
highly skilled jobs because they are not technically gifted. They are
seen as unfit for supervisory positions because they lack qualities of
independence, leadership, and responsibility. However, firms that have
female supervisors were more approving of them. It was concluded
that sex differentiation in employment is the result of both the
traditional prejudices of employers and the cultural expectations of
employees. (No references)

326
Vimont, Claude M., and Gontier, Genevieve. A survey of female employees. [Une enquête sur les femmes fonctionnaires.] *Population,* 20(1):21-52, 1965.

France. Civil service. Female employment.

This study investigated why women work in the French public sector and how they organize their family life, in relation to their educational attainment, marital status, and work status. Female Government workers (N=2,889) completed a mailed questionnaire pertaining to their work. Results indicate that most French Government employees must work, with 93 percent citing financial reasons for working, most often to supplement their husbands' salaries. Only 10 percent cited personal preference as a reason. Another 22 percent cited intellectual reasons, and this percentage increased with educational level. The reason most often cited for working in the public sector was the security the job offered (55 percent). Overall, these women liked their work but were not happy with the pay they receive. In regard to their family situation, the average time spent at household tasks was 26 hours per week, although 34 percent had some household help. Relatives or babysitters provided child care for the working mothers. This study refutes some of the myths about why women work and how they organize their family life. (2 references)

327
Waldman, Elizabeth. Changes in the labor force activity of women. *Monthly Labor Review,* 93(6):10-18, 1970.

Female employment. Employment trends. Career patterns.

This discussion considers American women's current participation in the labor force and briefly reviews their employment status during the past 50 years. Census data and manpower studies are presented and discussed.

The major elements affecting the work patterns of women are marital status, presence and age of children, family income, race, education, and job opportunities. Currently, nearly two out of every five American workers are women. Most of these women are married, and half are over 39 years old. Studies show that women work for a variety of reasons, with economic necessity the most frequently cited. A recent analysis of the lifetime work expectancy of women shows that they typically take a job in their late teens or early twenties, leave the labor force after marriage, resume work when their childrearing responsibilities decrease, and retire from the job world in their late fifties or early sixties. Varying lifetime work expectancies of women are outlined according to marital status and number of children. Labor force data of the last decade indicate that younger wives are staying in the labor force longer before starting their families. Moreover, apparently changing patterns in the spacing of childbirths are also increasing female labor force participation and lifetime work expectancy. (11 references)

328
White, Rodney F. Female identity and career choice: The nursing case. In: Theodore, Athena, ed. *The Professional Woman.* Cambridge, Mass.: Schenkman, 1971, pp. 275-289.

Sex-typed occupations. Self-concept. Career aspirations. Nurses.

The hypothesis of this study is that key components of identity influence the kind of occupation a woman chooses and the extent to which she views her occupational role in career terms. These components are the degree to which a woman regards herself as instrumental (productive), expressive (nurturant), and committed to a particular set of values and objectives. Career choice is seen as involving a matching of perceived characteristics of various occupational roles with those of the individual's evolving identity. Data on 4,000 freshman nursing students, 1,677 female freshmen preparing for other than nursing careers, and 1,000 registered nurses were provided by self-administered questionnaires and by interviews.

Both nursing and nonnursing students viewed nurses as respected and hardworking; however, more of the nonnursing than nursing students considered nurses to be overbossed and to have little chance for advancement or independent thinking. The self-ratings of a majority of the nursing students were higher than those of other students on hard-working and submissive characteristics, and lower on leadership and originality. Similarly, girls training for various other careers rated themselves highest on the characteristics they viewed as most necessary for their specific fields—medical students on IQ, and education majors on originality. Ninety-four percent of nursing students and 80 percent of the other students stated that a career was important to them. Only a small proportion of highly committed students selected career in preference to family as the most important satisfaction in life, and their responses varied among occupational groups. Strongly committed girls were also more likely to say that they would continue their education if they should marry before finishing or that they intended to go for advanced degrees. Satisfaction with the nursing career was directly related to degree of commitment for both single and married registered nurses. However, almost all married nurses' careers were secondary to family considerations. Older single nurses tended to be more committed to their careers than the younger ones. (20 references)

329

Wilensky, Harold L. Women's work: Economic growth, ideology, structure. *Industrial Relations,* 7:235-248, 1968.

Female employment. National differences.

International statistics and employment studies are used to investigate female nonagricultural labor force participation in industrialized societies. An examination of 33 countries on the basis of per capita income and official sex-role ideology reveals that level of economic development is the crucial determinant of rate of women's occupational participation; official ideology is but a minor influence. In contrast to underdeveloped countries where female labor participation is patterned according to rural to urban migration, family instability, or religious custom, industrialized countries have relatively homogeneous female employment rates.

The similarities between Soviet and American female job assignments are probably greater than the differences. American women workers are concentrated in jobs involving one or more of the following characteristics: Traditional household tasks, a few strenuous physical activities or hazards, patience, manual dexterity, a welfare orientation, contact with young children, and sex appeal. More Soviet than American women are involved in heavy industrial labor and professional careers. However, the United States and the Soviet Union both lack female engineers, managers, and top political officials. Although women comprise three-fourths of all Soviet doctors, the position of physician in the Soviet Union is considerably less prestigious and important than in the United States.

Male dominance of positions of authority in Western society is discussed in terms of traditional cultural norms. Women have longer working hours resulting from the combination of paid labor and household labor. Most working women would prefer more flexible schedules, shorter hours, or part-time jobs to allow them to spend more time with their families. Possible changes suggested to expand female labor participation include policies of fertility control, equalization of educational and occupational opportunity, subsidized retraining of older women, and the organization of leisure activities around the work locale, rather than around the school or home. (35 references)

330

Williams, Phoebe A. Women in medicine: Some themes and variations. *Journal of Medical Education,* 46:584-591, 1971.

Medicine. Professional women. Role conflict.

This study explored the personal characteristics, attitudes, and experiences at various career stages of women who aspired to become doctors. The sample was 212 Radcliffe alumnae who had enrolled in medical school sometime during the past 60 years and who returned mailed questionnaires. The sample included 203 M.D.'s or current medical students and nine medical school dropouts.

Findings showed that the subjects represented an urban, affluent, highly educated, business- and profession-oriented milieu. They decided on medical careers in the last 2 years of college or after, and most were motivated by interest in biological science and desire to help people. The desire for independence and need to pursue a challenging vocation emerged in open-ended questionnaires. Frequently subjects were aided by an encouraging adult. Most of the subjects were married, had children, and devoted long hours to medical practice.

Although the women still in school expressed the greatest concern about the problems of pursuing medical careers, two-thirds of the doctors in the M.D. subgroups admitted experiencing one or more critical times in their work lives regarding the marriage-career conflict. These crises were most often resolved by reducing work hours or changing to a less demanding specialty. Solutions mentioned less often were withdrawing temporarily from medicine or relinquishing some aspect of family life. Although the women over 65 had faced the polarized choice of having a medical career or getting married, most members of later generations were able to combine medicine with marriage and a family. (5 references)

331
Ziegler, Harmon. Male and female: Differing perceptions of the teaching experience. In: Ziegler, Harmon. *The Political Life of American Teachers.* Englewood Cliffs, N.J.: Prentice-Hall, 1967. Also in: Theodore, Athena, ed. *The Professional Woman.* Cambridge, Mass.: Schenkman, 1971. pp. 74-92.

Teachers. Sex-typed occupations.

This discussion draws on interviews with 803 Oregon high school teachers (three-fifths male and two-fifths female) and other empirical studies to examine the effects of sex, income, and teaching experience on the outlook of secondary school teachers. The central assertion is that male secondary school teachers, despite their numerical predominance, find it difficult to establish male authority in an occupational role that most of society associates with women. It is further asserted that, in job satisfaction, political values, educational values, and personal orientation toward life, males more than females personify the conservative, rigid, security-seeking teacher.

Overall, two patterns of reactions to the teaching experience emerged from the interviews and polls. The high-income females were more satisfied with their jobs, had less need for respect, indicated less opposition to change, were more politically conservative, and were more educationally progressive in their views. The low-income males were less satisfied with their jobs, had greater need for respect, and were more likely to oppose change. They were more politically liberal than females but less educationally liberal. For all behaviors examined, the greatest congruence of values for male teachers was with those of other males. Females were less likely to show adoption of values according to sex.

In contrast to a majority of the female teachers, only one-third of the males polled said they would choose teaching again if given an opportunity to relive their careers. More than one-half of the low-income females and one-third of the males were satisfied with their positions, regardless of amount of teaching experience. While increasing income and teaching experience lead to greater satisfaction among women, there is a decline over time in job satisfaction among high-income male teachers. It is suggested that this dissatisfaction results from the degradation of the male ego, in that male teachers are paid on a par with females whereas other occupations pay men more than women. (13 references)

Law and Politics

332
Constantini, Edmond, and Craik, Kenneth H. Women as politicians: The social background, personality, and political careers of female party leaders. *Journal of Social Issues,* 28(2):217-236, 1972.

Politicians. Career patterns. Personality differences.

The background, personality, and distinctive roles of women at high levels of political party leadership in California are the focus of this interdisciplinary study. The sample consisted of 264 respondents to a statewide survey of 1,000 party leaders. Among the respondents were 46 Republican and 51 Democratic women.

Women party leaders had relatively less education and lower incomes than the men, although the educational and socioeconomic levels of their parents were higher than those of the men's parents. The Gough-Heilbrun Adjective Check List showed that female leaders are forceful, effective, ambitious, and socially ascendant individuals. However, this achievement orientation and purposeful style is complicated by their doubts and concerns about woman's place in society. Male leaders expressed the same personal style without these added concerns.

Women are less likely than men to hold public office above the local level. Women of both parties were more likely than the men to have been active in partisan affairs for 10 or more years, to hold a current party post, and to have served as a national convention delegate. Women were more intraparty oriented and men more public office oriented in their patterns of political activity. Although both men and women ranked concern for public issues and a sense of community obligation as their most salient motivation, significant sex differences emerged on secondary motives. Male leaders appeared to follow generally self-serving patterns, and female leaders appeared to follow more public-serving patterns.

These career style and motivational differences between men and women politicians resemble typical sex-role patterns in the family (expressive-internal versus instrumental-external). The career patterns of female party leaders, in part a result of traits and attitudes of the women themselves, may contribute to male dominance in public and high party offices. (34 references)

333
Gradin, Anita. Sex difference in the application of social security. [Olika social trygglet.] In: *Könsroller.* Falköping, Sweden: Prisma, 1965. pp. 110-121.

Sweden. Social security. Sexual discrimination.

This examination of Swedish social law shows that there are considerable differences in the treatment of men and women. It is posited that, in creating social security for men and women in Sweden, the lawmakers have started from traditional sex roles. In general, the man is considered to be the prime supporter of the family and the woman the caretaker of the children. In the case of death from work, the widow always receives a life-annuity from social insurance, whereas the widower only receives benefits after a special investigation of his income. Under the public pension plan, the retired male can get a special allowance if his wife is 60 years old. However, should the wife be the prime family supporter, the same allowance is not paid when she retires regardless of the age of her husband.

Several of the private insurance funds show similar inequities. For example, in the pension plan for industrial employees, the woman retires at 60 whereas the man does so at 65. The man's annuity is based on his working period from age 25, whereas the woman's benefits do not start to accrue until she has reached the age of 30. Public health insurance gives better protection to the family that is supported by the husband. For example, the wife gets a small compensation if she is home and is ill. However, if a working woman is absent from work because of health but is in a position to do limited housework, her compensation may be reduced from the entitlement a working man would have under similar circumstances.

The person staying home to care for the children, man or woman, does not have the same social insurance as the person working outside the home. For example, the base for retirement pension should be changed to allow accrual of points during the time when a person is temporarily absent from the labor market to take care of children. It has been shown that the single mother with children who receives welfare while the children are young remains on welfare long after the time when she could have entered into the labor market to support her family. This is explained by the lack of effort by welfare administrators to actively support her entrance into the labor market and of resources to train the single mother to start work. The single father is normally given assistance in finding day care for his children, but he is seldom supported directly in such a way that he can stay home. (No references)

334

Haavio-Mannila, Elina. Sex roles in politics. In: Safilios-Rothschild, Constantina, ed. *Toward a Sociology of Women.* Lexington, Mass.: Xerox College Publishing, 1972. pp. 154-172.

Finland. Political participation. Historical trends.

This study, which examines sex roles in Finnish politics, is based on official statistics of Finnish parliamentary and municipal elections from 1907-68 supplemented by interview data. A representative sample of men and women ages 15-64 was interviewed in Helsinki, two small towns, and five rural communes.

It was found that modernization and urbanization increased the amount of political activity of both sexes and decreased the differences in political participation between men and women. Urban men were more exposed to social pressures to vote than rural men, but no differences in the expectations concerning women's political interests were observed between urban and rural areas. In spite of this, urban women were more politically active than rural women.

In comparing men and women as candidates, it was found that a high voting turnout of women did not necessarily mean that more women became elected to political offices. A majority of women everywhere voted for men. Women were more likely to be elected as political representatives in urban than in rural areas. In general, urban residents were overrepresented in the parliament. The proportion of women among candidates, among those receiving votes, and among those elected to parliament was highest in the socialist parties. Socioeconomic development, conservative conformity, traditions of equality in the social structure, and ideologies concerning equality of the sexes are some of the factors influencing sex roles in Finnish politics. (24 references)

335
Jennings, M. Kent, and Thomas, Norman. Men and women in party elites: Social roles and political resources. *Midwest Journal of Political Science*, 12(4):469-492, 1968.

Political delegates.

This study investigated whether or not sex-related differences in mass political behavior persist among party elites. The social role differentiation model suggests sex-related differences will persist even in party elites, whereas the elite socialization model predicts that the self-selection and socialization of the elite will tend to counter institutionalized sex statuses and thus reduce sex-related differences. Subjects were 134 male and 156 female Michigan delegates to the 1964 Republican and Democratic National Conventions. Questionnaires provided data on socioeconomic origins; family political background; party careers and service activity; candidacy for elective office; and attitudes toward the political process, their party, and on major political issues.

Male delegates were more likely than female delegates to have completed college. and to be self-employed or employed in a professional or business capacity. One-half of the female delegates did not work. Women delegates were older and of lower economic status than the men. For the most part, neither spouses nor parents of delegates were politically prominent. However, nearly one-half of the housewife delegates had husbands with high political status. Men were much more likely to have performed key campaign activities, to have held appointive public office, and to have sought and succeeded in election to public office. Men and women were more similar with respect to political orientation, where the definition of political roles and norms accords more with the model of elite socialization rather than the differentiated social roles model. However, some sex differences were evident, especially regarding delegates' self-reliance as political actors. Males more than females said delegates should rely on personal judgment rather than on party leaders or public opinion when voting at a convention. Overall, working women delegates resembled the men in behavior more than did housewife delegates. This tendency suggests that the role of jobholder helps to overcome sex differences. Women delegates' lack of political ambition is discussed in terms of role socialization and the political system. (27 references)

336

Jennings, M. Kent, and Niemi, Richard G. The division of political labor between mothers and fathers. *American Political Science Review,* 65(1):69-82, 1971.

Political behavior. Marital roles.

As a test of the role-sharing versus the instrumental-expressive model of parental behavior, conditions related to varied balances of conjugal political role sharing were investigated. A sample of 430 couples 35 to 55 years old was weighted to represent a national cross-section of pairs of mothers and fathers of high school students. Political activity studied included political resources (political knowledge, understanding of party differences, political efficacy), spectator politics (general interest, exposure to politics in media), and political participation (electoral activities, school affairs, community affairs). Data on these variables and personal background information were obtained by interviews.

Moderate to high homogeneity within couples was found on the political activity measures, thus supporting the role-sharing view of parents' political participation. Where heterogeneity within couples was indicated, men on the average exceeded their mates in most forms of political behaviors. Husbands scored considerably higher than their wives on political resources and higher on all aspects of spectator politics except watching television and reading magazines. Husbands indicated more overt participation in electoral activities; wives, in school affairs. Thus, total political activities emanating from the home had an input from each partner, although when the spouses had differing degrees of activity, the husband tended to score higher.

In considering the effects of background variables on the relative advantage of one spouse in level of political activity, the husband's net advantage decreased as his relative edge on education decreased. The effect of relative education was greater among working-class couples than among middle-class couples, perhaps due to the overall high level of schooling and participatory opportunity in the middle-class. Similarly, the wife's employment increased her political activity relative to her husband's more in working-class than in middle-class families. Within this sample, age of youngest child had no significant effect on the wife's relative political activity. Relative ego strength, determined by three forced-choice questions, was strongly associated with relative political activity for both men and women. It is concluded that the husband is most often the instrumental interpreter of the external world of politics, but not exclusively. The degree of sharing in division of political activity within couples is conditioned by the characteristics of each spouse and the interaction of these characteristics in marriage. (17 references)

337

Kanowitz, Leo. *Women and the Law: The Unfinished Revolution.* Albuquerque: University of New Mexico Press, 1969. 312 pp.

Legal processes. Sexual discrimination.

This book identifies continuing areas of sex-based legal discrimination for the purpose of promoting courtroom and legislative reform by stimulating a greater awareness of existing sex discrimination in American life. Unequal and differential treatment of the sexes is examined in light of underlying sociological factors. Data are provided from sociological studies, law review articles, and legal and legislative records. Discussion of laws particularly relevant to single women focuses on differences regarding age of majority; marriage qualifications; regulations about prostitution, rape, and abortion; and political rights. A chapter on law and married women compares married women's property rights under common law and community property systems and outlines inequalities affecting married women in other areas of civil and criminal law. The sex provisions of the 1964 Civil Rights Act and the Equal Pay Act of 1963 are also examined. Discussion of State protective legislation concerns both its benefits to women and its propensity toward allowing sex discrimination. A chapter on constitutional aspects of sex-based discrimination in American law describes and analyzes decisions and recent develop-ments and considers the desirability of the proposed Equal Rights Amendment.

From these analyses, it is concluded that the legal status of both married and unmarried American women has improved considerably. Specific events contributing to this include the termination of sex prohibitions in jury duty, the institution of Federal laws providing for equal pay for equal work, and nondiscrimination in employer and union hiring practices. However, women are still treated differently and less favorably than men in several areas. Common law traditions prevail in laws governing a married woman's name, domicile, and right to sue for loss of consortium. Discriminatory laws continue in the regulation of sexual conduct, and loopholes remain in recent legislation against sex-based inequalities in employment. Appendixes include Title VII of the Civil Rights Act of 1964, the Equal Employment Opportunity Executive Order, and two illustrative legal briefs. (30-100 references per chapter)

338
Levitt, Morris. The political role of American women. *Journal of Human Relations,* 15(1):23-25, 1967.

Political participation. Sex-typed behavior. Female role.

This discussion includes a review of literature on women's political behavior and a report of the author's study on the effects of work status and education on women's political attitudes and activities. Data for this study were obtained from three nationwide surveys, each conducted shortly after the presidential elections in 1956, 1960, and 1964.

When working women and nonworking women in the national surveys were compared at each educational level, working women at every educational level were found to be more politically involved and to participate more in the political process than did nonworking women. Furthermore, working women had a higher sense of political efficacy and of citizen obligation. There was no consistent pattern in terms of educational level and politicalization. Thus, it is concluded that working experience is a primary factor in American women's political role and education a secondary factor. Three additional conclusions are drawn on the basis of the literature review: Women suffer from the stereotyped image of a nonpolitical role in a man's world. Women do not participate in or get involved with the electoral process to a high degree because it is viewed as being inconsistent with their social role. Women hold political attitudes, such as a low sense of individual efficacy, which contribute to their withdrawal from active participation. It is suggested that the extension of women's political participation depends on both men and women refuting the idea that public life is a male realm. (19 references)

339
Means, Ingunn Norderval. Women in local politics: The Norwegian experience. *Canadian Journal of Political Science,* 5(3):365-388, 1972.

Norway. Politicians.

This exploratory study of the recruitment of women for municipal office in Norway is based on government statistics, newspaper articles, political party documents and publications, and interviews with 22 of the 24 women serving on the municipal councils of Bergen, Tromsø, and Volda in 1970. Factors in the political setting which could influence female recruitment and characteristics of women councilors were investigated.

Discussion of the political setting provides some historical background and focuses on the national effort to improve women's political position at the local level. This effort resulted in large gains in numbers of female councilors in the 1967 and 1971 elections. Other political factors promoting women's involvement in government are the parties' active recruitment of balanced tickets and women's subsequent increased awareness of political opportunities, the vigorous Scandinavian sex-role debate of the past decade, and the emphasis on political participation as a civic duty.

Norwegian women councilors are characterized by politicized childhood environments, modest though above-average education, and middle-class backgrounds. Contrary to recruitment theories that politicians are drawn from occupations associated with politically useful skills, a high proportion of the female councilors are middle-aged housewives. This is explained in terms of party apprenticeship compensating for deficiencies in formal education and occupational qualifications and the paucity of women candidates. This scarcity of political women allows even modest achievements in nonpolitical contexts to lead to a political career. Because better educated and occupationally qualified women have full-time careers, they are less available for time-consuming political duties. The councilors interviewed were anxious to perform their duties competently, but not to rise to higher office. It is concluded that Norwegian women are unlikely to attain an increasingly influential role in politics until a larger proportion of skilled career women becomes involved. (55 references)

340
Nagel, Stuart, and Weitzman, Lenore J. Double standard of American justice. *Society,* March 1972. pp. 18-25.

Legal processes. Sexual discrimination.

Data from studies of differences in the treatment of men and women under the law are examined in terms of length of sentence; favoritism in criminal, personal injury, and divorce proceedings; sex of the jury;

and comparative black-white and male-female sentencing practices. Specifically, the inquiry concerns whether American courts treat men and women equally.

A review of the findings indicates two basic syndromes—the disadvantaged pattern and the paternalistic pattern of discrimination. Women litigants are affected under both syndromes and do not receive the same treatment as men. In criminal cases, women are much less likely to be jailed before or after conviction and are less likely to have a jury trial than men charged with the same crime. In personal injury cases, women are less likely to win than men, and they collect substantially smaller awards, especially for injuries related to earning power or to sexual functioning and especially before male-dominated juries. Female-dominated juries, however, were found to favor female plaintiffs. In divorce cases, the woman more often wins the decree, but with a high probability of nonenforced child support and alimony orders. A paternalistic protectiveness, at least toward white women, characterizes the general legal treatment of women. However, women are more likely to be slighted in the allocation of monetary awards.

Suggested remedies for these disparities involve improving and equalizing the legal process for men and women. In personal injury and child support cases, society should perhaps seek collective action, such as no-fault insurance and expanded Social Security. (No references)

341
Pedersen, Inger Margrete. Status of women in private law. *Annals,* 375:44-51, 1968.

Legal processes. National differences. Sexual discrimination.

This historical review of the status of women, particularly married women, in private law throughout the world traces efforts of the feminist movement, of governments, and of international organizations such as the United Nations to remedy existing discriminatory practices. Unmarried women have generally attained legal equality before married women, who still face many unresolved legal issues. Minimum age for marriage, mutual consent to marriage, and registration of marriages are generally agreed upon as desirable safeguards. Ensurance against repudiation of wife by husband on insufficient grounds and ensurance that both parties have an equal right to obtain a separation or divorce also offer protection for women. The importance of all these safeguards has been agreed on in international conferences, but national laws do not always uphold them.

In regard to marital property rights, there has been a general trend away from common property toward separate property and the recognition of husband and wife as independent persons before the law. However, the institution of separate property raises the problem of recognizing the financial contribution of the wife who works only in the home, particularly if the marriage ends. There appears to be less consensus internationally on the question of responsibility for family support—whether the husband is the primary supporter or both spouses have an equal duty—than on any other issue. The situation of unmarried mothers is a special problem. Although discrimination against them in private law has been abolished in most countries, they are seldom awarded the right to exercise parental duty to the same extent as the married parent. Their position seems to be most favorable in Europe, particularly in Scandinavia. Overall, even in countries where the principle of equal rights for men and women is generally accepted, reform of private law remains a serious need. (6 references)

342
Sartin, Pierrette. Women, work and politics in contemporary society. [La femme, le travail et la politique dans les sociétés modernes.] *Res Publica* 9(1):111-121, 1967.

Political participation. National differences. France.

This article reviews statistics pertaining to women's participation in politics in the Western European countries. Although 30 to 50 percent of women work in the Western countries, an insignificant number is elected to political posts, except in Scandinavia and Germany. Even in the U.S.S.R., where women do occupy political posts, their numbers are not representative of the number of women in the population. In France, the number of women elected has declined drastically in the last 15 years. The leadership role is rarely taken by women who are elected, and most of their political work is done in social areas.

Discussion of this lack of female participation in politics centers on two French studies. One study indicates that the political domain is the one where male opposition to women is the strongest. Another study shows that women are not convinced of the necessity of their participation; in fact, in 89 percent of households surveyed, husband and wife vote the same way, often with the wife voting according to her husband's advice. Political behavior of European women is contrasted with the influence which American women have in politics. Although, again, participation is not proportional to the total female population in the United States, it is substantial. American women also participate more in civic affairs than do French women.

Finally, French women who do participate in politics in spite of the obstacles are described as being government employees or liberal professional women. It is suggested that educational programs to help women understand their social, political, and economic roles might be warranted. (4 references)

343
Simons, Harold Jack. *African Women: Their Legal Status in South Africa.* Evanston, Ill.: Northwestern University Press, 1968. 299 pp.

South Africa. Social Equality. Racial differences. Discrimination.

This book describes in detail the statutory, customary, and common law rules relating to native women in South Africa, evaluates these laws in relation to social change, and indicates possible lines of reform. Data sources include court reports, legislation, legal and demographic studies, and historical accounts. The evolution of relevant policies and legislation, including the continuing conflict of tribal and European legal systems, is traced. A discussion of marriage systems considers polygyny, lobolo (dowry paid to the bride's family), preferred and prohibited unions, and divorce. Women's rights and disabilities are discussed in reference to legal capacities of married, unmarried, and widowed females; property rights, child custody; seduction; and inheritance. A concluding section examines the effect of racial segregation on the position of women regarding land rights, work, urban migration, and politics. (20-100 references per chapter)

344
Snyder, Eloise C. Sex role differential and juror decisions. *Sociology and Social Research,* 55:442-448, 1971.

Jury decisions.

Actual jury decisionmaking was studied to determine the extent to which jury composition affects jury decisions on similar cases. Decisions of all-male, six-person juries in civil suits in one South Carolina court during 3 months of 1966 were compared with those of mixed male-female, six-person juries for the same court and same time period during 1967, after a change in law permitted women to be jurors. Aspects of the jury decisions investigated were favoring the plaintiff or defendant, favoring the superior-status or inferior-status litigant, and the amount of money awarded to the winner of the case.

During the period of mixed-sex juries, plaintiffs had a somewhat better chance of winning than defendants did, whereas all-male juries had awarded the decision equally to plaintiff or defendant. The difference was not statistically significant, however. The situation for status of litigants was the reverse: Mixed-sex juries awarded decisions to inferior- and superior-status litigants equally often, whereas all-male juries chose the higher status litigant in 74 percent of the cases. This difference in decision pattern was statistically significant. The mixed-sex juries awarded less money to the winners of cases than the all-male juries had. Proportionally, the difference was extreme: Mixed-sex juries were asked to award more than double what all-male juries had been asked for, yet they only awarded 20 percent of what was asked compared with 52 percent of requests to the all-male juries. It was concluded that the addition of women to juries increased the ability of inferior-status litigants to win decisions, but decreased the financial redress awarded. (7 references)

345
Stolte-Heiskanen, Veronica. Sex roles, social class and political consciousness. *Acta Sociologica,* 14(1-2):83-95, 1971.

Finland. Political behavior. High school students. Socioeconomic differences.

In support of a structural concept of political socialization, previous conceptualizations are reviewed, a new approach is outlined, and illustrative empirical data on sex differences in the political consciousness of youth are presented. The specific assumption tested was that women's lower political participation, which is particularly marked among lower-class \ women, has its source in concrete differences in the opportunity structures. The stratified sample of 1,048 students, composed almost equally of males and females, came from secondary and vocational schools in urban and rural and developed and underdeveloped regions of Finland. Standardized questionnaires focusing on attitudes toward and awareness of international and national issues were administered. The questionnaires also included some nonpolitical and standard family background questions. Degree of political articulation was measured indirectly by frequency or participation in discussions of world affairs, willingness or ability to express party preferences, and coherence of subject's politically relevant attitudes.

Results are interpreted as supporting the assertion that differences in opportunity structures are a crucial factor in producing differences in political awareness, articulation, and participation. Students from higher social strata were found to be overrepresented in the secondary, or general education, schools; students from lower strata were overrepresented in the vocational schools. No sex differences were found in the distribution of socioeconomic backgrounds within either type of school. Sex differences in questionnaire responses showed males to be better informed in general than females, and differences were even greater when political items were rated separately from nonpolitical items. More males than females reported high or medium participation in voluntary organizations, but the extent of newspaper readership did not differ between sexes. Irrespective of type of information considered, subjects were consistently ranked on informed awareness in the following high-to-low order: Males in secondary school, females in secondary school, males in vocational school, and females in vocational school. Differences in awareness were greater between type of school (secondary versus vocational) than between males and females. Type of region and urban versus rural residence were the variables least influential on both political and nonpolitical awareness. Political articulation followed the same pattern of results as informed awareness. (20 references)

Health and Mental Health

346
Alkire, Armand A. Enactment of social power and role behavior in families of disturbed and nondisturbed preadolescents. *Developmental Psychology,* 7(3):270-276, 1972.

Parental dominance. Family structure. Psychological adjustment.

As part of a larger evaluation of clinical intervention techniques for emotionally disturbed children, this study investigated possible authority role reversal in the families of these children. Subjects were 18 socioeconomically diverse Los Angeles families with children from 8 to 13 years old who had chronic, serious emotional problems. Normal control children from 14 families were matched with randomly selected disturbed children. Both groups were 84 percent boys.

A family communication task required the child to describe six graphic designs. The parents separately asked questions, received further information, and made guesses as to the design being described. Parents were then assigned one of two forms of social power to exert: The legitimate-expert, authoritarian role or the referent-expert, personalized role. Each parent was scored on success in enacting the assigned role, and the effects of this power display on family task-role behavior were observed in a subsequent task trial.

The findings gave evidence of a role reversal between parents of disturbed and normal preadolescents. In most cases, mothers of nondisturbed and fathers of disturbed children had similar difficulty in displaying authority over the child, and they were also alike in subsequent receiver behaviors. In contrast, fathers of nondisturbed and mothers of disturbed children were more authoritarian and also similar in task behaviors. These patterns suggest that parental role behavior toward a child is determined by that parent's particular domains of power within the family, rather than by generalized personality characteristics. (18 references)

347
Bart, Pauline B. Depression in middle-aged women. In: Gornick, Vivian, and Moran, Barbara K., eds. *Woman in Sexist Society*. New York: Basic Books, 1971. pp. 163-186.

Middle-aged women. Cultural differences. Maternal role loss. Depressions.

This investigation concerns the depression experienced by middle-aged women as the result of the loss of their maternal role. It was hypothesized that women whose identity is derived mainly from their role as mothers rather than their role as wives and workers encounter difficulties when their children leave home. As a cross-cultural inquiry into postparental roles, 30 societies were examined, using the Human Relations Area Files, and six cultures were intensively studied, using anthropological monographs. The records of 533 American women (ages 40 to 59) hospitalized for neurotic, involutional, psychotic, or manic depressive disorders were examined. At two of the five hospitals from which the sample was drawn, a total of 20 interviews provided personal information, questionnaire data on sex-role attitudes, and projective biography responses regarding life-cycle roles. Independent coders rated maternal role loss and relationship with children and husband from the case histories, which omitted references to symptoms, ethnicity, or diagnosis.

Anthropological data indicated that depressions in middle-aged women result from their lack of important roles and subsequent loss of self-esteem rather than from hormonal changes in menopause. It had been expected in the American sample that satisfying occupations, happy marriages, some children still at home, and children's residence near the mother would make it easier for mothers when the children left. It was also predicted that maternal role loss would be more painful for women who suffered loss of other roles (for example, wife or worker) or had unsatisfying relationships with the departing children.

Women having overprotective or overinvolved relationships with their children tended to suffer depression in the postparental period more than other women. Housewives had a higher depression rate than did working women. Jewish women were roughly twice as likely to be depressed than non-Jewish women, apparently owing to the traditional Jewish family ties between mother and children. When family interactive patterns were controlled, this difference diminished. Black women had a lower depression rate than white women. Possible reasons suggested for this difference are that middle-aged women in the black community are more likely to have relative's children to care for, to be employed, to still be regarded as sexually attractive, and/or not to be hospitalized if they are depressed. The traditional role explanation for middle-aged women's depression is discussed in relation to other sociological and psychiatric theories of depression, as well as to the depression experienced by many males at retirement. (13 references)

348

Bentzen, Frances. Sex ratios in learning and behavior disorders. *The National Elementary Principal,* 46(2):13-17, 1966. Also in: *American Journal of Orthopsychiatry, 33(1):92-98, 1963.*

Physiological maturation. Physical vulnerability. Psychological adjustment. Learning disorders.

This paper presents the theory that some of the male's learning and behavior disorders are a stress response to society's inability to take biological age differences into account in educational and developmental expectations for boys and girls. Data analyzed are from selected literature on biological development and the learning and behavioral problems of children and from a Maryland survey of 6,026 elementary school students.

The survey of elementary school learning problems indicates that the highest incidence of student referrals occurs in the first grade. Most students referred are boys cited for physiological, social, and emotional immaturity. It is suggested that these children, identified in the first grade, would be the ones most likely to have instructional and emotional difficulties in the fourth grade (the grade with the second highest incidence of referrals).

It is estimated that learning and behavior problems are 3 to 10 times more frequent among males than females of the same chronological age. This uneven sex distribution is linked to both the biophysical vulnerability and the slower maturation rate of males. Evidence for the male's greater vulnerability to stress includes sex ratios showing higher incidence of male still births, death and disease during infancy, stuttering, and schizophrenia. (16 references)

349
Broverman, Inge K.; Broverman, Donald M.; Clarkson, Frank E.; Rosenkrantz, Paul S.; and Vogel, Susan R. Sex-role stereotypes and clinical judgments of mental health. *Journal of Consulting and Clinical Psychology,* 34(1):1-7, 1970.

Sex-role perceptions. Mental health personnel. Sex-typed behavior.

Sex-role stereotyping among clinical psychologists, psychiatrists, and social workers was examined. It was hypothesized that clinical judgments about the characteristics of healthy individuals would differ as a function of sex of person judged, and that these differences in clinical judgments would parallel stereotypic sex-role differences. A second hypothesis predicted that behaviors and characteristics judged healthy for an adult would resemble behaviors judged healthy for men, but differ from those judged healthy for women.

A questionnaire of 122 bipolar items was administered to a sample of 79 clinicians (46 men, 33 women), each subject receiving one of three sets of instructions: To describe a mature, healthy, socially competent (a) adult, (b) man, or (c) woman. Agreement scores on the 38 sex-role stereotypic items and male and female health scores relative to an ideal standard of health (i.e., adult, sex unspecified) were developed from questionnaire responses.

Both male and female clinicians agreed on the behaviors and attributes characterizing a mentally healthy man, woman, and adult, independent of sex. The differing conceptions of what constitutes a mentally healthy man and a mentally healthy woman paralleled sex-role stereotypes. Clinicians did tend to ascribe male-valued traits more often to healthy men than to healthy women, whereas they ascribed only about half of the female-valued traits more often to healthy women than to healthy men. The adult and masculine concepts of health did not differ significantly, but a significant difference was found between the adult and feminine health concepts. (21 references)

350
Cheek, Frances E. A serendipitous finding: Sex roles and schizophrenia. *Journal of Abnormal Psychology,* 69(4):392-400, 1964.

Schizophrenia. Sex-role identification. Social interaction.

In the course of a study of the influence of the family environment of schizophrenics, an unexpected finding of differential interaction patterns for male and female schizophrenics emerged. It was expected that schizophrenics would show low total interaction rates and possibly low rates of dominance and/or social-emotional behaviors relative to nonpsychotics. It was also expected that, irrespective of illness status, females would be higher in rates of social-emotional behavior, and males would be higher in instrumental or task behaviors.

Subjects in the study were young adult convalescent schizophrenics (40 male, 27 female) and normal young adults of approximately the same age (31 male, 25 female). All subjects were single and living with their parents in New Jersey. However, the two groups were not matched on social class, religion, ethnicity of the family, or on age. Each subject, the mother, and the father completed a questionnaire regarding family problems. The three family members then took part in four recorded discussions, which were scored using the Bales Interaction Process Analysis. Additional information on subject's history and current adjustment was obtained from parent interviews and hospital records.

Schizophrenics as a group did not differ significantly from normals on total interaction rate, positive social-emotional behavior, expressions of tension or tension release, or amount of task behavior. However, they did differ on negative social-emotional behavior: Normals showed significantly more projected hostility and disagreement, and schizophrenics were more ego-defensive. Females, independent of clinical status, had significantly higher total interaction rates and showed more positive social-emotional behaviors and tension release than males. Females also showed somewhat more negative social-emotional behaviors and less task behavior than males. Separate analyses of results for male and female schizophrenics and normals and data from the questionnaires and records supported the overall conclusion that previously hospitalized male schizophrenics tend to be more passive and withdrawn than male normals, but female schizophrenics tend to be more active and dominating than female normals. (19 references)

351

Chesler, Phyllis. Women as psychiatric and psychotherapeutic patients. *Journal of Marriage and the Family,* 33(4):746-759, 1971.

Mental illness. Sex differences. Sociocultural determinants.

The effects of sex-role stereotyping and oppression on the mental health of women are examined. U.S. Government statistics on psychological distress show that more women (black and white) than men experience nervous breakdowns, impending breakdowns, psychological inertia, dizziness, and other neurotic symptoms. Studies of psychiatric and psychological practice patterns indicate that more women are involved in such treatment than men. Among the psychiatrically hospitalized, unmarried people of both sexes are disproportionately represented. Both male and female patients have a significant preference for a male rather than a female therapist. It is suggested that the reason for the greater number of women involved in psychotherapy is that women are oppressed and have no approved life recourse in this society other than marriage or psychotherapy, or both. Both are seen as maintaining the status quo of women. The analogy between "slave" and "woman" is analyzed in terms of symptoms exhibited by women patients as manifestations of "slave psychology" and oppression. Studies of practicing clinicians show that the majority are male and that they operate with stereotypic attitudes toward women. Recommendations to improve clinical practice involving women are made. (33 references)

352
Consentino, Fred, and Heilbrun, Alfred B., Jr. Anxiety correlates of sex-role identity in college students. *Psychological Reports,* 14(3):729-730, 1964.

Anxiety. Sex-role identification.

The relationships between sex-role adoption, aggression anxiety, and manifest anxiety were studied in a sample of 85 males and 156 females enrolled in an undergraduate psychology course. Tests used were the Adjective Check List to measure masculinity-femininity; an 80-item aggression questionnaire, which included 12 items related to aggression anxiety; and the Taylor Manifest Anxiety Scale.

Significant negative relationships were obtained between masculinity and both aggression anxiety and manifest anxiety. For both males and females, greater femininity was associated with greater aggression anxiety and manifest anxiety. From comparisons of these findings with those of an earlier study of 12-year-old children, it was concluded that the direction and magnitude of the relationship between aggression anxiety and sex-role identity is essentially the same at age 20 as at age 12. (5 references)

353
Gove, Walter R. The relationship between sex roles, marital status, and mental illness. *Social Forces,* 51(1):34-44, 1972.

Mental illness. Sex differences. Marital status. Female role.

Studies of sex, marital status, and mental illness in post-World War II industrial societies are reviewed to show that the sex role of married women accounts for the higher rates of mental illness among women. Four studies deal with the prevalence of mental illness, 12 with the incidence of mental illness, and one with termination of treatment. Since studies differ markedly in the severity, duration, and definition of disorders investigated, only categories within a particular study were compared.

The findings were examined in relation to three theoretical explanations for the high rates of mental illness in women: Females have greater biological susceptibility; some general sex-role characteristic makes more women appear to be mentally ill; and the roles women occupy are difficult and promote mental illness. The data suggest that the overall role explanation accounts for the sex differences in mental illness. The married of both sexes have lower rates of mental illness than the unmarried, possibly because of the nature of marital roles and because the selective processes prevent unstable persons from marrying. All studies found, however, that married women have higher rates of mental disorder than married men. In contrast, single, divorced, or widowed women tend to have somewhat lower rates of mental illness than their male counterparts. (59 references)

354
Gove, Walter R., and Tudor, Jeannette F. Adult sex roles and mental illness. *American Journal of Sociology,* 78(4):812-935, 1973.

Mental illness. Sex differences.

This attempt to clarify the relationship between adult sex roles and mental illness is based on earlier studies and new data which employ a more precise definition of mental illness. It is assumed that stress may lead to mental illness, and it is postulated that the difficulties associated with modern woman's role promote mental illness. In this analysis, which is limited to the United States and other Western industrial nations, "mental illness" includes functional disorders characterized by anxiety (neurosis) and/or mental disorganization (psychosis). Transient situation disorders, psychophysiologic disorders, and suicide are also included.

Data from the National Institute of Mental Health on first admissions to mental hospitals, psychiatric admissions to general hospitals, and psychiatric care in outpatient clinics were utilized. Data on private outpatient psychiatric care and on the practices of general physicians were derived from studies by other investigators. Additional data from 17 community surveys and from the Veterans Administration were examined.

All data indicated higher rates of mental illness for women than for men. Consistent results were found regardless of the process by which the person had been selected and treated as mentally ill. The sex-role explanation and alternative theories of why women show higher rates of mental illness than men are discussed. The societal reaction perspective, which asserts that a person becomes mentally ill primarily because of the perceptions and actions of others, fails to explain the patterned variations found in male and female mental illness. The theory that women more willingly express symptoms of mental illness has not yet been shown to account for sex differences in the rates of mental illness. (110 references)

355
Gump, Janice Porter. Sex-role attitudes and psychological well-being. *Journal of Social Issues,* 28(2):79-92, 1972.

Sex-role perceptions. Psychological adjustment. Career aspirations. Marriage aspirations.

Sex-role attitudes and their relationship to ego strength, happiness, and plans for further achievement were studied in a sample of 162 female University of Rochester seniors. Subjects' scores on a variation of the Fand Self/Other Orientation Inventory, Barron's Ego Strength Scale, and the Wessman-Ricks-Tyl Elation-Depression Scale were correlated with information on their personal and career goals, relationships with men, and demographic characteristics.

The majority of subjects believed it possible to assume the roles of wife and mother while pursuing extrafamilial interests. Neither happiness nor the establishment of relationships with men differentiated women who were traditional in sex-role orientation from women who were primarily concerned with self-actualization and achievement. Differences in ego strength were associated with plans for marriage and career: Subjects with the highest ego-strength scores were actively pursuing both objectives. Significantly more high scorers on ego strength were planning to pursue graduate study than low scorers. Yet, most of the high scorers were planning traditionally feminine careers. The data suggest overall that ego strength may be negatively related to conformity to a narrowly defined traditional female sex role. (12 references)

356
Kayton, Robert, and Biller, Henry B. Sex-role development and psychopathology in adult males. *Journal of Consulting and Clinical Psychology,* 38(2):208-210, 1972.

Sex-role identification. Mental illness.

This study investigated the relationship between sex-role development and degree of psychopathology in adult males. The sample consisted of matched groups of nonparanoid schizophrenics, paranoid schizophrenics, neurotics, and normals (N=20 in each group). Subjects lived or were hospitalized in the Chicago area, ranged in age from 18 to 49, had been raised in two-parent families, had from 9 to 18 years of education, and were primarily from lower- and middle-class backgrounds. The four groups were compared in terms of measures relating to masculinity-femininity of self-perceptions (Gough and Heilbrun's Adjective Check List) and of interests and attitudes (Gough's Femininity Scale). A psychosocial questionnaire was administered to the normals for prior psychiatric disturbance.

Resulting scores consistently indicated that all the disturbed groups were much less masculine than the normal subjects. However, these sex-role measures did not clearly differentiate the disturbed groups. Possible explanations for this finding are that schizophrenia and neurosis are both rooted in early gender development problems, or that diagnostic categories used in this study to distinguish levels of psychological disturbance were an inappropriate or too narrow criterion. It is concluded that inadequacies in sex-role development are involved in a variety of psychological disorders. (8 references)

357

Larson, Richard F. The influence of sex roles and symptoms on clergymen's perceptions of mental illness. *The Pacific Sociological Review,* 13(1):53-61, 1970.

Sex-role perceptions. Clergymen. Sex-typed behavior. Mental illness.

This is a report of an experimental investigation to determine whether clergymen perceive certain kinds of behavior as being more or less deviant according to the sex of the performer. It was hypothesized that examples of normal or extremely deviant behavior would be evaluated independently of the client's sex role, whereas judgments of mild to moderately deviant behavior would be influenced by sex of client. Four case histories describing a client showing erotomania, homosexual panic, simple schizophrenia, or hallucination; one case of schizophrenic behavior; and one normal case were presented in a questionnaire mailed to the 5,542 clergymen in a Southwestern State. The 34 percent who responded were the subjects for this study. Half of the clergymen received form A; half, form B, which differed only in the sex of the client described in each case history. For each case, subjects were asked to indicate to what extent the person was emotionally disturbed; to what extent the reader believed he could help the person; and whether there was anyone to whom he would refer the person.

As predicted, the paranoid schizophrenic was perceived as the most severely disturbed case, followed by the hallucinator, erotomanic, homosexual panic, simple schizophrenic, and the normal person. Sex role made a difference in the diagnosis of two cases: The male simple schizophrenic was seen as severely disturbed significantly more often than the female, and the female erotomanic was more likely than the male to be perceived as severely disturbed. Sex of client was also related to being perceived as severely disturbed. Sex of client was also related to the clergymen's professional role concept for the same two cases—in the treatment of the female simple schizophrenic and of the male erotomaniac, clergymen saw themselves as being of major assistance. Referral policy was influenced by sex of client in male simple schizophrenic and in female hallucinatory cases. Results supported the thesis that sex roles significantly influence perceptions of some deviant behaviors. Data also supported the conclusion that sex of client does not lead to different perceptions and judgments when the behavior involved suggests an overriding status, such as normality or severe disturbance. (14 references)

358
McClelland, David C., and Watt, Norman F. Sex-role alienation in schizophrenia. *Journal of Abnormal Psychology,* 73(3):226-239, 1968.

Sex-role identification. Schizophrenia.

Sex-role alienation in chronic schizophrenics and male and female normals was studied by means of unconscious and conscious sex-role measures. Subjects were 23 male and 22 female schizophrenics from the Boston State Hospital, 20 male and 20 female hospital employees and blue-collar workers, and 21 housewives. With the exception of the middle-class female hospital employees, the sample was lower middle-class. Personal data were gathered by interview. Sex-role measures were a Role Playing Test, a Body Parts Acceptance Test, a Figure Preference Test, the Thematic Apperception Test (TAT), and an interest and attitude questionnaire.

The schizophrenics showed sex-role alienation on tests containing self-image references (Role Playing, Body Parts, and Figure Preference). Female schizophrenics tended to react in the assertive manner of normal males, and male schizophrenics reacted in the less assertive manner of normal females. Nearly half of the schizophrenics but only 10 percent of the normals made three or more opposite-sex choices on the Role Playing Test. When the male role suggested assertion, aggression, or authority, male schizophrenics chose the female role significantly more often than the normal males. On the Body Parts Test, schizophrenic males replaced normal male concern for masculine parts with greater concern for their appearance; schizophrenic females showed less concern for all body parts. In the direct test of assertive versus yielding stories on the TAT, the sex-difference reversal was significant only when the housewives were used as normal female controls. The inclination of female schizophrenics toward assertive stories was similar to that of the hospital staff career women, suggesting that this role reversal is not as symptomatic of the schizophrenic condition as the self-image reversal. In conscious sex-typed interests and attitudes, schizophrenics did not differ from normals. A theory is proposed relating schizophrenia to sex-identity alienation in early life. (28 references)

359
Phillips, Derek L., and Segal, Bernard E. Sexual status and psychiatric symptoms. *American Sociological Review,* 34(1):58-72, 1969.

Psychiatric symptoms. Sex differences.

This study tested the hypothesis that women report more psychiatric symptoms than men, given an equal number of physical illnesses. A sample of 141 female and 137 male residents of Lebanon, N.H., were interviewed on two occasions a year apart. Subjects ranged in age from 21 to 50 and were married, but not to each other. Physical health was measured by subjects' medical checklist responses as to number of current illnesses. Psychiatric symptoms were estimated from responses to a 22-item Mental Health Inventory. The inventory consisted of indexes of psychological disorder symptoms, psychophysiological symptoms, physiological symptoms of organic disorder, and ambiguous symptoms possibly associated with either organic or psychological illness.

Data from both interviews revealed that a greater percentage of women than men had high scores on the two indexes of psychological and psychophysiological symptoms. On the two other indexes containing physiological and ambiguous items, men showed a tendency to have slightly higher scores. This pattern was reaffirmed in the analysis of turnover (the proportion shifting between high and low scores) during the 1-year period. There were no sex differences in the prevalence or number of physical illnesses, whether measured by subjects' reports or doctors' diagnoses. A further finding was that women are more likely to seek medical care than are men with the same number of physical illnesses and similar psychiatric symptoms. It was suggested that women's higher rate of reported psychological symptoms reflects men's reluctance to admit to certain unpleasurable feelings and sensations, since they are aware of cultural expectations regarding expressive control. (46 references)

360
Weissman, Myrna M. The depressed woman: Recent research. *Social Work,* 17(5):19-25, 1972.

Depression. Social interaction. Mother-child relations. Marital satisfaction.

This article summarizes recent research on the social functioning of acutely depressed women and discusses the marital, sexual, and parental dysfunctioning associated with depression. Implications of these symptoms for casework treatment are provided. The discussion is based on an ongoing study of acutely depressed female patients conducted by Yale University School of Medicine and Boston State Hospital, from a review of the literature, and from a comparison of the social functioning of 40 female patients, aged 25-60, and a control group of 40 matched normal women. A social adjustment scale derived from the Gurland scale was used to assess social functioning. Clinical materials were also analyzed.

When compared with the control group, the depressed woman was found to have diminished functioning in all roles. During acute illness, she derived little satisfaction from her marriage or sexual relations, felt considerable resentment toward her husband, and was reluctant to discuss her feelings with him. Depressed patients were less emotionally involved with and felt less affection for their children, had difficulty communicating with them, and suffered considerable resentment and guilt toward them. Whereas drug therapy is effective on a short-term basis, psychological intervention is usually necessary to achieve longer term goals of improved social functioning, interpersonal communication, and understanding of maladaptive behavior. (25 references)

361
Weissman, Myrna M.; Paykel, Eugene S.; and Klerman, Gerald L. The depressed woman as a mother. *Social Psychiatry,* 7:98-108, 1972.

Depression. Mother-child relations.

This article presents the results of two studies of maternal behavior among acutely depressed women. One study compares depressed women with a matched normal group; the other involves clinical investigation of maternal impairment at different points in the family life cycle.

In the first study, the performance of 40 depressed and 40 normal women was assessed in a variety of roles. Ranking the subjects by social adjustment scores revealed highly significant differences in parental role functioning. The depressed women felt only moderately involved in their children's daily lives, reported difficulty in communicating and lessened affection, and were having considerable friction with their children, in contrast to the relations that the normal women reported with their children.

In the second study, stages in the family life cycle from post partum to "empty nest" were examined in terms of the maternal role and the child's developmental role. Depressed mothers of newborns were overindulgent, overprotective, or compulsive. Depressed mothers of children at later developmental stages were unable to become emotionally or physically involved in helping their children to learn social skills, cultural mores, and to develop peer relationships. They lacked the resilience to allow adolescents to experiment with independent behavior and were unable to deal successfully with the termination of childrearing. Most school age children did not develop overt psychological symptoms. The most severe problems occurred with the adolescents. (34 references)

362
Zucker, Robert A. Sex-role identity patterns and drinking behavior of adolescents. *Quarterly Journal of Studies on Alcohol,* 29(4):868-884, 1968.

Sex-role identification. Sex-role preference. Adolescents. Alcohol consumption.

Four hypotheses were tested within an adolescent sample: Heavier drinking males show a more masculine conscious sex-role identity pattern than moderate drinking males; heavier drinking males show a more feminine unconscious identity pattern than moderate drinkers; heavier drinking females show a more masculine identity pattern than moderate drinking females; and nondrinkers of both sexes show greater signs of cross-sex identity than moderate drinkers. Subjects were 143 boys and 221 girls with a mean age of 15 years. On the basis of questionnaires on frequency and quantity of alcohol consumed, the sample was rated as heavy drinkers, moderate drinkers, and nondrinkers. Conscious sex-role identity of 68 boys and 76 girls was measured by the Gough Femininity Scale. Sex-typed fantasy preferences for books and movies provided data on the unconscious sex identity of 75 boys and 145 girls.

There were no significant differences in conscious sex identity among the female drinking groups. On the measure of conscious identity, the heavy drinking males were significantly more masculine than the moderate drinkers and the nondrinkers. The nondrinkers showed greater cross-sex identification than the heavy drinkers, but less than the moderate drinkers. Categorized by drinking frequency, male heavy drinkers and nondrinkers had almost identical masculinity scores, which were slightly higher than those of the moderate drinkers. On the fantasy preference measure, there were no significant differences in unconscious identity between drinking groups for either boys or girls. From comparisons of the conscious and unconscious sexual identity measures, it was concluded that the difference between the heavier and lighter drinking boys was that the heavier drinkers put up a facade, consciously representing themselves as hypermasculine. (26 references)

CROSS-CULTURAL OVERVIEWS OF THE STATUS OF THE SEXES

363
Auvinen, Riita. Women and work (II): Social attitudes and women's careers. *Impact of Science on Society,* 20(1):73-83, 1970.

Finland. Public opinion. Female employment. Education.

The effects of informal social attitudes on women's actual educational and career opportunities in Finland are discussed. A distinction is made between legal equality of the sexes and practical equality, based on educational and occupational statistics. Women's rights to the same training and professional opportunities as men are a formal national objective; yet social attitudes of both men and women pose a major obstacle to equal participation. Career choice is a long-term process which begins very early in life and depends largely on personal preferences and values acquired from the social environment. Changes in policy are ineffective in providing subjective freedom of choice when pervasive social attitudes set other norms. Marriage is still seen as a woman's main career, and women tend to be underrepresented in certain professional fields and to hold lower-level positions than comparably trained men.

Sex differences in level of education no longer exist, but the type of education obtained is still strongly influenced by discriminatory vocational guidance and by other traditional attitudes within the educational system. At all levels of schooling, and particularly in vocational education, the choice of field of study is strongly sex-role oriented. Girls are concentrated in fields such as health care, textile crafts, home economics, and commercial and office work; they are largely excluded from such areas as wood and metal crafts and technical subjects. Data on the proportion of women in various fields and at various levels of university education are reported. Greater training and involvement of men in household tasks and partial assumption of responsibility for childrearing by society are changes which must be accelerated to permit full utilization of the female labor resource. (No references)

364
Bernard, Jessie. *Women and the Public Interest: An Essay on Policy and Protest.* Chicago: Aldine-Atherton, 1971. 293 pp.

Sex-typed occupations. Women's liberation.

This book presents an analytic framework for consideration of sociological and other data on women in relation to public interest, manpower training and utilization, concepts of self-fulfillment and sex roles, and the current women's liberation movement. The public interest is defined as the optimal use of people in the division of labor and the performance of all other necessary functions. General sex-typed jobs and career patterns of women in the medical, engineering, and management professions are examined. Sexual specialization of functions, as distinct from the sexual division of labor, is discussed in detail. These include glamor, homemaking, childrearing, reproduction, emotional support, and industrial production. The supportive function of women is seen as incompatible with some aspects of the production function. The women's liberation movement has challenged national policymakers to reexamine this conflict and its consequences for women. Women's movement leaders and their strategies are described. The issues of sexism, marriage, and the nuclear family are examined in conjunction with such proposed solutions as communes, expanded childrearing by men, and other implementations of a shared-role ideology.

The conflict between women's supportive and productive functions requires policy choices which give priority either to the general welfare or to the pursuit of happiness as the most suitable criterion of the public interest. It is asserted that sexual division of labor contradicts the general welfare and that sexual specialization of functions is a form of sexism that influences personality and impedes the pursuit of happiness. A general reformulation of society's ideas about the sexual differentiation of functions is called for to resolve the current paradoxes of public policy related to women. (2-40 references per chapter)

365
Brown, Donald R., ed. *The Role and Status of Women in the Soviet Union.* New York: Teachers College Press, 1968. 139 pp.

U.S.S.R. Female employment. Family structure. Social equality.

This is a collection of studies and discussion papers from a symposium on the role and status of Soviet women. A demographic study of the female population of the Soviet Union with regard to education, employment, and childbearing draws on previous research and statistics to compare the actual situation of contemporary Soviet women with Leninist ideology and Stalin's constitutional provisions. Changes in the image of women in Soviet literature are considered in an analysis of recent Soviet poetry. The focus of this analysis is on symbols reflecting the conflict between Soviet women's roles as woman and worker. Soviet and Western studies and essays provide information for an article considering changes in the Soviet family and the psychosocial impact of communal, institutional childrearing practices on individual development and social structure. Three shorter discussion papers are concerned with the effect of state abortion policy on the childbearing functions of the Soviet family, values affecting marital and family living, and differences between women students at Soviet and American universities. (0-53 references per chapter)

366
Brown, Judith K. A cross-cultural study of female initiation rites. *American Anthropologist,* 65:837-853, 1963.

Initiation rites. Adolescent females.

This study explored variations in female initiation rites in 75 societies. A female initiation rite consists of one or more ceremonial events mandatory for all girls of a given society between their 8th and 20th years, excluding betrothal or marriage. Three hypotheses were proposed: Female initiation rites, as an announcement of change in status from child to woman, occur in societies in which the young girl continues to reside in her mother's home after marriage. In societies in which the infant sleeps solely with its mother and in which the young married woman moves to her husband's home, female initiation rites involve a genital operation or extensive tatooing as a preparation for the adult role. In societies where females have an important role in subsistence activities, female initiation rites indicate the importance of this role and the young girl's competence to perform it. Ethnographic accounts and ratings by anthropologists provided tests of the hypotheses.

Of the 75 societies studied, 43 were found to practice initiation rites. In 22 of these societies, young married women resided with their mothers at least 50 percent of their married lives. Painful female rites were practiced in 7 of the 11 societies in which infant girls slept with their mothers exclusively and then moved into a male-dominated domestic unit. Six of these societies also practiced male rites involving a genital operation and seclusion. It was suggested that the conflict in sexual identity necessitates painful resolution for both sexes. Women played an important role in subsistence activities in 38 of the societies studied; and in 26 of these, female initiation rites were practiced. (23 references)

367
Brown, Judith K. Economic organization and the position of women among the Iroquois. *Ethnohistory*, 17(3-4):151-167, 1970.

Preindustrial societies. Social structure. Matriarchy.

The relationship between the status of women and their economic role is examined by comparing ethnohistoric and ethnographic data on the Iroquois of North America and the Bemba of Northern Rhodesia. A review of studies of these two matrilineal and matrilocal cultures shows that the economic organization of subsistence activities must be considered in determining the status of women.

Unlike Bemba women, Iroquois women controlled the factors of agricultural production. Iroquois male contributions to food production were not culturally emphasized, and the elected female leaders controlled food distribution. Through their power to supply or withhold food for council meetings, war parties, religious festivals, and daily meals, Iroquois matrons exercised control over tribal economic organization. These economic realities were institutionalized in the power of the matrons to nominate council elders, to influence council decisions and treaties, to elect religious leaders, and to control domestic life.

Although Bemba women enjoyed a higher status than women in many tribal societies, it was not nearly as high as that of the Iroquois, in spite of the similarities in rules of descent and marital residence between the two tribes. The unusual role of Iroquois women cannot be explained by historical circumstance, the social structure, or the extent of women's economic contributions. The high status of Iroquois women appears to result from their economic control of the tribe. (39 references)

368
Chafe, William Henry. *The American Woman: Her Changing Social, Economic and Political Roles, 1920-1970,* New York: Oxford University Press, 1972. 351 pp.

Female role. Historical trends. Employment. Social equality.

This historical study investigates whether the status of women has altered in the United States since 1920, why this social change has occurred, and how it is manifested. The book focuses on public perceptions of woman's "place" and on the impact of such events as war and depression on women's roles. The economic role of women is given special attention, since the issue of earning a living is seen as central in defining masculine and feminine responsibilities.

An introductory discussion traces the women's movement prior to 1920. For the period 1920-40, the topics of women and politics, women and economic equality, women in industry, women in professions, and the Equal Rights Amendment are examined. The impact of World War II is discussed in terms of the paradoxical situation of persistent sexual inequality despite rapid changes in female labor force participation. The debate on woman's place and the revival of feminism which have characterized the period since the 1940's are examined. The concluding section includes a discussion of the interplay of attitudes and behavior in effecting social change. Attitudes concerning sex roles are seen as so deeply rooted that behavioral change must precede any attitudinal change. It is postulated that, because World War II forced changes in the behavior of men and women, former attitudes concerning women became irrelevant. The increased employment of women has led to a gradual overlapping of sex roles, which is seen as a necessary precondition for an ideology of equality. It is speculated that the existing family structure will be modified rather than eliminated, and that women will accept discrimination and less competitive achievement for some time. In the long run, however, history is viewed as supporting continued change in women's status. This book is extensively footnoted and lists 51 private manuscript collections as data sources in addition to a selective bibliography. (305 references)

369
Chombart de Lauwe, M. J. Some changes in the situation of women in society. [Représentation des changements de la situation de la femme dans la société.] *Psychologie Francaise,* 9:86-101, 1964.

France. Social equality. Female role. Public opinion.

The Social Ethnology Group of France undertook this study, based on previous research on women in society, to determine people's awareness that women's situation in society is changing and the ways that different categories of people perceive these changes. Small, systematic samples were selected from different social milieux (working, middle, and upper class) to permit comparisons by specific variables, including sex, socioeconomic status of father, age, and region of the country. The total sample of French men and women included 360 married individuals (180 couples) and 100 single students, with an equal division of men and women in both samples.

In the married sample, the husband and wife were interviewed separately and then together. A pilot-tested questionnaire was administered to both samples.

Analysis of the data indicated that awareness of changing women's rights is related to awareness of general societal change, and that anticipated societal changes include changes in the economy; in professional, social, and political life; in domestic family life; and in female behavior and personality. Subjects expressed fears about the disruption of family relationships and unemployment; they expressed hope for humanizing professional relationships through the presence of women and for raising family income. The middle-class sample showed the greatest awareness of changes taking place and the most positive attitudes toward change. Whereas women tended to be both sensitive to and positive toward changes in the growth of their rights, men were more likely to express resentment and fear. Subjects born before the end of World War II were also more skeptical about changes in the status of women than younger people. With respect to region, new-town inhabitants were the most acutely aware of changes. For a majority of respondents, however, changes concerning women were uniformly perceived as symbols of the evolution of society at large. (4 references)

370
Chombart de Lauwe, Paul-Henry, ed. *Social Roles of Women: An International Study. [Images de la Femme dans la Société: Recherche Internationale.]* Paris: Les Éditions Ouvrieres, 1964. 280 pp.

Female role. Sex-role perceptions. National differences. Social equality.

This book contains 12 chapters on the roles of women in various countries by 10 researchers. The book reports the results of a sociological study sponsored by UNESCO to discover male and female perceptions of the role of women in France, Poland, Morocco, Ivory Coast, Canada, Togo, and Austria. Cultural and intellectual influences as well as the technological advances of the society were considered important determinants of change. This project reflects coordinated research, as opposed to a single international study. Although separate questionnaires were developed for each country, a nucleus of common questions were included in each survey. Subjects for the most part were of working-class origin, and from 60 to 250 subjects were interviewed in each country.

The discussion focuses primarily on the role of women at work and the equality of the sexes. Polish men and women appeared to be least opposed to the idea of women working, with Moroccan subjects the most vocal in their opposition. Male subjects in all countries most often pointed out the drawbacks of having women work. Equality of the sexes was examined regarding financial matters in the home. In most countries, men still hold the financial pursestrings, and household tasks are considered woman's work. It is concluded that women's role is changing throughout the world. Suggestions for new lines of research following from the present study are included. (1 to 19 references per chapter)

371

Cole, Johnneta B. Black women in America: An annotated bibliography. *Black Scholar,* 3(4):42-53, 1971.

Women's liberation. Female role. Family structure. Black women.

This selective bibliography includes materials on black women in America under 10 general headings: General reference works on black America; general reference works on women in the United States; socialist writings on women; women in revolutionary societies; woman's liberation; black women on women's liberation; women in Africa; black families in Africa, the Caribbean, and the United States; black women in the United States; and autobiographical and biographical materials on black women in the United States. (185 references)

372

Dahlström, Edmund, ed. *The Changing Roles of Men and Women.* Boston: Beacon Press, 1971. 302 pp.

Sweden. Social equality. Sex-role ideology.

This book by a team of Scandinavian social scientists examines the modern debate on sex roles from the disciplines of sociology, psychology, social psychology, industrial sociology, and economics. This revised English language version of the original 1962 Swedish book *Kvinnors Liv och Arbete* (Women's Life and Work) discusses the data available on the family and work roles of both men and women and introduces new ideas to the ideological debate. Specific chapters concern the family and married women who work, sex roles and the socialization process, parental role division and the child's personality, the positions of men and women in the labor market, and analysis of the current sociological debate on sex roles. Also included are a historical sketch of the women's movement in Sweden and the full text of *The Status of Women in Sweden,* a 1968 report to the United Nations reviewing Government reforms in family law, family policy, education, and labor market policy. (0-22 references per chapter)

373
De Vos, George, and Wagatsuma, Hiroshi. Status and role behavior in changing Japan. In: Seward, Georgene H., and Williamson, Robert C., eds. *Sex Roles in Changing Society.* New York: Random House, 1970. pp. 334-370.

Japan. Family structure. Marital roles.

This discussion draws on existing sociological and psychological studies to assess the relationship between Japan's social sex roles and the relatively successful modernization of Japanese culture. Continuities from past to present society are examined in relation to the instrumental and expressive role components of the three generational and two sex-role positions found in the traditional Japanese family. These instrumental vectors are achievement, competence, responsibility, and control. Expressive vectors considered are pleasure-pain, harmony-discord, affiliation-separation, and nurturance-deprivation.

Evidence is presented to counter the Western view of the overbearing Japanese male and his totally self-abnegating wife. It is suggested that the interdependent structure of the family allows for direct and indirect expression of achievement-oriented, nurturant, and nurturance-seeking behaviors by both sexes. The primacy of role over the individual results in status satisfaction and ego protection as well as in inhibition of individualism. Marriage in Japan is increasingly oriented toward companionship and intimacy. However, the degree of gratification in one's interpersonal relations is still related to underlying expectations concerning the obligations and satisfactions of traditional roles. (48 references)

374
Domenach, Jean-Marie, ed. Woman at Work [La Femme au Travail.] *Éspirit,* 295:721-1020, 1961.

Female employment. France.

In the introduction to this special issue of *Éspirit* on women at work, it is pointed out that the traditional balance of the sexes has been disturbed. Thrown into the workday world of men, women have experienced changes in their lives that are little understood, especially by women themselves. The articles are divided into four topics: Dimensions of the problem, including the evolution of the working woman, women's rights in Russia, and a discussion of myths and realities about women's capacity to work and their implications for her other roles; biological data on women; social contradictions, emphasizing the need for concrete legal and social reform to facilitate women's work; and ambiguity in women's attitudes toward their own condition.

In addition to the collected articles, this issue presents the results of an opinion survey of organizations considered representative of French attitudes about working women. Included in the sample are professional, social, and civic associations; unions; public and private companies; and politicians. (30 references)

375
Dowty, Nancy. To be a woman in Israel. *School Review,* 80(2):319-332, 1972.

Middle-aged women. Cultural differences. Israel. Psychological adjustment.

A broad-scale survey was conducted to explore cultural responses to aspects of middle age among women from five Israeli subcultures. The study utilized data from a pilot investigation, followup psychiatric interviews, and survey information from 1,148 middle-aged women to determine whether the modern or the traditional culture presents greater rewards to women in their middle years. Brief histories of the Muslim Arab villagers and of Jewish immigrants from North Africa, Persia, Turkey, and Central Europe are presented to define a traditional-to-modern continuum in terms of equality of rights, education, religion, and size of family.

European and Arab women were found to be the best adjusted to middle age, with Persian women the least adjusted. Women in more modern cultures evaluated menopause as the welcome end of fertility and as an improvement in their marital relationships, but they perceived a decline in social status and possible negative changes in their emotional health. Traditional women perceived their emotional health and status as improved with middle age, but were less optimistic about their marriages and the end of their fertility. Transitional women, having neither value system and being no longer matriarchs, had the least positive perceptions of middle age. Comparisons between the Arabs and Europeans showed that obedience to tradition does not preclude actively coping with changes. These findings suggest that in cultures in transition, rather than in modern or traditional cultures, problems for middle-aged women arise from the demands for new roles in a changed environment. (10 references)

376
Field, Mark G., and Flynn, Karin I. Worker, mother, housewife: Soviet woman today. In: Brown, Donald R., ed. *The Role and Status of Women in the Soviet Union.* New York: Teachers College Press, 1968. pp. 7-56. Also in: Seward, Georgene H., and Williamson, Robert C., eds. *Sex Roles in Changing Society.* New York: Random House, 1970. pp. 257-284.

U.S.S.R. Female role.

This discussion utilizes Soviet Government statistics, empirical studies, and other publications to examine the current economic, political, and social status of the Soviet woman. Women have become an integral part of the Soviet labor force, due not so much to egalitarian ideology as to manpower shortages caused by the two wars and the industrialization and collectivization initiated by Stalin. Employed women are underrepresented in managerial and executive functions and overrepresented in subordinate positions and menial productive labor. Although women are now heavily represented in medicine, engineering, and teaching, their proportions are dropping as shortages of males lessen. On the other hand, as consumer production gradually replaces heavy industry and as automation increases, it is expected that more women will be found in white-collar and professional positions. Although the educational status of Soviet women is less than that of men, it is surpassed by few other countries. The role of women in the Communist Party is more than token, but does not approach equality. However, women are fairly well represented in the Communist Youth League, in the Soviet, and in labor unions. Women were awarded one-third of all medals and awards of distinction in the period 1918-67.

Four social roles of Soviet women are discussed, ranging from the heroine of the factory and home to the "socially regressive parasite," who is dependent on a husband or father. The woman who chooses occupational achievement is likely to be considered exemplary, provided she does not neglect her family functions. There is evidence from the Soviet press that hard physical labor for women is becoming less acceptable and that childrearing is being recognized as an important function, with status. (47 references)

377
Ford, Clellan S. Some primitive societies. In: Seward, Georgene H., and Williamson, Robert C., eds. *Sex Roles in Changing Society.* New York: Random House, 1970. pp. 25-43.

Preindustrial societies. Sex-typed behavior. Physiological determinants.

This examination of the roles of men and women in primitive (preindustrial) societies is based on ethnographic data from the cultural anthropology literature and from the Human Relations Area Files. A brief summary is presented of some secondary biological differences between the sexes which seem to have cultural significance.

The assumption that the activities of males and females are strongly influenced by biological heritage is supported in the literature. The reproductive role is the single most important biological fact among primitive peoples in determining how men and women live, and categorization of the members of society by sex is universal. Since polygamy is permitted in nearly every primitive culture and practiced in varying degrees, marriage is a possibility for most women. In many societies the woman's reproductive role reaches beyond the matter of giving birth to young and suckling them, and most restrictions imposed by primitive societies upon a woman's freedom stem directly from some aspect of her reproductive role. In societies where adults attempt to control the sexual activities of the young, a double standard is likely to prevail, with the more strict control applied to the females. Men are also generally permitted more freedom than women where restrictions are in force for adult sexual behavior. The training of children for their sex roles in adult life begins at an early age, and the differential sex typing that characterizes early phases of the life cycle is generally carried on into old age, with the ascription of higher status roles to men.

In primitive societies, there is always some division of labor between the sexes, with some tasks performed exclusively by men and others by women. Although the number of sex-typed activities varies among societies and the particular activities assigned to each sex role vary markedly, in no society are all tasks interchangeable. Overall, it is not anticipated that advanced technological development or conscious striving for sexual equality will fundamentally change sex roles. (14 references)

378
Frederiksson, Ingrid. Why sex roles? [Varför könsroller?] In: *Samlevnad i Överflöd.* Lund, Sweden: RFSU, 1966. pp. 69-82.

Sweden. Social equality. Sex-role ideology.

This article discusses some basic questions about the male-female role in Swedish society. It is suggested that societies with a racial problem base social attitudes on biological signs. The same is true of many modern societies where rights, responsibilities, and work are divided according to sex rather than individual skills or talents. Moreover, because of social expectations, persons of different sex behave in accordance with accepted roles and thus give apparent confirmation of the prejudices. The debate about sex roles involves the role of men in society as well as of women. The goal is not to give a woman the same role as a man, but to consider both men and women as individuals who have equal responsibility for their economy, work, and childrearing.

It is argued that a very small part of what is considered masculine or feminine behavior is a result of biological differences. The average differences between the sexes are often less than the differences between individuals of the same sex. In the area of sexuality, there is frequent misunderstanding regarding what is biologically "natural."

The question is raised why politicians have failed to realize the necessity of sufficient child care facilities to aid working parents and support sex-role reforms presently underway. Apparently, many politicians are unaware of the problem because they have domestic help themselves; they may also not want to offend traditionally oriented female constituents. Many older people prefer that the man work and the woman stay at home. On the other hand, many middle-aged people develop psychological problems from lack of postparental activities. Without knowledge of employment opportunities for which they are qualified, older women are under pressure to take underpaid jobs. (17 references)

379
Gerson, Menachem. Women in the kibbutz. *American Journal of Orthopsychiatry,* 41(4):566-573. 1971.

Kibbutzim. Social equality. Female role. Israel.

This historical article focuses on the three stages of kibbutz evolution and the changing concept of sexual equality, from the early exaggerated and male-oriented egalitarianism through the gradual recognition and positive differences in the interests and capabilities of men and women. Despite the realization of many goals of social, sexual, and economic equality, women in the kibbutz are currently dissatisfied with their work and their society.

A major consideration is whether altered social conditions bring change in feminine characteristics, or if there is indeed an essential feminine character rooted in biological structure. This idea is discussed in relation to the movement for familial tendencies, the disillusionment of many now middle-aged founding-generation females, the current trend among the young toward early marriage and noncareer involvement, and the future of the kibbutz.

It is concluded that radical change in social conditions does not immediately produce a corresponding psychological change. Changes in fundamental attitudes take time. Several suggestions are offered for deepening the involvement and satisfaction of women in kibbutz life and for increasing the existing choices of roles and prestige occupations. (No references)

380

Haavio-Mannila, Elina. Activity and passivity among women in Finland. [Aktivitat och passivitet bland kvinnor i Finland.] In: *Kynne eller Kön.* Stockholm: Raben o Sjögren, 1966. pp. 105-131.

Scandinavia. Social equality. National differences.

This study evaluates female sex roles in Finland and compares them with those in other Nordic countries (Sweden, Denmark, Norway, and Iceland). Data show that the percentage of women among university students and the employed population is much higher in Finland than in other Nordic countries. This is explained by the less patriarchal tradition in Finland. Data also partially support the hypothesis that the patriarchal tradition is stronger in rural areas than in towns and among farmers compared with workers.

Women's rights emerged earlier in Finland, but the movement was less radical and aggressive than in other Nordic countries. Also, in Finland the movement spread very rapidly within rural as well as urban areas. As a result, women were granted the right to vote in 1906, earlier than in any other European country. In other women's rights developments, Finland has tended to follow Sweden's lead. For example, Finnish women were allowed in government departments in 1926, one year after Sweden. However, women were granted equal rights with men in marriage laws in 1929 in both countries. Even though women's participation in society has increased, particularly in education and employment, there are indications that women tend to cling to traditional roles more than men. This tendency varies among different classes and between rural and urban populations in all the Nordic countries. (22 references)

381

Haavio-Mannila, Elina. The position of Finnish women: Regional and cross-national comparisons. *Journal of Marriage and the Family,* 31(2):339-347, 1969.

Scandinavia. U.S.S.R. Social equality. National differences.

This review of official demographic statistics, interview data, and earlier research studies discusses both formal and informal sex-role behavior and attitudes in Finland as compared with the rest of Scandinavia and the Soviet Union.

Finnish women participate with relative emancipation on the formal level of society, and Finnish behavior and attitudes related to employment of women are fairly consistent. In Finland, women are active in national politics, in higher education, and in the labor force, although less active in local politics or volunteer organizations. However, informal behavior and attitudes toward women are more traditional in terms of power in the society and division of household tasks. Although vigorous discussion of sex roles has taken place in Finland since 1965, no national child care system exists, and husbands help out little in the home. Finland's unique historical and geographical circumstances largely explain why women there are active and hard working in the society, but are not very powerful or appreciated.

A comparison of sex-role behavior in Scandinavia and the Soviet Union shows that the formal activity of women increases from west to east. In the home, however, the informal division of labor between the sexes is most traditional in the Soviet Union, less so in Finland, and least traditional in Sweden. (7 references)

382
Havio-Mannila, Elina. Convergences between East and West: Tradition and modernity in sex roles in Sweden, Finland and the Soviet Union. *Acta Sociologica,* 14(1-2):114-125, 1971.

Household tasks. Employment trends, National differences. Scandinavia. U.S.S.R.

Changes in the participation of men and women in the labor force during the 20th century and the present division of household tasks are examined in Sweden, Finland, and the Soviet Union. Sex-role attitudes in Finland and Sweden are also studied. Trends within each country and differences between them are explained in terms of time and rate of industrialization, and of economic, educational, and ideological factors. Census statistics, surveys, and opinion polls provide data.

The division of household labor in urban areas is very similar in the three countries. Despite different proportions of working wives in the samples, division of tasks generally follows traditional sex roles. This finding suggests that changes in the economic and political roles of women have not filtered down to the family level.

Sweden, the first of the three countries to industrialize, has experienced some phenomena not evidenced in the other two. For example, ideologies favoring female economic independence and the training of women for skilled occupations make it unlikely that Finland or the Soviet Union will duplicate the 1930's Swedish women workers' "return-home" movement. In both Finland and the U.S.S.R., the proportion of women in nonagricultural occupations has steadily increased while the proportion in agriculture has decreased. Industrialized Sweden has been the country most able to support the institution of the nonemployed housewife, but because of a labor shortage in the 1960's, the Swedish Government began improving child care centers and encouraging more women to work. Finland, unlike Sweden, has a tradition of rural equality which merged in the late 1960's with modern urban egalitarian sex-role standards. (11 references)

383
Havel, Jean Eugene. The Condition of Women. [La Condition de la Femme.] *Paris: Librairie* A. Colin, 1961. 219 pp.

Female role. Historical trends.

This book outlines the history of woman's role in Western civilization based on historical facts and on the way women have been portrayed in literature. Beginning with ancient Greece, woman's lot in public life, work, marriage, and motherhood is described. The topic of prostitution is treated in some historical detail. The discussion emphasizes the growing status of women in the economy. Two pervasive historical frameworks by which women have been viewed are noted: In biological comparisons of the sexes, sometimes men and sometimes women have been considered superior; when the discussion centers on human identity, no clear, consistent sexual hierarchy emerges. The remaining discussion focuses on the complexities and inconsistencies in these two perspectives of women's role. (19 references)

384
Holmberg, Per. The economic and social consequences of today's sex roles in society. [Om de ekonomiska och sociala konsekenserna av nu varande könsroller.] In *Kynne eller Kön.* Stockholm: Raben o Sjogren, 1966. pp. 15-30.

Sweden. Social equality.

The social and economic effects of traditional female sex roles in Sweden are discussed. Changes in sex roles are seen as an economic

and social need of highest priority, as well as a question of justice.
Economic effects of traditional sex discrimination are manifested in
unused human resources and underutilized skills in the labor market,
poor distribution of labor, and in the loss of private and public
consumption and investment potential. Social effects of traditional
sex roles are discussed in relation to the declining fertility rate,
increasing class discrepancies, social-medical problems (alcoholism,
suicide, etc.), political organizations and political change, unequal
social and tax regulations, and the disproportionate number of
widows in the population. The effects on single persons, and
especially widows, are discussed in terms of suffering imposed as well
as economic and social losses. It is suggested that the material
standard of living in Sweden could double with the institution of
equal roles in society for men and women. (5 references)

385
Holstrom, Engin Inel. Changing sex roles in a developing country.
Journal of Marriage and the Family, 35(3):546-553, 1973.

Turkey. Sex-role perceptions. Marital roles. Urban-rural differences.

This study identified groups of Turkish families with different degrees
of exposure to urban life styles to compare the self images, attitudes,
and husband-wife interactions of couples. A traditionally patriarchal
society, Turkey is currently undergoing industrialization and is thus
appropriate for studying how new behaviors and attitudes regarding
the role of women affect the family structure.

Data were obtained from three female populations on a rural-urban
continuum: 53 rural-born wives living in squatter-house areas in and
around Istanbul; 25 rural-born wives married to *Kapici* (doormen) in
Istanbul; and 65 upper middle-class, educated, urban wives. The
interview probed family structure and dynamics, including the wife's
attitudes toward the husband and her self-perception, as measured by
the Kuhn and McPartland procedure and by a list of adjective pairs
describing self and Turkish people in general.

Contrary to expectation, discrepancies between prevailing cultural
norms and actual daily behavioral patterns do not invariably produce
strains and dissatisfactions. The upper middle-class urban wives were
much more active, participant, and modern than dictated by
traditional Turkish mores. More autonomous life patterns also have
evolved for women in both rural-migrant groups. However, the urban
wives seemed to consider themselves a cultural elite; the squatter
housewives saw themselves and the society as still quite traditional;
and only the *Kapici* wives were dissatisfied with their semimodern
lives as compared with the adjacent urban life style.

Personal stress and satisfaction outcomes vary in industrializing countries, depending on such factors as the perceived status of the husband as breadwinner, the role of exemplary cultural elites, and the perception of self in relation to reference groups and the society at large. (6 references)

386

Holter, Harriet. *Sex Roles and Social Structure.* Oslo, Norway: Universitetsforlaget, 1970. 299 pp.

Norway. Sex-typed behavior. Sex-role development. Social interaction.

This book describes patterns of sex-role differentiation in contemporary Norwegian society and discusses some of the processes that maintain sex-role differentiation. A primary aim is to broaden the investigative context of gender roles from the family to the social system as a whole. Data relevant to political, occupational, and educational life in Norway are considered in terms of normative and ideological aspects of sex-role differentiation and sex differences in behaviors and attitudes. Sources are psychological and sociological studies by the author and others. It is postulated that the sociological and sociopsychological meaning of sex roles can be analyzed without considering the exact implications of physical and biological sex differences, and that understanding of one gender role requires consideration of the complementary role.

When discussed as part of the social structure, differentiation is viewed as one system of norms and patterned behavior. However, a discussion of patterns of sex differentiation concerns relationships among the values, norms, and behaviors that differ by sex. An introductory essay summarizes prominent theories of sex-role differentiation and elaborates on general propositions concerning the social foundations of sex differentiation. Other theoretical topics include the development of sex roles, the maintenance of gender-differentiated behavior in individuals, and the effect of sex differentiation on other components of the social system and on interaction patterns between men and women and within same-sex groups. (248 references)

387

Horoszowski, Pawel. Woman's status in socialistic and capitalistic countries (I). *International Journal of Sociology of the Family,* 1(1):35-52, 1971.

National differences. Sex-ratios. Birth rates. Marital status. Education.

This article comprises part one of a two-part comparative analysis of woman's status in socialist and capitalist countries. Part one presents statistical data on population by age and sex, women's marital status, birth rates, and male and female education for various capitalist and socialist nations.

No substantial differences in male-female population ratios exist among most socialist and capitalist countries. Although the Soviet Union has a distinctly larger proportion of women to men, capitalist countries such as Austria and West Germany have a similar ratio. No differences in male-female proportions are connected unequivocally with the socialist or capitalist system. No difference exists between socialist and capitalist countries in percentages of married women of various ages. However, from 1950 to 1965 the divorce rate in capitalist countries generally declined, while it increased substantially in Poland, Hungary, and the Soviet Union. Despite the greater availability of birth control devices and state-approved abortions in many socialist countries, no consequential differences in birth rates were found between the two types of countries. In regard to women's participation in education, socialist and capitalist countries did not differ overall. (No references)

388
Horoszowski, Pawel. Woman's status in socialistic and capitalistic countries (II). *International Journal of Sociology of the Family,* 1(2):160-180, 1971.

National differences. Female employment. Political participation. Poland.

This conclusion of a two-part comparative analysis of women's status in socialist and capitalist countries concerns sex differences in occupational activity and in crime and suicide rates. Data are provided by national and international statistical yearbooks, sociological reports, and a 1968 study of women's role in Poland.

Women's economic activity is slightly higher in socialist than in capitalist countries because of greater participation in agriculture. Single women in capitalist countries generally tend to be more economically active than married women; in socialist countries, the opposite tendency appears. The discussion of women's role in Poland examines male and female economic, political, and social participatory rates in detail. Although high percentages of physicians, dentists, and pharmacists in Poland are women, health service in Poland (as in other socialist countries) is neither well-paid nor a prestigious field. Of the deputies in the Polish Parliament (1965-69), 12.4 percent were women. In 1966, 19.1 percent of all party members were women. Although women made up 34.8 percent of all union members in 1966, only 19 percent of the managerial board members were female. A survey of 5,708 Polish women indicated that 25 percent of the working women questioned were unhappy with their work situation and that 58 percent of all subjects believed women should not be economically active. Over half of the working women reported no help with housework, over 75 percent did not vacation away from home, and large percentages did not attend various kinds of cultural entertainment.

Data available for capitalist and some socialist countries indicate that male-female crime and suicide rates do not differ between the two types of countries. It is suggested that it will be several decades before the effects of changes in women's role can be assessed for rates of suicide, crime, and other social phenomena. For the present, women's emancipation is seen as being far from a reality in both capitalist and socialist countries. (17 references)

389

Huang, Lucy Jen. A re-evaluation of the primary role of the Communist Chinese woman: The homemaker or the worker. *Marriage and Family Living,* 25(2):162-166, 1963. Also in: Bardwick, Judith M., ed. *Readings on the Psychology of Women.* New York: Harper & Row, 1972, pp. 231-235.

Female role. People's Republic of China.

This report on changes in women's roles in Communist China since 1949 analyzes a discussion of values and attitudes in the socialist society initiated and reported by the magazine, *Women of China.* The magazine described a female worker who was preoccupied with her family and home, and invited opinions from its readers. A majority of women responding were critical of the worker's "individualistic," "hedonistic," and "middle-class" thinking. Predominant attitudes were that love of family is secondary to work for the people, and that only through group welfare in the perfect socialist society is there happiness for anyone. The magazine editors summed up the discussion by suggesting that the errant worker concern herself with the revolution and "the warmth of the people's large family."

In evaluating this magazine discussion, the report notes that the Communist Party continuously strives to promote the idea that female employment promises not only more labor for the state, but liberation of women from the confines of household chores and economic dependence on men. However, during the initial period of socialist reconstruction, there have been problems of family instability and dissatisfaction on the part of some female workers. This report concludes that full-time participation in the labor force will continue to raise the status of women in China, and that, for many, the void left by the demise of the traditional consanguineal family will be filled by loyalty toward the "people's large family." (2 references)

390
Lehr, Ursula, and Rauh, Hellgard. Male and female in the German Federal Republic. In: Seward, Georgene H., and Williamson, Robert C., eds. *Sex Roles in Changing Society*. New York: Random House, 1970. pp. 220-239.

German Federal Republic. Stereotypes. Family structure. Female role.

Sex-role stereotypes still prevalent in German social science literature are compared with actual sex roles and public opinion in the German Federal Republic. Evidence disputing stereotypes is provided by statistics on education and employment, work-life histories of men and women from different age groups, and studies comparing male and female behavior, family roles, moral standards, and ideals.

Although the father-centered family is no longer accepted as the norm, many social scientists sustain traditional ideas concerning feminine characteristics and "women's work." Other investigators refer to the wife's dominance in the family since the middle of the century, especially with respect to her educational functions. It is concluded from the various empirical sources that neither the traditional patriarch nor the dominating wife is an accurate conception. Even at the turn of the century, women had prominent social positions, although within the bounds of home and family. Sex-role changes since 1900 are largely attributable to women's access to higher education, political life, and equal rights regarding major family decisions. Actual changes in sex roles in West Germany have usually concerned degree of expectation and attitudes, rather than behavior patterns. Although no essential changes in the male role in work or the family are indicated, there has been a leveling of sex-role differences in the urban, higher social class, younger generation. (76 references)

391
Liljeström, Rita. The Swedish model. In: Seward, Georgene H., and Williamson, Robert C. eds. *Sex Roles in Changing Society*. New York: Random House, 1970. pp. 200-219.

Sweden. Social equality. Government policy. Female role. Sociocultural determinants.

The official position of the Swedish Government on sexual equality is compared with the current division of roles in Sweden regarding education, the family, the labor market, and organizational participation. The 1968 report to the United Nations on the status of women in Sweden and other empirical studies provide data. Prior to the 1960's, prevailing official and liberal public opinion was that women had a right to an occupational role before and after the period of childrearing. More recently, the Government and "cultural radicals" have come to agree that social reform in education, employment, and Government benefits should enable both parents to engage in work and/or childrearing with equal economic status regardless of role.

The Government has removed legal obstacles to equality and has attempted to stimulate the interest of both sexes in occupational alternatives. Nevertheless, deeply rooted conceptions of women and of their employers, fellow workers, and families have sustained a strongly traditional orientation to sex roles. This orientation persists in Swedish students' vocational choices and in mass media socialization. Content analysis of Swedish children's books revealed that girls' stories emphasize emotionalism and outward appearance, whereas boys' stories emphasize knowledge and individual achievement. Although female employment has tended to increase with completion of childrearing at a younger age and Government programs of adult education, division of jobs by sex has hindered achievement of equal wages. Women's voting participation equals that of men, yet their political knowledge is less and they hold few political offices. More women are found to participate in organizations of a religious or charitable nature than in male-dominated labor unions, economic groups, and sports clubs. (16 references)

392
Lundin, Åge. Sex roles and democracy. [Könsroller och demokrati.] In: Kynne eller Kön.~Stockholm: Raben o Sjögren, 1966. pp. 161-175.

Denmark. Working wives. Working mothers. Family structure.

This discussion of changes in sex roles in Danish society during the last 20 years asserts that changes have become more obvious and rapid during the last 2 years, not because of a more mature society or a democratization of the family, but because there is now a need for women in the labor market. The housewife is more and more regarded as a luxury. This has made it easier for many women to enter the labor market, but it has also forced some women to work without previous education or other preparation for their new role. Also, the rest of the family is not prepared for a change in women's roles. The result is that a majority of working women have to adopt a dual role. If traditional female roles must be performed under new conditions, the male role and the role of the whole family must change as well.

The majority of studies exploring women and the labor market deal with problems in connection with mother and child. The role of the father is seldom mentioned, although a woman's experience of her own sex role is closely linked with the male role and male expectations of the female role. Men often tend to cling to their old position and to emphasize their traditional role when they feel their authority crumbling. The traditional "pater familias" role can only with difficulty be combined with the role of a working woman.

Women often must accept dull, monotonous work because of their lack of training and poor education. An ongoing study of the atmosphere of the place of work found that persons in management positions preferred women for dull jobs, and that women were willing to accept monotonous work because it allows them to think about what to do when they return home. Many regard their work as merely an extension of their roles as housewives.

This discussion also considers women in leadership roles and the training of both sexes to work together. The role of day care facilities in allowing women to work and in training children to accept new roles in concert with new ideas regarding personal freedom in these roles is discussed. (5 references)

393
Mandel, William M. Soviet women in the work force and professions. *American Behavioral Scientist*, 15(2):255-280, 1971.

U.S.S.R. Female employment. Professional women.

Recent statistical data and some personal observations of the investigator are presented to provide up-to-date knowledge of the changes in women's employment status in the Soviet Union. The major thesis is that women have advanced in the Soviet labor force approximately in direct proportion to the elimination of handicaps inherited by the Soviet regime. Residual sex differences in employment are attributed to an inevitable time lag. Prerevolutionary, post-World War II, and the most recent census data are compared to refute the common Western view that the current employment situation of Soviet women is static or has worsened.

In the 1970 census, women comprised 50.5 percent of the Soviet labor force and 54.3 percent of the total Soviet population. Sex differentials persist within individual fields of employment, primarily because of women's own initial patterns of interest. Women are the majority in the two professions in the middle of the pay scale, medicine and teaching, and the minority in the engineering (highest paying) and law (lowest paying) fields. The rise of professional women is greatest in fields not associated with traditional women's roles. More jobs are actually available in skilled physical labor than in the professions and academia, and the most rapid rate of increase in female employment has been in the most highly skilled mechanical trades. Evidence of prejudice against women, special protective legislation for women, and the employment problems of women are also discussed and briefly compared with conditions elsewhere. It is concluded that the Soviet Union has consistently implemented its original revolutionary social policy regarding women in the work force and professions. (30 references)

394
Michel, Andrée, and Texier, Geneviève. *The Condition of the Contemporary French Woman: Myths and Realities. [La Condition de la Francaise D'aujourd'hui: Mythes et Réalités.]* Geneva: Gonthier, 1964. 237 pp.

France. Female role. Stereotypes. Sexual discrimination. Historical trends.

This book traces changes in women's roles since the early 19th century, drawing heavily on the literature of attitudes about women who work and mythology about characteristics of women. Part I examines myths and preconceptions about women in society with respect to procreation, the family, professions, and politics, with emphasis on feminine dependency, the preeminence of man, women's presumed inabilities, and feminine passivity.

Part II historically examines women's real status in society. An analysis of specific laws affecting wives and mothers is included. A review of the stages of women's movement into professions since the last half of the 19th century emphasizes discriminatory employment practices and attitudes as well as other impediments, such as repressive tax laws. The status of women in political life is described, including the extent to which they are represented, their political rights, discrimination in party politics, and traditional and innovative models or solutions to their political problems. It is concluded that women are repressed as a result of specific laws and the arsenal of myths forged by society. Sexism, like racism, requires administrative and legal reform, but women must undertake demythification themselves, since men tend to be traditional in their views of woman's place in society. (14 references)

395
Moberg, Eva. The conditional liberation of women. [Kvinnans villkorliga frigivning.] In: *Unga Liberaler.* Stockholm: Bonniers, 1961. pp. 68-87.

Sweden. Female role. Social equality.

This essay considers the burden of contemporary Swedish woman's double role. She has the right to develop her capabilities and interests by choosing any form of education and employment; at the same time, she has to fulfill her role as wife and mother. The role of the mother has always been the main task for the woman, and the scope of this role has substantially limited the possibilities for women to be independent individuals. The ideological aim of women's liberation is to give every individual the best possible means to develop himself or herself. However, governments tend only to support individual development when its benefits to society are obvious. An example of this tendency is the support provided for women in industrial production during World War II; after the war, support was reduced or withdrawn.

Three explanations are offered as to why women do not engage more actively in attempting to liberate themselves: Their childbearing functions make them periodically dependent for subsistence and security; the desire to abolish traditional sex roles is interpreted as a symptom of deficiencies in relations with the opposite sex; and marriage and motherhood bring social prestige not available to the single woman. Also, marriage does not require competitiveness or occupational development. A necessity for the achievement of equality between men and women is that women become socially and economically independent of men. A salary to the housewife is not a solution, because wives would still be dependent on husbands as employers.

Discussion of the possibilities for equality within the marriage suggests the following: With total integration of women into the labor market, the workday could be reduced to 6 hours; the parents' personalities and emotions are important for a child's development and harmony, not the number of hours the parents spend with the child; and home duties should be shared because studies show that children exclusively brought up in day care centers develop less rapidly, both emotionally and intellectually.

In conclusion, the article calls for a public debate which would bring out all hidden conceptions and prejudices, in particular those present in the weekly magazines. Social reforms in relation to the role of children and women in the labor market should be stepped up. Sex differences should be abolished in education, upbringing, and the public media. Social reforms have given women their double role in society, and many more changes in society are needed before these goals are met. (6 references)

396

Munroe, Robert L., and Munroe, Ruth H. A cross-cultural study of sex gender and social structure. *Ethnology,* 8(2):206-211, 1969.

Language. Social structure.

This study tested the hypothesis that the relative frequency of masculine and feminine nouns in languages with sex gender is partially determined by social structural factors. Although social structure probably does not account for the origins of gender in language, already existing gender forms may reflect a structural societal bias. Thus, a society with a patribias would be expected to have a relatively high proportion of masculine nouns.

Six Indo-European languages—one each from the Celtic, Germanic, Hellenic, Indic, Romance, and Slavic subfamilies—and four non-European languages were investigated. Six of the languages are spoken by societies listed in the *Ethnographic Atlas,* and data were available on social structural sex biases. Closely related languages represented in the *Atlas* were substituted for the languages of three societies not listed. Three characteristics coded in the *Atlas* were used to measure the degree of male and female bias in the social structure: Marital residence, kin groups, and inheritance. The ratios of male-to-female nouns for six of the languages were available from an earlier study. A sex-gender count was computed for the three remaining languages.

A significant relationship was found between structural sex bias and male-female gender proportions. The five societies with a majority of male-bias items also had a majority of male-gender nouns. The four societies with a minority of male-bias items had a minority of male-gender nouns. Because no society with a female structural bias had been included in the study, data from the Khasi of Assam were added. The Khasi data also confirmed the hypothesis. (26 references)

397

Patai, Raphael, ed. *Women in the Modern World.* New York: Free Press, 1967. 519 pp.

National differences. Social equality.

This book presents an international review of changes in the status of women during recent decades, particularly since World War II. Developments encompass the legal, sexual, social, occupational, economic, political, and cultural realms. The introduction presents a thesis regarding patterns of development in women's emancipation from the home. The 22 articles are written by social scientists, the majority of whom are native to the countries or geographic areas they discuss. Countries examined are grouped according to similarities in degree of traditionalism or modernity of sex roles.

India and Pakistan are the most traditional in the status and freedom of their women, followed by the Muslim Middle East and the Latin-Mediterranean areas. France, West Germany, Israel, and Japan have both traditional and modern elements in their sex roles. Sub-Saharan African, Burmese and Southeast Asian, and Indonesian women have historically had a degree of freedom not attained by women in some Western countries until recently. In the Soviet Union and mainland China, economic, political, and social equality between the sexes has been notably enforced by governmental measures. Finally, Scandinavia, Great Britain, and the United States are generally considered the "Western spearhead" of women's rights. (0-37 references per chapter)

398

Prokopec, Jiri. The married woman in family life and at work. [La femme marieé dans sa famille et son emploi.] *La Nouvelle Critique,* 42:152-171, 1964.

Poland. Czechoslovakia. Working wives. Working mothers.

This study of the working wife's condition in society was undertaken in Poland and Czechoslovakia by the Czech State Commission on Population and the Polish Central Institute of Statistics. Women's opinions were solicited about the current trend toward population decline and the number of children they personally prefer to bear. Of 7,955 women interviewed, 61 percent were employed and 39 percent were housewives. Findings from the study were that most women who do not work cite health or raising children as their reasons for not doing so; industrial companies are more concerned with elevating women's work status than are agricultural organizations; most employed women are satisfied with their work; women who work are more active in political and public life than nonworking women; and most women would prefer to have no more than two children under any circumstances. For those who would like to have a third child, improved financial status and good health were frequently cited as prerequisites.

The article suggests that the economic and cultural development of society requires favorable public opinion toward having families and raising children. Working conditions will have to be improved so that women can successfully lead a double life of wife-and-mother and worker. (2 references)

399
Rabin, A. I. The sexes: Ideology and reality in the Israeli Kibbutz. In: Seward, Georgene H., and Williamson, Robert C., eds. *Sex Roles in Changing Society.* New York: Random House. 1970. pp. 285-307.

Kibbutzim. Social equality. Sex-typed occupations. Family structure. Israel.

This discussion draws on a number of studies to examine the historical background and current status of the discrepancy within the kibbutz between sex-role ideology and reality. The ideology of the politically leftist kibbutzim has always been one of complete economic, political, and social equality for all members. Initially, an attempt was made to promote equality of role and status by denying any differences between the sexes other than physiological ones. Collective childrearing and coeducation deemphasized sex differences, and women were transferred from traditional housekeeping functions to such activities as agricultural work.

However, over time, equality of roles has diminished and the traditional division of labor has resumed. Women have assumed responsibility for child care, education, health, and food services, while men have taken over productive and managerial positions. The men appear to be largely unaware that women are dissatisfied with this situation. Although women express dislike for their traditionally feminine occupations, they would also like to spend more time with their own children. Politically, women do not participate in as large numbers as frequently or as actively as men in the governing bodies of the kibbutzim. It is concluded that a gradual accommodation between ideology and reality will bring increased family-centeredness and changes in education—training women for the feminine functions they are already performing. The kibbutz principles of economic collectivism and legal equality will be preserved. (21 references)

400
Ridley, Jeanne Clare. Demographic change and the roles and status of women. *Annals of the American Academy of Political and Social Science,* 375:15-25, 1968.

National   differences.   Female   role.   Demographic   determinants.
Economic development.

United Nations data and national census data for 37 countries
provided the basis for this analysis of the impact of demographic
factors on women's roles and status. Findings from the data are
discussed in relation to the redefinition of social and economic roles
produced by the Western industrial revolution. As expected, of the
three groups of countries—high natality and mortality, high natality-
low mortality, and low natality and mortality—the third group had
the highest female economic participation rates. Other effects of
demographic change considered were the length and patterns of
married life, the reduced importance of the female reproductive role,
the ratio of marriageable males to females, and the number of single
women and their educational and occupational status. Current
demographic changes in many parts of the world are proceeding more
rapidly and under different conditions than in the industrial
revolution. It is suggested that the increasing age at marriage and
proportion of single women now found in some developing countries,
as well as other demographically induced social changes, will produce
the educational and occupational advances and egalitarian marital
roles found in industrialized countries. (26 references)

401
Rocheblave-Spenlé, Anne-Marie. *Masculine and Féminine Roles:*
Stéréotypes, the Family, Pseudohermaphrodites. [Les Roles Masculins
et Féminins: Les Stereotypes, la Famille, les États Intersexuels.]
Paris: Presses Universitaires de France, 1962. 346 pp.

Sex-role perceptions. Stereotypes. Marital roles. National differences.
Sex-role development.

This book reports on three studies of sex roles from different
perspectives. The first study deals with sex-roles at the societal level.
Sex-role stereotyping differences between French (N=143) and
German (N=102) psychology students were assessed by questionnaires. Results indicated that French students were more likely to
dichotomize traits as masculine or feminine than were German
students. French men tended to ascribe to themselves more traits
overall than did French women, whereas the opposite was true for
the German sample. This section of the book concluded with an
elaboration of male and female stereotypes in each country, and a
description of what are held to be ideal roles for men and women.

The second study deals with the interaction of male and female roles
in the family. Families of engineers from France, England, and

Germany were interviewed. Husbands and wives were interviewed separately regarding their attitudes toward domestic roles. Questions were asked about care of the children, authority figures in the family, and civil rights of women. Results indicate that there is more equality of authority in families in France and England than in Germany. Overall, respondents felt that women had enough civil rights. Attitudes toward working women were more liberal in England, followed by France and then Germany. In England it is acceptable for the man to help with the housework, and in both England and France, it is acceptable for the man to help with the children.

The third part of the book deals with the development of sex roles at the personality level. Three clinical profiles of pseudohermaphrodites are cited and the effects of their genital abnormalities on their sex-role development are discussed. Overall, the book aims to explain masculine and feminine behavior as being the result of the sociocultural environment. (289 references)

402
Rosenberg, Carroll Smith. Beauty, the beast and the militant woman: A case study in sex roles and social stress in Jacksonian America. *American Quarterly,* 23:562-584, 1971.

Female role. Historical trends.

Women's role in antebellum America (1830-60) is considered in this analysis of the Female Moral Reform Society, a female association dedicated to the eradication of sexual immorality. Primary and secondary historical sources, particularly the society's newspaper and minutes of its meetings, provide data. Discussion of the Society centers on the thesis that, because respectable middle-class 19th century women were psychologically unable to directly defy the restrictions of traditional sex roles, they turned to moral reform movements in an attempt to define and limit the sexual behavior of men. Sexual promiscuity and alcohol consumption were regarded as components of the role-defining masculine ethos underlying man's social preeminence. The Society's efforts to combat the double standard and to raise the status of women in the home and society are discussed, and the reform crusade is compared with the suffrage movement that followed. Although less radical in its view of women's role, the Female Moral Reform Society was the first organized effort to combat women's traditional passivity and promote unity in asserting female worth and values in American society. (63 references)

403
Rosenmayr, Leopold. The Austrian woman. *International Social Science Journal,* 14(1):157-165, 1962.

Austria. Working wives. Work motivation. Marital dominance.

The relationships between practical role tasks of husbands and wives, the demands of occupational roles, and the culturally established images of man and woman are discussed as background to a description of actual role situation and role practice in Austria. This description is intended to facilitate understanding of a proposal for the systematic study of female role images. Data on the Austrian situation came from research carried out by the Social Science Research Centre at Vienna University.

Austrian demographic data reveal that regular work outside the family shapes everyday life for a high percentage of the female population, particularly if women over 60 years of age are excluded from the calculations. The degree of financial motivation for work is said to be clearly connected with husband's income. In one large-scale attitude study, the percentage of women who worked because they liked the job was significantly lower than the percentage of men who were enthusiastic about their jobs. The percentages of women who said they worked for other than financial reasons were highest among teachers, artists, medical care and social workers, and similar professions; medium among white collar clerical workers; and lowest among manual laborers. A small-scale, indepth interview study showed that financial motives for work were professed most frequently by mothers with three or more children. Women demonstrated a high degree of readiness to give up their jobs if requested to do so by their husbands.

The conclusion is drawn that the wife's work outside the family operates as an extension of her function within the family, especially in families where the husband belongs to the lower income groups and/or where there are many children. In the realm of friendship and social relations, the husband's position was found to be dominant over the wife's, perhaps because his role is traditionally seen as the determiner of outside relationships, whereas the wife's traditional concern is with internal family affairs. (11 references)

404
Safilios-Rothschild, Constantina. A cross-cultural examination of women's marital, educational and occupational options. *Acta Sociologica,* 14(1-2):96-113, 1971.

Female role. National differences. Economic development.

A cross-cultural examination of available census and other official data about women's marital, educational, and occupational behavior was undertaken to investigate the relationship between GNP per capita and indicators of social modernity pertaining to women's options; to find possible correlations among the different indicators of social modernity related to women's options; and to construct a typology of societies based on the latitude of women's options. The restricted availability of censuses and other official publications or nationwide studies necessitated using different countries and varying numbers of countries for each variable examined. Rank-order coefficients and biserial coefficients of correlation were calculated to test a curvilinear model for the data.

The evidence indicates that women in different types of societies may have many options via very different combinations of social, political, cultural, and economic factors. No linear relationship exists between a country's level of economic development and the range of women's options in different life sectors. The option not to marry is greater in the less economically developed countries. On the other hand, more women have the options to work in general, to work after marriage, and to gain a college education when a country is at a medium-high level of economic development than at higher or lower levels. Countries at a medium level of GNP provide a wider range of occupations for women, including "masculine" occupations such as pharmacy, dentistry, law, and medicine, than countries at higher or lower levels. No single configuration of conditions provides women with the maximum range of options. A widespread ideology about sexual equality is, however, the strongest factor in increasing women's options. (20 references)

405
Safilios-Rothschild, Constantina, ed. *Toward a Sociology of Women.* Lexington, Mass.: Xerox College Publishing, 1972. 406 pp.

Female role. Sex-role development. Women's liberation.

This cross-cultural collection of 31 articles on women's role is intended to provide a foundation for the development of a sociology of women. Experimental and speculative approaches and personal views are presented by the various authors. Each chapter includes a discussion by the editor synthesizing cross-cultural evidence related to the topic. Major topics are the formation of sex roles by means of socialized sex differences; images of women in the mass media; women as sex objects in economic terms; women's options for conventional and professional roles; and discussions of the women's liberation movement and future sex roles. Eleven of the articles were commissioned for the book; the remainder were reprinted from professional journals. (0-66 references per chapter)

406
Saleh, Saneya. Women in Islam: Their status in religious and traditional culture. *International Journal of Sociology of the Family*, 2(1):35-42, 1972.

Middle East. Social equality. Islam.

The relative influences of Islamic and non-Islamic cultural influences on the role and status of women in the Middle East are evaluated by examination of the Koran and its associated body of religious law, the Shariah, in conjunction with interviews with Islamic scholars. It is posited that writers who have attributed the generally low status of women in the Middle East to the Islamic laws and culture have failed to distinguish between Islamic and non-Islamic elements in the present Moslem culture. This study demonstrates that the Islamic influence historically tended to raise the status of women to one of practical equality with men, in contrast to pre-Islamic culture and colonial European culture and law. The material and spiritual rights, obligations, and status of women in Islam are discussed in detail. Their current low status is attributed to nonreligious influences and to the mixture of laws and traditions initiated during the European colonial period. (13 references)

407
Sartin, Pierrette. *The Liberated Woman? [La Femme Libérée?]* Paris: Stock, 1968. 287 pp.

France. Women's liberation.

This book is a treatise on women's place in present-day France. Beginning with depictions of women in literature, some statistics are presented on female participation in politics; legal rights of women, including rights over their own bodies; economic liberation of women; the education of women; barriers to hiring women; and the plight of the woman alone. It is noted that, in the last 20 years, the number of women elected to the National Assembly has decreased. Many women believe it is their duty to stay out of politics. Types of work open to women and unequal pay are related to the fact that only 37 percent of university graduates in 1961 were women. In France, one out of every three women lives alone. Reference is made in the discussion to the sociological and psychological literature. (50 references)

408
Schuster, Alice. Women's role in the Soviet Union: Ideology and reality. *Russian Review*, 30:260-267, 1971.

U.S.S.R. Female employment. Political participation.

Economic and sociological studies, newspaper articles, and political works are examined to evaluate the impact of Communist ideology on the role of women in the Soviet Union. Women gained political equality in the Soviet Constitution of 1918 and gained economic, social, and cultural equality in the Constitution of 1936. Communist ideology recognized that the revolution depended on female support and emphasized the political organization of women workers and peasants. Female workers were used as a labor resource to fulfill the first and subsequent Five-Year Plan quotas in heavy industry and later to offset labor shortages during and after World War II. However, under Stalin, women were not appointed to high political office and the Women's Section of the Communist Party's Central Committee was abolished.

The majority of employed women continue to be engaged in manual labor on collective farms and in factories. Currently, only 20 percent of agricultural administrative workers are women. Women now predominate in the fields of medicine, dentistry, and pharmacy, and the Soviet Government is attempting to achieve more equal distribution in other professions. Seventy percent of elementary and secondary school teachers are women, but the proportions of women academic administrators, technical experts, and teachers in higher education are considerably smaller. Whereas 20 percent of Communist Party members are female, the upper ranks of leadership are almost exclusively male. Related to these inequalities are Russian traditions of female subordination and equality in hardship. It appears that Soviet women continue to bear the double burden of responsibility for the home and family and full-time labor for the state. (15 references)

409
Scott, Ann Firor, ed. *The American Woman: Who Was She?* Englewood Cliffs, N.J.: Prentice-Hall, Inc., 1971. 182 pp.

Female role. Historical trends.

This collection of chiefly primary documents represents an examination of the changing role of women in American society in relation to changes in women's education, patterns of work, participation in various reform movements, and views of family life. Letters, memoirs, essays, and speeches by noted feminists and lesser known men and women are used to trace changes in women's role since the Civil War. Some selections from secondary historical sources are included to highlight particular developments such as increased opportunities in education or changing patterns in female employment. The various documents and sources used illustrate how women fit in a society; how society regards them; the restraints placed upon women's activities and development; the way these restraints are embodied in social norms and laws; and the changes produced by education and professional opportunities, industrialization, and urbanization. (76 references)

410
Scott, Anne Firor. *The Southern Lady: From Pedestal to Politics, 1830-1930.* Chicago: University of Chicago Press, 1970. 247 pp.

Female role. Historical trends.

The purpose of this book is to describe the culturally defined image of the Southern lady, to trace the effect of this image on women's behavior, to outline discrepancies between the image and reality, and to characterize women's efforts to free themselves from cultural expectations and achieve self-determination. Part I concerns the antebellum and war years (1830-1864) and draws on diaries and letters from various manuscript collections to describe the Southern lady as visualized by others and herself. Part II (1865-1930) additionally relies on public records and secondary historical sources to discuss the post-Civil War conditions which created new professional and political opportunities for women. It was during this period that Southern women used unlikely organizations such as missionary societies, clubs, and the Women's Christian Temperance Union to advance their own development without openly throwing off their traditional roles. (450 references)

411
Seward, Georgene H., and Williamson, Robert C., eds. *Sex Roles in Changing Society.* New York: Random House, 1970. 419 pp.

Sex-typed behavior. Sex-role development. National differences.

This book presents discussions and data on the origins of sex-role patterning and on sex roles in contemporary Eastern and Western cultures. The sex-role behavior of men and women is explored by a variety of social scientists. Societies examined are the United States, the Soviet Union, Sweden, East and West Germany, Greece, Latin America, Africa, the Israeli kibbutz, India, Japan, and China. Sex-role behavior in the industrially advanced countries is viewed sociologically in terms of group norms and statistical comparisons. The less technological cultures are treated by means of ethnological descriptions and personal impressions. Some attention is also given to the historical development of sex roles in Western culture and to the psychological problems and processes of sexual identity development. The book places a special emphasis on women because of recent changes in the social role of women in many cultures. (10-98 references per chapter)

412
Stolte-Heiskanen, Veronica, and Haavio-Mannila, Elina. The position of women in society: Formal ideology vs. everyday ethic. *Social Science Information,* 6:169-188, 1967.

Finland. Hungary. Social equality. National differences.

The status of women in two countries, Finland and Hungary, is compared to determine some of the formal and everyday conditions associated with variations between societies. Most of the data reported come from United Nations statistical compilations and from survey studies. Based on historical trends and events in the two countries, greater formal or doctrinal equality was expected in Hungary, with greater informal or attitudinal equality predicted in Finland.

A lower percentage of the female population is economically active in Hungary than in Finland, but participation in the labor force among those who do work seems to be more in conformity with the principles of equality of the sexes in Hungary. The educational distribution of the total population is about the same in the two countries, but differences in the educational levels of men and women are much greater in Hungary. Hungary, however, has a more even distribution of female students by field of study than Finland. Data are provided on the relative amounts of time men and women in the two countries spend on such daily activities as sleep, leisure, productive activity, and housekeeping. These data reflect the private, everyday ethic, as contrasted with the formal ideology, and suggest that the traditional division of labor between the sexes is less persistent in Finland than in Hungary. The data also indicate some material conditions which may affect the position of women in society, such as differences in the agricultural system or the level of industrialization of the different countries. Overall, the expectation regarding relative conditions in the two countries was supported. (11 references)

413
Sullerot, Evelyne. *Women Tomorrow. [Demain les Femmes.]* Paris: R. Laffont, 1965. 269 pp.

Female role. Historical trends. Women's liberation.

This book presents a historical overview of changes in the status of women. Following a discussion of the premises of women's liberation, favorable and unfavorable factors influencing women's freedom are discussed. Part I includes a discussion of biological factors as they affect women, including the potential effects of such scientific developments as birth control. Various myths about biology, morality, psychology, and the normal balance of power between the sexes are described and challenged. Part II presents a historical account of woman's place in the economy in terms of the effects of increasing leisure time, specific laws, and prevailing ideologies about women's employment. Part III presents the cultural stereotypes of woman as reflected in the mass media. (37 references)

414
Sullerot, Evelyne. *The History and Sociology of Women at Work.* *[Histoire et Sociologie du Travail Féminin.]* Paris: Gonthier, 1968. 383 pp.

Female employment. Historical trends. National differences.

This book presents cross-cultural comparisons of the history of the employment of women. Part I covers working women from ancient times to the present, with particular attention to attitudes of men and women toward the employment of women, including biological arguments against it; characteristics and conditions of women's work; the feminist movement in France, the rest of Europe, and the United States; the role of women during and between wars; the consequences of Nazi doctrines on women's work; and Soviet efforts to improve women's working conditions. Numerous tables showing comparative statistics on employment of women, such as wages and percentage of the labor force represented by women in various professions and levels, are included.

Part II examines the role of working women today. Extensive cross-cultural comparisons of the female work force in Russia, America, and European countries are presented. Included are discussions of "feminine" and "masculine" trades, types and conditions of women's work by age and educational level, analysis of wage or salary levels, and women's professional associations. Attitudes and opinions concerning working women are described, with particular reference to recent literature in France and the United States. (135 references)

415

Sullerot, Evelyne. *Woman, Society and Change.* New York: McGraw-Hill, 1971. 256 pp.

Female role. Cultural differences.

This book presents general economic and sociological cross-cultural data in a comprehensive discussion of the position of women in the modern world. The topics covered include changes in social attitudes, demography, economics and employment, education, legal codes, political life, and the influence of the Catholic Church. Although the discussion is concerned with current developments, changes are considered in their historical context. Differences in women's roles in selected countries are discussed in relation to educational opportunities and technology and industrialization. Discussion of education in underdeveloped nations of Africa and South America focuses on the problem of female illiteracy. Possible future developments in women's lives are outlined. The role of women in solving such world problems as overpopulation and illiteracy is noted. This book is translated from its original French edition and extensively illustrated. (48 references)

416

Talmon. Yonina. Sex-role differentiation in an equalitarian society. In: Lasswell, Thomas; Burma, John; and Aronson, Sidney, eds. *Life in Society.* Glenview, Ill.: Scott, Foresman and Co., 1965. pp. 144-155.

Kibbutzim. Social equality. Household tasks. Sex-typed occupations. Israel.

This study analyzes the emergence of sex-role differentiation in the kibbutz, a society originally based on a denial of sex-role differences in the performance of the work of the settlement. Interviews with kibbutz members on their sex-role attitudes and work histories provide the data. Major aspects analyzed were sex-role differentiations of internal family tasks, external activities, role allocation, and redefinition of sex-role models. The mechanisms that have evolved to reconcile the ideology and reality of sex roles are also discussed.

Role differentiation was found to be most prevalent in the occupational sphere and comparatively less so in community affairs and within the family. Sex-role attitudes regarding the family tended to be most equalitarian on the level of ideological generalization, but less so in reference to specific tasks. Child care was least differentiated along traditional lines, care of the family quarters more so, and care of clothing most differentiated. Work histories for the past 10 years indicated gradual but increasing sex-role specialization in work assignment. Men were concentrated in agriculture, production services, and central public offices. Women were concentrated in health services and education.

Although the governing committees of the kibbutz were not as sex-segregated as the occupations, they reflected a similar occupational differentiation: Men predominate in overall leadership, in central committees, and in production management; women predominate in committees on education, health, and welfare. The dynamics of differentiation are examined in terms of the reemergence of sex roles and how differentiation in one of the three spheres (family, occupation, committee membership) affects the other two. Institutional mechanisms bridging the gap between sex-role ideals and reality are the increasing mechanization of service institutions, professionalization of housekeeping and child care services, diversification of feminine occupations to include social work and craft industries, recruitment of women for predominantly male committees, and participation of men and women in highly visible positions normally associated with the other sex. (No references)

417
Ward, Barbara E., ed. *Women in the New Asia: The Changing Social Roles of Men and Women in South and South-East Asia.* Paris: UNESCO, 1963. 529 pp.

Southeast Asia. Social equality. Female role. Family structure.

This cross-cultural collection of sociological reports and autobiographical memoirs concerns the effects of recent changes in women's public status on their family life. Specific countries examined are Burma, Ceylon, India, Indonesia, Laos, Malaysia, Pakistan, the Philippines, Singapore, Thailand, and Vietnam. The material, gathered under the auspices of UNESCO, focuses on how changes in women's political, legal, economic, and educational status have influenced the roles of men and women within the home. The sociological chapters were written by social scientists using earlier research findings, and the memoirs were written by female nationals recalling sex-role developments in their own families since the days of their grandmothers. Also included are a history of women's emancipation movements in South Asia and a demographic survey, with appendices, on the existing state of women's rights and family planning measures in the countries concerned. (1-6 references per chapter)

418

Williamson, Robert C. Role themes in Latin America. In: Seward, Georgene H., and Williamson, Robert C., eds. *Sex Roles in Changing Society*. New York: Random House, 1970. pp. 177-199.

Latin America. Sex-role development. Family structure. Historical trends.

Relations between the sexes in Latin America are discussed, based on a number of sociological and psychological studies. Related issues considered are marriage and family patterns, sex roles and societal values, and socialization and parental identification.

Historical influences on the Latin American family structure include the initial conquistador-male/native-female contact and the patriarchal nature of the Catholic Church. Values tending to affect sex roles are respect for personal dignity, sense of hierarchy, emotionalism and mysticism, use of language as a verbal facade rather than a conveyor of reality, and fatalism. The predominant characteristic of male socialization is the machismo cult. Historical factors such as the Argentine gaucho legend and anxiety about excessive identification with the quasi-mystical mother figure contribute to the development of an overmasculinized role. Women are revered as images of the Virgin Mary and as central figures of the home and family. Yet they have been traditionally considered innately inferior and subordinate to males. Variations in this sex-role pattern occur in every Latin American country, depending on social class and cultural factors. Recent studies have shown that, among the urban middle class, increased industrialization, education, and family planning are gradually resolving the inferior status of women. However, it is concluded that industrial and technical changes must be accompanied by shifts in values and political stability to bring about overall equality in status in Latin America. (54 references)

419

Young, Frank W. The function of male initiation ceremonies: A cross-cultural test of an alternative hypothesis. *American Journal of Sociology,* 67(4):379-396, 1962.

Initiation rites. Sex-role development. Social structure.

This analysis offers an alternative hypothesis to previous explanations of male initiation ceremonies offered in two studies—Whiting, Kluckhohn, and Anthony, 1958; and Burton and Whiting, 1961.

Evidence against the conclusions of these two studies, Whiting's defense, and the author's rejoinder are included in this article.

The 1958 study interpreted male initiation rites as a means of controlling potentially disruptive emotions generated in childhood. These emotions presumably result from exclusive mother-infant sleeping arrangements for the first year of life or more, during which time the father is prohibited from having sexual relations with the mother. The infant feels dependency toward the mother and hostility toward the father who eventually returns to displace him.

In the 1961 study, the disruptive-emotions explanation was replaced by a sex-role conflict hypothesis, positing that an adolescent male identifies with both parents and consequently has to give up identification with the mother through male rites. The counter-hypothesis in this study uses symbolic interaction theory to explain initiation as the dramatization of the sex-role characteristic of societies with a high degree of adult male solidarity. To test this hypothesis and refute the other two, the variables of exclusive mother-son sleeping arrangements, postnatal sex taboo, and exclusive male organizations as evidence of male solidarity were each examined as predictors of male initiation rites in 54 societies.

It was found that the relationship of male initiation rights and male solidarity is stronger than either exclusive mother-son sleeping arrangements or postnatal sex taboo. It is suggested that the exclusive mother-infant sleeping arrangement results from the father's absence while he is with other wives, and that the postnatal taboo is a norm protecting wives from too frequent pregnancies, both representing aspects of polygynous families. (19 references)

REVIEWS AND THEORETICAL EXPOSITIONS

420
Acker, Joan. Women and social stratification: A case of intellectual sexism. *American Journal of Sociology,* 78(4):936-945, 1973.

Social stratification. Methodological issues.

The social stratification literature is reviewed to examine the conceptual and methodological problems arising when sex is considered a relevant stratification variable. Six assumptions about determinants of social status and their validity as indicators of women's social position are discussed: That the family is the unit in the stratification system; that the family's social position is determined by the status of the male head of the household; that a female's status is determined by and equal to that of the male to whom she is attached; that a woman determines her own social status only when not attached to a male; and that the disadvantaged position of women in the hierarchies of wealth, power and prestige is irrelevant to the study of stratification systems.

It is suggested that sex affects evaluation of persons and positions, forms the basis of sexual division of labor and sex-based inequalities, and prevails as a dichotomy cutting across all classes and strata. To integrate these sex-based inequalities into conceptual stratification models, the individual rather than the family must be regarded as the central unit.

Alternatives to present models may consider sex as a dimension cutting across class lines and producing two interrelated hierarchies, or as a basis of evaluation affecting the placement of individuals in particular hierarchies. Another possibility is to view females as constituting castes within traditional social classes. The individual social status of the nonemployed wife could be defined by a combination of the ranking of housewife and conferred status from her family of origin. Regarding sex as a salient stratification variable would facilitate a more thorough understanding of mobility processes, class structure, and distribution of power in a variety of cultures. (32 references)

421
Angrist, Shirley S. The study of sex roles. *Journal of Social Issues,*
25(1):215-231, 1969.

Methodological issues. Role theories.

Previous research on the definitions of sex role is reviewed, and the
usefulness of the sex-role concept in studying how men and women
learn to enact sex-related roles is discussed. Key dilemmas in role
analysis research are highlighted, and two approaches for studying sex
roles are suggested.

The three predominant meanings of role are said to be position,
behavior, or relationship, depending on the discipline within which it
is studied—anthropology, psychology, or sociology, respectively. Sex
role involves four elements: Label, behavior, expectations, and
location or social context. Attempts to isolate definitions of sex role
are complicated by varying and inconsistent terminology and by the
wide range of contexts in which roles can be located.

The concept of role constellation is proposed as a useful way to
handle the location problem in the study of sex roles, as well as the
operation of sex as a modifier of ongoing social interactions and
relationships rather than a dominant, isolated role to be enacted.
Role constellation is the combination of roles one individual can play
at a given stage in life. Role flexibility—maneuverability within the
roles available to any given individual—is also advanced as a key
phenomenon in sex-role behavior. The extent of role flexibility is
illustrated by data from studies of women's roles at various stages of
life. Women are hypothesized to operate within a contingency
orientation in both early and adult socialization in adjusting to and
preparing for various possibilities in their marriage and work roles.
(43 references)

422
Bardwick, Judith M. *Psychology of Women: A Study of Bio-Cultural
Conflicts.* New York: Harper & Row, 1971. 242 pp.

Female role. Sex-role development. Physiological determinants. Sociocultural determinants.

This book draws on research data from psychological, biological, and
cultural sources to examine the motives, behaviors, and conflicts of
contemporary American middle-class women. Traditional psychoanalytic and exclusively cultural sex-role theories are disputed, and
alternative explanations of psychological sex differences are offered.

These explanations stress the interaction of genetic temperamental differences, differences in the adult reproductive system, and sex-linked values specific to each culture.

Specific chapters concern psychoanalytic theory; the effect of body states on the psyche; psychology and the sexual body; psychosomatic dysfunctions of the female reproductive system; differences between male and female brains; sex differences in personality and learning ability; dependence, passivity, and aggression; identification; the ego and self-esteem; the motive to succeed; and changes in motives and roles during different stages of life. Sex similarities as well as differences in goals and motives, in productivity and creativity, and in traditional and work roles are described.

The ambivalence engendered by the culturally defined female role is emphasized. A concluding essay suggests that, for women's self-esteem to be raised from its present low level, either the socialization of girls will have to encompass the currently esteemed masculine qualities of independence, activity, and assertiveness, or society will have to value more highly the feminine humanistic goals of empathy, nurturance, and sensitivity. (7-58 references per chapter)

423

Bardwick, Judith M., ed. *Readings on the Psychology of Women.* New York: Harper & Row, 1972. 335 pp.

Sex-role development. Female role.

This book is a collection of theoretical analyses, clinical observations, research studies, and essays on the psychology of women. Sources are the professional literature on psychology, sociology, anthropology, endocrinology, obstetrics, and psychosomatic medicine. Major topics in these articles encompass female role expectations, conflicts, and status of women. Each topic section is preceded by an editorial introduction. Specifically, topics include the development of sex differences, socialization, cultural values, and the development of motives; the traditional female role and its gratifications, frustrations, and stresses; the women's liberation movement; intercultural comparisons; women in relationship to their bodies; and women and criteria for mental health. (0-100 references per article)

424

Bem, Sandra L. *Psychology looks at sex roles: Where have all the androgynous people gone?* Paper presented at the UCLA Symposium on Women, May 1972. (Mimeo) 14 pp. Available from the author.

Sex-typed behavior. Methodological issues.

SEX ROLES: A RESEARCH BIBLIOGRAPHY

This review of the psychological literature indicates that psychologists have neglected the study of androgynous people—those who do not conform to an exclusive sex role. Rather, nearly every existing sex-role inventory treats masculinity and femininity as two ends of a single continuum which are, by definition, inversely correlated. Also, investigators use such inventories to divide the population into sex-typed and sex-reversed categories. The existence of a group of people to which neither label applies is either ignored or excluded from the sample.

Two assumptions may be responsible—psychology's own version of the sex-role ideology of America, and the use of a set of questionable assumptions about the nature of personality. The process by which boys and girls become psychological males or females—the developmental process of sex-typing—dominates psychological investigation. Moreover, the assumptions that sex-typing is a desirable process and that children will be better off if their behavior conforms to society's stereotype of sex-appropriate behavior consistently bias the empirical literature. However, current empirical evidence on the consequences of sex-role differentiation indicates that a high level of sex-appropriate behavior does not necessarily facilitate general psychological or social adjustment.

The assumption that there are pervasive cross-situational consistencies in an individual's behavior is questioned. Evidence suggests that behavior is situation-specific, rather than consistent. Evidence also supports the proposition that sex-typing can produce consistent defensive behavior traits. Research to test this and related hypotheses and to validate the concept of androgyny and its components is underway. (34 references)

425
Brown, Daniel G. Sex-role preference in children: Methodological problems. *Psychological Reports,* 11(2):477-478, 1962.

Sex-role preference. Methodological issues.

The conflicting findings on children's sex-role preferences from studies using the subjects' direct choices and from those using the indirect, It Scale choices are discussed. Evidence indicates that school age children of both sexes tend to see the It figure as male. Consequently, both boys and girls make masculine choices as the figure's preference. In a traditionally masculine-oriented culture, any human figure not clearly structured as female will tend to be seen as male. Other projective techniques using sexually ambiguous figures are mentioned. Possible changes in the It Scale might involve replacing the existing It with an imaginary child, an It figure from the waist up, a drawing of a face, or a baby doll. (11 references)

426

Carlson, Rae. Understanding women: Implications for personality theory and research. *Journal of Social Issues,* 28(2):17-32, 1972.

Methodological issues. Personality differences.

This paper addresses the need for research in feminine psychology as it reflects the broader need for contemporary research in personality. Constraints imposed by current research paradigms are discussed in terms of the theoretical concepts of agency and communion. Masculine (agentic) modes of psychological inquiry involving manipulation, quantification, and control need to be complemented by the naturalistic, qualitative, and open (communal) research styles which women have developed in other disciplines.

It is hypothesized that a serious consideration of the psychology of women would cause reformulations of personality theory. Three issues are proposed for personality research: Duality in human nature, typology and qualitative patterning, and biological bases of personality. These issues are consonant with the nature of femininity, engage the talents of female investigators, and could foster development of the new research paradigms required for serious inquiry in personality. Suggestions for conceptual elaboration and empirical research are proposed. (48 references)

427

Dahlström, Edmund. Analysis of the debate on sex roles. In: Dahlström, Edmund, ed. *The Changing Roles of Men and Women.* Boston: Beacon Press, 1971. pp. 170-205.

Sweden. Social equality. Sex-role ideology.

This broad discussion of the general assumptions and values regarding the status of women in society and in the labor market compares the Swedish moderate and radical sex-role ideologies. Soviet Communist views on sex roles are also briefly discussed. The moderate and radical positions and suggested means of their implementation are considered in reference to disagreement on the equality and freedom of the sexes, which involves the benefits of vocational and family life, political power and influence, personal esteem and prestige, and satisfaction and adjustment. Arguments bearing on the family draw on the relationships between women's employment and the birth rate, child development and adjustment, and family harmony. The value of women's work input is pivotal to the examination of economic arguments on sex roles. In all areas of dispute, disagreement exists not only on values, but on facts regarding the present roles of women in the labor market and how they have developed, and on the consequences of previous changes, the conceivable effects of new measures, and the question of ultimate goals. (8 references)

428
D'Andrade, Roy G. Sex differences and cultural institutions. In: Maccoby, Eleanor E., ed. *The Development of Sex Differences.* Stanford, Calif.: Stanford University Press, 1966. pp. 174-204.

Sex-typed behavior. Social structure.

Some of the ways in which sex differences have been culturally institutionalized are reviewed from an anthropological perspective. Using data from numerous field studies, the discussion emphasizes reductionistic (resulting from psychological or physiological mechanism) explanations of empirically observed behavioral sex differences. Cross-cultural trends are presented for male-female differences in the performance of daily activities; the ascription of social status; interpersonal behavior; sexual behavior; authority and deference; aggression, conflict, and responsibility; gender identity; and fantasy and cognition. Although not intended to be a comprehensive review, this comparison of many anthropological studies reveals a number of cross-cultural trends from which some general conclusions are drawn:

The division by sex of labor involved in subsistence and other activities is strongly influenced by primary and secondary sex characteristics. Sex bias in forms of social organization is related to subsistence activities and the division of labor by sex. The cross-cultural mode in interpersonal behavior is that males are more sexually active, more dominant, more deferred to, more aggressive, less responsible, less nurturant, and less emotionally expressive than females. However, the extent of these differences varies by culture, and in some instances the differences are nonexistent or even reversed.

Maleness and femaleness are institutionalized as statuses in all cultures and become psychological identities for most individuals. Usually the desired sex status is the same as the assigned one, but special cultural conditions can affect the degree to which one sex envies the status of the other. In projective tests, males from a number of cultures have been found to be more insecure and anxious than females, a condition which may be the result of greater stress and danger involved in the male role. (39 references)

429

DeLucia, Lenore A. The Toy Preference Test: A measure of sex-role identification. *Child Development,* 34:107-117, 1963.

Sex-role identification. Toy preference. Methodological issues.

This study examined the validity of the Toy Preference Test as a measure of sex-role identification. In developing the test, experimenters asked 19 female and 28 male college students with a mean age of 21 to rank 48 children's toys on sex-appropriateness. Pairs of these toys were then presented to 120 kindergarteners, 46 first graders, 20 second graders, 20 third graders, and 20 fourth graders. There was an equal number of boys and girls in each group. Each subject was asked to choose which of two toys a pictured child of the same sex as the subject would like to play with. The same set of 24 toys (Set A) was used for all subjects, except for 30 kindergarteners who were tested with the other 24 rated toys (Set B).

There was an orderly increase in the number of sex-appropriate choices for both boys and girls through the third grade. Fourth graders made fewer appropriate choices than did third graders. Boys made more sex-appropriate choices than girls, and this trend consistently increased in the later school years. When subjects were presented with two toys rated sex-appropriate for them, they chose the more appropriate toy less often than when they were asked to choose between two toys which were both inappropriate for their sex. The reliability of the Toy Preference Test was greater when administered by an opposite-sex experimenter. The increase in the number of appropriate choices from kindergarten through the third grade suggests the face validity of this test. However, as the test now exists, it would be inappropriate for use with boys over 8 and girls over 10 years old. (14 references)

430

Douvan, Elizabeth. New sources of conflict in females at adolescence and early adulthood. In: Bardwick, Judith M.; Douvan, Elizabeth; Horner, Matina S.; and Gutmann, David. *Feminine Personality and Conflict.* Belmont, Calif.: Wadsworth, 1970. pp. 31-43.

Adolescent females. Sex-role development. Puberty. Physiological determinants. Sociocultural determinants.

This examination of existing empirical studies of adolescent development explores hypotheses concerning the effect of physiological changes and cultural pressures on the psychic and interpersonal life of the adolescent girl. Mood recognition and visual judgment tests have shown that menstruation and the cyclic character of female internal cues disrupt the adolescent girl's developing self-concept and make her dependent on external information for self-direction.

The girl is confronted at puberty by a sexual development that is inherently more ambiguous and diffuse than that of the boy. This ambiguity requires the exploration and definition provided by close, like-sex friendships. Sexual expression in overt behavior and fantasy is significantly lower for adolescent girls than for boys, but projective tests indicate increased anxiety and defensiveness.

Identity is further disrupted during adolescence by the codified norms of dating and the intensified need for peer acceptance. Boys develop a positive self-concept and peer acceptance through such measurable achievements as athletics; girls' self-concept is dependent on interpersonal skills measured only by social feedback. As interest in popularity and social leadership rises, educational aspirations decline. A girl's physiology urges her to turn inward to self-exploration, but the culture's narrowly conceived sex-role expectations push her outward. (29 references)

431
Emmerich, Walter. Socialization and sex-role development. In: Baltes, P. B., and Schaie, K. W., eds. *Life-span Developmental Psychology: Personality and Socialization.* New York: Academic Press, 1973.

Sex-role development. Socialization variables. Methodological issues.

This theoretical review of sex-role development indicates that, although recent secular trends have attenuated long-term continuities in sex-role socialization, sex differences within age periods can be considered as aspects of one or more ontogenetic series. Knowledge about sex-role development remains fragmentary at all age periods largely because underlying theoretical assumptions have not been satisfactorily incorporated in research designs. It is suggested that each theory of socialization be translated into a distinct set of predictions for the several parameters of developmental trends in behavior and for the impact of socializing influences upon these developmental trends.

Certain concepts are suggested for sex-role measurement, including the competence-performance distinction. In illustrating these points, particular attention is given to psychodynamic and cognitive theories of sex-role identity and to internalized normative structures as regulators of sex-role behaviors and development. Implications for a life-span developmental framework are discussed, including the issue of ontogenetic versus secular changes in sex roles. differences between early and later sex-role socialization, and the possibility that sex-role development is subordinated to other ontogenetic sequences during much of the life cycle. (94 references)

432
Erikson, Erik H. Inner and outer space: Reflections on womanhood. In: Lifton, Robert Jay, ed. *The Woman in America.* Boston: Houghton Mifflin, 1965. pp. 1-26.

Sex-role identification. Physiological determinants. Female role.

This essay uses psychoanalytic, anatomical, and historical observations to argue that women's family leadership roles of preservation, responsible upbringing, peacekeeping, and nurturance have ethical and political implications for potential public leadership roles. Women's unique qualifications for public roles are rooted in their commitment to human life. In play construction, preadolescent boys and girls structure discernably different scenes: Boys are preoccupied with exterior space and girls with interior space. The girls' preoccupation, it is suggested, is a reflection of their awareness of a productive inner body space. This view suggests that it is this positive awareness of inner potential that shapes development in the normal female, rather than solely the sense of loss and penis envy. Women do not fatalistically renounce male activity for the masochism of periodicity and childbirth; they turn with satisfaction to their own role. Further, inwardness and sensitive indwelling are neither confined to women nor constantly foremost in female life, especially in the psychosocial moratorium of young adulthood. However, a basic female schema does exist for individual fulfillment and for the collective survival of the culture. Although women are citizens and workers as well as somatic individuals, they never cease to be women. As such, they see their long-range goals only in activities which include and integrate their natural dispositions. It is concluded that it is these nurturing and preserving dispositions which mankind's inventions and institutions require. (No references)

433
Foa, Uriel G.; Triandis, Harry C.; and Katz, Evelyn Walker. Cross-cultural invariance in the differentiation and organization of family roles. *Journal of Personality and Social Psychology,* 4(3):316-327, 1966.

Family structure. Role perceptions. Cultural differences.

A theoretical analysis of family-role development was proposed and tested using data from four cultures. The hypotheses were that the child first learns to differentiate between self and others as actor and object of behavior; the child then learns to differentiate on the basis of sex (same-different) and of generation (parents-different, siblings-same). The hypotheses were tested by two sets of data. American and Greek male college students and Japanese-Hawaiian and Japanese students of both sexes were given written sentence-completion tests of whether various behaviors occurring between actor and object role pair were appropriate for members of their cultures. A content analysis of interrelations between family members in 50 American short stories provided the second set of data.

Findings from both data sources suggest that the proposed order of roles appears in different cultures. The Greek data suggest, however, the possibility that in some cultures differentiation by generation may precede differentiation by sex. The degree of invariance in role development across cultures would seem to indicate that the model proposed could provide a framework for investigation of cultural differences in family roles. (15 references)

434
Garai, Josef E., and Scheinfeld, Amram. Sex differences in mental and behavioral traits. *Genetic Psychology Monographs,* 77:169-299, 1968.

Sex differences. Physiological determinants. Sociocultural determinants.

A comprehensive review of psychological and other social science literature was undertaken to assess the current state of knowledge about sex differences. The earliest works discussed are from the late 19th century. Specific considerations are whether sex differences in performance and occupational achievement exist, and, if they do exist, whether they are determined by biology or environmental conditioning or a combination of the two. Also considered are the developmental stages at which differences in abilities, interests, and psychological traits are sufficiently manifested for empirical measurement.

It is concluded that certain sex differences in temperament, interests, abilities, and needs or drives manifest themselves cross-culturally. These sex differences condition members of each sex toward the assumption of roles; these roles, in turn, become institutionalized into occupational roles and cultural expectations. Latitude of sex roles and their variations are, to some extent, determined by societal norms. An integrated theory of sex differences is presented, based on 14 interrelated differences between the sexes. The significance of sex differences is discussed as it involves educational reforms and teaching techniques to improve the motivation and achievement of males and females. (474 references)

435

Gutmann, David. Female ego styles and generational conflict. In: Bardwick, Judith M.; Douvan, Elizabeth; Horner, Matina S.; and Gutmann, David. *Feminine Personality and Conflict.* Belmont, Calif.: Wadsworth, 1970. pp. 77-96.

Ego styles. Sex differences. Cultural differences.

This speculative discussion describes two ego styles—ways of creating and managing experience—that distinguish the sexes in predictable ways. The autocentric ego style, in which the order of events is seen as related to the self, is said to characterize women more than men. It is distinguished from the allocentric ego style, in which the order of events is seen as having a direction and logic of its own. The relationship between gender, ego style, and adjustment is discussed, as are examples of cross-cultural differences in the ego styles typical of each sex. It is contended that the autocentric ego state reflects nurture more than nature.

For the American woman, as for the American Indian man, autocentric ego functioning may be the result of an adaptive fitting of ego to special psychoecological circumstances which differ from those of allocentric environments. It is suggested that the conditions prevailing in preliterate, rural societies are comparable with those in the traditional domestic realm of women, in contrast to the conditions of the literate, urban society experienced by most American men. The autocentric and allocentric ego states are compared with respect to space, time, constancy and change, self-other relationships, instrumentality, and morality.

The autocentric orientation is said to be appearing more frequently among men in Western society and to be both a cause and a correlate of alienation among men. The hippie, "flower child" culture is used as an example, based on interviews conducted with alienated young men associated with it. The origins of their autocentric style are traced to hyperintensive relationships with autocentric mothers and consequent alienation from the traditional male allocentric ego style. Fixed and intrinsic sex differences are not denied in relation to this process. However, an overview of the "autocentric revolution" leads to the conclusion that the inherent contradiction of impersonal, mass society is that it does not nurture the development of an allocentric ego. (9 references)

436

Hochschild, Arlie Russell. A review of sex role research. *American Journal of Sociology,* 78(4):1011-1029, 1973.

Sex differences. Sex-typed behavior. Methodological issues.

This broad but selective review of articles and books offers a guide to questions and theories fundamental to sex-role research. Most of the literature discussed is based on sociological research written since 1960; literature reviewed ranges from empirical studies to theoretical discussions. The content, methodology, and biases of sex-role research in general are discussed.

Four main research perspectives are presented in detail in relation to specific studies of sex differences, which focus particularly on measuring cognitive and emotional traits and on debating the nature-nurture question; sex roles, which discuss role behaviors and norms and draw on role theory; women as a minority group, which draw on minority group theory; and the politics of caste, which view the sexes in terms of power relations.

The sociology of sex roles is defined in terms of research that reflects the assumptions and propositions of these perspectives and that treats sex roles as an important independent variable. The possible effects of sex-role research on the field of sociology and its assumptions are discussed. (155 references)

437
Holter, Harriet. Sex roles and social change. In: Safilios-Rothschild, Constantina, ed. *Toward a Sociology of Women.* Lexington, Mass.: Xerox College Publishing, 1972. pp. 331-343.

Sex-typed behavior. Social equality. Social structure.

This discussion of changing sex roles in present-day society summarizes and elaborates on various theories of sex-role establishment and maintenance. The focus is on recent changes in sex roles and their links with the society at large. Social change strategies are also evaluated.

The analysis assumes that the extent and modes of sex differentiation are results rather than primary determinants of change in social and economic domains. Sex differentiation is viewed as a social arrangement which always exists, but which may take on different forms and functions. Sociological, anthropological, and social psychological theories discuss these shifts as resulting from changes in the requirements of the economic system.

Strategies which aim for sexual equality in present Western societies differ from those which envision a radically changed economic and political order. Covert sex differentiation and discrimination, as well as the psychological maintenance of sex roles, involve more than economic factors, however. Individual consciousness-raising, solidarity among women, and cooperation between men and women are discussed as initiators of social change. (16 references)

438
Kagan, Jerome. The emergence of sex differences. *School Review,* 80(2):217-227, 1972.

Sex differences. Infant behavior. Maturation.

Current knowledge about sex differences in the first 2 years of life is summarized on four dimensions: Susceptibility to fear, cognitive functioning, variability, and social class. Most studies have reported a slight tendency for the female to display fear and anxiety more frequently and more intensely than the male. One possible reason is a greater tendency in an uncertain situation for the male infant to issue a response which buffers fear, whereas the female infant is more likely to inhibit motor responses and to withdraw. A second possible explanation is that psychological precocity may parallel the known biological precocity of the female, making her conscious of discrepant events in her environment at an earlier age than the male. Evidence of babbling in infant girls and from brain surgery on epileptic adults supports the hypothesis that females are precocious in language development, possibly because of precocious brain development, with earlier attainment of left-hemisphere dominance within the brain.

In addition to sex differences in precocity, females show less variability than males for many biological attributes, such as height, weight, bone growth, and also for tested intelligence. Many studies of children in various Western countries show a closer correlation between social class and indexes of cognitive development for girls. Early social experience seems to affect girls' development more consistently than that of boys. This difference may result from greater male variability in maturational pattern and display of temperamental attributes, as well as from differences in maternal behavior toward boys and toward girls in different social classes. (13 references)

439
Kagan, Jerome. Acquisition and significance of sex typing and sex role identity. In: Hoffman, Martin L., and Hoffman, Lois Wladis, eds. *Review of Child Development Research, Vol. 1.* New York: Russell Sage Foundation, 1964. pp. 137-167.

Sex-role identification. Sex-typed behavior. Sex-role perceptions.

An examination of research literature pertaining to sex differences in sex typing and sex-role identity was undertaken to evaluate the premise that the desire to conform to an internal standard is the basic motivation for sex-role identification.

Literature from the last four decades on sex typing of masculine and feminine characteristics reveals the existence of sex-role standards comprised of culturally approved characteristics for males and females, such as physical attributes and overt and covert behaviors. Empirical evidence shows that children as young as 4 years old are aware of these standards. The degree to which an individual regards himself or herself as masculine or feminine comprises sex-role identity, and the acquisition of sex-role identity is through a model. Establishment and maintenance of sex-role identity are effected through an individual's expectations of affection and acceptance and prevention of social rejection by displaying the traits of the standard.

Evidence shows a strong relationship between sex-role identification and continuity of sex-typed behavior. Also, the literature indicates a relationship between sex-role identification and intellectual mastery and sexuality.

The analysis concludes that the desire to achieve congruence between an ideal representation of the self as derived from a standard and everyday behavior is a compelling behavioral motive. Deviation from sex-role standards can produce anxiety and unnecessary conflicts. However, sex-role standards are modifiable during the early developmental years. Moreover, society should consider the desirability of changing some aspects of the current standards of sex role. (103 references)

440
Knox, William E., and Kupferer, Harriet J. A discontinuity in the socialization of males in the United States. *Merrill-Palmer Quarterly,* 17(3):251-261, 1971.

Male role. Socialization variables. Sex-typed behavior.

This discussion draws on existing empirical evidence to assert that there is a discontinuity between the American male's youthful socialization and the roles he later undertakes in his adult family life. It is suggested that, if male power, aggression, independence, and achievement were less emphasized in socialization practices, and if the definition of permissible male behavior were enlarged to include some female role behaviors, the family group would be a more effective cooperating unit. Other factors involved in the discontinuity are structural changes in the middle-class family, economic and technical factors affecting the division of labor, increasingly complex joint conjugal role relationships and marital role definitions, and the comparative difficulty boys face in avoiding culturally forbidden objects and behaviors and in learning to identify with a same-sex role model.

Two cross-cultural propositions are offered as possible tests bearing on this argument: (1) Societies with clear and exclusive sex-role differentiation in division of labor will tend to have clear and exclusive prohibitions on the cross-sex socialization experience available to one or both sexes; and (2) as societies with clear and exclusive sex-role differentiation in the division of labor change in the direction of less clear and exclusive differentiation, they will show uncertainty or stress. (30 references)

441

Lipman-Blumen, Jean. Role de-differentiation as a system response to crisis: Occupational and political roles of women. *Sociological Inquiry,* 43(2):105-129, 1973.

Role theories.

This research paper develops a theoretical model for the analysis of crisis-induced change in social roles, with reference to occupational and political roles of women. It is proposed that all social systems are subject to periods of crisis, during which the system is more vulnerable to change than in periods of stability.

Basic stages in role development are defined. Role dedifferentiation is discussed, and alternative role responses to crises are explored: The retraction, expansion, immobilization, highlighting, and increased differentiation of roles. The conservation and repression of resources during periods of stability are examined.

Implications of the theoretical model include allowance for preparedness to implement change in times of greatest permeability of the social structure; provision of supports to prevent too rapid or comprehensive dedifferentiation of roles without adjustments in other areas; and precipitation of crisis by attempts to introduce change in periods of relative stability. (45 references)

442

Lynn, David B. The process of learning parental and sex-role identification. *Journal of Marriage and the Family,* 28(4):466-470, 1966.

Sex-role development. Parental models.

An attempt is made to provide a comprehensive and coherent framework for theory and research concerning sex-role identification.

This overall theoretical formulation begins with the hypothesis that males tend to identify with a culturally defined masculine role, whereas females tend to identify with their own mothers. Since both sexes identify more closely with the mother than with the father, each sex must achieve sex-typical identification by different methods of learning. Hypotheses are advanced concerning such topics as male sex-role difficulties and anxieties, male and female problem-solving methods, male feelings of hostility toward women, and female opposite-sex role preference. (15 references)

443
Lynn, David B. Determinants of intellectual growth in women. *School Review,* 80(2):241-260, 1972.

Intellectual maturation. Cognitive styles. Female role.

This theoretical discussion draws on pertinent research literature to postulate that the intellectual development of women is based on an interaction of biologically rooted potentials which predispose them toward certain roles, parent-child relationships within the typical family which predispose them toward certain cognitive styles, and cultural reinforcement of their traditionally prescribed roles.

Males surpass females on measures of skills considered essential to scientific, technical, professional, and administrative excellence. Males have also surpassed females in actual intellectual achievement. Evidence from research studies suggests that certain sex differences appear in earliest infancy and are biologically based. These differences function to keep women closer to home and childrearing activities, and most cultures reinforce these biological potentials. It is hypothesized that the process of learning appropriate identification habituates each sex to a different method of perceiving, thinking, and learning, which is subsequently applied generally. The male cognitive style primarily involves defining the goal, restructuring the situation, and abstracting principles. The female cognitive style primarily involves a personal relationship and lesson learning. Traditional feminine role prescriptions are culturally reinforced through the image of females presented in school readers, discriminatory vocational counseling, family disciplinary patterns, advertising images of women, and the patriarchal foundations of the society. Research and educational practices should be aimed at changing stereotypic attitudes and at improving female intellectual performance. Certain experimental procedures for researchers, teachers, and parents are described and suggested. (56 references)

444
Maccoby, Eleanor E., ed. *The Development of Sex Differences.* Stanford, Calif.: Stanford University Press, 1966. 351 pp.

Sex-differences. Sex-role development.

This book presents five articles reviewing previous research on the development of sex-typed differences in temperament, behavior, and ability. Contributors are psychologists, biologists, and sociologists. Specific chapters deal with the effects of sex hormones on behavior, sex differences in intellectual functioning, a social-learning view of sex differences, the relationship between cognitive development and the processes of sex typing, and cross-cultural studies on the institutionalization of sex differences. A lengthy, two-part bibliography includes abstracts of research works on sex differences and a summary classifying these research findings by behavioral attribute studied. (39-159 references per chapter)

445
Mead, Margaret. The life cycle and its variations: The division of roles. *Daedalus,* 96(3):871-875, 1967.

Lifestyle. Social structure.

This essay suggests some male and female role alternatives that could occur in the world as the more affluent societies adapt to new life styles. The contemporary American style of relations between men and women is characterized by early marriage, marriage as the principal form of adult male-female relationship, parenthood for all couples, separate housing for each nuclear family, the exclusion of adults other than the parents from the family, female education that emphasizes homemaking, and increasing involvement of men in domestic activities. At the same time, women are under pressure to work outside the home to support the nuclear family's high standards of consumption. It is asserted that the failure of this form of family organization has produced such reactions as juvenile delinquency, alcoholism, addiction, and sexual deviation. However, recognition of the significance of their world role in style setting may cause affluent societies to limit their population growth rates and to change their mode of living. Having fewer families functioning as childrearers would free other individuals in the society to operate as individuals unhampered by sex roles. Alternatively, personality typing by sex could continue, with women in nurturant, teaching, or curing roles outside the home. Still another possibility is that any attempt to introduce radical new behavior styles could result in ideological or religious counterrevolutions to reassert traditional sex roles and the primacy of the home. In light of these possibilities, it is suggested that transculturally viable institutional arrangements be made to assist men and women during the transition to new styles of behavior. These arrangements could include social support for women learning to function economically on their own and education for young boys that emphasizes masculine identity. (No references)

446
Millman, Marcia. Observations on sex role research. *Journal of Marriage and the Family,* 33(4):772-776, 1971.

Methodological issues.

Five papers which comprised the Session on Sex Roles in the 1970 meeting of the American Sociological Association are reviewed as representative of current research on sex roles. Several trends in current research are criticized, and suggestions are made for an alternative approach.

Although most researchers profess an interest in discovering whether there is a change taking place in American sex roles, the reported research focuses on places in society which are most stable and least likely to reveal any changes in sex roles. Studies may also be constructed and interpreted so as to minimize the opportunity to observe changes in sex roles. Characteristic of sex-role research in general, four of the five studies reported actually examined only women's sex roles, not those of men, and four of the five dealt with sex roles in the family. It is suggested that sex roles be studied in relation to men and to nonfamilial settings, such as government agencies, political organizations, military groups, and corporations.

Finally, the striking absence of any consideration of sex roles from a functional point of view is noted; that is, it is important to understand not only what sex roles are and how individuals learn them, but why these roles develop and why they do or do not change. It is suggested that one way to understand roles is to see them as a device which enables a social system to preserve contradictory qualities or features by assigning them to different actors. The American value system and traditional male and female roles in America are discussed as an example of this process. The suggestion is made that, in times of very rapid social change, it may be best that social behavior cease to be characterized by sexual differentiation or specialization, and that both males and females reincorporate the qualities which they lost in the role division. Discussion of the corporation manager role is used to suggest that the study of sex roles, when carried out in institutions other than the family and when it includes a functional perspective, may reveal rapid and broad changes in our society. (10 references)

447
Mischel, Walter. A social-learning view of sex differences in behavior. In: Maccoby, Eleanor, ed. *The Development of Sex Differences.* Stanford, Calif.: Stanford University Press, 1966. pp. 56-81.

Sex-role development. Social learning.

Basic social-learning principles are reviewed in terms of their relevance to major research findings on sex differences in social behavior. Research on sex differences has relied heavily on self-report measures, but the social-learning viewpoint indicates that the determinants of self-reports may affect behavior differently than more natural (nontesting) situations. Sex-typed behaviors are defined as behaviors that typically elicit different rewards for one sex than for the other. Acquisition of sex-typed behaviors is examined in relation to the processes of observational learning, imitation and identification, reinforcement, attention, and contiguity in learning.

Through observation and experience, children gradually acquire information about the kinds of behavior that are socially approved for the two sexes. This learning provides information about probable outcomes for responses before they are actually performed. Differences in the attitudes and emotional responses of the sexes to specific stimuli arise from differences in their conditioning histories.

The social-learning view does not deny intrapsychic activities or mediating cognitive processes; but discriminable antecedent events, rather than inferred intrapsychic activities, are used to predict and analyze behavior. It seems likely that some of the major differences in the behaviors of the sexes reflect differences in the standards adopted for self-reward in different performance areas. Similar response patterns are manifested in different situations because of learned stimulus generalization for that response pattern and the specific contingencies in the situation, rather than because of relatively situation-free underlying traits. Various research findings on differences between the sexes in aggression, dependency, and their environmental correlates are examined and interpreted in social-learning terms. (64 references)

448
Mussen, Paul H. Early sex-role development. In: Goshlin, David A., ed. *Handbook of Socialization Theory and Research.* Chicago: Rand McNally, 1969. pp. 707-731.

Sex-role development.

This is a review of major theories of early childhood sex typing and sex-role development found in the literature. Interpretations of research findings on sex typing differ because of the use of different and uncorrelated measures. However, findings show that the first 2 years of a child's life are crucial in sex-role development, and that sex-typed characteristics developed during the first 2 years are stable and continuous over time.

Three general theories of sex-role development are discussed—social learning, identification, and cognitive developmental theory. Although evidence can be found in the literature to support each theory, no one theory accommodates all the observed phenomena or completely explains the process of the acquisition of sex-typed behavior. Thus, it is proposed that a comprehensive theory should incorporate elements from all three theories. Moreover, labeling, training, and identification are suggested as comprising the sequence of critical events in sex-role development. (54 references)

449
Niel, Mathilde. *The Problem of Women's Libération. [Le Drame de la Liberation de la Femme.]* Paris: Le Courier du Livre, 1961. 219 pp.

Women's liberation. Discrimination. Stereotypes.

This book considers sexual inequality to be on a psychological continuum with racial or class inequality. Following a historical review of women's place in various cultures, sexual inequality is discussed primarily as the result of stereotyping. The discussion includes a list of characteristics deemed "proper" for women, how they developed, and how they affect the lives of women today. Difficulties of liberation are also considered, with an examination of the roles of guilt, the Catholic Church, and of literature as obstacles to liberation. Finally, the need for liberation of men is discussed in a third section, Western European statistics are offered concerning the percentages of women in politics, in the professions, and in higher education. (81 references)

450
Orr, Douglass W. Anthropological and historical notes on the female sexual role. *Journal of the American Psychoanalytic Association,* 16:601-612, 1968.

Sexual behavior. Social structure. Historical trends.

This discussion cites anthropological, historical, and psychoanalytical data to refute an assertion that the sexuality of prehistoric women was insatiable and was gradually and coercively suppressed. It is argued that, if inordinate sexuality ever existed, it was prehuman rather than prehistoric. The psychological and economic forces leading to the sexual domestication of both men and women and to the formation of relatively stable family groups appear to be almost as old as mankind.

Other evidence is cited to dispute one investigator's claims that the transition from nomadic to urban life required the curbing of previously uncontrolled female sexuality and that this suppression took as long as 5,000 years. It is suggested that the nature of the female sexuality has caused women throughout history to find satisfaction in the "subjugation" of pregnancy and motherhood. The amount of sexual freedom, as well as of intellectual and emotional freedom, varies according to culture and historical era. Intrapsychic variables such as incest taboos and oedipal conflicts combine with cultural attitudes and institutions to influence the childrearing practices affecting future generations.

Variations in myths about the Amazons, Spartans, and other cultures and figures are documented to demonstrate the difficulties of drawing conclusions from history. It is concluded that any statement about the sexual role of women in history should be made in the context of race, class, and economic position within a given culture or subculture and within a given historical era. (24 references)

451

Ridley, Jeanne Clare. The effects of population change on the roles and status of women: Perspective and speculation. In: Safilios-Rothschild, Constantina, ed. *Toward a Sociology of Women.* Lexington, Mass.: Xerox College Publishing, 1972. pp. 372-386.

Female role. Demographic determinants. Historical trends.

The demographic factors of mortality, fertility, and migration are used in this essay to explore historical population changes which have contributed to altering the roles and status of women. Possible future changes and their implications are also discussed.

Equality between the sexes prior to and following urbanization and industrialization in western societies is examined in terms of differentiating economic from familial roles. Whereas the industrial revolution restricted women from the economy, men increased their status by acquiring the economic role previously shared by the entire family. In the 19th century, a sharp decline in female mortality and an increase in male emigration affected the age and sex composition of the overall population, resulting in a "marriage squeeze" for women in industrializing countries. The marriage squeeze effect produced higher proportions of educated and working single women. In the 20th century, increased life expectancy, reduction in fertility, and increasing migration within and between societies continue to change the patterns of women's lives and relations within marriage and the family.

In historical perspective, the almost exclusively male-run economy of industrialized societies must be regarded as only a transitional phenomenon. More women in the future will resume an economic role in society, and their status will cease to depend on that of their husbands. The structure and functions of the family will change, and husband-wife relationships will become more egalitarian. Zero population growth will be a necessity. Child care will become less the complete, long-term responsibility of women. In general, societies will have to redefine the role and status of both men and women. (46 references)

452
Roessler, Richard T. Sexuality and identity: Masculine differentiation and feminine constancy. *Adolescence,* 6(22):187-196, 1971.

Sex-role development.

This essay, based on existing studies and group discussions with female college students, postulates the theory that the processes of identity formation differ between males and females. Development of the female role involves a fundamental constancy, commencing with identification with the mother and continuing through her own motherhood. The male role, it is suggested, must be developed through differentiation from the maternal matrix of home and school. Differences between a male child's filial role and his adult role and the frequent absence of a male model make his development less certain than the female's. Cultural cues, many of them from the females surrounding him, have a distinct impact on how he defines his male role.

Since the certainty of instrumental, active masculine identity in the male is necessary for the constancy of the nurturant, passive female role, adolescent girls tend to involve adolescent boys in a set of cultural expectations that provide the link between masculinity and identity. Increasing female education and the dissolution of career restrictions within the culture are seen as producing conditions of possible conflict between a female's role constancy and her human potential. Finding the male not truly instrumentally superior, the female alters her expectations for him. The students questioned still want the male to be head of the household, but in a democratic, nondomineering sense. Further changes in the female role may bring changes in female expectations of the male and consequently in the formation of the male role itself. (8 references)

453
Rosenberg, B. G. *Sex, Sex Role, and Sex Role Identity: The Built-In Paradoxes.* Paper presented at the annual meeting of the American Association for the Advancement of Science, Washington, D.C., 1972.

Sex-role identification. Sex-typed behavior.

This paper draws on existing empirical and theoretical studies to assert the need for updating the traditional model of sex-role identification. Several failings of the model are discussed, such as the prevailing emphasis on sex differences at the expense of similarities, the concept of human behavior as primarily conflict induced, the assumption that diverse behaviors must fit into either a masculine or feminine role, and the overemphasis on the power inherent in the masculine role. These failings are partially explained by analysis of the traditional model's biological and psychoanalytical roots. The conflict between biological and personal tendencies and socialized sex stereotypes is examined in the context of feminine sex-role identity models. The restrictiveness of the male sex role's commitment to strength and achievement is compared with the greater range of personality differentiation and role behavior of the female. It is concluded that sex differences and sex-role identity are precursors to the more advanced levels of individual identity and human relationships. Changes in society and in role content indicate that an integrated model of human sex-role development must consider the effects of a variety of familial and societal factors. (No references)

454

Rossi, Alice S. Sex equality: The beginnings of ideology. *The Humanist,* 29:3-6, 16, 1969. Also in: Safilios-Rothschild, Constantina, ed. *Toward a Sociology of Women.* Lexington, Mass.: Xerox College Publishing, 1972. pp. 344-353.

Social equality. Sex-role ideology.

This essay examines the manifestations of sexual inequality and evaluates possible goals of equality between the sexes. Inequality based on sex is compared with inequality based on race, religion, or nationality, and the similar problems in effecting social and political change are noted. However, sex inequality differs from other forms of discrimination in several respects: Although women outnumber members of other minority groups, their even distribution throughout the population makes it difficult for them to exert pressure as a group. Women's early sex-role socialization trains them for intimate dependence on men. Sex solidarity, unlike racial or national solidarity, is restricted by the conflict it could engender in the heterosexual relations of marriage.

Of the three possible models of social equality available, the pluralist model says the woman's nurturant nature finds its best expression in maternity; the assimilation model says women must be motivated to seek professional careers similar to those of men. In the hybrid model, societal values and structures would have to be radically changed. The eventual goal would be a society in which family, community, and play activities are valued equally with politics and work for both sexes of all races and classes. (No references)

455

Shainess, Natalie. The formation of gender identity. *Journal of Sex Research,* 5(2):75-85, 1969.

Sex-role development.

This discussion draws on existing psychosexual research to explore possible factors affecting the formation of gender identity. Topics include the development of conscious anatomical awareness and emotional conviction of gender identity, and the relationship between sexual and personal identity. Distinctions are made among various forms of sexual abnormality in men. It is concluded that gender formation is a complex process in which particular aspects of the self develop in relation to a core concept of self. Contributing to gender preference and gender consolidation are experiences within the range of parental anticipation and fantasies; early differentiation from the mother and identification with her; later maternal expectations and demands; identification and relationships with the father, with siblings, and with significant others; and cultural role demands. Due to the number of developmental factors and the complexity of their inter-action, neither normal nor distorted gender identity formation is completely explicable. (21 references)

456
Sherman, Julia A. *On the Psychology of Women: A Survey of Empirical Studies.* Springfield, Ill.: Charles C. Thomas, 1971. 304 pp.

Female role. Sex-role development. Physiological determinants.

This book reviews biological, anthropological, sociological, psychological, and psychoanalytical research literature on the psychology of women. Specific topics are the biological and psychological determinants of sex differences, Freudian and non-Freudian theories of moral and sex-role development, adolescence, cyclic changes, female sexuality, pregnancy, motherhood, and the post-menstrual period. Emphasis is placed on the influence of biological factors because of the feminine psychology of certain biological events, the lack of material on the female biological cycle and alterations resulting from normal chemical change, and the importance of the psychology of reproduction in producing healthy offspring. (890 references)

AUTHOR INDEX

SUBJECT INDEX

Ability (*see* academic ability, athletic ability, cognitive ability, intelligence, mathematical ability, motor coordination, verbal ability)

Absenteeism 271, 296

Academic ability 9, 17-19, 20, 84, 213 (*see also* aptitude maturation, intellectual maturation, intelligence, mathematical ability, verbal ability)

Academic achievement 14, 16, 19, 20, 27, 39, 43, 85, 91, 96, 134, 182, 183, 213, 234, 245, 250, 256

Academic interests 259

Achievement (*see* academic achievement, mathematical achievement, verbal achievement)

Achievement motivation 22, 39, 45, 50, 79, 106, 137, 143, 182, 255, 256, 268, 304, 422

Achievement tests 14, 16, 91, 96, 146, 245, 250

Adolescent females 100, 105, 123, 173, 175, 293, 321, 366, 430, (*see also* adolescents)

Adolescent males 40, 77, 99, 123 (*see also* adolescents)

Adolescents 6, 8, 35, 45, 71, 123, 129, 135, 155, 181, 189, 221, 229, 345, 362 (*see also* adolescent females, adolescent males, high school students, junior high school students)

Affective Sensitivity Scale 23

Africa 299, 370, 371, 397, 411, 415 (*see also* Ghana, Kenya, Nigeria, Union of South Africa)

Age differences 102, 152, 154, 160, 162, 165, 182, 183, 200

Aggression 2, 45, 57, 60, 61, 68, 75, 103, 113, 119, 128, 133, 144, 145, 203, 257, 422, 447

Agricultural societies 222 (*see also* preindustrial societies, urban-rural differences)

Alcohol consumption 362

American Indians 13, 367, 435 (*see also* preindustrial societies)

Animal studies 54, 57, 58, 60, 61, 64-67, 93, 107, 125

Anxiety 45, 49, 113, 177, 352, 442

Anxiety tests 68, 79, 105, 177, 245, 352

Aptitude maturation 9, 17-19, 64

Aptitude tests 9, 14, 16, 41, 63, 88, 110, 146, 249, 292

Argentina 185

Artistic activities 10, 15, 40, 41, 150, 182

Aspirations (*see* career aspirations, educational aspirations, marriage aspirations, material aspirations)

Children's Picture Story Test 115
Chile 189
China, People's Republic of 389, 397, 411
Chromosome disorders 59 (*see also* genetic determinants)
Civic participation 193, 199 (*see also* politics)
City planning 212
Civil service 285, 286, 326
Clergymen 357
Coeducation 250 (*see also* education)
Cognitive ability 49, 55, 132, 304
Cognitive styles 1, 4, 29, 32, 48, 51, 88, 112, 135, 443
College attendance 85, 248, 260
College educated women 195, 196, 208, 252, 262, 268, 284, 289, 292
College men (*see* male college students)
College students 3-5, 7, 10, 15, 17, 21, 23, 25, 27, 29, 33, 43, 47, 48, 101, 139, 148, 151, 153, 167, 178, 248, 249, 255, 352 (*see also* female college students, male college students, married students)
College Student Questionnaire 156
College women (*see* female college students)
Competitiveness 47, 255
Concept Mastery Test 249
Community agencies 193 (*see also* politics)
Conditioning 11, 38 (*see also* social learning, negative reinforcement)
Coopersmith Self-Esteem Inventory 35
Coping behavior 33, 208
Creativity 19, 40-42, 304
Cross-cultural studies 13, 87, 126, 200, 206, 222, 223, 225, 232, 363-419, 423, 428, 435 (*see also* cultural differences)
Cross-sex identity 19, 77, 86, 87, 99, 104, 113, 362 (*see also* sex-role identification)
Cultural differences 13, 87, 111, 126, 144, 145, 148, 162, 185, 221, 232, 234, 235, 272, 299, 347, 370, 375, 411, 415, 433, 435 (*see also* cross-cultural studies, national differences)
Czechoslovakia 398

Delinquency 6, 25, 97, 121, 131, 145, 146, 238, 388
Demographic determinants 310, 387, 400, 451 (*see also* fertility)
Denmark, 150, 295, 307, 380, 392
Dentists 322
Dependency 19, 45, 90, 103, 107, 116, 120, 128, 203, 227, 238, 257, 422, 447 (*see also* autonomy)
Depression 347, 360, 361
Differences (*see* cultural differences, national differences, racial differences, sex differences, socioeconomic differences, urban-rural differences)
Differential Aptitude Test 63